The Auchinleck Manuscript: New Perspectives

YORK MEDIEVAL PRESS

York Medieval Press is published by the University of York's Centre for Medieval Studies in association with Boydell & Brewer Limited. Our objective is the promotion of innovative scholarship and fresh criticism on medieval culture. We have a special commitment to interdisciplinary study, in line with the Centre's belief that the future of Medieval Studies lies in those areas in which its major constituent disciplines at once inform and challenge each other.

All enquiries of an editorial kind, including suggestions for monographs and essay collections, should be addressed to: The Academic Editor, York Medieval Press, Department of History, University of York, Heslington, York, YO10 5DD (E-mail: pete.biller@york.ac.uk).

Other volumes in the Manuscript Culture in the British Isles series are listed at the back of this volume.

Details of other York Medieval Press volumes are available from Boydell & Brewer Ltd.

The Auchinleck Manuscript
New Perspectives

Edited by
Susanna Fein

THE UNIVERSITY *of York*

YORK MEDIEVAL PRESS

First published 2016
Paperback edition 2018

A York Medieval Press publication
in association with The Boydell Press
an imprint of Boydell & Brewer Ltd
PO Box 9, Woodbridge, Suffolk IP12 3DF, UK
and of Boydell & Brewer Inc.
668 Mt Hope Avenue, Rochester, NY 14620–2731, USA
website: www.boydellandbrewer.com
and with the
Centre for Medieval Studies, University of York

ISBN 978-1-903153-65-9 hardback
ISBN 978-1-903153-78-9 paperback

A CIP catalogue record for this book is available
from the British Library

Contents

Illustrations

Contributors

Venetia Bridges	University of Leeds
Patrick Butler	University of Connecticut
Siobhain Bly Calkin	Carleton University
A. S. G. Edwards	University of Kent
Susanna Fein	Kent State University
Ralph Hanna	Keble College, Oxford
Ann Higgins	Westfield State University
Cathy Hume	University of Bristol
Marisa Libbon	Bard College
Derek Pearsall	Harvard University
Helen Phillips	University of Cardiff
Emily Runde	University of California at Los Angeles
Timothy A. Shonk	Eastern Illinois University
Mícéal F. Vaughan	University of Washington

Acknowledgements

I am grateful to Ruth Kennedy and Simon Meecham-Jones for settling on the Auchinleck manuscript as the theme for the 2008 London Old and Middle English Seminar, and convening a magical set of speakers. I sincerely thank those who participated at that conference, offering stimulating perspectives and, thereafter, moral support for this volume (and, in many cases, ripened versions of their talks): Siobhain Bly Calkin, Tony Davenport, Tony Edwards, Rosalind Field, Ralph Hanna, Ann Higgins, Cathy Hume, Marisa Libbon, Helen Marshall, Maldwyn Mills, Derek Pearsall, Helen Phillips, Tim Shonk, Míceál Vaughan and Alison Wiggins. I also thank Venetia Bridges, Patrick Butler and Emily Runde for adding more fresh outlooks to this conversation on Auchinleck. At the manuscript's home, the National Library of Scotland, Dr Ulrike Hogg, Curator of Manuscripts and Archive Collections, and Lynsey Halliday, Special Collections Assistant, provided expert assistance whenever called upon for details of the manuscript and reproductions from it. Kent State University granted material assistance through the Institute of Bibliography and Editing, the English Department and the Office of Research and Sponsored Programs. Editors and staff at Boydell and Brewer and York Medieval Press have been wonderfully supportive of this endeavour from the start. Profound gratitude goes to the indefatigable Caroline Palmer, and to Peter Biller, Rob Kinsey, Rohais Haughton, Rosie Pearce and Nicholas Bingham. As ever, I am deeply grateful to David Raybin, my most discerning reader.

For initiating this conversation some forty years ago, when he chose Auchinleck as the subject for one of the earliest facsimiles of an early English book, this collection is warmly dedicated to Derek Pearsall. We are deeply fortunate to be graced in this volume by his cumulative reflections on Auchinleck. Without his foresight and wisdom, the field of manuscript studies—grounding for this book— could not have advanced to where it is today.

Abbreviations

AND	W. Rothwell *et al.*, *Anglo-Norman Dictionary*, 2nd edn (London, 2005), http://www.anglo-norman.net
ANTS	Anglo-Norman Text Society
Archiv	*Archiv für das Studium der Neueren Sprachen und Literaturen*
Burnley-Wiggins	*The Auchinleck Manuscript*, ed. D. Burnley and A. Wiggins (Edinburgh, 2003), http://auchinleck.nls.uk
Pearsall-Cunningham	*The Auchinleck Manuscript: National Library of Scotland Advocates' MS. 19.2.1*, intro. D. Pearsall and I. C. Cunningham (London, 1977)
BL	British Library
CCCM	Corpus Christianorum, Continuatio Mediaevalis
CUL	Cambridge University Library
DIMEV	L. R. Mooney, D. W. Mosser, E. Solopova, and D. H. Radcliffe, *The Digital Index of Middle English Verse*, http://www. dimev. net
EETS ES	Early English Text Society, Extra Series
EETS OS	Early English Texts Society, Original Series
EETS SS	Early English Text Society, Supplementary Series
FRETS	French of England Translation Series
Kms	*Karlamagnús saga*, in *La Saga de Charlemagne*, trans. D. W. Lacroix (Paris, 2000)
LALME	A. McIntosh, M. L. Samuels, and M. Benskin, with M. Laing and K. Williamson, *A Linguistic Atlas of Late Mediaeval English*, 4 vols. (Aberdeen, 1986)
LOMERS	London Old and Middle English Research Seminars
MED	H. Kurath, S. H. Kuhn *et al.*, *Middle English Dictionary* (Ann Arbor MI, 1954–2001), http://www.quod.lib.mich.edu/m/med
NIMEV	J. Boffey and A. S. G. Edwards, *A New Index of Middle English Verse* (London, 2005)
NLS	National Library of Scotland
NLW	National Library of Wales
OED	*Oxford English Dictionary*, http://www.oed.com
PL	*Patrologiae cursus completus … series latina*, ed. J.-P. Migne.

PMLA	*Publication of the Modern Language Association of America*
STC	*Short-Title Catalogue*, ed. A. W. Pollard and G. R. Redgrave, 2nd edn (London, 1976)
The Riverside Chaucer	Geoffrey Chaucer, *The Riverside Chaucer*, ed. L. D. Benson *et al.*, 3rd edn (Boston, 1987)

Note on the Presentation of Auchinleck Texts

In the naming of works from the Auchinleck manuscript, the forms of titles and the use of modern item numbers (1–44) correspond to Pearsall-Cunningham, 'Contents of the Manuscript', pp. xix–xxiv. The manuscript possesses a contemporary numbering of contents by roman numerals set at the top centre of rectos; this numbering system may also be found in Pearsall-Cunningham, pp. xix–xxiv. The sources for quotations taken from Auchinleck texts are supplied in the notes for each chapter. As indicated there, individual contributors may have used any of the following methods for accessing texts: scholarly editions, transcriptions drawn from the digital Burnley-Wiggins facsimile, or independent transcriptions made directly from the manuscript or from the print Pearsall-Cunningham facsimile. The Bibliography lists all editions, including the Burnley-Wiggins transcriptions, cited in this volume.

The Auchinleck Manuscript: New Perspectives

Susanna Fein

T HIS volume owes much of its genesis to an event sponsored under the aegis of the London Old and Middle English Research Seminars (LOMERS), held at Senate House, University College London, in July 2008. Focused on the Auchinleck manuscript (Edinburgh, NLS, MS Advocates 19. 2. 1), the presentations were, as I recall, meticulous in delivering new ways to perceive the book's array of tangible clues, often daring in how they used these clues to assess contents and reconstruct new scenarios of the book's making and purpose, and – more often than not – contentious in knocking down old theories in order to replace them with explanations of finer nuance and better historical grounding. The organizers of the conference, Ruth Kennedy and Simon Meecham-Jones, had pulled together a group of keenly interested scholars to take on, whole, this tantalizing volume that embodies in its very existence a massive amount of material evidence as to London commercial book production and the demand for vernacular texts in the early-fourteenth century, c. 1330–40.

Displaying reproduced folios alongside the cogent aids provided by Derek Pearsall and I. C. Cunningham, the 1977 facsimile of Auchinleck had already become an indispensible resource – and the magnet that drew many a scholar of medieval English literature into manuscript studies. As Pearsall noted in the introduction to the facsimile, Auchinleck holds crucial significance 'in its early date, in the range, variety and intrinsic interest of its contents, and in the evidence it provides for English poetry, of book-production and readership in the period before Chaucer'.[1] In the present volume, Pearsall returns, some forty years later, to affirm that statement and speculate further that, in its own time, Auchinleck was a rare book and 'perhaps quite famous' (p. 23). Other notable voices chime in. For A. S. G. Edwards, the massive Auchinleck is a landmark of 'unprecedented comprehensiveness' (p. 34), and, for Ralph Hanna, the book holds 'deserved cultural centrality' in our understanding of fourteenth-century English poetry and book production (p. 213).

Each of these three experts of medieval English manuscripts spoke at the LOMERS Auchinleck conference, and each has refined, updated, and formalized

---

[1] D. Pearsall, 'Literary and Historical Significance of the Manuscript', in *The Auchinleck Manuscript: National Library of Scotland Advocates' MS. 19.2.1*, intro. D. Pearsall and I. C. Cunningham (London, 1979), pp. vii–xi (p. vii).

his observations for this volume. Many other chapters included here also date their inception to this productive event, specifically those by Siobhain Bly Calkin, Ann Higgins, Cathy Hume, Marisa Libbon, Helen Phillips, Timothy A. Shonk, and Mícéal F. Vaughan. These contributions have likewise been revisited and deepened for this collection, having gained from post-conference reflection, ongoing conversations, and the changing ideas and new research swirling in the several fields under study. And, because much of that new research is being generated by a new batch of scholars, it too is represented here, in chapters written by Venetia Bridges, Patrick Butler, and Emily Runde.

At the same time, given the vigorous, ongoing activity in Auchinleck studies, several other papers from the LOMERS conference do not appear here, because they have already evolved into publications in other venues. Of note are: Rosalind Field's important work on Auchinleck's essential, underlying Anglo-French character[2] (a matter now largely settled, but which in 2008 struck everyone as both fresh in conception and in need of being asserted); Helen Marshall's innovative work on Auchinleck's paraph styles[3] (expanded upon here in the chapter by Shonk); and my own work on the West Midlands flavour of many of the lyric 'fillers' added by Auchinleck's Scribe 1, items that correspond interestingly with items found in two important Western books contemporary with Auchinleck: London, BL, MS Harley 2253; and Oxford, Bodleian Library, MS Digby 86.[4] Meanwhile, the field has peered steadily into further nooks through such new and provocative studies as Christopher Cannon's probing of Laura Hibbard Loomis's idea that Chaucer 'knew' the Auchinleck manuscript[5] (a discussion revived from a new angle here in Phillips's chapter); Matthew Fisher's assessment of Auchinleck Scribe 1 as potentially the 'scribal author' of Auchinleck's *Anonymous Short English Metrical Chronicle*;[6] Arthur Bahr's ideas on medieval compilations, paying special attention to Auchinleck's booklet 3 and Scribe 3[7] (Runde's chapter reconsiders the arguments of both Fisher and Bahr); and Linda Olson's conceptualization of Auchinleck as a book for family

---

[2] See R. Field, 'Romance', in *The Oxford History of Literary Translation in English, Volume 1: To 1550*, ed. R. Ellis (Oxford, 2008), pp. 296–331, esp. pp. 302–6; and R. Field, 'Patterns of Availability and Demand in Middle English Translations *de romanz*', in *The Exploitations of Medieval Romance*, ed. L. Ashe, I. Djordjević, and J. Weiss (Cambridge, 2010), pp. 73–89.

[3] H. Marshall, 'What's in a Paraph? A New Methodology and Its Implications for the Auchinleck Manuscript', *Journal of the Early Book Society* 13 (2010), 39–62.

[4] S. Fein, 'The Fillers of the Auchinleck Manuscript and the Literary Culture of the West Midlands', in *Makers and Users of Medieval Books: Essays in Honour of A. S. G. Edwards*, ed. C. M. Meale and D. Pearsall (Cambridge, 2014), pp. 60–77.

[5] C. Cannon, 'Chaucer and the Auchinleck Manuscript Revisited', *Chaucer Review* 46 (2011), 131–46, referring to L. H. Loomis, 'Chaucer and the Auchinleck MS: "Thopas" and "Guy of Warwick"', in *Essays and Studies in Honor of Carleton Brown*, ed. P. W. Long (New York, 1940), pp. 111–28.

[6] M. Fisher, *Scribal Authorship and the Writing of History in Medieval England* (Columbus OH, 2012), pp. 146–87.

[7] A. Bahr, *Fragments and Assemblages: Forming Compilations of Medieval London* (Chicago, 2013), pp. 105–54.

reading (a view Hume explores in her chapter).[8] There has also been, since 2008, a steady stream of other new scholarship, mainly on Auchinleck's romances or on its distinctive yet controversial 'Englishness' – subjects that permeate the chapters of this volume.[9]

It is useful to recall the interesting situation in Auchinleck studies at the time of the LOMERS conference. Major developments had followed from the emergence of the Pearsall-Cunningham print facsimile in 1977. With this advance in scholarly access to the book came increasing clarity as to its contents, layout, booklets, scribal hands, miniatures, fragments, and lacunae. The conversations in London were greatly stimulated by Timothy A. Shonk's ground-breaking article on 'Bookmen and Bookmaking' (1985), Thorlac Turville-Petre's *England the Nation* (1996), Ralph Hanna's *London Literature, 1300–1380* (2005), Siobhain Bly Calkin's *Saracens and the Making of English Identity* (2005), and Rhiannon Purdie's *Anglicising Romance* (2008), to name a few.[10] Most notable among the recent developments had been the arrival, twenty-six years after Pearsall-Cunningham, of a monumental, 'second-generation' facsimile made available online – a true pioneer of the form and still very alive and functional – edited by David Burnley and Alison Wiggins,

---

[8] L. Olson, 'Romancing the Book: Manuscripts for "Euerich Inglische"', in K. Kerby-Fulton, M. Hilmo, and L. Olson, *Opening Up Middle English Manuscripts: Literary and Visual Approaches* (Ithaca NY, 2012), pp. 95–151.

[9] A sampling of other post-2008 publications bearing on Auchinleck studies includes: several essays in *A Companion to Medieval Popular Romance*, ed. R. L. Radulescu and C. J. Rushton, Studies in Medieval Romance (Cambridge, 2009); D. Battles, '*Sir Orfeo* and English Identity', *Studies in Philology* 107 (2010), 179–211; E. Runde, 'Reexamining Orthographic Practice in the Auchinleck Manuscript through Study of Complete Scribal Corpora', in *Variation and Change in English Grammar and Lexicon: Contemporary Approaches*, ed. R. Cloutier, A. M. Hamilton-Brehm and W. Kretzschmar, Jr (Berlin, 2010), pp. 265–87; T. Summerfield, '"And she answered in hir language": Aspects of Multilingualism in the Auchinleck Manuscript', in *Multilingualism in Medieval Britain (c. 1066–1520): Sources and Analysis*, ed. J. A. Jefferson and A. Putter, with A. Hopkins (Turnhout, 2013), pp. 241–58; M. Johnston, *Romance and the Gentry in Late Medieval England* (Oxford, 2014); M. Turner, 'Guy of Warwick and the Active Life of Historical Romance in *Piers Plowman*', *Yearbook of Langland Studies* 28 (2014), 3–27; *The King of Tars*, ed. J. H. Chandler (Kalamazoo MI, 2015); and M. Ailes and P. Hardman, 'Texts in Conversation: Charlemagne Epics and Romances in Insular Plural-Text Codices', in *Insular Books: Vernacular Manuscript Miscellanies in Late Medieval Britain*, ed. M. Connolly and R. Radulescu, Proceedings of the British Academy 201 (Oxford, 2015), pp. 61–79.

[10] T. A. Shonk, 'A Study of the Auchinleck Manuscript: Bookmen and Bookmaking in the Early Fourteenth Century', *Speculum* 60 (1985), 71–91; T. Turville-Petre, *England the Nation: Language, Literature, and National Identity, 1290–1340* (Oxford, 1996); Ralph Hanna, *London Literature, 1300–1380*, Cambridge Studies in Medieval Literature 57 (Cambridge, 2005), and his earlier 'Reconsidering the Auchinleck Manuscript', in *New Directions in Later Medieval Manuscript Studies: Essays from the 1998 Harvard Conference*, ed. D. Pearsall (York, 2000), pp. 91–102; S. B. Calkin, *Saracens and the Making of English Identity: The Auchinleck Manuscript* (New York, 2005); and R. Purdie, *Anglicising Romance: Tail-Rhyme and Genre in Medieval English Literature*, Studies in Medieval Romance 9 (Cambridge, 2008).

sponsored by the National Library of Scotland.[11] In it, each folio may be viewed in high-resolution digital colour image, and one may readily access, in addition, a folio-by-folio transcription of every item.

The contributors to the present volume take full advantage of this remarkable resource and also the print facsimile that preceded it, frequently choosing to cite manuscript items directly from the scribes' handwriting (in lieu of, or alongside, critical editions), reading them by means of either facsimile or both – and sometimes, too, by visiting the manuscript in Edinburgh and its fragmentary bits there or in St Andrews or London. Interestingly, neither facsimile has made the other obsolete. Both provide essential information about Auchinleck, and, on balance, the authors of these essays rely on them equally. Few other manuscripts of key interest to medieval English literary scholars have achieved this level of option, accessibility, clarity, and advantage for scholars, and Auchinleck would seem to be the first.[12]

The issues most at stake in the study of Auchinleck tend to be about finding answers to a group of related questions. Who were its makers? Its users? How was it made? And what end did it serve? To propose answers, scholars must turn, first of all, to the physical features of the object itself – a massive compendium now consisting of 331 parchment folios, fourteen stubs, and ten fragmentary folios (recovered in early book and notebook bindings).[13] There were originally at least fifty-two gatherings, at least five of them now missing. The surviving gatherings are of eight leaves, with one exception, quire 38, a gathering of ten. The normal layout of a page consists of forty-four ruled lines in two columns. Most texts were headed with an opening miniature and large initial, but, unfortunately, a good number of folios are now damaged because, at some point in the book's history, most of

---

[11] *The Auchinleck Manuscript*, ed. D. Burnley and A. Wiggins (Edinburgh, 2003), http:// auchinleck.nls.uk.

[12] Through very recent developments, one can currently work this way with the Harley manuscript (London, BL, MS Harley 2253), the Vernon manuscript (Oxford, Bodleian Library MS Eng. poet. a. 1), and the *Gawain* manuscript (London, BL, MS Cotton Nero A. x). For Harley, see the print *Facsimile of British Museum Ms. Harley 2253*, intro. N. R. Ker, EETS OS 255 (London, 1965); the online colour facsimile at 'MS Harley 2253', British Library Digitised Manuscripts, http://www.bl.uk/manuscripts/FullDisplay. aspx?index=9&ref=Harley_MS_2253; and the edition/translation in *The Complete Harley 2253 Manuscript*, ed. and trans. S. Fein, with D. Raybin and J. Ziolkowski, 3 vols. (Kalamazoo MI, 2014–15). For Vernon, see *The Vernon Manuscript: A Facsimile of Bodleian Library, Oxford MS. Eng. poet a. 1*, intro. A. I. Doyle (Cambridge, 1987); and the DVD-Rom colour facsimile with transcription in *A Facsimile Edition of the Vernon Manuscript, Bodleian Library MS. Eng. poet. a. 1*, ed. W. Scase, software N. Kennedy, Bodleian Digital Texts 3 (Oxford, 2011). For *Gawain*, see *Pearl, Cleanness, Patience and Sir Gawain Reproduced in Facsimile from the Unique Ms. Cotton Nero A.x in the British Museum*, intro. I. Gollancz, EETS OS 162 (London, 1923); and the colour digital facsimile with transcription at 'The Cotton Nero A.x Project', ed. M. McGillivray *et al.* (Calgary, 2010), at http://gawain-ms.ca/.

[13] See I. C. Cunningham, 'Physical Description', in Pearsall-Cunningham, pp. xi–xiv. Higgins provides a detailed account of the fragments and their history in her chapter in this volume.

the miniatures were removed. These excisions have damaged not only textual openings; invariably, they have also created a lacuna on the reverse side. Thus it is normal for Auchinleck texts to survive with some loss, sometimes light, at other times substantial. For texts that also have missing gatherings, as is true for *Kyng Alisaunder* and *King Richard* (discussed here by Bridges and Libbon, respectively), the losses are substantial, and speculative 'restoration' depends on estimates of the length of missing text, assessments of fragmentary half-columns, and judicious comparisons to sources or analogues.

Structurally, Auchinleck is made up of twelve booklets copied by either five or six different scribes.[14] The hand of Scribe 1 dominates the project, and he is often presumed (based on physical evidence) to be the compiler and/or overseer of the project – that is, someone who handed off, piecemeal and with instructions, portions of the task to other scribes whose handiwork is evident in five or six of the booklets.[15] The true number of scribes – five or six –depends on whether Scribe 6 is actually Scribe 1, as Hanna argues here that he is, on palaeographical grounds, also pointing out how the theoretical sixth scribe rests on a weak line of scholarly reasoning based on little evidence. Postulating that 'Scribe 6' is indeed Scribe 1 at a different temporal moment leads Hanna to ruminate on the chronological evolution of the Auchinleck project. He notes how 'the book may have [once] been imagined in very different conformations than what we have received' (p. 221).

Of the twelve booklets, Scribe 1's hand appears in nine, and Scribe 6 is responsible for a tenth. Scribe 1's independently copied booklets are 1, 6, 8, 9, 10, and 11. Scribe 6 copied booklet 7; Scribe 2 copied booklet 12; and the hands of Scribes 2–5 appear in booklets 2, 3, 4, and 5. In booklets 2, 4, and 5, Scribe 1 shares copying work with Scribes 2, 5, and again 5, respectively. Ultimately, the section that goes most 'off script' in terms of content and layout is booklet 3, copied by Scribes 2–4, with Scribe 3 being responsible for four of its six gatherings. In the present volume, this aberrant third scribe receives a fair amount of scrutiny. Edwards calls his work less planned and 'messier' (p. 28), and Hanna observes that he is uninformed as to the design of the larger project (pp. 217–19), while Runde argues that this anomalous scribe exhibits a level of conscious agency and thoughtfulness for developing 'pedagogies of [moral] reading' that deserve close attention within the whole scheme of Auchinleck (p. 81).

Even though it is the textual work of scribes that remains core to answering the question 'Who made Auchinleck?', the authors of the chapters in this volume venture beyond the scribal evidence to also look at the book's whole design apparatus. There were also, of course, illuminators, decorators, paraphers, and correctors who had a hand in producing the finished volume. The present studies open up paths to knowing about these ancillary rubricators and artists with whom

[14] See D. Pearsall, 'Literary and Historical Significance of the Manuscript', in Pearsall-Cunningham, pp. vii–xi (p. xi).

[15] On Scribe 1's supervisory role, the conclusions of Shonk, 'A Study', are widely accepted. In her chapter in this volume, however, Runde warns against too readily accepting Scribe 1 as a 'comfortingly authorial figure' (p. 69).

the scribes worked.[16] Some corrections could have been made by the scribes themselves – Vaughan is here able to identify much of Scribe 1's correction work, for example – but how did they do these operations? Scribes might have corrected their own work, checked that of other scribes, or used outside correctors, thereby introducing more hands into the manuscript. And, as Vaughan observes, some correcting hands are undoubtedly those of readers from later decades or centuries (p. 206). Examining the paraphs, Shonk expands here upon his earlier important codicological work on Auchinleck while also building on the work of Marshall. He identifies five distinct types of paraphs in Auchinleck, and he generally agrees with Marshall that Scribe 2 is reponsible for one of these types. In detecting palaeo-graphically distinct paraphers, Shonk expresses a wish for further work by others on the manuscript's miniatures, coloured initials, and borders (p. 191). It is this kind of evidence that Hanna surveys in a portion of his chapter (pp. 219–20). Thus, in these three essays and also some others, the methodical observation of new categories of data leads to valuable new ideas – sometimes speculative yet also quite plausible – about the different operations of the scribes, the chronological sequencing of booklets in the making of Auchinleck, and the distribution of textual units to other professional bookmen for final details of correction, paraph, and visual ornament.

Of course, there is another side to the coin of 'Who made Auchinleck?', namely the poet-translators and authors of the forty-four items contained in it as it survives today. It seems that many items, particularly the romances, were commissioned works, frequently derived from Anglo-French sources and refashioned into English couplets and tail-rhyme stanzas.[17] So who were these wordsmiths who created numerous first-time-in-English literary works for edification and entertainment? Because so many of Auchinleck's texts are either unique copies or the earliest extant versions, it seems probable that (at least in part) the task of translation operated as a division of the bookmaking process. It is tempting to implicate the scribes in the endeavour, imagining a situation in which acts of composing, translating, and scrivening were merged operations. Whether this is plausible or not is a tricky matter, and it is such a question as this that Pearsall dissects with great precision and perception in his chapter in this volume. He examines what we can and cannot know of early-fourteenth-century minstrel performance in England, and how far is 'the leap from performance to written copies' (p. 21). Scholars tend to not believe that written texts would ever truly give us actual scripts for 'raucous performances in tavern and village square', so they prefer to imagine, instead, those texts we have in manuscripts being performed in more refined settings, such as the manor hall of a gentleman.

The underlying minstrel question returns, interestingly, in Phillips's probing not into *whether* Chaucer might have actually known the Auchinleck manuscript

---

[16] The style of the Auchinleck miniatures is affiliated with that of the Queen Mary Psalter. See L. Dennison, '"Liber Horn", "Liber Custumarum" and Other Manuscripts of the Queen Mary Psalter Workshops', in *Medieval Art, Architecture and Archaeology in London*, ed. L. Grant, British Archaeological Association Conference Transactions 10 (London, 1990), pp. 118–34; and the chapters in this volume by Shonk and Hanna.

[17] Edwards also notes a substrate of largely Latin sources for the religious texts in Auchinleck (p. 32).

but, instead, 'what looking from Auchinleck to Chaucer might reveal about Chaucer, and perhaps about Auchinleck' (p. 139). She reads *Sir Thopas* as a playful yet potent comment upon the romance formulae exemplified in Auchinleck, with Chaucer impishly fashioning himself as the pilgrim one might call the Minstrel, and she concludes, provocatively, that, to Chaucer, the Auchinleck romances 'may have appeared not so much outdated as threateningly well established, as a national narrative canon, and not so much provincial as associated with regional power and the entrenched interests (entrenched also in literary culture) of great dynasties' (p. 152). The romance metrics of English tail-rhyme stanzas also become, for Phillips, a point of interest in comparing Chaucer to Auchinleck, while Pearsall points to the odd instances of Auchinleck works starting in one metre and shifting to another (as, for example, in *Guy of Warwick* and *Sir Beues of Hamtoun*).

Other contributions to this volume shine light on romances that have been somewhat invisible in general estimations of Auchinleck because they have suffered extensive losses. For one of these, *Kyng Alisaunder*, Bridges points out how, were we to conceptualize its hefty presence in its original form in Auchinleck (8,000-plus lines), we would comprehend just how much this romance – presently a 'ghost text' of just 704 lines (pp. 90–1) – inclined the book towards a valuation of Latinate learning, bookishness, and multilingualism, that is, features we have not been accustomed to associate with the Auchinleck project. Regarding another fragmentary Auchinleck romance, *King Richard*, Libbon points out how distinctively different it is from the sensational aspects of the later *Richard Coer de Lion*: it lacks the cannibalism and the fairy mother. Libbon finds the English hero-king to be fashioned in Auchinleck in ways that imitate the legendary Charlemagne, so that 'instead of excising the French canon, Auchinleck reinvents it as England's rightful inheritance and reinvests that inheritance in its own English corpus' (p. 137). In her analysis, the Auchinleck romance of Richard Lionheart illustrates 'the real and present fourteenth-century difficulty of what to do when your own cultural identity cannot be cleanly distinguished from that of your (renewed) enemy' (p. 137).

Geography, politics, international relations, and the formulation of a national English identity become pressing subjects in the chapters of Bridges, Libbon, and others concerned with romance texts in Auchinleck. Butler's essay, in particular, illustrates how Auchinleck has become, in recent years, a flashpoint for such matters, which are pivotal in our desire to know the cultural valence of English vernacularity in the early fourteenth century. Butler situates Auchinleck in a period of political tension, c. 1323–37, and reads the Prologue to *Of Arthour and of Merlin* as a warning on the perilous loss of multilingualism in England. He positions this prologue vis-à-vis other contemporary comments on the use of English (for example, in *Cursor Mundi* and the *Northern Homily Cycle*), and he finds more instances in Auchinleck, noting how interesting it is that remarks on multilingualism recur in 'a manuscript often noted for its nearly monolingual composition' (p. 66). His essay represents a recurring thread in the volume that reevaluates Auchinleck's avowed 'Englishness', showing how deeply French and Latinate substrates inform every effort at establishing an English identity.

Another way of situating Auchinleck in its geographical and political setting may require us to revise a long-standing tenet that its main affiliation is with London. Higgins uses the Auchinleck romance of *Sir Tristrem* to support her hypothesis that the book travelled to North England very soon after its making. She comments that:

> Insofar as the book is the product of the scribes who ruled its pages, copied its texts and numbered its items, of the artists who decorated its pages, of the stitchers who assembled its booklets and of the binder who bound them into a codex, Auchinleck is without question a London book. However, insofar as it is the product of the person who thought of it, brought that idea to a bookmaker and commissioned its production, it is, I would argue, something else entirely. (p. 109)

A share of the evidence Higgins adduces is literary: the romance of *Sir Tristrem* was apparently known in the North in the decades immediately following the making of Auchinleck (perhaps even from this book), but there is nary a trace of it in the rest of England. Other evidence is codicological: the discovered fragments and the early history of the book prove its presence in Edinburgh in the early seventeenth century (and perhaps earlier). Higgins sets up a plausible scenario in which the first owner took the book home to North England, from which it eventually migrated to Scotland by family connections.

So there is more to be considered than scribes and bookmen, more than trans-lators and authors, in grasping the making and purpose of Auchinleck. Certainly of critical importance, too, are the first readers, real or intended – that is, the patron who commissioned the book, his family, his affiliates – what Higgins refers to as the pressing matter of 'patron-centred identification' as opposed to 'production-end identification' (p. 109). Issues of readership cannot always be isolated from production, but there is no question that keeping audience in view adds a crucial dimension to how we are able to understand the contents and their presentation in the book. As the essays of Hume and Runde, in particular, show, the Auchinleck versions of certain items evince a strong awareness of the planned-for user. Found towards the beginning of the manuscript as it survives today, *The Life of Adam and Eve* is designed, according to Hume's analysis, for edifying family reading, with affecting portraits offered of Adam, Eve, and their son Seth, and exemplary lessons tucked in for good measure. The threesome are portrayed as 'a unified family whose love for one another strengthens their ability to combat the devil' (p. 47). Runde looks at devotional 'pedagogies of reading' in Auchinleck booklet 3, and sees Scribe 3's opening religious texts *On the Seuen Dedly Sinnes* and *The Pater Noster Vndo on Englissch* as setting forth a programme to induce prayerful activity and 'call upon a reader's consciousness of his or her inner spiritual state' (p. 80).

As Hume and Runde's essays illustrate, religious texts possess authority in Auchinleck, and this may well be another way in which the essays in this volume work to shift the standard characterization of the book away from its being seen primarily as a manuscript of romance. Edwards's chapter gives thoughtful attention to how the opening of Auchinleck as we have it – from *The Legend of Pope Gregory* to *The Assumption of the Blessed Virgin* (items 1–16) – is virtually all about religion, how the five lost texts at the start (numbered by a scribe 'i'–'v') may have delivered more religion, and how there may even be a point of demarcation before the romance section begins (p. 30).[18] He asks us to consider what might have been the original balance of religious and secular contents, and to see how the religious contents help to establish 'the full range of the compiler's concerns' (p. 34).

When we speak of such matters, the lines between compiler and patron, or author and audience, begin to blur a bit. When does the textual evidence show a compiler's interests versus a reader's needs and demands? In some instances, there are no easy answers. A recurring puzzle of this type pertains to how texts open and close. Beginnings that ask an audience, in minstrel style, to 'listen up' may directly counter rubrics that instruct a reader in how to read. Phillips and Pearsall each provide interesting accounts of how such openings – of both kinds – exist in Auchinleck and what they might mean. The provocative prologues distinctive to Auchinleck (discussed in the chapters by Butler, Runde, and Libbon) form another category of opening that may reveal a compiler's concerns or, equally, indicate an audience's widespread sentiments. Of course, many openings in Auchinleck are damaged by the excision of miniatures, and so another matter to consider is the original visual appearance, to which Hanna's chapter pays attention. The miniatures would have given the book a *de luxe* appearance, to please a patron's eye.

Calkin's chapter takes on the wide-ranging subject of the ways in which Auchinleck texts close. Like openings, many endings are damaged, but among those that are 'perfect' there is a tremendous variety of method. Traditional types of closure are certainly present – a prayer, a hero's death, a text recapitulated. But others are oddly open-ended. One of the most intriguing instances marks the close of the romance *Of Arthour and of Merlin*, which leaves Arthur feasting after a battle without the war having been concluded. Calkin speculates that this 'ending' relies on knowledge shared between redactor/compiler and audience:

> Perhaps … we are expected to draw on knowledge of the Arthurian tradition to fill in the ending for ourselves, either by knowing that Arthur does triumph and unify his realm in other texts, or by knowing that in the end Arthur's realm falls apart, riven by conflict and destruction. In some ways, reflecting on the larger tradition supplies readers with a 'choose-your-own-adventure' conclusion. (pp. 173–4)

The *Of Arthour* ending is 'perfect' in the sense that it gives us everything the scribe wrote. The text simply stops on fol. 256vb, mid-column, and then something else begins beneath a miniature. Ironically, had the miniature been excised (like most others), this strange, inconclusive yet 'perfect' ending would have been lost, and the romance would have simply become another Auchinleck item that 'ends imperfect' instead of one that physically concludes but at a puzzling moment.

---

[18] Unlike Pearsall, Edwards excludes *The King of Tars* and *Amis and Amiloun* (items 2, 11) from the list of Auchinleck secular romances on account of their religious orientations. Appearing with other religiously themed texts on the first seventy-seven folios of Auchinleck, they share narrative form with many of the other texts found there (e.g., saints' lives, legends, miracles).

Ultimately, it seems most helpful to try to maintain a mental division of the differently shaded agencies – of authors, of scribes, of users – that led to the Auchinleck project taking shape, even if these roles must certainly have overlapped here and there in practice. Whether we contextualize the Auchinleck manuscript in fourteenth-century London, in seventeenth-century Edinburgh, in unknown spots in between, or at later moments in its history after arriving at the NLS, the task of scholars is, as Higgins insists, to strive for sound 'conclusions – some founded on the rock of physical evidence, some resting on the shifting sand of speculation, but all … worth our consideration if we are ever to come close to understanding what the Auchinleck manuscript really is' (p. 124). Certainly, standing as one of the chief compendiums of literature in the Middle English period, gathering up so many national and dynastic romances in one place at such an early date, and made in the capital, Auchinleck draws the map lines for massive areas of our current understanding of literary bookmanship and readership before Chaucer, and all of this makes our intense attention paid to it tremendously worthwhile.

CHAPTER ONE

The Auchinleck Manuscript Forty Years On

Derek Pearsall

T HE facsimile of the Auchinleck manuscript was published in 1977 on the break of a wave of published facsimiles of manuscripts of Middle English verse.[1] There had been facsimiles published by the Early English Text Society of the *Gawain* manuscript and the Harley manuscript as 'one-off' ventures, a very old facsimile of the Ellesmere manuscript, and a recent one of the Lincoln Thornton manuscript.[2] But Auchinleck was immediately followed by facsimiles of the Findern manuscript, CUL Ff. 2. 38, Fairfax 16, CUL Gg. 4. 27 and a stream of others, mostly published by either the Scolar Press or D. S. Brewer.[3] The characteristic target was a miscellany or manuscript of varied contents such as would provide literary scholars with the kind of excitement that archaeologists take in a midden. The facsimile of the Hengwrt manuscript of the *Canterbury Tales*, which was published in 1979 by Pilgrim Books as part of the University of Oklahoma Variorum Chaucer project,[4] itself followed by facsimiles of several manuscripts of Chaucer and Chaucer-related manuscripts from the same source, was part of the same production revolution, though with somewhat different literary objectives. The general outbreak of facsimile publication coincided with a vigorous and widespread new interest in the 'material manuscript', that is, the physical evidence in all its aspects – script, ornament,

---

[1] *The Auchinleck Manuscript (Edinburgh, National Library of Scotland Advocates' MS 19.2.1)*, intro. D. Pearsall and I. C. Cunningham (London, 1977), hereafter 'Pearsall-Cunningham'.

[2] *Pearl, Cleanness, Patience and Sir Gawain Reproduced in Facsimile from the Unique Ms. Cotton Nero A.x in the British Museum*, intro. I. Gollancz, EETS OS 162 (London, 1923); *Facsimile of Brtish Museum Ms. Harley 2253*, intro. N. R. Ker, EETS OS 255 (London, 1965); *The Ellesmere Manuscript of Chaucer's Canterbury Tales*, intro. H. C. Shulz (San Marino CA, 1966); and *The Thornton Manuscript (Lincoln Cathedral MS. 91)*, intro. D. S. Brewer and A. E. B. Owen (London, 1975).

[3] *The Findern Manuscript (Cambridge University Library Ms. Ff.1.6)*, intro. R. Beadle and A. E. B. Owen (London, 1977); *Cambridge University Library Ms. Ff.2.38*, intro. F. McSparran and P. R. Robinson (London, 1979); and *Bodleian Library, MS Fairfax 16*, intro. J. Norton-Smith (London, 1979); *Poetical Works: A Facsimile of Cambridge University Library MS Gg. 4.27*, intro. M. B. Parkes and R. Beadle (Norman OK, 1979).

[4] *The Canterbury Tales: A Facsimile and Transcription of the Hengwrt Manuscript with Variants from the Ellesmere Manuscript*, ed. P. G. Ruggiers, intro. D. C. Baker, A. I. Doyle and M. B. Parkes (Norman OK, 1979).

layout, binding, annotation, readers' scribbles – of the medieval literary text. It only subsided when the functions that facsimiles had performed for medieval scholars and readers began to be taken over by digital forms of manuscript publication.

The introduction to the Auchinleck facsimile was written by myself and I. C. Cunningham, then Keeper of Manuscripts at the National Library of Scotland. Dr Cunningham's contribution, comprising a physical description of the manuscript, a detailed collation, and a description of script and ornament and of binding, has mostly stood the test of time. My own contribution to the introduction dealt with the literary and historical significance of the manuscript, including the organization of its production in the form of booklets, its origins in a London 'bookshop', its prospective audience, and its contents. Unfortunately, the 'bookshop' idea was soon overtaken by events. It was based on the assumption that the manuscript was the work of a number of scribes working together on the instructions of a patron in a kind of shop, perhaps with translators, versifiers, and decorators on the same premises. This was the influential theory put forward by Laura Hibberd Loomis in 1942 and, in the absence of any other explanation, generally accepted.[5] It accorded with the equally generally accepted assumption that the explosion in the commercial production of English literary manuscripts (of Chaucer, Gower, Langland, Trevisa, Hoccleve) in the early fifteenth century was likewise generated in bookshops or literary 'scriptoria'. This assumption underwrote the lengthy descriptions of the manuscripts of the *Canterbury Tales* by John Manly and Edith Rickert in Volume 1 of their edition of the poem.[6]

The misfortune that I spoke of was that the foundations of the bookshop theory were seriously undermined by the argument of the landmark essay by A. I. Doyle and M. B. Parkes on Cambridge, Trinity College, MS R. 3. 2, published in the year after the Auchinleck facsimile.[7] The manuscript, containing Gower's *Confessio Amantis*, was written by five scribes about 1420, working simultaneously on different portions of the exemplar, and would seem on the face of it one of the manuscripts most likely to have been produced collaboratively in a London bookshop. The examination of the manuscript by Doyle and Parkes demonstrated conclusively that there was no evidence of close collaborative activity between the scribes, and woefully little evidence of supervision. This seemed incompatible with any notion of the activity of scribes working under supervision on the same premises, as did the absence of historical evidence of any such 'bookshop' at the time. Though the authors did not discuss the Auchinleck manuscript, the same conclusion seems unavoidable with a manuscript produced nearly a century earlier. The immediate point of the article by Doyle and Parkes was to test and dismiss the bookshop theory, though its long-term importance was much greater. It may be said to have marked

[5] L. H. Loomis, 'The Auchinleck Manuscript and a Possible London Bookshop of 1330–1340', *PMLA* 57 (1942), pp. 595–627.

[6] J. M. Manly and E. M. Rickert, eds., *The Text of the Canterbury Tales: Edited from All Known Manuscripts*, 8 vols. (Chicago, 1940).

[7] A. I. Doyle and M. B. Parkes, 'The Production of Copies of the *Canterbury Tales* and the *Confessio Amantis* in the Early Fifteenth Century', in *Medieval Scribes, Manuscripts and Libraries: Studies Presented to N. R. Ker*, ed. M. B. Parkes and A. G. Watson (London, 1978), pp. 163–210.

the beginning of the study of the 'material' evidence of medieval literary texts, how they were written and decorated, how they were laid out and produced, and what they were able to reveal of scribes who can be shown from palaeographical analysis to have worked on more than one manuscript.

To provide a context for the discussion that follows, a brief description of Auchinleck is needed. Written down in London in 1330–1340, it is a massive book – 355 surviving leaves, including stubs, and also fragments now in other libraries – and would have been even more massive with all that it once contained. It is almost exclusively in English, and within it are represented many of the types of English verse writing of the period, including saints' legends, religious tales, and didactic works (altogether nineteen of forty-four items), but it is dominated by popular romances – eighteen items, accounting for three-quarters of the surviving bulk of the manuscript, eight of them in unique copies.[8] The audience for which the book was designed was one that wished to be both edified and entertained, one that relished familiar piety and instruction, but one that also desired access, in the native tongue, to the historical dignities and fashionable *haut monde* of romance (nearly all the romances are based on known or putative French or Anglo-Norman sources). The taste that it is designed to appeal to is that of the aspirant middle-class citizen, perhaps a wealthy merchant. It would have been a fairly expensive book, not in the *de luxe* class, perhaps, since the quality of the illustration, decoration, and penwork is modest, but the very presence of miniatures in such a manuscript at such a date in England is a sign of some ambition.

Since the publication of the Auchinleck facsimile in 1977, there has been considerable further work on the manuscript, notably the important essay by Timothy Shonk, which added to the work of Cunningham in the introduction to the facsimile and above all established the primacy of the role of Scribe 1, responsible for more than three-quarters of the copying, as in effect a kind of 'supervisor' of the manuscript.[9] It was Scribe 1 who accepted the commission of the patron, did a certain amount of initial planning, procured a number of scribes to help with the copying, farmed out exemplars, and at the end added the finishing touches: the ordering of the finished gatherings, the catchwords, the Arabic numbering of the leaves, and the titles. Scribes share gatherings but never poems. All the scribes leave space of the same kind for miniatures, and there is a consistent plan of decoration throughout. Scribe 1, the organizer, tried to begin each gathering with a big poem, but it didn't always work. So, there was planning but it was not perfect. There would subsequently be need for rubricators, decorators, and binders, all of whom could be found in the network of lanes and alleys around St Paul's. Contact, collaboration, and consultation would be possible but not necessarily close or common. Without wishing to resurrect

---

[8] See Appendix. There are eighteen romances if *The Seven Sages of Rome* is counted as a romance and if the three poems into which the Anglo-Norman *Gui de Warewic* has been divided – the couplet *Guy of Warwick*, the stanzaic continuation, and the sequel *Reinbrun Gij Sone of Warwike* – are counted as three.

[9] T. A. Shonk, 'A Study of the Auchinleck Manuscript: Bookmen and Bookmaking in the Early Fourteenth Century', *Speculum* 60 (1985), pp. 71–91.

the bookshop theory, it is perhaps worth picking around among its debris, for it is possible that its pernicious influence has been exaggerated. There may have been no 'bookshops' until the middle of the fifteenth century, but there is certainly evidence of collaborative activity long before then. If it was done by a number of scribes hired for the occasion, working loosely together in the same warren of streets, the net effect might not be so very different from an extremely ill-organized imaginary bookshop. Not that much imagination is needed. One also has to allow for the rather unusual nature of Trinity R. 3. 2, as a manuscript where the exemplars were shared out among five scribes for simultaneous copying. Such practice was not unknown in the making of literary manuscripts in the fifteenth century, but it was not common, being fraught, as one might think, with possibilities for disaster.

Other important work has been done on Auchinleck in the last forty years, especially on the individual contents of the manuscript, and Ralph Hanna, in addition to refining on Shonk's model of the making of the manuscript, has also questioned the 'exceptionalization' of Auchinleck, the view that it is isolated in its culture and in need of special explanations.[10] He provides a context for it in civic and royal books and in legal and historical writings, and much enriches our under-standing of the London book culture of the time. He also produces a number of comparable manuscripts of different kinds and varied contents, including one or two romances. Some of these manuscripts are big like Auchinleck, but never much like nor so exclusively in English.

Some of the questions surrounding the making of the Auchinleck manuscript have been resolved. Others remain, and the rest of this essay will be devoted to what seems to me one of the outstanding questions still unresolved: who were the authors of the poems in Auchinleck, and in particular of the romances, and what associ-ation did they have with the translators of the many derived from Anglo-Norman and French? There is some speculation on this subject in the introduction to the Pearsall-Cunningham facsimile, evidence of apparently arbitrary changes of metre without change of scribe in the course of a single romance being taken, for instance, to suggest the collaborative workaday activity of professional 'hacks'. I have stopped using this term for medieval writers, but one can see how the writing of these romances might for such reasons be thought of as a kind of 'job', passed around as people dropped out or became available. 'Aesthetic' reasons for such changes are hard to find, though in the case of the continuation of *Guy of Warwick* the choice of tail-rhyme in place of couplet may have to do with the greater emotional charge of the former, as Guy and the story undergo their religious transformation.[11] But such changes of metre may be just everyday working practice.

---

[10] See R. Hanna, *London Literature, 1300–1380*, Cambridge Studies in Medieval Literature 57 (Cambridge, 2005), pp. 74–81. The remarks on Auchinleck are anticipated in R. Hanna, 'Reconsidering the Auchinleck Manuscript', in *New Directions in Later Medieval Manuscript Studies: Essays from the 1998 Harvard Conference*, ed. D. Pearsall (York, 2000), pp. 91–102.

[11] Some scepticism about this interpretation has been expressed by R. Purdie, *Anglicising Romance: Tail-Rhyme and Genre in Medieval English Literature*, Studies in Medieval Romance 9 (Cambridge, 2008), p. 5.

Sir Beues of Hamtoun switches from tail-rhyme to octosyllabic short couplet at line 475, apparently arbitrarily. But there are also changes of metre in the Anglo-Norman original of *Beues*. In the first 2,338 of the total of 3,850 lines, the long lines of the *laisses* are bound by rhyme, but in the remaining 1,512 by assonance.[12] In addition, the length of the *laisses* undergoes a change after *laisse* 66, which ends at line 415 (the point in the poem corresponding to line 475 in the English poem). Up to that point, the *laisses* have been short, usually about six lines, giving the effect of six-line monorhymed stanzas. After that, they get longer, often much longer: there is one *laisse* of 187 lines – this with assonance, of course. The English writer simply followed the Anglo-Norman and made his change at the same point. However, the change of metre in the English poem, from tail-rhyme to couplet, was a different change of metre from that in the Anglo-Norman poem, with different resonances, and could still have had significance in a promotional aesthetic. This is less likely with *Roland and Vernagu*, which switches from normal tail-rhyme (with octosyllabic couplet) to a version of tail-rhyme with three stresses for all twelve lines of the stanza, including the tail (like the stanza of *Degrevaunt*) at line 425: but this is the point at which it begins to share lines with *Otuel and Roland* in the Fillingham manuscript (London, BL, Additional MS 37492).

More significantly, *King Richard*, after twenty-four lines of tail-rhyme (two stanzas), switches to short couplet. Such changes might be the arbitrary result of a change of composer/translator, as assumed above; but it is something of a coincidence that it takes place after what might well be regarded as a kind of prologue. In that case, Scribe 1, the 'organizer', may have introduced a practice of leading off a poem with some lines of tail-rhyme, the fashionable new metre for various kinds of English verse, but especially for romance, much as a greengrocer might put his freshest fruit at the front of the stall. This assumes a close relationship between the 'organizer' of the manuscript and the everyday work of the composers/translators. This is a large assumption. Something similar about the organization of Auchinleck may be deduced from the fact that *Roland and Vernagu* begins imperfect, with four lines that are identical with the last four lines of the forty-four-line prologue to the romance of *Otuel and Roland* in the Fillingham manuscript. This suggested to R. N. Walpole that the prologues were based on a lost composite Middle English 'Charlemagne and Roland' romance translated from a lost Anglo-Norman redaction of the Latin pseudo-Turpin chronicle.[13] This may have been one of the 'working translations' made

---

[12] There is other evidence of arbitrary change of metre in the non-Auchinleck Middle English *Ferumbras*, which switches from the old accentual long line or septenary to six-line tail-rhyme at line 3,410 of a total of 5,890 lines. See *The English Charlemagne Romances I: Sir Ferumbras*, ed. S. J. H. Herrtage, EETS ES 34 (London, 1879).

[13] See R. N. Walpole, 'Charlemagne and Roland: A Study of the Source of Two Middle English Metrical Romances, *Roland and Vernagu* and *Otuel and Roland*', *University of California Publications in Modern Philology* 21 (1944), 385–451; and R. N. Walpole, 'The Source MS of Charlemagne and Roland in the Auchinleck Bookshop', *Modern Language Notes* 60 (1945), 22–6. See also H. M. Smyser, '*Charlemagne and Roland* and the Auchinleck MS', *Speculum* 21 (1946), 275–88. For detailed critique of the Walpole theory see Purdie, *Anglicising Romance*, pp. 115–25.

available to the professional versifiers, especially to be 'poeticized' into tail-rhyme. The presence of the same prologue in two romances suggests they were designed to introduce, in a promotional and enthusiastic way, the groups of romances on the Matter of France. The presence of the same prologue at the head of *Lay le Freine* and also, it is presumed, at the beginning of *Sir Orfeo* (where the preceding page is lost) may suggest something of the same sort to introduce the Breton lays.

The last two romances have been attributed, reasonably enough, to the same author, which would reduce by one the number of Auchinleck authors that we know nothing about. Apart from that, there is the supposition that *Of Arthour and of Merlin, Kyng Alisaunder*, and *King Richard* (and perhaps also *The Seven Sages of Rome* – all four are in Auchinleck) are by the same author, because of their similar Kentish-influenced dialect. G. V. Smithers accepts this hypothesis in the introduction to his edition of *Kyng Alisaunder*, but O. D. Macrae-Gibson, in the introduction to his edition to *Of Arthour*, having examined the hypothesis in detail, concludes that it is strong only for *Of Arthour* and for *Kyng Alisaunder*.[14] There is also the further possibility, in view of the large amount of internal stylistic and verbal resemblance between the Auchinleck romances, that there may be other instances of common authorship. However, the evidence is flimsy, and diminishingly persuasive in the face of the large common stock of phrases and formulae. The extensive imitation of *Guy of Warwick* in *Amis and Amiloun*, as well as in other romances, argues not so much for common authorship as for the importance of *Guy* as the central and most prestigious item in the collection. The division of the English version of the Anglo-Norman *Gui de Warewic* into three romances – the couplet account of his adventures, the tail-rhyme account of his 'conversion' and further adventures, and the sequel *Reinbrun* about his son – adds to its weight of importance.[15] With the two long poems that follow it, *Beues* and *Of Arthour*, it perhaps formed the nucleus of the collection: 148 of 355 folios, including stubs and fragments (fols. 108–256, almost exactly central), 'historical', national, the Matter of England.[16] Also important in this context is the inclusion in Auchinleck of *The Anonymous Short English Metrical Chronicle*, and conceivably also the list of names of Norman barons at Hastings (*The Battle Abbey Roll*).

All this contributes to our understanding of working practice in Auchinleck, but not to knowing who exactly the authors were or what kind of profession they followed. There is of course Thomas Chestre, who is reputed to have been the author of three popular romances: *Sir Launfal, Libeaus Desconus*, and the southern

---

[14] *Kyng Alisaunder*, ed. G. V. Smithers, 2 vols., EETS OS 227, 237 (1952, 1957), II, 41; and *Of Arthour and Of Merlin*, ed. O. D. Macrae-Gibson, 2 vols., EETS OS 268, 279 (1973, 1979), II, 65–75.

[15] To ensure that no aspect of the hero's popularity should remain unexploited, there was also included in the manuscript the *Speculum Gy de Warewyke*, a familiar treatise of basic religious instruction extant in many later manuscripts, here loosely attached to Guy's 'conversion'.

[16] For the 'Englishness' of Auchinleck, see T. Turville-Petre, *England the Nation: Language, Literature and National Identity, 1290–1340* (Oxford, 1996), pp. 108–41; and Purdie, *Anglicising Romance*, pp. 96–102.

Octavian.[17] The first is in Auchinleck, and Thomas Chestre is the kind of person we might be looking for, but we know nothing of him but his name.

Surely there ought to be someone we can lay a finger on. After all, France had its well-documented poet-minstrels or *jongleurs*, and Germany too, most of them itinerant but some integrated into the lives and schedules of court and city.[18] These are poet-minstrels – that is, composers as well as musicians. David Wallace makes a lengthy comparison of the Tuscan *cantare* tradition to that of the Middle English popular romances.[19] The *canterini* were street-minstrels who recited their poems in the piazza. Some even have names, like Antonio Pucci, who was also a town-crier in Florence. The earliest surviving *cantare* manuscript, from about 1340, contains, as it happens, like Auchinleck, a version of the French *Floire et Blancheflur*. Wallace points out how Boccaccio was indebted to the *cantare* tradition, and compares the *Filostrato* and *Sir Thopas* as expressions of the poets' indebtedness to the traditions of popular romance, which would bring us back to another influential essay by Laura Hibberd Loomis arguing that Chaucer at some point had access to the Auchinleck manuscript.[20]

Of course, minstrels are frequently mentioned in English records and writings, though not in ways that would make them obvious candidates for the translation or composition of romances such as we find in Auchinleck. Often, 'minstrels' is the word used to refer to instrumental musicians of the higher professional caste, such as those employed by Edward III or those in attendance at the great feast for Edward of Caernarvon in London in 1306.[21] These, as they are described in the marvellous account by Constance Bullock-Davies of a surviving payroll, were often citizens or squires in everyday life, or royal messengers, or heralds, or watchmen, or waferers (high-class pastry-cooks who made fancy sweet biscuits to have with *ypocras* at the end of a feast): all doubled as musicians on big occasions, and some organized spectacles and interludes, as well as musical entertainments.[22] There would on such occasions be no 'romanz reding on the bok' such as we hear of at the celebration of Havelok's coronation.[23] But these part-time minstrels may provide some of our

---

[17] See M. Mills, 'The Composition and Style of the "Southern" *Octavian*, *Sir Launfal* and *Libeaus Desconus*', *Medium Ævum* 31 (1962), 88–109.

[18] M. Dobozy, *Re-Membering the Present: The Medieval German Poet Minstrel in Cultural Context* (Turnhout, 2005). The classic study of French minstrels is L. Gautier, *Les épopées françaises: Etude sur les origines et l'histoire de la littérature nationale*, 3 vols. (Paris, 1865–68). But A. Taylor, 'The Myth of the Minstrel Manuscript', *Speculum* 66 (1991), 43–73, is sceptical about the 'manuscrit de jongleur' (see pp. 44–53).

[19] D. Wallace, *Chaucer and the Early Writings of Boccaccio*, Chaucer Studies 12 (Cambridge, 1985), pp. 75–93.

[20] L. H. Loomis, 'Chaucer and the Breton Lays of the Auchinleck Manuscript', *Studies in Philology* 38 (1941), 14–33.

[21] C. C. Olson, 'The Minstrels at the Court of Edward III', *PMLA* 56 (1941), 601–12.

[22] C. Bullock-Davies, *Menestrellorum Multitudo: Minstrels at a Royal Feast* (Cardiff, 1978).

[23] *Havelok the Dane*, line 2327, in *Four Romances of England: King Horn, Havelok the Dane, Bevis of Hampton, Athelston*, ed. R. B. Herzman, G. Drake, and E. Salisbury (Kalamazoo MI, 1999), pp. 72–185 (p. 142).

romance composers. Although harpists might simply have accompanied recitation of narrative verse, it was a herald who wrote *The Siege of Caerlaverock*.[24]

The term 'minstrel' was also used to refer to the professional entertainers who travelled around with a repertoire of stories, songs, and 'turns'. There is no written evidence of their work as writers until those late-fifteenth-century manuscripts that contain what might be polished-up versions of their performances, like *The Greene Knight* and *The Turke and Sir Gawain*.[25] Such minstrels have been relegated by modern scholars to a rather disreputable role, and to some extent remain a shadowy presence.[26] Minstrels are commonly denounced in homiletic and other similar kinds of writing as purveyors of filth, but it is significant that Robert Mannyng, writing the prologue to his verse translation of the Anglo-Norman Chronicle of Pierre de Langtoft about 1338, makes no reference to 'minstrels', perhaps because of the ambiguity of the term, but reserves his wrath for a class of what appear to be poet-minstrels that he calls 'disours'. Though both 'disour' and 'segger' in the passage quoted below are usually glossed 'reciter' or 'minstrel', it seems clear from the way Mannyng speaks of them that they are also thought of as the composers of the rhymes they recite. Mannyng himself declares that he writes 'not for the lerid bot for the lewed', those who speak English and know neither Latin nor French, and who desire to hear of the history of their country when they sit down together in fellowship (at dinner, presumably). He makes a distinction between his own simple style and the artificial verse-forms and 'strange Inglis' of modern poets.

> I mad noght for no disours,
> ne for no seggers, no harpours,
> Bot for þe luf of symple men
> þat strange Inglis can not ken;
> ffor many it ere þat strange Inglis
> In ryme wate neuer what it is; ...
> If it were made in ryme couwee,
> or in strangere or enterlace,

[24] *The Roll of Caerlaverock*, a roll of arms in verse written by English heralds, describes the feats of arms performed by English knights at the siege of Caerlaverock in 1300 (*The Roll of Arms, of the Princes, Barons, and Knights who Attended King Edward I to the Seige of Caerlaverock, in 1300*, trans. J. Wright [London, 1864]). But of course it is in French as, much later, is the Chandos Herald's *Life of the Black Prince*. As to harpists, at the 'Romance in England' conference in Bristol in 2014, Linda Zaerr recited/ sang the romance of *Sir Orfeo* to the accompaniment of a rather plaintive rising and falling musical figure, repeated for each couplet, played on the harp. It was effective in imaginatively realizing something of the nature of minstrel performance.

[25] *Sir Gawain: Eleven Romances and Tales*, ed. T. Hahn (Kalamazoo MI, 1995), pp. 309–35, 337–58, respectively. Some of these poems appear in the early-seventeenth-century Percy Folio (London, BL, Additional MS 27879), a late relic of minstrelsy.

[26] For vigorous questioning of the role of minstrels as authors or in relation to manuscripts see Taylor, 'The Myth of the Minstrel Manuscript'; and A. Taylor, 'Fragmentation, Corruption, and Minstrel Narration: The Question of the Middle English Romances', *Yearbook of English Studies* 22 (1992), 38–62.

þat rede Inglis it ere inowe,
þat couthe not haf coppled a kowe,
þat outhere in couwee or in baston
som suld haf ben fordon. (lines 75–80, 85–91)[27]

These 'disours' write in such complicated schemes 'in ryme couwee / or in strangere or enterlace' and in such 'strange Inglis' that their poems cannot be understood nor recited without errors. Fine poems like *Sir Tristrem* (unique in Auchinleck) by the semi-mythical Thomas of Erceldoune are routinely mangled, he says (lines 92–104). Mannyng makes a clear distinction between the ordinary prosaic short couplet that he writes and the fancy new tail-rhyme ('ryme couwee') with musical associations, alliterative embellishments, and a generally 'poetic' quality. The distinction made earlier (above), between the two verse-forms seems to be confirmed here. If Mannyng had known the Auchinleck manuscript, written down about the same time, he might be talking about it.

Langland too thinks ill of 'disours': he calls those who tell tales of harlotry the 'deueles dysors' (C. VIII. 52), and the fat doctor at the Feast of Patience dismisses Patience's eloquent speech in praise of the virtue of patience as 'a *dido* ... a dysores tale' (C. XV. 170).[28] But he is ambiguous about 'minstrels'. Minstrels are worthy of respect if they serve in the household of a great lord, and there are others, loosely associated with minstrels, who are in fact 'lered' men (C. VII. 104), and who can 'fithele the withoute flaterynge of god Friday the geste' (C. VII. 106) and 'telle of Treuthe and of the twelue apostles' (C. XI. 30). But more often they are chastized as tellers of ribald stories and as crude entertainers, and Langland's opinion of them seems to harden in the later text.[29] Activa Vita (Haukyn in B) calls himself a minstrel, but he says he is unable to do any of the things a minstrel does – except make wafers. Langland seems to want to speak well of minstrels (perhaps he thought of himself as a kind of minstrel), but the only way he can do so is to metaphoricize them. He speaks of honest humble beggars as 'goddes munstrals' (C. VII. 99), and of 'lunatyk lollares' – those other beggars who roam the land, apparently 'witteles', yet 'profecye of the peple, pleyinge as hit were' – as 'munstrals of heuene' (C. IX. 107, 111, 114, 127). Again, Langland seems to have himself in mind. E. Talbot Donaldson, who writes best on Langland's minstrels, thinks that Langland in his youth may have been a minstrel, 'one of the irregulars of minstrelsy, of whom there seem to have been

---

[27] Robert Mannyng of Brunne, *The Story of England*, ed. F. J. Furnivall, 2 vols, Rolls Series 34 (London, 1887), I, 3. See also J. Coleman, 'Strange Rhyme: Prosody and Nationhood in Robert Mannyng's *Story of England*', *Speculum* 78 (2003), 1214–38. Mannyng's nostalgia for older verse forms of verse-making is echoed in *Wynnere and Wastoure*, ed. S. Trigg, EETS OS 297 (Oxford, 1990), lines 19–30; and in *Piers Plowman* (see note 28 below). The verse-terms are: *strangere*, 'foreign'; *enterlace*, 'with alternate rhymes such as *abab*'; *couwee*, 'with a tail'; and *baston*, 'complex stanza'.

[28] William Langland, *Piers Plowman: A New Annotated Edition of the C-Text*, ed. D. Pearsall, Exeter Medieval Texts and Studies (Exeter, 2008). Unless otherwise stated, all quotations from Langland are from this edition.

[29] Compare B. Prol. 33–4 with C. Prol. 35–40. The B-Text is cited from William Langland, *Piers Plowman: The B Version*, ed. G. Kane and E. T. Donaldson (London, 1975).

thousands'.[30] Perhaps he was one of those recruited for Auchinleck – maybe for *The Simonie*, which of course is one of the poems most reminiscent of *Piers Plowman*.[31] He would have been very young. He seems an unlikely candidate, yet many such clerics of lost vocation were probably marketing their skills among the growing London bourgeoisie.

Mannyng and Langland both provide evidence that minstrels might be composers as well as performers – composers not just of short pieces and religiously edifying material but, as Mannyng suggests, of full-scale romances in fashionable metres. Other kinds of evidence of minstrel activity are more difficult to assess. Romances often begin with direct address to a listening audience, as in these examples from Auchinleck (quoted direct from the facsimile):

> Herkneþ boþe ȝinge & olde
> Þat willen heren of batailles bolde …
>
> > *(Otuel*, lines 1–2, fol. 268ra)

> Lordinges herkneþ to me tale
> Is merier þan þe niȝtingale …
>
> > *(Beues*, lines 1–2, fol. 176ra)

There are many other examples, in Auchinleck as well as in the corpus of romances generally, and it seems unlikely that they are transcripts of oral performance. The manuscript evidence of 'oral delivery', often cited as proof of the ubiquity of minstrels, may be part of the traditional atmosphere of conviviality that the writer wants to create, or it may be the relic in written form of the memory of oral delivery on the part of a minstrel-turned-writer. Cries for cups of ale accompanying transitions to new matter are frequent in medieval romances, and the article by Ruth Crosby collects large numbers of examples.[32] Again, they are most likely to be the work of writers trying to create the traditional atmosphere of conviviality associated with minstrel recitation. The best-known examples are in *Wynnere and Wastoure*: 'Full freschely and faste for here a fitt endes'.[33] Here it is perhaps the scribe Robert Thornton who, in the mid-fifteenth century, has added these 'evidences' of oral delivery by minstrels. Stephanie Trigg calls them 'a stylistic remnant of the minstrel's art'.[34]

Most internal reference in the romances to minstrels and minstrel performance is uninformative about who actually wrote the texts they recite or perform, whether

---

[30] E. T. Donaldson, *Piers Plowman: The C-Text and Its Poet*, Yale Studies in English 13 (New Haven, 1949), p. 135. For his full, rich and suggestive discussion of Langland's minstrels, see pp. 136–55.

[31] See E. Salter, '*Piers Plowman* and "The Simonie"', *Archiv* 203 (1967), 241–54.

[32] R. Crosby, 'Oral Delivery in the Middle Ages', *Speculum* 11 (1936), 88–110. The most up-to-date study of aurality is J. Coleman, *Public Reading and the Reading Public in Late Medieval England and France*, Cambridge Studies in Medieval Literature 26 (Cambridge, 1996).

[33] *Wynnere and Wastoure*, ed. Trigg, line 217 (repeated at line 367).

[34] Ibid., p. 31.

minstrels or not. The Auchinleck *King of Tars* describes a marriage-feast and makes a special point of mentioning the rich robes and many jewels that were given to the minstrels on that occasion:

> For þer was melodi wiþ þe mest
> Of harp and fiþel & of gest[35]
> To lordinges of renoun;
> Þer was ȝeuen to þe menstrels
> Robes riche & mani iuweles
> Of erl & of baroun. (lines 556–61, fol. 10ra)

This might serve as a none-too-subtle reminder to the audience to reward the minstrel-performers likewise, but the gifts are extravagantly lavish, as befits an attempt to create the ideal old-world atmosphere in which minstrels had flourished. The author of the non-Auchinleck romance of *Emare* begins with a stanza of prayer to Jesus and Mary and in the next tells that what he has just done is exactly what minstrels should do:

> Menstrelles þat walken fer and wyde,
> Her and þer in euery a syde,
>   In mony a dyuerse londe,
> Sholde at her bygynnyng
> Speke of þat ryghtwes kyng
>   That made both see and sonde.[36]

There follows a famous account of minstrels, how they walk far and wide, and deserve to be warmly welcomed, and the author says he is one such minstrel as he begins his story of *Emare*. Both stanzas have the character of those officious recitals of 'correct' behaviour that are associated with attempts to keep a tradition alive, if not to 'invent' it. Minstrels undeniably did exist, but the difficulty is in making the leap from performance to written copies. Perhaps it was the minstrels themselves who adapted to new circumstances and prepared copies of romances they knew well. The leap to the humdrum routines of 'publication' would be less great if it was from sober readings with written copies before respectable audiences and not from raucous performances in tavern and village square. The editors of the non-Auchinleck *Ywain and Gawain* think this version of *Yvain* was written by a minstrel to be read or recited, not in a tavern or marketplace but to 'the sober realistic audience of a provincial baron's hall'.[37] This hall has become one of the favourite haunts of minstrels for modern scholars looking for an alternative to the

---

[35] The manuscript reads *grest*. On the emended reading – accepted by Burnley-Wiggins, Perryman, and Chandler – see *The King of Tars*, ed. J. Perryman, Middle English Texts 12 (Heidelberg, 1980), p. 111; and *The King of Tars*, ed. J. H. Chandler (Kalamazoo MI, 2015), p. 66.

[36] *The Romance of Emaré*, ed. E. Rickert, EETS ES 99 (Oxford, 1908), lines 13–18.

[37] *Ywain and Gawain*, ed. A. B. Friedman and N. T. Harrington, EETS OS 254 (London, 1964), p. xvii.

tavern and market square. For Auchinleck and its merchant-patron, we can imagine readings aloud after dinner in the hall of a merchant's great house.

Whether the actual manuscript texts of romances show evidence of minstrels composing for performance is much debated. W. E. Holland thinks that the Auchinleck text *Of Arthour* was clearly written to be read, while the later texts bear evidence of memorial corruption in the process of transfer from performance.[38] A. C. Baugh, in an early and very important article on 'Improvisation in the Middle English Romances', argued conclusively against the application of the then-current oral-formulaic theories of composition to the Middle English romances, pointing out that the longer romances like *Beues* and *Guy* follow their Anglo-Norman originals with fair fidelity, and that the differences between texts, given the ubiquity of stock phrases, go back to the reciter substituting phrases of his own for those he did not immediately recall, that is, they are due to improvisation.[39] He excludes the possibility that all the changes are due to scribal corruption. But modern editorial techniques and the experience of editing *Piers Plowman* have given scholars encouragement to think that the mistakes that used to be thought impossible for a scribe to have made are simply part of the normal scribal chatter or 'static', the kind of thing that scribes could quite customarily produce by transferring text, line by memorized line, from an exemplar. And, whereas it has often been said by adherents of *mouvance* that manuscripts of texts derived from the narratives designed for oral delivery are not capable of being edited except by the use of parallel texts, *King Horn*, often thought to be an example of such a text, has been edited with a fair degree of success by Rosamund Allen, who takes the three manuscripts back to a single original from which all surviving copies can be shown to be derived by the usual processes of scribal corruption.[40]

'Holster-books', small tallish narrow manuscripts of varied contents which were supposed to fit in the holster of a travelling romance-reciter, have been scepti- cally examined by Andrew Taylor.[41] London, Lincoln's Inn, MS 150, which seems a likely candidate, certainly contains texts that have undergone some process of oral transmission, as through minstrel recitation.[42] But Taylor allows only Oxford, Bodleian Library, MS Douce 228 as a true minstrel-manuscript, describing it as a notebook in which a travelling entertainer would jot down bits he especially wanted to remember, while he memorized the rest. Such things as 'holster-books' did exist,

---

[38] W. E. Holland, 'Formulaic Diction and the Descent of a Middle English Romance', *Speculum* 48 (1973), 89–109.

[39] A. C. Baugh, 'Improvisation in the Middle English Romance', *Proceedings of the American Philosophical Society* 103 (1959), 418–54. Similar points are made by N. M. Bradbury, *Writing Aloud: Storytelling in Late Medieval England* (Urbana IL, 1998).

[40] *King Horn: An Edition Based on Cambridge University Library MS Gg. 4. 27 (2)*, ed. R. Allen, Garland Medieval Texts 7 (New York, 1984).

[41] Taylor, 'The Myth of the Minstrel Manuscript', pp. 57–60.

[42] Writing of the Lincoln's Inn MS of *Kyng Alisaunder*, Smithers says that it is full of gross blunders that cannot possibly be due to scribal transmission but must go back to oral transmission of a text partly memorized by a reciter (*Kyng Alisaunder*, ed. Smithers, II, 11–13). But see Taylor, 'The Myth of the Minstrel Manuscript', pp. 55–7.

but they were mostly used as account books by travelling collectors; there are some, such as Cambridge, St John's College, MS S 54, which also contain lyrics and songs, but not longer poems, and may have been the repertoire of travelling minstrels. Similarly, small pocket-sized books containing sermons were carried around by itinerant Lollard preachers.[43]

Not all the romances of Auchinleck have the same kind of origin, whether or not at some remove, in minstrel composition or the work of *disours*. *Kyng Alisaunder*, for instance, offers a sophisticated rendering of the Anglo-Norman *Roman de toute chevalerie* that could not possibly be the work of a backroom hack. The author borrows material from other relevant sources, including Latin, and is 'exceptionally well versed in the French language and so widely read in French literature'.[44] He is expert, too, in adapting the stylistic and rhetorical conventions of the *chanson de geste* to Middle English romance. Several romances, without aspiring to the sophis-tication of *Kyng Alisaunder*, follow their Anglo-Norman originals with sufficient fidelity to eliminate the idea of derivation from minstrel copies. The sequence of *Guy of Warwick* romances is one example, and *Sir Beues of Hamtoun* is perhaps another. Whether the authors of *Guy* and *Beues* wrote their poems direct from the Anglo-Norman originals before them, or whether they versified a rough working translation made by themselves or others, is a question impossible to answer. Some romances were evidently written well before the Auchinleck manuscripts came to be copied down, and found their way into the manuscript by the usual processes of scribal transmission. *Floris and Blauncheflur* is one such poem. Karl Brunner proposed that *King Horn* and *Floris*, along with a poem on *The Assumption of Our Lady*, which all appear in a single late-thirteenth-century manuscript (CUL, MS Gg. 4. 27 (2)), were composed by a clerk in a lord's house for the ladies of the household who did not know French.[45] More and more, as these exceptions multiply, it seems that the Auchinleck romances most confidently to be associated with minstrels or former minstrels are the tail-rhyme romances.

Writing a conclusion to such a series of speculative arguments is worth attempting, even if much will have to remain speculative. In reconstructing the origins of Auchinleck, we have to imagine something like the following sequence of events. Scribe 1, a stationer-bookseller-scribe, was approached by a well-off London citizen and asked to provide English translations of the big Anglo-Norman ancestral romances that had made such a stir. It was as much a matter of practical conven-ience as English *amour propre*, though the latter is not to be excluded, especially if *King Richard* was included in the commission. He wanted a 'Great Book of English Romance': it turned out to be a very large book indeed and a rare one, perhaps quite famous (famous enough to come to the notice of Chaucer?). To this the

[43] A. Hudson, *The Premature Reformation: Wycliffite Texts and Lollard History* (Oxford, 1988), p. 185.

[44] *Kyng Alisaunder*, ed. Smithers, II, 40.

[45] See K. Brunner, 'The Middle English Metrical Romances and Their Audience', in *Studies in Medieval Literature in Honor of Albert Croll Baugh*, ed. M. Leach (Philadelphia, 1961), pp. 219–27.

stationer was asked or decided for himself to add poems on Arthur, Alexander, and Charlemagne, as predecessors among the traditional 'Nine Worthies' of our modern English heroes. *King Richard* acted as a bridge, given the mention of Charlemagne in its prologue. Exemplars were acquired, some already put into circulation by established writers like the *Kyng Alisaunder* poet. Others may have been commissioned as major translations of the Anglo-Norman poems that were to be central to the volume, whether versified from 'working translations' or not. Further exemplars were the work of minstrels who had decided to take advantage of the new form of employment. Some of these would bear the marks of oral transmission because of their previous life in performance or recitation. It was largely a matter of what was available, but the stationer might also have commissioned new poems from such former minstrels as understood the principles of verse composition, and especially of tail-rhyme. *Sir Degare*, with its hectic accumulation of popular romance motifs (mistaken identity, fairy intervention, incest, father fighting son incognito), might stand as the type of such up-to-the-minute, made-to-order romances.[46] One does not need to imagine a basement or backroom full of hack writers waiting for work, but simply a network of contacts. Mercantile piety also required that the romances should be balanced by a quantity of religious poems, most of them quite short. At the last moment, there came into the stationer's shop a vivid topical satirical diatribe against simoniacal and other kinds of greed and corruption, written by a graduate drop-out up from the country transfixed with horrified fascination by the London he found.

---

[46] N. Jacobs, reluctant to abandon the idea of a London bookshop, argues, with *Degare* in mind, that 'the redaction or even composition of some of the texts took place in a single bookshop' (*The Later Versions of Sir Degarre: A Study in Textual Degeneration*, Medium Ævum Monographs, n.s. 18 [Oxford, 1995], p. 4).

APPENDIX

The Auchinleck romances

No.	Title	Metre	Number of manuscripts	Derivation
2	*The King of Tars*	TR (tail-rhyme)	2 other MSS	
11	*Amis and Amiloun*	TR	3 other MSS	AN
17	*Sir Degare*	couplet	5 other MSS	
18	*The Seven Sages of Rome*	couplet	4 other MSS	AN
19	*Floris and Blauncheflur*	couplet	3 other MSS	Fr. (but an AN copy)
22	*Guy of Warwick*	couplet	other versions	AN (many MSS)
23	*Guy of Warwick* (stanzaic)	TR		AN
24	*Reinbrun*	TR		AN
25	*Sir Beues of Hamtoun*	couplet + TR	4 other MSS (& another version)	AN
26	*Of Arthour and of Merlin*	couplet	4 other MSS (of abbrev. version)	Fr.
30	*Lay le Freine*	couplet	unique	Fr.
31	*Roland and Vernagu*	TR	unique	AN
32	*Otuel a Kniʒt*	couplet	unique	AN
33	*Kyng Alisaunder* (fragment)	couplet	2 other MSS	AN
37	*Sir Tristrem*	5-line stanza	unique	Fr.?
38	*Sir Orfeo*	couplet	2 other MSS	Fr.?
41	*Horn Childe*	TR	unique	AN
43	*King Richard*	TR + couplet	7 other MSS	AN?

CHAPTER TWO

Codicology and Translation in the Early Sections of the Auchinleck Manuscript

A. S. G. Edwards

T HE early sections of the Auchinleck manuscript – that is, roughly the first hundred or so leaves – differ markedly in content from the later, predominantly romance sections that have been the chief focus of the attention the manuscript has received from literary critics. [1] These early sections comprise poems on religious subjects that are assembled in several distinct booklets, differentiated to varying extents by scribal stints and quire boundaries from each other and from the later booklet divisions in the manuscript. [2] The organization of these booklets, their contents, and what they may signify about the overall conception of the manuscript are questions that invite greater consideration than they have received. As I will suggest, the details of physical construction and content in these sections indicate that the achievement of the Auchinleck manuscript is more wide-ranging than scholarly discussion has generally indicated.

The opening six quires of Auchinleck (fols. 1r–38v) form the surviving part of the first of these booklets. Preceding sections of an indeterminable length are now lost, as are also ten leaves from different points in the surviving sequence of these quires. [3] This booklet includes nine texts, all relatively brief: even allowing for lost leaves, no single work seems likely to have exceeded about twelve hundred lines in length. These works are: item 1, *The Legend of Pope Gregory* (beginning imperfectly,

---

[1] Cf. the comment of Murdoch and Tasioulas, in *The Apocryphal Lives of Adam and Eve, Edited from the Auchinleck MS and from Trinity College, Oxford MS 57*, ed. B. Murdoch and J. A. Tasioulas, Exeter Medieval Texts and Studies (Exeter, 2002): 'studies of the Auchinleck Manuscript as such have tended to neglect the religious writings in favour of the romances' (p. 4). There are some brief but helpful observations on the religious writings by M. Görlach, 'The Auchinleck *Katerine*', in *So meny people, longages and tonges: Philological Essays in Scots and Mediaeval English Presented to Angus McIntosh*, ed. M. Benskin and M. L. Samuels (Edinburgh, 1981), pp. 211–28, esp. pp. 211–15. His interests are primarily textual, however, rather than codicological.

[2] There are probably twelve such booklets in the manuscript; they are detailed in D. Pearsall, 'Literary and Historical Significance in the Manuscript', in Pearsall-Cunningham, pp. vii–xi (p. ix).

[3] For details see the analysis of the quire sequences in I. C. Cunningham, 'Physical Description', in Pearsall-Cunningham, pp. xi–xiv (p. xii).

fols. 1r–6v; *NIMEV* 209); item 2, *The King of Tars* (fols. 7ra–13vb; *NIMEV* 1108); item 3, *The Life of Adam and Eve* (beginning imperfectly, fols. 14ra–16rb; *NIMEV* 1873.5); item 4, *Seynt Mergrete* (fols. 16rb–21ra; *NIMEV* 203); item 5, *Seynt Katerine* (21ra–24vb; *NIMEV* 1159); item 6, *St Patrick's Purgatory* (beginning imperfectly, fols. 25ra–31vb; *NIMEV* 303.6); item 7, *The Desputisoun bitven þe Bodi and þe Soule* (fols. 31vb–35ra; *NIMEV* 351); item 8, *The Harrowing of Hell* (fols. 35vb–37ra; *NIMEV* 185); and item 9, *The Clerk Who Would See the Virgin* (beginning imperfectly, fols. 37rb (?)–38vb; *NIMEV* 282.5). These works are all copied by Scribe 1, who is the principal scribe of the manuscript.[4]

These poems are all religious narratives, possibly, but not certainly, linked in some instances by common authorship.[5] The final work in the section, *The Clerk Who Would See the Virgin*, seems to function as a filler. Even allowing for its imperfect state, it is unlikely to have exceeded two hundred lines, which makes it one of the shortest poems in the manuscript. And it ends partway down fol. 38vb with the rest of the column blank. Such codicological evidence clearly marks this point as a booklet boundary.

The new quire that begins on the next leaf, fol. 39r, marks the start of the next booklet. The first text in it begins at the top of the recto. This booklet, extending from fol. 39ra to fol. 69va, consists of a further group of religious poems, again mainly narrative; that is: item 10, *Speculum Gy de Warewyke* (fols. 39ra–48rb; *NIMEV* 1101); item 11, *Amis and Amiloun* (fols. 48rb–61va; *NIMEV* 821); item 12, *Life of St Mary Magdalene* (beginning imperfectly, fols. 61va–65vb; *NIMEV* 304.5); item 13, *Nativity and Early Life of Mary* (beginning imperfectly, fols. 65vb–69va; *NIMEV* 213, 3452). This booklet is copied by two scribes. The first of these, Scribe 2, makes his first of several appearances here. At the start of the booklet, he copied the complete text of *Speculum Gy*, which occupies most of the first ten leaves, after which Scribe 1 returns to copy the remaining twenty-one leaves. The final text here ends at the very top of the verso of fol. 69 and the rest of this page is blank. The overall design of this booklet is as clear as that of the first booklet, both in its boundaries and in its emphasis on religious subject and narrative.

The next booklet occupies fols. 70r–107v. Its contents and scribal organization are more diverse than are those of the earlier booklets. It begins with two shortish religious poems: item 14, *On þe Seuen Dedly Sinnes* (fols. 70ra–72ra; *NIMEV* 1760), and item 15, *The Pater Noster Vndo on Englissch* (fol. 72ra–b; *NIMEV* 206). Item 16, the longer *Assumption of the Blessed Virgin*, follows (beginning imperfectly, fols. 72ra–78ra; *NIMEV* 4119.5). There then occur the first three major romances – item 17, *Sir Degare* (ending imperfectly, fols. 78rb–84rb; *NIMEV* 1895); item 18, *The Seven*

---

[4] Throughout, unless otherwise indicated, I follow the designations of scribes and their stints established by T. A. Shonk, 'A Study of the Auchinleck Manuscript: Bookmen and Bookmaking in the Early Fourteenth Century', *Speculum* 60 (1985), 71–91.

[5] As in the cases of the consecutive lives of Saints Margaret and Katherine; see A. J. Bliss, 'The Auchinleck "St. Margaret" and "St. Katherine"', *Notes and Queries*, 201 (1956), 186–8. Bliss's view of common authorship has been resisted by Görlach, 'The Auchinleck *Katerine*'.

Sages of Rome (beginning and ending imperfectly, fols. 84rb–99vb; *NIMEV* 3187);[6] and item 19, *Floris and Blauncheflur* (beginning imperfectly, fols. 100ra–104vb; *NIMEV* 2288.8) – before the booklet ends with the short item 20, *The Sayings of the Four Philosophers* (fol. 105ra–b; *NIMEV* 1857), and item 21, the prose *Battle Abbey Roll* (fols. 105v–107r). Three scribes, numbers 2, 3, and 4, appear in this booklet, and the implications of their involvement are discussed below.

The sequencing of texts here is rather messier than in the first two booklets. The romances (items 17–19) are sandwiched between the continuing sequence of religious narratives at the start of the booklet (items 14–16) and the concluding, possibly 'filler' texts at the end of the booklet (items 20–1). It may be that the form (or lack thereof) of the booklet was the consequence of some organizational miscalculation, of which occasional indications seem to remain. Particularly interesting is *Four Philosophers* (item 20), the shortest poem in the manuscript (ninety-eight lines), copied by Scribe 2. It may well have been intended to be placed elsewhere since it is misnumbered 'xxvi' in the contemporary manuscript sequence of texts, the same number as the immediately preceding *Floris and Blauncheflur*. It is possible that this poem was initially intended for the largely blank fol. 69v at the end of the previous booklet after *Nativity* (item 13), and that it had to be inserted later after a slight miscalculation in the casting off of copy that left it just too long for this page.

The same sort of miscalculations may have some bearing on other aspects of the possible difficulties in ordering the sequence of texts in this booklet as they had been originally planned. It seems possible that this third booklet was initially intended to continue the sequence of religious narratives, but that not all of those that were planned for inclusion in it finally became available. This possible lack of material may have created particular organizational difficulties around quires 11 and 12 (fols. 70r–84v), where, as I have noted, *Assumption* (item 16) overlaps these two quires and is followed by *Degare*, *Seven Sages*, and *Floris* (items 17–19) and then by *Four Philosophers* (item 20). If this last work preceded *Degare*, then the codicological distinction between religious works and romances would have been largely preserved. The confusions in the contemporary numbering in this section give some support to a hypothesis of a disruption to the envisaged design of the manuscript at this point, with the omission of numbers 'xix' and 'xx' from the original numerical sequence. These missing numbers indicate some sort of loss of overall control in the organization of this booklet that seems to have led to some confusion about the ordering of texts here and consequently the need for some hurried modification to and/or replacement of the envisioned sequence of texts.

The seeming breakdown in the projected execution of this third booklet may have been connected with the untypical nature of the scribal organization involved in it. This booklet is one of the few of the probably twelve booklets from which the manuscript was constructed in which the hand of Scribe 1, seemingly the organizing

---

[6] To designate *The Seven Sages of Rome* as a romance may seem problematic, but in Cambridge, University Library, MS Ff. 2. 38 it is also grouped in the sequence of verse romance texts.

scribe, does not appear.[7] Here Scribe 3 copied items 14–19, then Scribe 2 reappeared to copy item 20, while Scribe 4 copied the anomalous *Battle Abbey Roll* (item 21), with which this booklet concludes.[8] The presence of this last text, a list of names in Anglo-Norman orthography, is one of the manuscript's most curious features, both because this scribe's hand does not appear anywhere else in the manuscript and because this work, the only one not in Middle English verse, is copied in a four-column format not employed elsewhere in it.[9]

The inclusion of this work is inexplicable on grounds of language and form, given the clear design otherwise consistently expressed in Auchinleck. Its anomalous nature prompts the hypothesis that its inclusion may indicate a desperate, last-minute effort to find any sort of material to hand to fill out the booklet, to paper over an unplanned-for gap. This in its turn may suggest both that this booklet was produced outside of Scribe 1's normal control, and that the following booklet had already been transcribed or was already being transcribed, thus limiting any organizational room to manoeuvre. The nature of *The Battle Abbey Roll* and the unique appearance of its scribe give support to this hypothesis.[10]

In general terms, though, these early booklet sections of Auchinleck clearly bring together, sometimes with an evident degree of local planning, cognate works in religious genres and/or on religious themes or topics that are evidently distinct from the romance works that begin to appear in the third booklet and were possibly originally envisaged as following on from them. Henceforward, the generic predominance of romance texts is self-evident and the only departures from it are a few brief didactic fillers inserted near booklet boundaries.[11]

---

[7] The only other booklet where his hand does not appear is the final one, which contains *The Simonie* (fols. 328r–334v) copied by Scribe 2. The possibility remains that booklets 7–8 (fols. 268r–280v) are really a single unit, copied in part by Scribe 1 and in part by Scribe 6; see D. Pearsall, 'Literary and Historical Significance', p. ix.

[8] On the apportioning of scribal stints for the six scribes involved in preparing the manuscript and their overall significance, see A. J. Bliss, 'Notes on the Auchinleck Manuscript', *Speculum* 26 (1951), 652–8; and, particularly, Shonk, 'A Study'. Shonk calculates that Scribe 1 copied 'approximately seventy percent of the manuscript' (p. 73). I am especially indebted to Prof. Shonk for his interest in this paper and his encouragement to publish it. The existence of six scribes has been confirmed by the subsequent work of A. Wiggins, 'Are Auchinleck Scribes 1 and 6 the Same Scribe?: The Advantage of Whole-Data Analysis and Electronic Texts', *Medium Ævum*, 73 (2004), 10–20. But see also the chapter by R. Hanna in this volume.

[9] Two verse texts are macaronic: item 20, *The Sayings of the Four Philosophers* (in Anglo-Norman and Middle English); and item 36, *Dauid þe King* (a translation of Psalm 50 in Latin and Middle English).

[10] For a different view, see H. M. Smyser, 'The List of Norman Names and the Auchinleck Bookshop', in *Mediaeval Studies in Honor of Jeremiah Denis Matthias Ford*, ed. U. T. Holmes and A. J. Denomy (Cambridge, MA, 1948), pp. 257–87; and the recent subtle analysis by A. Bahr, 'Fragmentary Forms of Imitative Fantasy: Booklet 3 of the Auchinleck Manuscript', in his *Fragments and Assemblages: Forming Compilations of Medieval London* (Chicago, 2013), pp. 140–51.

[11] For example, item 29, *Hou Our Leuedi Saute Was Ferst Founde* (fols. 259rb–260vb; NIMEV 1840), at the end of quire 36; and items 35–36, *The Sayings of St Bernard* (fol.

If the point at which the modal shift from religious texts to romances can be fairly clearly identified in Auchinleck, it is worth stressing that the current predominance of romance materials in it as it now survives may not be an accurate reflection of the balance of content in the original construction of the manuscript. The first surviving item, *The Legend of Pope Gregory*, is numbered 'vi' and begins imperfectly. It lacks probably the opening 268 short lines that appear in other manuscripts of this work. In Auchinleck, these lines are copied in single columns, as long lines, the only point in the manuscript where this format is employed except at the very end of it with *The Simonie*, which forms a distinct booklet unit of its own. Hence 134 long lines, or just over three pages of text, have been lost.[12] In the case of *Legend*, such a single-column format would not have filled the entirety of the quire but would have left room for an antecedent text, the missing work numbered 'v', which must have occupied the approximately two and a half leaves of the missing first part of the quire that had been left unfilled before the transcription of *Legend*. This text, assuming the same single-column format, would have amounted to about 220 lines of verse, and, of course, more if it extended back into another preceding lost quire, as seems quite likely, since few poems in Auchinleck are this short.

It seems a reasonable guess (though, of course, it can be no more than that) that the five missing works at the start of Auchinleck were also religious in nature, in view of the clear distinctions in content that the manuscript seems to have originally sought to preserve between such works and the romances that predominate in its later sections. One may doubt that the missing contents would have included major religious verse compilations, like the *South English Legendary* or the *Northern Homily Cycle*. Such works are very different in their conception from the freestanding ones in the opening surviving sections of Auchinleck.[13] Their size and the consequent time required for copying would probably have taxed both the resources of those organizing the manuscript's production and the patience of its commissioner (and perhaps his purse). It seems more probable that the now missing early contents were of the same kind as those that still survive from Auchinleck's present beginning: discrete religious works, with emphasis on narrative, and of moderate length.

The likelihood that this was the case serves to bring into focus an aspect of the achievement of Auchinleck that has been less fully examined than is warranted. Much has been made in academic discussion of the significance of the romance texts in the manuscript. This importance is indisputable: it contains at least sixteen romances, of which eight are unique.[14] But the religious works at the beginning of

---

28orb–vb; *NIMEV* 3310) and *Dauid þe King* (fol. 28orb–vb; *NIMEV* 1956), at the end of quire 41.

[12] In the surviving portion of the text, there are 44 lines to a page – that is, 88 to the leaf.

[13] M. Görlach, *The Textual Tradition of the South English Legendary* (Leeds, 1974), notes the inclusion of a 'temporale' section related to the *South English Legendary* as item 13 (p. 127).

[14] As always, the use of the term 'romance' is inexact: I regard here *The King of Tars* and *Amis and Amiloun* (item 11) as religious narratives, and also do not include *The Wenche þat Loued a King* or *How a Merchant Did His Wife Betray* (items 2, 11, 27, 28). My count

the manuscript have not excited comparable interest. It may be that current thinking about the manuscript still lives under the shadow of the work of Laura Hibbard Loomis, whose emphasis on the number of romance texts Auchinleck contains and the implausible links she posits to Chaucer and *Sir Thopas* seem to have had a disproportionate influence on subsequent thinking about the manuscript.[15]

But not to give proper weight to the religious poems in Auchinleck is to overlook a body of material that is substantial and unusual in its own terms. No earlier vernacular English manuscript that now survives is comparable in the number and range of English verse texts it contains on such subjects. One instructive point of comparison is with Oxford, Bodleian Library, MS Laud misc. 108, most of the contents of which were probably copied in the earlier part of the fourteenth century, at least a couple of decades before Auchinleck, in a non-metro-politan environment. It comprises primarily saints' lives in English, largely taken from the *South English Legendary*, as well as two romances, *Havelok the Dane* and *King Horn*.[16] Hence the content of this manuscript rather reverses the emphases of Auchinleck. It lacks both the number of romances that appear in Auchinleck and the generic range of religious materials in it, which, as it now survives, amount to about a quarter of the surviving items and (as seems likely) originally rather more. And both the extent and the diversity of the religious verse in Auchinleck suggest the need for a proper appreciation of its compilational range. In terms of categories, its variety of religious verse is striking: saints' lives, biblical narratives, devotional stories, dialogue, and other didactic and expository works, which in totality seem to amount to an unusually expansive collection of such materials. The only notable formal omission is the lyric. Therefore this part of the manuscript does not appear to have had any evident recoverable antecedent models that could have provided a basis for shaping its content nor any parallels among contemporary manuscripts in such content. And the probability that the religious materials in this manuscript were once much larger makes it even more noteworthy in terms of this aspect of its content.

It seems therefore worth asking: is it possible to determine the source or sources of this collection of religious materials? The question of origins is obviously crucial to all aspects of Auchinleck. For example, Derek Pearsall posits a team of

---

does include items 17–19, 22, 23–6, 30–3, 37–8, 41, 43. Of these, items 23–4, 30–2, 37, 41, and 43 are unique. For a slightly different view of the number of romance texts, see D. Pearsall's chapter in this volume.

[15] See L. H. Loomis, 'Chaucer and the Auchinleck MS: "Thopas" and "Guy of Warwick"', in *Essays and Studies in Honor of Carleton Brown* (New York, 1940), pp. 111–28, 'Chaucer and the Breton Lays of the Auchinleck Manuscript', *Studies in Philology* 38 (1941), 14–33, and 'The Auchinleck MS and a Possible London Bookshop of 1330–40', *PMLA* 57 (1942), 595–627. For a recent critique of Loomis's arguments see C. Cannon, 'Chaucer and the Auchinleck Manuscript Revisited', *Chaucer Review* 46 (2011), 131–46. On the subject see also H. Phillips's chapter in this volume.

[16] For the most recent description of the manuscript see A. S. G. Edwards, 'Oxford, Bodleian Library, MS Laud. Misc. 108: Contents, Construction and Circulation', in *The Texts and Contexts of Oxford, Bodleian Library, MS Laud Misc. 108: The Shaping of English Vernacular Narrative*, ed. K. K. Bell and J. N. Couch (Leiden, 2011), pp. 21–30.

'professional hacks' engaged in turning Anglo-Norman romance into English verse specifically for inclusion in the manuscript.[17] Even if there seems to be no clear evidence to support such a view, yet we are conscious of the general linguistic and generic indebtedness of the romance portions of it to French-derived originals and the scale of the assemblage of these materials. But, if we look more closely at the earlier sections of Auchinleck and the religious verse they contain, we may perceive some degree of different linguistic implications in this part of the manuscript's compilation. For it seems that its codicological distinctiveness may gesture towards a different kind of vernacularity from that indicated by its later contents. It can be argued that there is not clearly the same degree of direct indebtedness in this section of the manuscript to the Anglo-Norman-derived originals that appear to have been the sources for the romances.[18]

Thus, *Speculum Gy de Warewyke* seems in part a translation from the Latin, in part an original creation.[19] *Seynt Katerine* appears to derive from a Latin version.[20] *Saint Mergrete* was, it has been argued, a free translation from the Latin of Mombutius.[21] *The Desputisoun bitven þe Bodi and þe Soule* clearly derives from a tradition of debate poetry.[22] *The Life of Adam and Eve* appears to derive from either a Latin or an English source.[23] *Nativity and Early Life of Mary* has been characterized by its editor as 'a largely original Middle English composition.[24] Some of the shorter of these religious poems, like those on the Seven Deadly Sins and the Paternoster, obviously demonstrate the continuing consequences of the Fourth Lateran Council and its commitment to vernacular religious instruction. It is unnecessary to posit any direct Anglo-Norman source for any of these poems. This is not invariably the case. Some among the early religious poems in Auchinleck do derive directly from Anglo-Norman originals. Sometimes these are themselves translations from the Latin, as Robert Easting has shown was the case with *St Patrick's Purgatory*, which was a translation from an Anglo-Norman verse translation of the Latin

---

[17] See Pearsall, 'Literary and Historical Significance', p. x, and modifications in his chapter in this volume (p. 14).

[18] *Amis and Amiloun* may be the exception to this generalization.

[19] On *Speculum Gy*, see most recently A. S. G. Edwards, 'The *Speculum Guy de Warwick*: and Lydgate's *Guy of Warwick*: The Non-Romance Middle English Tradition', in *Guy of Warwick: Icon and Ancestor*, ed. R. Field and A. Wiggins (Cambridge, 2007), pp. 81–93, esp. pp. 81–6.

[20] Görlach, 'The Auchinleck *Katerine*': 'we must treat *Katerine* as a very free rendering of the *Vulgata*' (p. 216).

[21] E. Krahl, *Untersuchungen über vier Versionen der mittelenglischen Margaretenlegende*, dissertation, Königlische Friedrich-Wilhelms-Universität (Berlin, 1895).

[22] See *Middle English Debate Poetry: A Critical Anthology*, ed. J. W. Conlee (East Lansing, MI, 1991), esp. pp. xiii–xx. Conlee observes specifically, of the early Middle English versions including Auchinleck, that they are 'closer in conception to the Latin *altercatio*' than to any Anglo-Norman analogues (p. 26).

[23] See *The Apocryphal Lives*, ed. Murdoch and Tasioulas, p. 23.

[24] *The South English Nativity of Mary and Christ*, ed. O. S. Pickering, Middle English Texts 1 (Heidelberg, 1975), p. 23.

prose *Tractatus de purgatorio sancti Patricii* of Henry of Sawtry.[25] And *The Legend of Pope Gregory* appears to have been derived from an Anglo-Norman source or sources.[26] Some instances do not seem to permit of the possibility of certain source identification. *The King of Tars* exists in an indeterminate relationship to any Anglo-Norman original.[27] And the treatment of *Amis and Amiloun* suggests a marked degree of independence in its handling of any putative source of like kind.[28]

It is also worth being conscious that a number of these religious poems, like a significant number of the romances, are unique to Auchinleck. Eight of the first sixteen poems in the first part of the manuscript are not recorded elsewhere: item 3, *The Life of Adam and Eve*; items 4–5, the lives of Saint Margaret and Saint Katherine; item 9, a miracle of the Virgin (*The Clerk Who Would See the Virgin*); item 12, the *Life of St Mary Magdalene*; items 14–15, the poems on the Seven Deadly Sins and the Paternoster; and item 16, the longer *Assumption of the Blessed Virgin*. There is no evidence, beyond the absence of other copies, to suggest that some of these unique religious poems were compositions or translations made specifically for inclusion in Auchinleck, as has been argued was the case for a number of the unique romance texts.[29] But the number of such poems could imply a close relationship of some kind between those involved in the conception of the manuscript and those who created these poems. The existence of so many poems unrecorded elsewhere does seem to provide testimony to the overall ambition of the compilers of the manuscript to achieve a degree of formal inclusiveness. As it is, of these early poems, only *Desputisoun*, *Speculum Gy*, and *Nativity* (items 7, 10, 13) seem to have enjoyed any relatively extensive circulation, if the number of surviving manuscripts is a valid indicator of the extent of their appeal. The first survives in six other manuscripts, the second in nine, and the third in five for the Prologue and eight for the main text.[30] Most of these copies seem later, as do those others that survive in smaller numbers.[31] The range of materials included in the early sections of Auchinleck (and those that may once have been there) suggests an unusually focused ambition of

---

[25] *St Patrick's Purgatory*, ed. R. Easting, EETS OS 298 (Oxford, 1991), p. xliv.

[26] This is the conclusion of, *inter alia*, Keller, in *Die mittelenglische Gregoriuslegende*, ed. C. Keller, Alt-und Mittelenglische Texte 6 (Heidelberg, 1914).

[27] R. J. Geist, 'On the Genesis of the King of Tars', *Journal of English and Germanic Philology* 42 (1943), 260–8, suggests some possible influence from the French *Florence de Rome*, but argues that 'the English *Otuel and Roland* influenced the romancer more directly' (p. 268).

[28] See D. Mehl, *The Middle English Romances of the Thirteenth and Fourteenth Centuries* (London, 1967): 'The English version ... is ... markedly didactic and less courtly than the Anglo-Norman poem *Amis e Amilun* which have may been its source, although in a different version from those extant' (p. 105).

[29] See note 17 above.

[30] See *NIMEV* 351, 1101, and 213B (Prologue) and 3452, respectively; it should be noted that *NIMEV* 3452, no. 1 is incorrect and should be deleted. In addition, *Owayne Miles* survives in the Auchinleck form in one other manuscript, but occurs elsewhere in different versions; see *NIMEV* 982, 1767.

[31] See note 35 below for details.

comprehensiveness that could have been met, at least in part, by commissioning specific poems.

Even without such speculation, what survives of the religious verse in Auchinleck suggests that at least a significant amount of it was transmitted by a different translational route from that by which the romances were. The overall range of sources for the poems in Auchinleck would seem, then, to encompass works rendered into English from both Latin and Anglo-Norman sources. Such different lines of transmission invite the possibility that the manuscript in its overall form constitutes a synthesis, an attempt to assimilate different forms of translation into English within a single linguistic and codicological entity, in which differences in content and source were quite clearly distinguished by their sequence in the manuscript, but also integrated into a whole that sought to achieve, through its treatment of these larger questions of organization and construction in the manuscript, a clear and unprecedented comprehensiveness in its representation of the range of Middle English verse.

The range of Auchinleck's content has some bearing on our larger sense of its situation in the continuing debate about the place of the vernacular in earlier-fourteenth-century manuscript production in England. The manuscript must have taken a considerable time to achieve its final shape, one that we, of course, cannot fully grasp from its present form. What seems most likely is that the manuscript's shape was not accretive – an evolving series of responses to the demands of the 'perhaps imperious' patron Ralph Hanna has envisaged[32] – nor formed by some other sense of scribal organization, nor simply by pragmatic sequencing. Rather, the evidence of its overall shape, of the broad sequential topical distinctions it embodies between religious and secular materials, suggests some deliberate controlling principle that probably existed from the outset. In this respect, the early religious sections are important in establishing the full range of the compiler's concerns.

And consciousness of this range relates to the manuscript's apparent deployment of a sequence of different kinds of vernacular translation, in which genre is often linked to sources in different languages. No other surviving Middle English manuscript bears comparison with Auchinleck in such respects. And no manuscript until the very end of the fourteenth century, in the writings of Chaucer and Gower, demonstrates on such a scale the diverse literary potentialities of the native tongue.

Such facts ought to be set against Loomis's contention that the manuscript provides a demonstration of cultural impoverishment by its presentation of its contents in a language 'avowedly not for the *lered* but for the *lewed*'.[33] The distinction seems to devalue English, presenting it as a self-evidently inferior form. As I have sought to suggest, such a view fails to appreciate the liminal status of Auchinleck, of what a consideration of the totality of its contents signifies about its programmatic status for literary English. Thorlac Turville-Petre's view seems more historically sensitive in his perception that Auchinleck should be seen as a

---

[32] R. Hanna, *London Literature, 1300–1380*, Cambridge Studies in Medieval Literature 57 (Cambridge, 2005), p. 76.

[33] See Loomis, 'The Auchinleck Manuscript', p. 600.

confident affirmation of a new, insistently vernacular culture in which 'the use of English ... is an expression of the very character of the manuscript, of its passion for England and its pride in being English'.[34] The size of Auchinleck, the range of its contents, and the cost of its production all provide evidence of a controlling and coherent taste. But, if it is to be seen in such terms, it must also be acknowledged as a special case, the product of a specifically metropolitan form of book production whereby a perhaps fortuitous conjunction of patron, literary materials, and production resources made possible a form of manuscript production that had no precedent and little discernible influence on later manuscript production.[35] Yet, whatever the specific motives behind the preparation of the Auchinleck manuscript and their relationship to questions of contemporary culture and class, the extent of the vernacularizing ambition that underlies its creation needs to reflect a fuller appreciation of the earlier religious verse than it has hitherto received, and of the place of these poems in the larger context of the manuscript's achievement. These earlier sections, as I have tried to suggest, are not simply generically different from what follows. They are also distinct in their linguistic derivation – translations not, most significantly, shaped by Anglo-Norman sources, but often demonstrably from Latin sources and perhaps, at times, of native composition. As such, they clearly suggest the widening capacity of literary English, its ability to take on new literary challenges in the vernacular, forms that extend generically considerably beyond vernacular romance. Such forms of translation, and the consequent 'Englishness' that the Auchinleck manuscript consistently demonstrates, show the emergence of English as a more ubiquitous literary language than hitherto. This is perhaps the ultimate achievement of this remarkable collection.

---

[34] T. Turville-Petre, *England the Nation: Language, Literature, and National Identity, 1290–1340* (Oxford, 1996), p. 138.

[35] Among the religious texts, two – *Nativity and Early Life of Mary* (item 13) and *The Sayings of St Bernard* (item 35) – appear earlier in MS Laud misc. 108, as does a variant version of *The Desputisoun bitven þe Bodi and þe Soule* (item 7). Both *Hou Our Leuedi Saute Was Ferst Founde* and *The Sayings of St Bernard* (items 29, 35) appear earlier in Oxford, Bodleian Library, MS Digby 86; see Turville-Petre, *England the Nation*, pp. 113–14; and S. Fein, 'The Fillers of the Auchinleck Manuscript and the Literary Culture of the West Midlands', In *Makers and Users of Medieval Books: Essays in Honour of A. S. G. Edwards*, ed. C. M. Meale and D. Pearsall (Cambridge, 2014), pp. 60–77. Three works, *The Legend of Pope Gregory*, *The King of Tars*, and a version of *The Sayings of St Bernard* (items 1, 2, 35), occur later in the fourteenth century in the Vernon manuscript (Oxford, Bodleian Library, MS Eng. poet. a. 1), together with a variant version of *Desputisoun*. And two works – *Legend* and a different version of *Nativity* (items 1, 13) – also appear in the early-fifteenth-century Oxford, Bodleian Library, MS Rawlinson poet. 225.

CHAPTER THREE

The Auchinleck *Adam and Eve*: An Exemplary Family Story

Cathy Hume

T HE idea that Auchinleck was compiled for a family audience is now well established.[1] Newer scholarship has moved away from Laura Hibbard Loomis's and
P. R. Robinson's view that the manuscript was produced speculatively, to the belief
that it was a bespoke production, which to some extent reflected the preferences of
an individual purchaser.[2] We do not know anything about this individual's social
status or geographical location, much less his or her actual identity, though various
possibilities have been suggested.[3] But the way in which Auchinleck's contents are
at once varied in terms of genre – including romance, chronicle, hagiography, and
doctrinal texts – and also unified by vernacularity and a certain lack of sophistication suggests that it was a household or family manuscript. That term can be
used quite broadly to mean that it was designed to meet the varied reading needs
of an entire secular household. More specifically, though, Nicole Clifton, Phillipa
Hardman, and Linda Olson have all suggested a child or adolescent audience for
some of the Auchinleck texts.[4] Here I want to think further about how Auchinleck
seems to have been designed for family reading, in relation to a text Clifton

---

[1] See T. A. Shonk, 'A Study of the Auchinleck Manuscript: Bookmen and Bookmaking in
the Early Fourteenth Century', *Speculum* 60 (1985), 71–91; and R. Hanna, *London Literature,
1300–1380*, Cambridge Studies in Medieval Literature 57 (Cambridge, 2005), pp. 75–82.

[2] See esp. L. H. Loomis, 'The Auchinleck Manuscript and a Possible London Bookshop of
1330–1340', *PMLA* 57 (1942), 595–627; and P. R. Robinson, 'A Study of Some Aspects of the
Transmission of English Verse Texts in Late Mediaeval Manuscripts', unpublished B.Litt
thesis, University of Oxford (Oxford, 1972), and 'The "Booklet": A Self-Contained Unit of
Composite Manuscripts', *Codicologica* 3 (1980), 49–69.

[3] Hanna, *London Literature*, p. 82; see also L. Olson, 'Romancing the Book: Manuscripts
for "Euerich Inglische"', in K. Kerby-Fulton, M. Hilmo, and L. Olson, *Opening Up Middle
English Manuscripts: Literary and Visual Approaches* (Ithaca NY, 2012), pp. 95–151, esp. pp.
105–6, 112–16.

[4] N. Clifton, '*The Seven Sages of Rome*, Children's Literature, and the Auchinleck
Manuscript', in *Childhood in the Middle Ages and the Renaissance*, ed. A. Classen (Berlin,
2005), pp. 185–201; P. Hardman, 'Popular Romances and Young Readers', in *A Companion
to Medieval Popular Romance*, ed. R. L. Radulescu and C. J. Rushton, Studies in Medieval
Romance (Cambridge, 2009), pp. 150–64; and Olson, 'Romancing the Book', pp. 99–116.

mentions only in passing: the unusual and relatively little-read Auchinleck *Life of Adam and Eve*. It is a small gem of vivid narrative, and, I will argue, it surprisingly presents Adam and Eve as positive exemplars for a medieval Christian family.[5]

The verse *Life of Adam and Eve* is now the third item in Auchinleck, and was originally numbered eighth.[6] It appears in the mainly religious booklet 1 after *The King of Tars* and before the stanzaic lives of *Seynt Mergrete* and *Seynt Katerine*. The poem as we have it is incomplete. The title and the opening section of the poem are lost; the first extant 352 lines appear in the fragment of Auchinleck that is now Edinburgh, University Library, MS 218, after which there is a further missing section. The poem begins again on fol. 14ra of Auchinleck and continues for a further 427 lines. It is copied entirely by Scribe 1 in his South-Eastern dialect.[7] The *Life* appears uniquely in Auchinleck and may well have originated in London.[8] As the *Life* turns out to be an edifying biography, it has similarities both with the saints' lives it precedes and the exemplary romance it follows.[9] It could also be grouped with the other broadly biblical narratives in Auchinleck: *The Harrowing of Hell*, *Nativity and Early Life of Mary*, *Life of St Mary Magdalene*, and *The Assumption of the Blessed Virgin*.[10]

The frequent focus on family relationships and lineage in Middle English romance is widely acknowledged, and has led to the conclusion that many romances were written for family audiences.[11] But the same is true of Middle English biblical literature, though much less attention has been paid to it.[12] Like romances, Middle English biblical poems often concern themselves with love and marriage (for example, *Susannah* and *The Storie of Asneth*) and with relationships between parents and children (for example, *Jacob and Joseph*), and feature child protagonists (for example, the Middle English *Childhood of Christ* stories).[13] And there are

---

[5] Clifton, '*The Seven Sages of Rome*', p. 188.

[6] *The Apocryphal Lives of Adam and Eve, Edited from the Auchinleck MS and from Trinity College, Oxford MS 57*, ed. B. Murdoch and J. A. Tasioulas, Exeter Medieval Texts and Studies (Exeter, 2002). All citations from the Auchinleck *Life of Adam and Eve*, cited in the text by line number, are taken from this edition.

[7] See discussion in *The Apocryphal Lives*, ed. Murdoch and Tasioulas, pp. 5–6.

[8] Hanna, *London Literature*, p. 104, suggests that most of the booklet 1 texts came from outside London, but there is no evidence for that in this case.

[9] On the close relationship between hagiography and romance in terms of their edifying and exemplary functions, see D. T. Childress, 'Between Romance and Legend: "Secular Hagiography" in Middle English Literature', *Philological Quarterly* 57 (1978), 311–22; and J. Boffey, 'Middle English Lives', in *The Cambridge History of Medieval English Literature*, ed. D. Wallace (Cambridge, 1999), pp. 610–34.

[10] For further details of these texts, see the Burnley-Wiggins facsimile.

[11] See, for example, Hardman, 'Popular Romances'; and F. Riddy, 'Middle English Romance: Family, Marriage, Intimacy', in *The Cambridge Companion to Medieval Romance*, ed. R. L. Krueger (Cambridge, 2000), pp. 235–52.

[12] For a useful guide see J. H. Morey, *Book and Verse: A Guide to Middle English Biblical Literature* (Urbana IL, 2000).

[13] *Susannah: An Alliterative Poem of the Fourteenth Century*, ed. A. Miskimin (New Haven, 1969); *The Storie of Asneth*, in *Heroic Women from the Old Testament in Middle English Verse*, ed. R. A. Peck (Kalamazoo MI, 1991), pp. 1–67; and *Iacob and Iosep: A Middle*

other connections between the two groups of texts. Both tend to combine entertainment with didactic messages conveyed through exemplary figures. Authors seem to choose from a shared menu of verse forms for both groups of texts, and can similarly treat short episodes (a Breton lay, perhaps, or the ballad *Judas*) or present huge narrative cycles.[14] And they appear together in manuscripts that suggest a secular audience – for example, *Cleanness* and *Patience* appear alongside *Sir Gawain and the Green Knight* in London, British Library, MS Cotton Nero A. x, while the fifteenth-century *Life of Job* appears in San Marino, Huntington Library, MS HM 140, where it is bound together with advice for apprentices and *The Libelle of Englyshe Polycye*, a London mercantile text.[15] So the Auchinleck *Life of Adam and Eve* is not unusual among Middle English biblical poems in telling a positive and entertaining exemplary story about a family to a family audience – who might have enjoyed it in much the same way that they enjoyed romances.

However, the Auchinleck *Life* looks more surprising within the wider reception of the Adam and Eve story in medieval England. So I will begin this essay by summarizing that wider tradition before going on to discuss the *Life*'s idiosyncratic treatment of Adam, Eve, and their son Seth as a loving, supportive, pious and doctrinally knowledgeable family. I hope to show that the text is designed to both entertain and instruct, and that its message appears to be directed towards a family audience – that is, for shared reading by married men and women and their children. Finally, I want to consider how this affects our wider conception of Auchinleck as a family manuscript.

I

Adam and Eve are everywhere in medieval England, and a full description of their complex meanings and representations would take more than a single volume. As well as appearing in the liturgy, sermons, and didactic literature, they are frequently portrayed in the visual arts, and in both plays and narrative literature in Latin, French, and English.[16] We need to understand some of the dominant strands in their portrayal in order to see what is distinctive about the Auchinleck *Life*.

The *Middle English Genesis and Exodus*, c. 1250, is a typical instance of the main meaning Adam and Eve carried in medieval England: it holds them individually

---

English Poem of the Thirteenth Century, ed. A. S. Napier (Oxford, 1916). On the treatment of the child protagonist in the Middle English Childhood of Christ stories, see M. Dzon, 'Joseph and the Amazing Christ-Child', in *Childhood in the Middle Ages and the Renaissance*, ed. A. Classen (Berlin, 2005), pp. 135–57.

[14] *Judas*, in *The English and Scottish Popular Ballads*, ed. F. J. Child, 5 vols. (Mineola NY, 1965), I, 243–44 (no. 23).

[15] *The Poems of the Pearl Manuscript: Pearl, Cleanness, Patience, Sir Gawain and the Green Knight*, ed. M. Andrew and R. Waldron, 5th edn, Exeter Medieval Texts and Studies (Exeter, 2007). For San Marino, Huntington Library MS HM 140, see C. W. Dutschke, *Guide to Medieval and Renaissance Manuscripts in the Huntington Library*, 2 vols. (San Marino CA, 1989), II, 185–90.

[16] For a summary focused on visual representations, see L. Réau, *Iconographie de l'art Chrétien*, 3 vols. (Paris, 1956), II, 77–93.

responsible for bringing misery to all mankind.[17] The same idea is articulated in the fourteenth-century *Lay Folk's Catechism*: we would all be innocent, except that 'we bere the wickednesse of thaire misdede'.[18] The *Metrical Paraphrase of the Old Testament* (c. 1400) takes this negative portrayal one step further. There they are not just sinful, but entirely without dignity: they live like 'bestes wyld' after the Fall.[19]

Another common emphasis is on Eve as the temptress and deceiver of Adam. In the fourteenth-century Cornish play the *Ordinalia*, for example, Eve insists that Adam eat the apple by threatening: 'Not to believe me is to lose me and my love. You'll never see me again as long as you live'.[20] The *Mirour of Mannes Saluacioun* (an English translation of a fourteenth-century Latin text) develops this into a more general misogynist rant, declaring: 'For thogh the Bibles text apertely noght it write,/ No doubt sho broght him inne with faging [flattering] words white,' and explaining that, if Eve had been content to meekly help Adam, no man would ever have 'done woman distresse', but, since she tempted him because of her own pride, womankind 'hase deserved forthi to soeffre of manes rod'.[21] Here, as in many treatments of the Fall, Adam's love for Eve is an unfortunate weakness: the *Fall and Passion* (c. 1300) expresses it regretfully as 'womman is lef euer to man'.[22]

These negative portrayals dominate, but it is also possible to present the pair as worthy forefathers in some respects. In the fifteenth century in particular, Adam and Eve's inauguration of the sacrament of marriage is a frequent subject in the visual arts.[23] As Ann Eljenholm Nichols has shown, it is mentioned in *St Edmund's Mirror*; and the sacrament is prominent in the Chester Drapers' play.[24] Adam and Eve also appear in the Harrowing of Hell tradition, where they are authoritative mouthpieces for orthodox theology: for example, in the York Harrowing of Hell play.[25] And, as John Flood notes, Eve sits at Mary's feet in Dante's *Paradiso*.[26]

---

[17] *The Middle English Genesis and Exodus*, ed. O. Arngart (Lund, 1968), lines 239–42.

[18] *The Lay Folk's Catechism, or the English and Latin Versions of Archbishop Thoresby's Instruction for the People*, ed. T. F. Simmons and H. E. Nolloth, EETS OS 118 (London, 1901), text T, line 23.

[19] *The Middle English Metrical Paraphrase of the Old Testament*, ed. M. Livingston (Kalamazoo MI, 2011), line 231.

[20] *The Cornish Ordinalia*, ed. and trans. M. Harris (Washington DC, 1969), p. 8.

[21] *The Mirour of Mans Saluacioun: A Middle English Translation of Speculum Humanae Salvationis*, ed. A. Henry (Aldershot, 1986), lines 339–59.

[22] *Fall and Passion*, in *Die Kildare-Gedichte: Die ältesten mittelenglischen Denkmäler in anglo-irischen Überliefung*, ed. W. Heuser, Bonner Beiträge zur Anglistik 14 (Bonn, 1904), pp. 106–12 (line 56).

[23] See Réau, *Iconographie*, II, 82.

[24] A. E. Nichols, *Seeable Signs: The Iconography of the Seven Sacraments 1350–1544* (Woodbridge, 1994), pp. 279–80; and 'Drapers' Play', in *The Chester Mystery Cycle*, ed. R. M. Lumiansky and D. Mills, 2 vols., EETS SS 3 (Oxford, 1974, 1986), I, 13–41 (lines 157–60).

[25] *The York Plays*, ed. R. Beadle, 2 vols., EETS SS 23, 24 (Oxford, 2009, 2013), I, 354–65. The Harrowing of Hell tradition is discussed in J. Flood, *Representations of Eve in Antiquity and the English Middle Ages* (New York, 2011), pp. 116–22.

[26] Flood, *Representations of Eve*, p. 80. See Dante, *Paradiso*, 32.4–6, in *The Divine Comedy of Dante Alighieri*, ed. and trans. R. M. Durling, 3 vols. (Oxford, 1996, 2003, 2011), III.

Then there is the *Vita Adae et Evae*, the source of the Auchinleck *Life*, whose positive slant on the couple is rather different from the examples I have mentioned so far. This piece of biblical apocrypha, composed in Latin probably between AD 100 and 400, seems to have circulated widely in medieval England – close to twenty manuscripts of English provenance survive.[27] It tells the story of Adam and Eve's lives after they were expelled from Paradise, beginning with their attempts to find food, their penance in the rivers of Jordan and Tigris, their second encounter with the devil during this penance, their separation, and the birth of Cain and Abel. Cain and Abel's lives and deaths follow, and then the birth of another son, Seth, who returns to Paradise to try to get the oil of mercy for the dying Adam. Finally, Adam and Eve die and are buried, and Seth records their lives on tablets of stone and clay. The *Vita* is not a stable text, and different manuscripts can include additional legends or paraphrases of parts of the Bible, but common to all is an emphasis on Adam and Eve's regret and penance rather than their sin. Moreover, the *Vita* form lends it a hagiographical shape, which encourages the presentation of Adam and Eve as positive exemplary figures. There are several versions of the *Vita* in Middle English: three in prose, one of which is in the Vernon manuscript and one of which appears in several manuscripts of the *Gilte Legende*; and another verse version, the *Canticum de Creatione*, which states that it was composed in 1375.[28] But, despite the generally more positive slant of these texts, Flood's characterization of the *Vita* Eve as 'dependent, despairing, and lacking in moral judgement' seems accurate and can be extended to all these English versions.[29] The one exception is the Auchinleck *Life*, which presents Adam, Eve, and Seth as a whole family of positive exemplars.

II

The status of the Auchinleck *Life* as an exemplary narrative is made clear at the end of the poem. Its narrative is retrospectively described as a 'liif', as its modern (but editorial) title suggests, and in keeping with its *Vita* source:

> Now haue ȝe herd of Adames liif,
> and of Eue, þat was his wiif,
> Whiche liif þai ladden here on mold,
> And seþþen diden, as God wold. (lines 725–8)

[27] See M. D. Johnson's English translation of the 'Life of Adam and Eve', in *The Old Testament Pseudepigrapha*, ed. J. H. Charlesworth, 2 vols. (London, 1985), II, 249–95. On the circulation of the *Vita* in medieval England, see *The Apocryphal Lives*, ed. Murdoch and Tasioulas, pp. 7–25.

[28] For the Vernon version, see *Middle English Religious Prose*, ed. N. F. Blake (London 1972), pp. 103–18; for the *Gilte Legende* version, see *The Wheatley Manuscript*, ed. M. Day, EETS OS 21 (1921), pp. 76–100; for the version in Oxford, Bodleian Library, MS Bodley 2376, see C. Horstmann, 'Nachträge zu den Legenden', *Archiv* 74 (1885), 327–65. There is a version closely related to the Bodleian text in Cambridge, Trinity College, MS 601 (R. 3. 21). The *Canticum de Creatione* is included in *The Apocryphal Lives*, ed. Murdoch and Tasioulas, pp. 63–98.

[29] Flood, *Representations of Eve*, p. 95.

The term 'lyf' was, as Paul Strohm demonstrates, the normal term for a saint's life in Middle English. The strongly exemplary function of that genre, which can be traced back to Gregory of Tours's *Liber Vitae Patrum* (c. 591), was well established by the fourteenth century, so that readers would expect exemplary lessons to emerge from any saint's life they encountered.[30] Moreover, the final lines of the poem present Adam as our exemplar, describing Christ's action in bringing 'Adam out of helle' (line 778) and praying:

> 3if ous grace for to winne
> Þe ioie þat Adam now is inne. (lines 779–80)

We must hope to follow Adam, whose clear need for Christ's assistance to escape Hell (because he was born before the Incarnation) helps to make him more like the average Christian than the typical saint.

That the average Christian layperson is indeed the intended audience of the *Life* is implied by its doctrinal content. A few doctrinal messages are given a prominent place in the *Life* without much precedent in the Latin *Vita*. All are fairly simple, and consistent with the core pastoral teaching of the medieval Church.[31] In its current acephalous state, the poem begins with an account of the Fall of Lucifer (which is not normally part of the *Vita*). This account repeatedly labels the sin of Lucifer and his fellow fallen angels as 'pride' (lines 14, 25, 34, 47) before concluding:

> In heuen pride first bigan
> In angel, ar it cam in man,
> And for it com out of heuen,
> And was þe form sinne of seuen,
> Þerfore, wiþouten lesing,
> Of alle sinnes, pride is king. (lines 59–64)

The *Life*'s other main doctrinal message is, as one might expect, the gravity of breaking God's commandments. This was linked with pride in interpretations of the Fall going back to Augustine, and more generally was a commonplace of medieval pastoralia.[32] The message that Adam and Eve broke God's commandment is repeated again and again for emphasis: at lines 70, 103, 119, 189, 276, 364, 413, 560, 607, and 624. Other messages include the importance of proper Sunday observances

---

[30] P. Strohm, 'Passioun, Lyf, Miracle, Legende: Some Generic Terms in Middle English Hagiographical Narrative', *Chaucer Review* 10 (1975), 62–75, 154–71 (pp. 155–6). On the origins of the exemplary function for saints' lives, see T. J. Heffernan, *Sacred Biography: Saints and Their Biographers in the Middle Ages* (New York, 1988), esp. pp. 3–30.

[31] On pastoral messages in fourteenth-century England, see H. L. Spencer, *English Preaching in the Late Middle Ages* (Oxford, 1993), pp. 196–227. The core curriculum from Pecham's 1281 *Ignorantia sacerdotum* included the Ten Commandments, Seven Works of Mercy, Seven Deadly Sins (including an emphasis on the first three, spiritual, sins, pride, envy, and wrath), and the seven sacraments (p. 203).

[32] On Augustine's theology of the Fall, see J. M. Evans, *'Paradise Lost' and the Genesis Tradition* (Oxford, 1968), pp. 93–9. For the more general association, see e.g. John Mirk, *Instructions for Parish Priests*, ed. G. Kristensson (Lund, 1974), lines 979–82.

(lines 656–68) – something that seems to have preoccupied late medieval priests – proper burial rites (lines 574–92) and, inevitably, penance, which I will discuss at greater length below.[33] These are mentioned in the *Vita* (burial in chapter 48 and the Sabbath in chapter 51) but given more attention in the *Life*. The treatment of the devil's temptation of Eve is especially interesting in terms of the poem's doctrinal content and imagined audience. He tempts her with the prospect of knowing all God's 'priuete' (lines 86) if she eats the forbidden fruit. This expression, which is familiar from Chaucer's *Miller's Tale*, 'Men sholde nat knowe of Goddes pryvetee',[34] is not used in other versions of the Adam and Eve story, as far as I know, but warns the reader against the danger of too much theological curiosity and speculation. Nicholas Watson has shown that such warnings are relatively common in late medieval English literature aimed at the laity.[35] All of these messages are clearly communicated, while other doctrinal details are clarified: for example, there is a clear distinction between Paradise and Heaven at lines 28–9, 113, 126, and 568. The emphasis on clear and unambiguous communication of important details probably reflects the text's hagiographic affiliations as much as it suggests a family audience.[36]

Formal signals and doctrinal content suggest, then, that the *Life* should be read as an exemplary text that offers moral lessons. But the most important criterion for such a text is that it should feature protagonists who are both virtuous and engaging.[37] Adam and Eve might seem unlikely candidates since their story centres on them being sinfully responsible for breaking God's commandment; the *Vita* story also involves Eve sinning by breaking penance. However, in the *Life*, both of these sins are minimized rather than being multiplied as they are in other versions of the story, leaving an overall impression of virtuous people who make a couple of very serious mistakes. This effect is achieved, first, by an unusually brief treatment of the events in Paradise. We do not see Adam and Eve assenting to God's prohibition on the forbidden fruit. They do not have well-developed wicked motivations for eating it: Eve simply tells Adam that he should 'do as ich þe rede' (line 93) and eat the apple in order to become as 'wise of alle þing' (line 98) as God. This is described as Adam's 'wiues enticement' (line 102), but she does not flatter or threaten, and Adam and Eve's pride in aspiring to be as wise as God is left implicit. Afterwards, they do not blame one another for their joint transgression, and they come across as less self-seeking and gluttonous than they do in the *Vita*. The first few chapters of the *Vita* focus on Adam and Eve's rather precious-sounding attempts to find 'food such as they had had in Paradise' (chapter 2), including Adam's complaint that 'for us there used to be the food of angels' (chapter 4). Eve goes on to break her penance

---

[33] For medieval preaching on Sunday observances, see G. R. Owst, *Literature and Pulpit in Medieval England* (Cambridge, 1933), pp. 98, 161, 359, 364, 423.

[34] *Canterbury Tales*, I 3454, in *The Riverside Chaucer*, p. 71.

[35] N. Watson, 'Christian Ideologies', in *A Companion to Chaucer*, ed. P. Brown, Blackwell Companions to Literature and Culture (Oxford, 2000), pp. 75–89. He cites *Piers Plowman*, *The Cloud of Unknowing* and *A Book for a Simple and Devout Woman*.

[36] Heffernan, *Sacred Biography*, p. 6.

[37] Ibid., p. 30.

of standing in the river because the devil lies that God has had a meal prepared for her (chapter 9). In the *Life*, their complaint is the more pathetic one that they are dying of hunger (line 152), and Eve abandons penance because she believes she is forgiven (line 251). The drama of this, her second transgression, is also diminished. In the *Vita*, Eve's flesh turns green from cold when she leaves the river; she swoons, and the devil raises her up – an image that implies she is in some sense in his care or under his power (chapter 10). In the *Life*, all of these details are cut, making the moment far less memorable.

At the same time, the poet takes pains to bring his narrative of the distant past closer to the experience of the English audience, and to present Adam and Eve sympathetically. Various exotica, such as 'nard, crocus, calamine and cinnamon' (chapter 43), are dropped from the story, and the fig-leaves with which Adam and Eve cover their nakedness in Genesis are replaced with 'more' (roots) and 'gras' (line 110). There is also a lovely passage about the cyclical movements of the moon and the sea, when Liȝtbern (Lucifer) presumes to sit on God's throne:

> And seyd he was worþier þan he,
> For þe mone bar him wittnesse,
> It wexeþ and waineþ more and lesse;
> Þe se, þurth vertu of Godes miȝt,
> Ebbeþ and flouweþ day and niȝt.
> Þis tvay no habbe neuer rest,
> Noiþer bi est no bi west. (lines 52–8)

The source of this image is mysterious, but it is undoubtedly powerful, creating the sense that the familiar phenomena of the natural world around us are implicated in the Fall of the Angels.[38]

Adam and Eve's emotional reactions also seem familiar and engage our sympathy. Eve repeatedly reproaches herself for her sins, and vivid speeches like the following couplet make her plight starkly pitiable:

> 'Adam, Adam, wele is te,
> And Adam, Adam, wo is me!' (lines 325–6)

Adam's response to Eve's suffering is also sympathetic:

> Adam was in gret care
> Þat seyȝe his wiif so iuel fare. (lines 285–6)

Neither detail is in the *Vita*, but both exemplify a programme of authorial changes that make the narrative more affecting and encourage audience identification with the characters.

The narrative interest of the *Life* is not confined to establishing that the story is relevant and that its heroes are worthy of imitation. It is more generally dramatic

---

[38] Parallels are suggested by Murdoch and Tasioulas, in *The Apocryphal Lives*, p. 101; and in G. Dunphy, 'The Devil's See: A Puzzling Reference in the Auchinleck *Life of Adam*', *Medium Ævum* 73 (2004), 93–8. However, they do not seem particularly close.

and entertaining. This is not a surprise in a hagiographical text, but does make it easy to imagine a lay family audience affording it enough attention to absorb its messages.[39] To give a few examples, the narrative is reordered so that it begins (in its current state) with the drama of Liȝtbern's rebellion, rather than this being conveyed in reported speech later. A vivid image is presented when Adam and Eve lie miserably 'al star naked' (line 144) under a crude shelter for six days and nights after their expulsion from Paradise, instead of being clothed at this point as in Genesis or the *Vita*. Enigmatic supernatural disappearances are added, apparently for the fun of a marvel, so that, after the devil harasses Seth and Eve:

> Þurth miȝt of þe heuen king
> Out of her siȝt oway he nam –
> Þai nist neuer whar he bicam. (lines 442–4)

The poet is apparently so keen on this device that he repeats it where it does not make complete sense, after the angel has delivered his lecture about Sunday observance:

> In to heuen þe way he nam;
> Þai wist neuer whar he bicam. (lines 671–2)

And short and vivid speeches are not the preserve of Eve, but are a major feature of the whole *Life*, as in God's single speech to Adam and Eve in Paradise once he knows what they have done:

> 'Adam, Adam, why destow þus?
> Þou hast ybrouȝt þiselue in wo
> And Eue þi gode wiif also,
> For þou hast min hest ybroke.
> Forsoþe, Adam, ichil be wroke –
> Ȝe haue ydon a sori dede;
> Forsoþe, ȝe schul haue ȝour mede'. (lines 116–22)

In seven short lines we get reproach, revenge, a vague and sinister threat, and a refreshing refusal to place the blame on Eve.

III

All the signs, then, are that a medieval audience would have read the *Life* as a positive and entertaining exemplary story. The most striking dimension of its exemplarity is the presentation of Adam, Eve, and Seth as a family whose love, mutual respect, and support give all of them greater moral and devotional strength. This depiction is in stark contrast to the negative portrayal of love as a source of manipulation and weakness and a gateway to sin that was common to many other treatments of Adam and Eve.

---

[39] On the importance of action and vivid scenes in saints' lives, see Heffernan, *Sacred Biography*, pp. 6, 20.

In the *Vita*, it is certainly clear that Eve loves Adam, to the extent that she suggests that he should kill her:

'My lord, would you kill me? O that I would die! Then perhaps the Lord God will bring you again into Paradise, for it is because of me that the Lord God is angry with you'. Adam answered, 'Do not wish to speak such words lest the Lord God bring on us some further curse. How is it possible that I should let loose my hand against my flesh?' (chapter 3)[40]

Adam's response is corrective – the words of someone with greater moral authority and wisdom – and gives no indication of emotion. In the Auchinleck *Life*, his tone is quite different:

> 'A, woman', quaþ Adam þo,
> 'Allas, whi seydestow so?
> Wostow make me so wode
> To sle min owhen flesche and blode?
> Boþe in flesche and in bon
> Jhesus Crist haþ made ous on –
> He made þe of mi ribbe –
> Þou miȝtest be me no ner sibbe!' (lines 161–8)

The content is similar, but we get a quite different impression of Adam's love for Eve: something deep, natural, and even divinely ordered, which makes the very thought of her death distressing to him. Much the same pattern is repeated when Adam lies dying.

The dynamics between the couple are more generally subtly redrawn to create a partnership between husband and wife. Adam still appears wiser and more authoritative than Eve in the *Life*, but he does not interrogate or upbraid her or lay down the law. In the *Vita*, Eve has to ask him what penance is (chapter 5), Adam commands her (chapter 6), and, when the devil tricks her into breaking penance, he says: 'Eve, where is the work of your penitence? How have you again been seduced by our enemy?' (chapter 10).[41] In the *Life*, Eve displays her own understanding of penance and the importance of not abandoning it (lines 199–206), and Adam advises a form of penance by saying 'mi rede it is' (line 191) – which may imply a suggestion rather than an order. When Eve is tricked into breaking penance, Adam's speech is sorrowful and explanatory rather than condemnatory and scolding:

> 'Eue, allas! allas!
> Now is wers þan it was!
> He þat comeþ in þi compeynie,
> Now he haþ ygiled þe tvie'. (lines 269–72)

And, when Eve realizes her mistake, she reacts so dramatically that our attention is focused on her own realization and self-reproach, rather than either Adam's words

---

[40] 'Life of Adam and Eve', trans. Johnson, p. 258.
[41] Ibid., p. 260.

or the preceding transgression. Some of the dramatic detail that the Auchinleck poet had removed from the moment when she left the river is transferred to this moment, where she now swoons and shakes for fear of God (lines 279–82). She does not complain, as she does in the *Vita*, that she has been 'cheated and deceived' (chapter 18).[42] Instead she again articulates an orthodox idea of penance:

> 'Þe foule flesche þat haþ agilt,
> In þesternesse it schal be pilt'. (lines 337–8)

We understand Eve, then, as someone with her own conscience and sense of moral responsibility, who nevertheless needs Adam's help.

So much for Adam and Eve's marital relationship. As parents, they are presented as holding joint responsibility and authority, and this impression is interestingly created by the way Adam speaks to Eve about their children. In the *Vita*, when Eve is upset by Adam's suffering on his deathbed, he tells her to 'rise and go with my son Seth' to Paradise (chapter 36).[43] Seth seems to be in charge of the expedition, and when they set off he leads the way (chapter 37). In the *Life*, Adam tells her to 'take Seþ in þi compeynie' (line 391), which suggests an inversion of the relationship. Eve leads the way, and she is to give Seth specific directions once they get there (lines 393–400). Seth is expected to follow his mother and do as she says. Later, the *Life* also treats Adam's dying words to Eve differently. In the *Vita*, Adam tells her accusingly that she will have to explain to the children that she was the cause of original sin and all their suffering (chapter 44). In the *Life*, this becomes something more positive. He takes joint responsibility for 'þe wo / Þat is ywakened of ous tvo' (lines 511–12), and the reason for Eve to explain original sin to the children is so that she can go on to instruct them 'niȝt and day merci to crie' (line 517).

Eve's role as a moral authority and teacher of her children is not completely without parallel outside this text. In the later Chester Drapers' Play, Eve tells Cain and Abel that they should be warned by her experience and avoid falling into sin, and, in the *Ordinalia*, she blesses Abel.[44] But, in the *Life*, Eve plays a larger role as moral educator, instructing her children much as a typical medieval mother might have done.[45] She passes on Adam's message about crying for mercy and offers her blessing, but also more significantly introduces the idea that the children should offer 'penaunce' (line 612) and explains how to make use of the exemplary story she is telling:

> 'Þo þat be now ȝong childre
> Mai it see, and her elder,

---

[42] Ibid., p. 264.

[43] Ibid., p. 272.

[44] 'Drapers' Play', ed. Lumiansky and Mills, lines 511–12; and *Cornish Ordinalia*, trans. Harris, p. 14.

[45] See D. M. Webb, 'Woman and Home: The Domestic Setting of Late Medieval Spirituality', in *Women in the Church*, ed. W. J. Sheils and D. Wood (Oxford, 1991), pp. 159–73, esp. pp. 159–61; and K. J. Lewis, 'The Life of St Margaret of Antioch in Late Medieval England: A Gendered Reading', in *Gender and Christian Religion*, ed. R. N. Swanson (Woodbridge, 1998), pp. 129–42 (p. 135).

> And oþer, þat here after be bore,
> Hou we han wrouȝt here bifore,
> Þat þai mowe taken ensaumple of ous
> And amenden oȝain Jhesus'. (lines 627–32)

Within the poem Eve is speaking to an audience of 'hir childer and hir childer childre' (604) – already a larger group than the children mentioned in the *Vita* – but here her authoritative advice on exemplary reading is extended to all of Eve's progeny, which of course includes the readers of the Auchinleck *Life*.

If Eve the teacher is an exemplary mother, Seth is also an exemplary child. (The Cain and Abel episode is missing from the manuscript, as mentioned above, so that we cannot tell whether they were treated as exemplary figures.) When he and Eve reach Paradise in the *Vita*, they prostrate themselves and sigh noisily for many hours (chapters 40–1). But, in the *Life*, Eve stands back and Seth weeps silently – 'alle stille' (line 453) – and simply awaits God's will. This sounds much more like the medieval ideal of youthful behaviour prescribed in *The Babees Book*, which emphasizes how boys in service should stand 'styl as stone', waiting in silence for their lord to address them.[46] Probably more importantly, he and his brothers and sisters are attentive listeners, good at absorbing important lessons. The angels had instructed the family about proper burial after Adam died, and when Eve dies they know what to do:

> Her children token hem to rede,
> And beren hir þilke selue day
> Vnto þe stede þer Adam lay,
> And biried hir in þilke stede,
> Riȝt as þe angels dede
> Þat biried Adam and Abel –
> Þerof þai token hede ful wel. (lines 640–6)

That final line signals the exemplary function of the passage.

Individually, Adam, Eve, and Seth are well-informed proto-Christians, and they also model the kind of good behaviour a medieval household might have wanted to encourage. But the sense of their mutual love, concern, and support is just as important, and is conveyed much more strongly in the Auchinleck *Life* than it was in the *Vita*. I discussed Adam and Eve's mutual love above. Adam and Eve's protective love for Seth is also emphasized when the adder bites him (lines 414, 494). When the adder goes on to speak aggressively to Eve afterwards, Seth's response is to call him a 'foule þing' (line 437) and tell him to get away 'fro mi moder' (line 438) and himself. The overall impression is of a unified family whose love for one another strengthens their ability to combat the devil.[47]

---

[46] *The Babees Book: Early English Meals and Manners*, ed. F. J. Furnivall, EETS OS 32 (London, 1868), pp. 1–9 (line 86).

[47] This may parallel the tendency Morgan sees in fourteenth-century Bible illustration to portray medieval family structures and feudal order: N. Morgan, 'Old Testament

IV

So, while all *Vita* texts are exemplary, the Auchinleck *Life*'s exemplarity, with its positive focus on family roles and relationships, seems distinctive. This is even more obvious if we compare the poem with its closest analogue, the *Canticum de Creatione*, as well as its neighbouring texts in Auchinleck.

The *Canticum* is the only other Middle English verse adaptation of the *Vita*. It appears uniquely in Oxford, Trinity College, MS 57, and is later than the Auchinleck *Life*, giving its date of composition as 1375.[48] Like the *Life*, it minimizes Adam and Eve's sin in Paradise and shares the *Life*'s tendency to emphasize exemplarity. And, like the *Life*, it adds various doctrinal messages: in the *Canticum*, the focus is primarily on proper tithing (see especially lines 328–44, 487–92). However, it does not present us with the same image of a loving family that the Auchinleck *Life* achieves, instead staying closer to the *Vita*. The *Canticum* poet does not choose to insert moments where Adam and Seth display love and concern of the kind that the Auchinleck poet adds. Indeed, there is actually *less* intimacy between Adam and Eve: after Eve breaks her river penance, she is too ashamed ever to look at Adam again and veils her face from him (lines 373–84). And, instead of having a partnership marriage with Eve, Adam is clearly the moral guardian of both her and their children. As in the *Vita*, Eve has to ask Adam what penance is (lines 103–8), and when she speaks to the children after Adam's death it is only to tell them to record the story of their lives (lines 899–903) rather than to give them a maternal lesson of her own devising as in the *Life*. Finally, the *Canticum* does not give Seth any of the moments of imitable good behaviour that I suggested could have made him an exemplary model for medieval children. The overall impression is that the *Canticum* is far less interested than the Auchinleck *Life* in creating a story with positive exemplars for every member of the family.

The Life of Adam and Eve appears, rather, to have more in common with other Auchinleck texts. Clifton's 2005 essay '*The Seven Sages of Rome*, Children's Literature, and the Auchinleck Manuscript' offers an extended consideration, centred on *Seven Sages*, of her claim that the manuscript 'testifies to a serious and sustained production and appreciation of medieval children's literature'.[49] Clifton identifies several common traits found in more recent children's literature and shared by *Seven Sages*, including child protagonists, an emphasis on action rather than reflection, and an explicit narrative style, where motivations and connections between events do not have to be guessed.[50] She also suggests that the English language of the manuscript may reflect the youth of its target readers, and notes that 'many of the texts contain didactic elements of the sort to be found in courtesy books aimed at children and teenagers'.[51] We have seen many of these features in

---

Illustration in Thirteenth-Century England', in *The Bible in the Middle Ages: Its Influence on Literature and Art*, ed. B. S. Levy (Binghamton NY, 1992), pp. 149–98 (p. 172).

[48] See *The Apocryphal Lives*, ed. Murdoch and Tasioulas, p. 5.

[49] Clifton, '*The Seven Sages of Rome*', p. 187.

[50] Ibid., pp. 190–1.

[51] Ibid., p. 187.

The Life of Adam and Eve. Seth is a young protagonist; the poet seems concerned to present a dramatic narrative, including more direct action than he found in his source; he improves the clarity of certain narrative details such as the identity of the adder, and gives Adam some additional motivation.[52] And we saw that aspects of Seth's behaviour reflected the advice given in *The Babees Book.* The *Life*'s combination of exemplary lessons with a lively narrative also fits neatly into what Clifton sees as the mode of reading invited by the manuscript and modeled in *Seven Sages*: that moral lessons should be extracted from entertaining stories. Clifton argues that this mode of reading is proposed in *Seven Sages* and that the texts that follow it fall into seven pairs, where 'one more pointedly moral or practical text' is presented 'alongside one more strongly fictional or entertaining'.[53] Her focus is on child readers of different ages and on the end of the manuscript. I think there are indications of an intended family audience in this early part of the manuscript, too, but I want to be specific about what exactly these various indications are.

In booklet 1 of the Auchinleck manuscript, the *Life* is followed by the stanzaic lives *Seynt Mergrete* and *Seynt Katerine*. Lives of both these saints commonly appear in household manuscripts, as Katherine J. Lewis has shown; and both suggest a readership of wives or mothers, as well as of children.[54] Katherine, virgin martyr, may on the face of it seem an unsuitable subject for family reading, but in fact she was considered a patron of nursing mothers – because her neck spurted milk when she was beheaded – and of women with cruel husbands like her suitor, the emperor. Sherry L. Reames notes that the Auchinleck version of her *Life* has an exemplary emphasis.[55] Margaret's primary association was with childbirth because she had successfully emerged from a dragon's belly. Women in medieval England commonly had her story fastened to their bodies as a protective amulet while in labour.[56] Margaret's *Life* also includes a section where she is a child being told stories of saints by her Christian nurse, which could appeal to a child and also function as an *exemplum* of a medieval woman's responsibility for teaching the Christian faith to children in the home.[57]

Preceding *The Life of Adam and Eve* is the pious romance *The King of Tars*. It features a Christian princess who is forced to marry a heathen Sultan, but converts him to Christianity when, at her instigation, God transforms their child – born as a lifeless lump of flesh – into a beautiful boy. As with *The Life of Adam and Eve*, then, the romance presents an active and pious role for a wife and mother, a prominent child, and the idea that love and family can lead to Christian salvation rather than being obstacles to it. Small differences exist between the Auchinleck version of this

---

[52] John Geck provided further examples of Auchinleck's avoidance of ambiguity in its narrative style and presentation of character in his LOMERS conference paper 'Auchinleck, among Others: Prevailing Themes in Multiple-Manuscript Romances'.

[53] Clifton, '*The Seven Sages of Rome*', p. 199.

[54] Lewis, 'The Life of St Margaret of Antioch', p. 135.

[55] *Middle English Legends of Women Saints*, ed. S. L. Reames (Kalamazoo MI, 2003), p. 170.

[56] Ibid., p. 111.

[57] Lewis, 'The Life of St Margaret of Antioch', pp. 131–5.

romance and that in the Vernon manuscript: in Auchinleck, God is referred to as 'þe fader' (line 758) where he is 'þat ilke Lord' in Vernon; Mary is Jesus's 'moder fre' (line 65) in Auchinleck, but a 'mayden freo' in Vernon.[58] The positive use of familial epithets in the Auchinleck *King of Tars* is telling. Similarly, the poem's editor, Judith Perryman, notes that Auchinleck portrays the Christian characters 'as having more human feelings of love and grief than the heathens'. The Auchinleck *Life of Adam and Eve* shares this implication that human love is a positive Christian force, but the idea is lost in the Vernon *King of Tars*.[59]

So, *The Life of Adam and Eve* and its neighbouring texts can be added to the growing list of Auchinleck contents for which a family audience has been proposed. The list includes, in addition to Clifton's *Seven Sages* and the fourteen texts that follow it, the romances *Amis and Amiloun*, *Sir Degare*, *Sir Tristrem*, and *Horn Childe*, whose child and family protagonists, and lessons for young people, Hardman has noted.[60] Olson has also suggested that the didactic texts *The Pater Noster Vndo on Englissch* and *On þe Seuen Dedly Sinnes*, as well as *Speculum Gy de Warewyke*, are directed to a family audience; the Seven Sins text makes its direction to 'children', 'wimmen and men' explicit. Olson argues, too, that *The King of Tars* and *Seynt Katerine* provide exemplary heroines for young women.[61]

Conclusion

How seriously should we take these various claims about family reading? While it is possible that a short text, in English, that avoids ambiguity and contains lots of drama may be aimed at children, it is also probable that these features would have appealed to other unsophisticated readers – those with relatively little education or just simple tastes. On the other hand, the explicit indications of audience that Olson notes are evidence of at least an intention to speak to families. Meanwhile, I would argue that texts like *Seynt Mergrete* whose subject matter suggests an audience of wives and mothers are best thought of in a third category, along with *The Life of Adam and Eve* and its family exemplars. In these texts the indication of a family audience is implicit rather than explicit, but it is stronger evidence than mere narrative simplicity.

All three kinds of evidence of family orientation appear in several Auchinleck texts. The sheer number of them suggests that this happened by design rather than by chance. But that raises the question of how the design came about. One possibility is that the purchaser chose texts that he thought suitable for his family, perhaps supplying exemplars or requesting particular items.[62] Alternatively, the compiler – whom we may assume to be Scribe 1 – could have chosen texts, or versions of texts, that he knew to be family-friendly. These possibilities in turn raise

---

[58] *The King of Tars*, ed. J. Perryman (Heidelberg, 1980), p. 65.

[59] Ibid., p. 65.

[60] Hardman, 'Popular Romances', p. 159.

[61] Olson, 'Romancing the Book', pp. 109, 113.

[62] This is suggested by Hanna, *London Literature*, p. 76.

the question of how much customer and scribe would have known about the range of texts in circulation in London, rival versions, and their specific emphases. Would either scribe or customer have known enough to choose, say, the family-friendly *Life of Adam and Eve* over something more like the *Canticum*, with its veiled Eve and tithing reminders? When differences between manuscript versions are as small and verbal as those we saw between the Auchinleck and Vernon texts of *The King of Tars*, it seems more likely that some adaptation was going on during the copying process. The scribe may have been consciously emphasizing family relationships and exemplary lessons with his customer in mind, adapting as he wrote.[63] That may be more likely if we are already envisaging a process of adaptation: for example, if the scribe was translating into English from French.[64] But *The Life of Adam and Eve* is distant from its ultimate, Latin source and appears uniquely in Auchinleck, and its acephalous state means we do not know whether it said anything about audience in its opening lines. Unfortunately, then, we cannot know when its family orientation was introduced or use that knowledge to deepen our understanding of how the Auchinleck texts were chosen and adapted.

More broadly, though, the family orientation of *The Life of Adam and Eve* directs our attention to other Middle English biblical poetry, the largely unexplored question of its audience, and an investigation of what it had to say about family roles and relationships. I have argued elsewhere that the fifteenth-century *Storie of Asneth*, another Middle English poem adapted from a piece of Latin biblical apocrypha, is deeply concerned with noble family values.[65] The same seems to me to be true of some other poems that retell Old Testament stories: *Jacob and Joseph*, *Susannah*, *Cleanness*, and the fifteenth-century *Life of Job*. I hope to explore all of these in more detail in future publications, but there are many more Middle English texts in both poetry and prose that would benefit from investigation of their messages, audience, and adaptation – treatments of the New Testament, and some of the much longer biblical poems such as *Genesis and Exodus* and *Cursor Mundi*.[66] Such examinations would both advance our understanding of biblical literature and contribute to our wider sense of how Middle English narratives combined the secular and the Christian, the entertaining and the exemplary.

---

[63] Shonk, 'A Study', p. 88, discusses scribal adaptation.

[64] See R. Field, 'Romance', in *The Oxford History of Literary Translation in English, Volume 1: To 1550*, ed. R. Ellis (Oxford, 2008), pp. 296–331, esp. pp. 302–6; and R. Field, 'Patterns of Availability and Demand in Middle English Translations *de romanz*', in *The Exploitations of Medieval Romance*, ed. L. Ashe, I. Djordjević, and J. Weiss (Cambridge, 2010), pp. 73–89.

[65] C. Hume, '*The Storie of Asneth*: A Fifteenth-Century Commission and the Mystery of Its Epilogue', *Medium Ævum* 82 (2013), 44–65.

[66] For details of all these texts, see Morey, *Book and Verse*.

CHAPTER FOUR

A Failure to Communicate: Multilingualism in the Prologue to *Of Arthour and of Merlin*

Patrick Butler

S CHOLARSHIP on the French of England has recently explored the relationship between English and French during the Hundred Years War.[1] However, the period of escalating political tension between England and France from the War of Saint-Sardos to the start of the Hundred Years War (1323–37) has received comparatively little attention. The Auchinleck manuscript (Edinburgh, NLS, MS Advocates 19. 2. 1), compiled during this time of strain between France and England, remains notable as a nearly monolingual manuscript. Previous studies have seen its high volume of Middle English texts as indicative of an increased demand for works in English.[2] Rather than being written in English for its own sake, however, the Prologue to the Auchinleck romance *Of Arthour and of Merlin* is written in English while communicating anxiety over a perceived loss of French. The Prologue depicts French as a means to avoid needless bloodshed before the Hundred Years War, and it helps reveal a militaristic shift in England's perception of French after that war began.

---

[1] See A. Butterfield, *The Familiar Enemy: Chaucer, Language, and Nation in the Hundred Years War* (Oxford, 2009); and C. Kleinhenz and K. Busby, eds., *Medieval Multilingualism: The Francophone World and Its Neighbors*, Medieval Texts and Cultures of Northern Europe 20 (Turnhout, 2010). For essays on the development of the French of England over a longer period, see U. Schaefer, ed., *The Beginnings of Standardization: Language and Culture in Fourteenth-Century England*, Studies in English Medieval Language and Literature 15 (Frankfurt am Main, 2006). For a politically attuned survey of the Middle English language that looks at the development of Chancery English as opposed to the Hundred Years War, see T. W. Machan, 'Politics and the Middle English Language', *Studies in the Age of Chaucer* 24 (2002), 317–24.

[2] For summaries of the exceptional nature of the Auchinleck manuscript's English composition see T. Turville-Petre, *England the Nation: Language, Literature, and National Identity, 1290–1340* (Oxford, 1996), pp. 112–14; and L. Olson, 'Romancing the Book: Manuscripts for "Euerich Inglische"', in K. Kerby-Fulton, M. Hilmo, and L. Olson, *Opening Up Middle English Manuscripts: Literary and Visual Approaches* (Ithaca NY, 2012), pp. 95–151 (pp. 99–101). For a recent study that challenges interpretations that favour the English emphasis of the Auchinleck manuscript, see T. Summerfield, '"And she answered in hir language": Aspects of Multilingualism in the Auchinleck Manuscript', in *Multilingualism in Medieval Britain (c. 1066–1520): Sources and Analysis*, ed. J. A. Jefferson and A. Putter, with A. Hopkins (Turnhout, 2013), pp. 241–58.

The Prologue to Of Arthour and of Merlin

The Auchinleck Prologue to *Of Arthour and of Merlin* does not appear in any other extant copies of the romance, and it might have been added to appeal to the specific tastes of a patron.[3] If the Prologue is an original creation for the Auchinleck manuscript, it would not be the only text adapted to fit the desires of the manuscript's compilers.[4] The Prologue's poetic style is noticeably different from the text that follows, and it makes no specific reference to the romance *Of Arthour*. In fact, the Prologue concerns itself more with education than with the following text.[5] As a space that primes readers' or listeners' expectations, the Prologue indicates the romance's intended audience and contributes to our understanding of the book's understood readership.[6] Although scholars have examined questions of audience for *Of Arthour*, they have not considered in detail its prologue's association between knowing French and Latin and enacting the reduction of violence:

> Childer þat ben to boke ysett
> In age hem is miche þe bett
> For þai mo witen and se
> Miche of Godes priuete
> Hem to kepe and to ware
> Fram sinne and fram warldes care,
> And wele ysen ȝif þai willen
> Þat hem no þarf neuer spillen –
> Auauntages þai hauen þare
> Freynsch and Latin eueraywhare. (lines 9–18)[7]

---

[3] See *Of Arthour and of Merlin*, ed. O. D. Macrae-Gibson, 2 vols., EETS OS 268, 279 (Oxford, 1973, 1979), II, 76.

[4] For a study of some changes made to *Of Arthour and of Merlin*, see E. Sklar, '*Arthour and Merlin*: The Englishing of Arthur', *Michigan Academician* 8 (1975) 49–57. For adaptations of other texts, see A. Wiggins, 'Imagining the Compiler: *Guy of Warwick* and the Compilation of the Auchinleck Manuscript', in *Imagining the Book*, ed. S. Kelly and J. J. Thompson (Turnhout, 2005), pp. 61–72; D. Battles, '*Sir Orfeo* and English Identity', *Studies in Philology* 107 (2010), 179–211; and L. H. Loomis, 'The Auchinleck *Roland and Vernagu* and the *Short Chronicle*', *Modern Language Notes* 60 (1945), 94–7. For articles on the production of the manuscript itself, see R. Hanna, 'Reconsidering the Auchinleck Manuscript', in *New Directions in Later Medieval Manuscript Studies: Essays from the 1998 Harvard Conference*, ed. D. Pearsall (York, 2000), pp. 91–102; and T. A. Shonk, 'A Study of the Auchinleck Manuscript: Bookmen and Bookmaking in the Early Fourteenth Century', *Speculum* 60 (1985), 71–91.

[5] For an argument in favour of the romance being designed, on some level, with children in mind, see N. Clifton, '*Of Arthour and of Merlin* as Medieval Children's Literature', *Arthuriana* 13.2 (2003), 9–22.

[6] For a summary of the different audiences for the manuscript, see Olson, 'Romancing the Book', pp. 101–16.

[7] All quotations from the Auchinleck *Of Arthour*, cited in the text by line number, are from *Of Arthour and of Merlin*, ed. Macrae-Gibson.

The Prologue uses the word 'spillen' to describe the unrestrained nature of killing as something that can be avoided by setting children to book-learning. *Spillen* means 'to kill', but it also emphasizes brutality, notably, 'to break apart' the victim. In addition, other definitions of *spillen* imply collateral damage. A land that is *spilt* is devastated. A soul that is *spilt* is damned to hell. Blood that is *spilt* not only kills the victim but flows out onto the ground, impacting the environment around it.[8] The etymology of *spillen* connects this particular form of violence to the English language, for the word derives from Old English *spillan*. In the next line, the word 'auauntage' contrasts with the definition and etymology of *spillen*. The first definition for *auauntage* means 'benefit' in general, but other definitions emphasize 'accumulation' or 'addition', sometimes pecuniary.[9] It is fitting that a French loan word describes what is gained from learning French, and a native English word alludes to what is lost from relying on English.

According to the Prologue, learning French and Latin means one would have no need to spill blood. It follows that those who can speak only English might be prone to spilling more blood than necessary. Previous readings of the Prologue have interpreted the sentiments towards English as positive,[10] but the association between language-learning and violence complicates such a position. Rather than celebrate the widespread presence of English, the Prologue tempers any praise of the language by commenting more explicitly on the absence of French:

> Of Freynsch no Latin nil y tel more
> Ac on I[n]glisch ichil tel þerfore:
> Riȝt is þat I[n]glische vnderstond
> Þat was born in Inglond.
> Freynsche vse þis gentil man
> Ac euerich Inglische Inglische can,
> Mani noble ich haue yseiȝe
> Þat no Freynsche couþe seye,
> Biginne ichil for her loue
> Bi Ihesus leue þat sitt aboue
> On Inglische tel mi tale –
> God ous sende soule hale. (lines 19–30)

The Prologue asserts what is expected rather than exceptional about the English language in England: 'Riȝt is þat Inglische vnderstond / Þat was born in Inglond'. This assumption, that the English language is known among the people of England, stands in stark contrast to other prologues that celebrate the English language's potential for artistry, as may be found, for example, in the prologues to the *Northern Homily Cycle* and the *Cursor Mundi*.[11] Instead, the Prologue to *Of Arthour* frames

---

[8] *MED*, s.v. *spillen*.

[9] *MED*, s.v. *avauntage*.

[10] See, for example, A. C. Baugh and T. Cable, *A History of the English Language*, 5th edn (London, 2002), pp. 131–6, who quote six lines of the Prologue (lines 21–6).

[11] J. Scattergood, 'Validating the High Life in *Of Arthour and of Merlin*', *Essays in Criticism*

English as neither the preferred means of expression nor the most beneficial language available.

The references to the widespread presence of English, such as 'euerich Inglische Inglische can', have been taken by Tim Machan to indicate that English represents the language of the land, 'lacking both political self-consciousness and linguistic rationalisation'.[12] The Prologue resists Machan's claim, however, by explaining that the increased presence of English is connected to an absence of French among the nobility. The Prologue's call for continued education in French and Latin relies on a self-conscious awareness of how languages form social and political identities. By including violence as a consequence of deficient language education, the Prologue expresses an anxiety that the languages of England are becoming, as Machan describes, 'socially undifferentiated'.[13] The manner of education described in the Prologue, book-learning, also reinforces social differentiation. Book-learning signals a group of people who have monetary and social means, and, in the case of French, would include merchants and clerks in addition to the nobility.[14]

Even after the Prologue asserts that 'Of Freynsch no Latin nil y tel more', the French language remains a topic for discussion. This inclusion initially seems odd as it appears that the Prologue contradicts itself in the space of four lines. However, the Prologue shifts from emphasizing literacy in French and Latin to emphasizing spoken languages in England. Here, the loss of French gains a different emphasis. The Prologue observes that there are many nobles who currently cannot speak French, 'Mani noble ich haue ysei3e / Þat no Freynsche couþe seye'. These lines have been previously read in favour of English's inclusivity, but the lines do not draw attention to the accessibility of English.[15] Rather, they stress that some of the nobility – those who should know French – cannot speak it. The text that follows explains why the romance will be told in English rather than simply justifying the use of England's most accessible vernacular. It is not out of a love for the English language or for what the English language can do. Instead, the Prologue will begin

54 (2004), 323–49, sees the Prologue to *Of Arthour* as 'part of a broader agenda justifying translation into English, as is clear from roughly contemporary works' (pp. 331–2).

[12] T. W. Machan, *English in the Middle Ages* (Oxford, 2003), pp. 89–90.

[13] Ibid, p. 89.

[14] For a brief survey of relevant sources, see A. Putter and K. Busby, 'Introduction: Medieval Francophonia', in *Medieval Multilingualism: The Francophone World and Its Neighbors*, ed. C. Kleinhenz and K. Busby, Medieval Texts and Cultures of Northern Europe 20 (Turnhout, 2010), pp. 1–13 (pp. 3–4). See also R. Britnell, 'Uses of French in Medieval English Towns', in *Language and Culture in Medieval Britain: The French of England c.1100–c.1500*, ed. J. Wogan-Browne, C. Collette, M. Kowaleski, L. Mooney, A. Putter, and D. Trotter (York, 2009), pp. 81–9.

[15] J. Scattergood writes that the romance 'seems to be part of a movement which was literary and educative, whereby what was previously available to the linguistically competent few became, through the efforts of translators, accessible to the many' ('Validating the High Life', p. 332). I would argue that the context for the discussions of language-learning, the content of the romance, and the expectations of the audience limit the role this text might have in opening up a romance to the many, without also dealing with an anxiety about the consequences of losing French among the noble and affluent.

'fore her loue' – that is, for those among the audience who cannot understand French.

The language of unrestrained violence

The murder of a French sergeant, which incited the War of Saint-Sardos (c. 1323), and the sentencing of Roger Mortimer for the murder of Edward II (c. 1330) were prominent events during the compilation of the Auchinleck manuscript. These events reveal the extensive political consequences that could develop from single acts of bloodshed. Other texts in the Auchinleck manuscript, such as *The Sayings of the Four Philosophers* and *The Simonie*, directly address the political context of their production. However, the Prologue to and the romance *Of Arthour and of Merlin* have not been considered in terms of the politically motivated violence in Saint-Sardos and Mortimer's sentencing. The language used to describe the murders, central to both events, resonates not only with the Prologue's concerns about spilling blood but also within the romance as well. The political environment of the Auchinleck manuscript's compilation may provide insight into the Prologue's concerns about the consequences of unrestrained violence.

The War of Saint-Sardos ruptured long-established communication between England and France over jurisdiction in the duchy of Aquitaine.[16] Ever since the Treaty of Paris in 1259, the kings of England had been negotiating with the kings of France over the form of homage that was to be paid for the duchy of Aquitaine. The kings of England wished to offer simple homage to the French crown for the duchy, granting recognition for the holding, whereas the kings of France wished for liege homage, which implies military service.[17] The hanging of a French sergeant (c. 1323) over the imminent construction of a *bastide* within English-controlled Gascony provided King Charles IV of France the pretext he needed to invade.[18]

Before the outbreak of the war, Edward II sent a letter to Charles expressing his distress over the event and his hopes to renew negotiations about the issue of homage. Edward's letter describes the murder in a manner similar to the Prologue's use of the word *spillen*. He describes the death of the sergeant as a *desconvenue*, an 'act of brutality or barbarity':[19]

> Mes de ceo naveoms uncore nulle certeinte; totez foitz, tresame frere, vous fesoms saver qe, si nule riote, descovenue ou outrages soient faitz el dit lieu ou aillours deinz nostre poair contre vous ou nul des voz, qe Dieu defende, ce ne feut unqes par nostre sceu, conscent ne volunte.

> More than this we did not have any certainty; every time, treasured brother, we have made known to you that, if any discord, barbaric or wanton acts were

---

[16] G. P. Cuttino, *English Diplomatic Administration* (Oxford, 1940), p. 17.

[17] Ibid., p. 15.

[18] For an excellent overview of the events of the War of Saint-Sardos, see S. Philips, *Edward II* (New Haven, 2010), pp. 461–71.

[19] *AND*, s.v. *desconvenue*.

made within the aforementioned place or elsewhere within our jurisdiction against you or anyone of yours, who God defends, this did not happen ever by our knowledge, consent, or desire.[20]

Edward attempts to distance himself from the murder that happened within his territory but does not deny the outrageous nature of the crime. He instead focuses on the fact that any such action was committed unjustly, without any legal sanction or even personal desire on his part. Similar concerns about excessive violence occur in the romance. The repeated attacks by the kinsmen of Angys not only spill blood but despoil the land around them: 'Ac amorwe he wold fond / Brennen and spillen al þis lond' (lines 6961–2). The blood spilt by the kinsmen of Angys upset the stability of the entire area and impact the environment. Similarly, the death of the French sergeant has destabilized diplomacy between France and England to the point of war, resulting in the devastation of English holdings in Gascony. Both acts of violence lack restraint and cause collateral damage.

The sentencing and execution of Mortimer in 1330 for the alleged murder of Edward II provides another narrative of political upheaval resulting from a single act of violence. Among the crimes in Mortimer's sentence, his role in the supposed murder of Edward features prominently. The language used to describe this crime reflects the unrestrained nature of the act. Also, the expedited procedure for Mortimer's sentencing demonstrated strong support for resolving the narrative of Edward's death. Rumors of the king's murder circulated widely after 1327, but it was not until the sentencing of Mortimer that the accusation of murder became official. He was described as moving the imprisoned Edward so as to have him 'treacherously, feloniously, and falsely murdered'.[21] Whether the charges were true or not, Edward III consolidated the legitimacy of his rule by portraying Mortimer as a murderer and bringing him to justice, all the while distancing himself from the deposition of his father. Parliament heard no evidence in support of the accusation nor any evidence for Mortimer's defence. The entire proceeding took place in his absence while he remained imprisoned elsewhere.[22]

Of Arthour and of Merlin also explores the consequences of regicide. Fortigern's conspiracy to murder King Constans resembles the alleged method Mortimer employed to kill the imprisoned Edward II, particularly the use of agents to isolate and kill the vulnerable king.[23] The romance uses *spillen* to emphasize the

---

[20] *The War of Saint-Sardos (1323–25): Gascon Correspondences and Diplomatic Documents*, ed. P. Chaplais, (London, 1954), p. 179 (translation mine).

[21] This is Philips's translation (*Edward II*, p. 565) of *Parliament Rolls of Medieval England*, Parliament of Nov. 1330, C 65/2, item I: 'et ordina q'il feust mande au chastell de Berke, ou par lui et ses soens feust treterousement, felonessement, et falsement murde et tue'.

[22] Philips, *Edward II*, p. 565.

[23] Fortigern uses knights loyal to him to kill King Constans while he is unaware (*Of Arthour and of Merlin*, ed. Macrae-Gibson, lines 185–291), and Mortimer allegedly employed his followers to aid in moving the imprisoned Edward II from Kenilworth to Berkeley Castle. For a summary of the conspirators, their charges, and ultimate fates, see Philips, *Edward II*, pp. 572–6.

particularly heinous crime of spilling royal blood. After the death of King Constans, the barons send his sons over the sea in order to prevent their deaths:

> To barouns þer weren gent
> Þat this treson vnderstode
> And sore hem rewe þe kings blod
> Þat it schuld be spilt so
> And tok rede bitvixen hem to
> Þe to childer ouer þe se bring. (lines 282–7)

Fortigern's treasonous murder of King Constans and the usurpation of royal power resemble the narrative that developed around Roger Mortimer once Edward III had claimed the throne. After being imprisoned, Mortimer was accused of usurping control of royal power for himself, in addition to murdering the imprisoned and deposed Edward II. By positioning Mortimer as responsible for spilling a king's blood, Edward III reclaimed the royal power that had been compromised by Mortimer's stewardship after Edward II's deposition. This episode is one of many points of similarity that Edward III's path to kingship had with the romance's various narratives surrounding the rise of Uther and Arthur Pendragon.[24] It also reinforces the Prologue's anxiety about unrestrained violence and the political consequences it can generate. The sentencing of Mortimer demonstrates how the execution of someone responsible for politically motivated bloodshed served to reinforce royal power.

Political poems of the Auchinleck manuscript

Two other poems in Auchinleck, *Four Philosophers* and *The Simonie*, connect the political consequences of unrestrained violence to language-learning in a manner similar to the Prologue to *Of Arthour*. As John Scattergood notes, *Four Philosophers* adapts Latin maxims to the political context of Edward II's reign, specifically the king's breach of the ordinances made to limit royal power in 1311.[25] While *Of Arthour* addresses the languages of England through direct references, the Auchinleck version of *Four Philosophers* is a macaronic poem containing lines of Anglo-Norman. Scattergood has previously identified these Anglo-Norman lines as related to a version of *De Provisione Oxonie* in Cambridge, St John's College, MS 112, which was adapted from earlier versions so as to criticize political events during the reign of Edward I. Scattergood explores how *Four Philosophers* changes, in turn, these political criticisms of Edward I to fit the reign of Edward II. References to violence in *Four Philosophers* resonate, however, not only with the *De Provisione*

---

[24] For a broader discussion of the political and legal aspects of a king returning from exile in English chronicles and romances, see L. Ashe, 'The Anomalous King of Conquered England', in *Every Inch a King: Comparative Studies on Kings and Kingship in the Ancient and Medieval Worlds*, ed. L. Mitchell and C. Melville (Leiden, 2012), pp. 173–93 (p. 180).

[25] J. Scattergood, 'Political Context, Date and Composition of *The Sayings of the Four Philosophers*', in J. Scattergood, *Manuscripts and Ghosts: Essays on the Transmission of Medieval and Early Renaissance Literature* (Dublin, 2006), pp. 95–106 (p. 103).

Oxonie but also with the Prologue to *Of Arthour*.[26] The author of *Four Philosophers* explains 'why "engelond is shent" and "brought adoun", and invites an interpretation of his lines in these terms'.[27] The Prologue provides more manuscript context for these terms, specifically on the role of violence in the downfall of England.

Both the Prologue and *Four Philosophers* address an audience that is accountable for violence and has the ability to change the current state of the country. While the Prologue indicates an intended audience by describing the type of education its author feels can mitigate violence, *Four Philosophers* refers directly to acts of creation and destruction:

> L'en puet fere & defere,
> Ceo fait-il trop souent;[28]
> It nis nouþer wel ne faire,
> Þerefore Engelond is shent. (lines 1–4)[29]

The two Anglo-Norman lines set the verbs *fere* and *defere* in opposition, positioning acts of creation and destruction in rhetoric traditionally associated with the nobility but also used as keys to wealth and commerce. *Trop* emphasizes the excessive actions of the nobility, and – given the different definitions of *defere*, in particular 'destroy', 'lay waste', and 'kill'[30] – the terms imply that uncontrolled violence has left England destroyed ('shent').[31] This commentary on violence in England occurs again in the speech of the fourth philosopher, 'For wille is red, þe lond is wrecful' (line 65). The English people are rash, leading to the land's ruination. *Four Philosophers* addresses its audience in a manner similar to the Prologue to *Of Arthour*. Specifically, *Four Philosophers* balances the accessibility of the English language with the political and social implications of French. This technique allows as many people as possible to understand the message while it directs that message to a particular audience familiar with the French language. Even as the poet directly addresses problems that occurred earlier in the century, it gives scope to the issue of unrestrained violence. England's problems of civil violence would continue until Edward III's declaration of war provided a means to channel violence towards the Continent.

The second poem, *The Simonie*, sometimes known as the *Poem on the Evil Times of Edward II*, catalogues the reasons for England's deterioration during Edward II's reign. The poet writes about how rampant violence among the nobility and ignorance among the clergy has brought England near to ruin. The rhetoric describing violence and the problems of relying on the English language resembles

---

[26] Ibid., pp. 99–101.

[27] Ibid., p. 98.

[28] 'One can make and unmake / What one does too often'.

[29] All quotations from *The Sayings of the Four Philosophers* and *The Simonie* are cited by line number from the online transcriptions of the poems found in the Burnley-Wiggins facsimile.

[30] *AND*, s.v. *defaire*.

[31] *MED*, s.v. *shenden*.

that of the Prologue to *Of Arthour*. Violence among the nobility has poised all of England to *spille*:

> Gret nede hit were to bidde þat þe pes were brouht
> For þe lordinges of þe lond þat swich wo han iwrouht
> Þat nolde spare for kin þat o kosin þat oþer;
> So þe fend hem prikede vch man to mourdren oþer
>   Wid wille,
> Þat al Engelond, iwis, was in point to spille. (lines 427–32)

The nobility is unambiguously blamed for their reckless violence, not sparing even their own kin. In addition, they are responsible for all mayhem provoked by their reckless behaviour. The political consequences of unrestrained bloodshed, such as the start of the War of Saint-Sardos and Roger Mortimer's alleged murder of Edward II, resonate with the poet's descriptions of violent acts that leave England vulnerable. In particular, the reference to civil conflict during Edward II's reign resembles other general descriptions of lords turning on their kin.[32]

The Simonie also describes the problems of relying on the English language, especially among members of the clergy. An entire parish can be brought to ruin because of a priest's ignorance, 'And þus shal al þe parish for lac of lore spille' (line 102). The poem specifies that the problem comes from a deficiency of Latin education. A clergy member unable to understand the Latin he reads is no better than a jay that speaks English:

> For riht me þinkeþ hit fareþ bi a prest þat is lewed
> As bi a iay in a kage þat (þat) himself haþ bishrewed:
> God Engelish he spekeþ, ac he wot neuere what;
> No more wot a lewed prest in boke what he rat
>   Bi day.
> Þanne is a lewed prest no betre þan a iay. (lines 103–8)

Far from being celebrated as a spoken practice within England, the use of English highlights deficiencies in a priest's education. The figure of the jay associates English with an imitated education, something that sounds pleasing but lacks substance. Furthermore, the poem distinguishes between language spoken and language understood through reading. Similar to the Prologue's concern with book-reading, the action of speaking a language – or even of reading words aloud – does not

---

[32] The violence of lords against their kin can be seen strongly in the baronial opposition to the favourites of Edward II, Piers Gaveston, Hugh Despenser the younger, and Hugh Despenser the elder. See *Vita Edwardi Secundi, monarchi cuiusdam Malmesberiensis*, ed. N. Denholm-Young (London, 1957), for the unusual circumstances of Thomas of Lancaster executing Gaveston: 'For they had put to death a great earl whom the king had adopted as a brother, whom the king cherished as a son, whom the king regarded as a friend and ally' (p. 28); and the barons turning on the Despensers: 'they requested the lord king to dismiss Hugh Despenser … otherwise they would no longer have him for a king, but would utterly renounce their homage and fealty and whatever oath they had sworn to him' (p. 109).

constitute sufficient knowledge. *The Simonie* advances the concerns of the Prologue by identifying an absence in reading comprehension. Even if everyone can under-stand the English spoken by the jay, the words have no value if a speaker doesn't know what he is saying.

Violence among the nobility and the clergy's reliance on English are brought together in the poem's discussion about the game England plays to insult the entirety of the world:

> Þer was a gamen in Engelond þat durede ȝer and oþer:
> Erliche vpon þe Monenday, vch man bishrewed oþer.
> So longe lastede þat gamen among lered and lewed
> Þat nolde þeih neuere stinten or al þe world were bishrewed,
>   Iwis. (lines 367–71)

The people of England bicker and insult one another until everyone has been scorned. All of England participates, the *lered* and the *lewed*, drawing attention to the previous connection made between *lewed* priests and communication in English. This insult-game must be taking place in English rather than in French or Latin, for *lewed* people would not be able to participate in the game with any language other than English. The description of the game implies that the people of England employ English for no better purpose than to insult one another, leaving their country not only to deteriorate but also to suffer divine wrath in the form of scourging cold weather.[33] The game itself is violent, damaging both the partici-pants and the country's very climate. According to Thorlac Turville-Petre, *The Simonie* describes the ruined state of England and the disillusionment of the people following the reign of Edward II.[34] While he addresses the poem's concerns with community, his observations can be aptly extended to include English as an isolated linguistic system. Over-reliance on English perpetuates stagnation. If a society only concerns itself with spite among its own individuals, cross-cultural communication becomes irrelevant.

The different audiences and genres of other fourteenth-century prologues

The prologues to *Cursor Mundi* and the *Northern Homily Cycle* have been previously grouped with the Prologue to *Of Arthour* as indicative of England's perspectives on French and English during the fourteenth century. However, the earlier dates of composition for these two texts and their differing considerations of genre and audience complicate this grouping. *Cursor Mundi* and the *Northern Homily Cycle* express views on the languages of England before the crises of communication presented by the War of Saint-Sardos and the sentencing of Roger Mortimer for the murder of Edward II. As a result, references to French and English in these two early-fourteenth-century prologues bear some similarity to those in the Prologue to *Of Arthour*, but they do not portray French as a means for limiting unrestrained

---

[33] *The Simonie*, lines 373–5.
[34] Turville-Petre, *England the Nation*, pp. 11–15.

violence. Both prologues seek to present their respective texts to the most expansive audience possible, not to an audience needing a discussion on book-learning in French and Latin. In addition, the two earlier prologues are composed in English because of its benefits, not because the writer sees a lamentable lack of French comprehension among the nobility.

The Prologue to *Cursor Mundi* (c. 1300) supports English as the most common means of expression, and references to French highlight its uselessness to those who cannot understand it:

> Ofter haly kirkis state
> This ilk boke ys translate
> Until Ingeles tonge to rede
> For the love of Englis lede,
> Englis lede of Engelande
> The commune for til understande.
> French rimes here I rede
> Communely in iche a stede
> That mast ys worth for Frenche man.
> Quat ys worth for him nane can?
> Of Engeland nacioun
> Ys Englis man thar-in commoun,
> The speche that man with sone may spede
> Mast tharwit to speke ware nede.
> Selden was for any chaunce
> Englis tong praysed in Fraunce! (lines 73–88)[35]

Emphasizing the usefulness of translating the text into English, this prologue captures a tone of celebration – 'For the love of Englis lede' – absent from the Prologue to *Of Arthour*. Rather than being invited to focus on the absence of French as a problem among the nobility, the *Cursor* poet addresses those who hold English in common. For the writer of the *Cursor* prologue, French is the language of another country and another group of people rather than an identifying factor of the affluent English citizens and the nobility. French rhymes and French men are presented as distinct from English writings for the English people. The *Cursor* poet goes on to observe that English has seldom been praised in France in the same manner French has been in England: 'Selden was for any chaunce / Englis tong praysed in Fraunce'. According to the *Cursor* poet, the fact that the English language is held in common is a point of pride.

The Prologue to the *Northern Homily Cycle* (c. 1315) expresses the importance of English to make interpretations of Scripture available to everyone. Its terms discussing differences among Latin, French, and English bear similarities to those in the Prologue to *Of Arthour*, but the audience for these homilies is said to embrace

---

[35] All text from *Cursor Mundi* is cited by line number and taken from *The Idea of the Vernacular: An Anthology of Middle English Literary Theory, 1280–1520*, ed. J. Wogan-Browne, N. Watson, A. Taylor, and R. Evans (University Park PA, 1999), pp. 267–71.

the accessibility of the English language in a way reminiscent of the *Cursor Mundi* prologue:

> Godes word for to her,
> Than klerkes that thair mirour lokes,
> And see hou thai sal lif on bokes.
> And bathe klerk and laued man
> Englis understand kan
> That was born in Ingeland,
> And lang haves ben tharin wonand.
> Bot al men can noht, i-wis,
> Understand Latin and Frankis.
> Forthi me think almous it isse
> To wirke sum god thing on Inglisse,
> That mai ken lered and laued bathe. (66–77)[36]

The author of the *Northern Homily Cycle* prologue here claims that it would be a good thing to create a work in English 'That may ken lered and laued bathe'. In contrast, the author of the Prologue to *Of Arthour* has a specific audience in mind – one aware of the potential value that French and Latin have for learning. Pious writings gain value through reaching as expansive an audience as possible; in this case, given the genre, English allows homiletic messages to reach many people in England. The increased accessibility of the English language does not mean that the language bears a heightened significance in relation to French and Latin. For this homiletic author, words in English are equivalent to alms for the poor, an act of charity.[37] Not only might the laity be poor financially, but laity and nobility alike may be poor linguistically. Therefore, they need generous acts of translation in order to understand homilies for their souls' salvation. Fundamentally, it is those conversant in both languages who can control what is disseminated and how it is disseminated, for the good of England.

The French of England and violence after Edward III declares war

The perception that knowledge of French among the nobility of England helps confer the benefit of limiting violence does not remain after the declaration of the Hundred Years War. The later writings of Jean Froissart in his *Chroniques* recount the role of the French language for the English. The vocabulary is similar to the Prologue to *Of Arthour*. However, the *auauntage* to knowing French becomes centred on its usefulness in war and for recognizing the dishonest practices of the French in negotiation. In Froissart's account of the parliament of 1337, Edward III encourages his noble, gentry, and merchant classes to educate their children in French:

[36] The *Northern Homily Cycle* is cited by line number and taken from *The Idea of the Vernacular*, ed. Wogan-Browne *et al.*, pp. 125–30.
[37] *Northern Homily Cycle*, line 75.

[T]out seigneur, baron, chevalier et honnestes hommes de bonnes villes mesissent cure et diligence de estruire et aprendre leurs enfans le langhe françoise par quoy il en fuissuent plus able et plus able et plus coustummier en leurs gherres.

All Lords, barons, knights, and respectable men from good towns should take care and be diligent to instruct and teach their children the French language so that they might become more able and more familiar with it as they go to the wars.[38]

Froissart's account frames the improvement of those who would have access to education as a forward-looking project, something that requires French to be an essential part of a country at war. The French language is a component of military preparation alongside parameters for coastal defence and recommendations for the peasantry to practice archery. French, in this moment, becomes a resource to be accrued for conquest.

The use of the word *auauntage* appears in the context of England negotiating with France in 1392, but with implications different from its use in the Prologue to *Of Arthour*:

Car en parlure françoise a mots soubtils et couvers et sur double entendement, et les tournent les François, là où ils veulent, à leur prouffit et avantage: ce que les Anglois ne sçauroient trouver, ne faire, car euls ne le veulent entendre que plainement.

For the French language has subtleties and hidden meanings, and where there are double meanings the French manipulate them the way they want to, for their own profit and advantage: which the English do not realize, nor can they do it themselves, for they only want to understand it clearly and plainly.[39]

'Avantage', in this instance, signals how the French use their language against the English, and how the French language itself enables the manipulation of others. According to Froissart, the French language possesses subtleties and hidden meanings that make the language more apt for manipulation. Every language will present advantages to a native speaker's familiarity, but the criticism of French centres on its role as a shared means of negotiation and communication. Deliberate manipulation of the language violates negotiating in good faith. The statement also implies that English, by comparison, must not have the same degree of subtleties as French. Complicating this statement on language even further is the fact that

---

[38] Jean Froissart, *Chroniques*, in *Oeuvres de Froissart*, ed. J. M. B. C. Kervyn de Lettenhove, 25 vols. (Brussels, 1867–8), II–V (Book II, p. 419); translation from Putter and Busby, 'Introduction', p. 4.

[39] Froissart, *Chroniques*, ed. Kervyn de Lettenhove, Book XV, p. 114. Translation from S. Lusignan, 'French Language in Contact with English: Social Context and Linguistic Change (Mid 13th and 14th Centuries)', in *Language and Culture in Medieval Britain: The French of England c.1100–c.1500*, ed. J. Wogan-Browne, C. Collette, M. Kowaleski, L. Mooney, A. Putter, and D. Trotter (York, 2009), pp. 19–30 (p. 26).

Froissart writes about the deceptive potential of French in French.[40] Characterizing it as nuanced and deceptive represents a rather drastic shift in describing French, compared with the Prologue to *Of Arthour*, which emphasizes instead the role that French has in making a man *gentil*.

Froissart explains that deficiencies in French among English people come from the condition of their education rather than from a lack of French education altogether:

> Le françois que ils avoient apris chiés eulx d'enfance, n'estoit pas de telle nature et condition que celluy de France estoit et duquel les clers de droit en leurs traittiés et parlers usoient.

> The French that they had afterward primarily of their childhood, it was not of such nature and condition that it was for those of France, but of which the clerks of law were using in their discussions and speech.[41]

No amount of education can shift the English position, for they are doubly disadvantaged in trying to communicate in a straightforward manner by means of a manipulative language to manipulative people.[42] Froissart's attempt to categorize the French of England as different from the French of France indicates a desire to differentiate two cultures sharing a common language. The desire to differentiate England and France in broad terms, such as their approaches to communication, was probably informed by ongoing war between the two countries. According to the Prologue to *Of Arthour*, French remains important for pre-war England precisely because it is *shared* in common with France, not because it is fundamentally different in some way.

Conclusion

England from 1323 to 1337 was fraught with failed communication, military defeat, and political upheaval. In the midst of this chaotic period, the Prologue to *Of Arthour* offers a way to reduce needless bloodshed by increasing linguistic education. On the surface, the Prologue's intervention on reducing bloodshed seems oddly placed. The romance *Of Arthour and of Merlin* has been noted for its long and repeated descriptions of violence, and the romance genre in general often idealizes the chivalric violence of its protagonists.[43] These features, however, make examining the romance's unrestrained violence all the more potent. The Prologue encourages readers to reflect on what distinguishes blood spilt needlessly from chivalric violence. It offers a potential intervention by means of language education,

---

[40] See Lusignan, 'French Language in Contact with English'.

[41] Froissart, *Chroniques*, ed. Kervyn de Lettenhove, Book XV, p. 115 (translation mine).

[42] For an extended discussion of English negotiations with the French during the Hundred Years War, see A. Butterfield, *The Familiar Enemy*, pp. 165–72.

[43] For a summary of the tepid scholarly reception of battles in *Of Arthour*, see S. B. Calkin, *Saracens and the Making of English Identity: The Auchinleck Manuscript* (New York, 2005), p. 167.

but it lays out no definitive solution for controlling violence in a troubled time. *The Simonie* and *The Sayings of the Four Philosophers* further this reflection on language and violence in the manuscript, extending beyond the genre of romance to political poetry. All of these texts frame their interventions as restorative rather than bellicose. England must rebuild after the disastrous reign of Edward II, and an increase in language education has a place in this process. Despite the fact that this perspective on language would not last through the Edwardian phase of the Hundred Years War, it expands our understanding of how England's perceptions on multilingualism shifted. It is striking that a message about multilingualism occurs in more than one text in a manuscript often noted for its nearly monolingual composition. The Prologue to *Of Arthour and of Merlin* complicates the scholarly perception of the use of Middle English in the Auchinleck manuscript. Instead of our thinking mainly about the languages that compose the texts themselves, it encourages us to re-examine how languages are represented to readers of the manuscript.

CHAPTER FIVE

Scribe 3's Literary Project: Pedagogies of Reading in Auchinleck's Booklet 3*

Emily Runde

I N the Prologue to the Auchinleck *Of Arthour and of Merlin*, English is emphatically not the language of privilege. Addressing the poem's Englishness in the context of a valorization of education, the writer asserts, 'Auauntages þai hauen þare / Freynsch & Latin eueraywhare' (lines 17–18).[1] This preface frames the choice of English as a potentially inclusive move, one that might render 'auauntages' accessible to every English person and not just to those with training in Latin or French – it claims, after all, that 'euerich Jnglische Jnglische can' (line 24). Although its contents occasionally incorporate some French and Latin themselves, it is tempting to view Auchinleck's own Englishness in light of this accessibility; indeed, this passage has been taken as an addition specific to the manuscript.[2]

More than an endorsement of Auchinleck's most prevalent vernacular, however, this passage articulates a valuation of reading that transcends the particularities of language. The preceding lines identify 'auauntages' with textual access:

> Childer þat ben to boke ysett
> In age hem is miche þe bett
> For þai mo witen & se
> Miche of Godes priuete
> Hem to kepe & to ware
> Fram sinne & fram warldes care,
> & wele ysen ʒif þai willen
> Þat hem no þarf neuer spillen. (lines 9–16)

* I would like to thank Matthew Fisher and Christopher Baswell for their incisive feedback on earlier versions of this chapter. I am also grateful to Christine Chism and Donka Minkova for reading and commenting upon the work, and to Susanna Fein for her helpful editorial advice.
[1] All quotations from *Of Arthour and of Merlin* are cited by line number from the online transcription in the Burnley-Wiggins facsimile.
[2] See R. Purdie, *Anglicising Romance: Tail-Rhyme and Genre in Medieval English Literature*, Studies in Medieval Romance 9 (Cambridge, 2008), p. 99. On further linguistic implications of the Prologue to *Of Arthour*, see P. Butler's chapter in this volume.

This passage makes book-based learning central to the 'auauntages' so often restricted to readers of French and Latin. Education that entails being 'to boke ysett' – that involves pursuing, in other words, a systematic programme of reading – is an ethical shield, warding off the spiritual ills of sin and the material ills of need and suffering. Knowledge of 'Godes priuete' furnishes guidance, a means of steering a wise and ethical course through life. This preface builds its Englishness upon a teleology of reading intrinsic not to the language of education but to education itself. It implies that access matters, that the Englishness of its accompanying text – and, by extension, other texts – answers a perceived moral need.

We might struggle to understand why a popular account of the origins and exploits of Merlin and Arthur occasions such an ambitious and ethically freighted claim, but the impenetrability of this juxtaposition is revealing in and of itself. For all that this preface resoundingly endorses reading's ethical potential and English's inclusivity, it sheds little light on how or why the accompanying text would have been read, or where, if not here, a lay reader of English might turn to be 'to boke ysett'. Like many contemporary English prefaces, it offers plentiful rhetorical assertions of the accessibility and even the potential utility of English texts, but it leaves a great deal unsaid. What sort of access and 'auauntages' did Auchinleck offer its medieval readers? How did they read the manuscript's vernacular texts and think about the ways in which they read? And what did it mean for them to read well in this vernacular context?

Here I adopt a seemingly counterintuitive approach to these questions, examining the moments of disruption that work against Auchinleck's broader visual, linguistic, and generic coherences, from the apparent predilection for Middle English verse romances to its harmonies of presentation. The contributions of Auchinleck's less prolific scribes – particularly those multilingual, non-narrative contributions that resist the manuscript's dominant literary/aesthetic programme – offer valuable means by which we might better understand the codicological circumstances of the book's production and the literary projects within the volume that exist independently of Auchinleck's major romances but also might usefully inform our reading of them.

Auchinleck's third booklet represents the largest eruption of difference – linguistic, visual, scribal, and so on – within the manuscript. Here I contend that its primary scribe, Scribe 3, undertakes an independent project, one anchored in the booklet's opening understudied texts: *On þe Seuen Dedly Sinnes* and *The Pater Noster Vndo on Englissch*. Booklet 3's project illuminates the issues towards which the Prologue to *Of Arthour* gestures, namely the pedagogical and ethical potential of Englishness, the access it grants, and the means by which readers, given this linguistic access, might read – and specifically read *well* – in their vernacular.

This argument depends, of course, on the probability that Scribe 3 was acting as an intelligent agent when he contributed his stint. Auchinleck's less prolific scribes have lately begun to receive well-merited scholarly attention. Concerning Scribe 3, Arthur Bahr has recently asserted the linguistic incompetence of this scribe and the likelihood that his scribal decisions were dictated by Scribe 1.[3]

---

[3] A. Bahr, *Fragments and Assemblages: Forming Compilations of Medieval London* (Chicago, 2013), pp. 105–54.

Before turning to a close examination of booklet 3's contents, then, it is necessary to contextualize Scribe 3's contributions within a broad picture of the manuscript's contents and the dynamic of their production. Far from finding Scribe 3 incapable of intelligent scribal agency, I suggest that his work be closely examined alongside that of Scribe 2. These two scribes operated with comparable independence from the predominant aesthetic of Auchinleck, and their work generates moments of productive rupture within the manuscript – that is, moments of linguistic- and generic-switching during which narrative is thrust aside and texts confront readers with matters of pressing socio-political or spiritual import. *Seuen Dedly Sinnes* and *Pater Noster* occasion such disruptions by situating the narratives of booklet 3 – and of Auchinleck – within a pedagogical framework prompting audiences to read self-consciously and with hermeneutical sophistication.

The eccentricities of booklet 3

The third extant booklet in Auchinleck is the hardest to reconcile with prevailing scholarly insights into the probable means by which the manuscript was produced in early-fourteenth-century London. Scholars of Auchinleck frequently turn to the comfortingly authorial figure of Scribe 1 as a way into understanding the manuscript's construction and its purpose as a kind of authored book.[4] He is presumed to have made many of the decisions that shaped the manuscript as we now encounter it, and his own scribal contributions to the book dwarf those of the four or five other scribes who penned Auchinleck's contents.[5] Even when we talk about these other scribes, Scribe 1 is often the implied if not explicit foil to their practices and the presumed manager of their activities. As one of the few booklets in which Scribe 1 did no copying – and the only one of these to which multiple scribes contributed – booklet 3 exhibits a richly significant tension with the project of the manuscript's putative mastermind.

Booklet 3's contents confound expectations based on Auchinleck's devotion to Middle English narrative. This booklet begins not with a substantial romance

---

[4] This perspective stems from the now widely accepted theory, advanced by T. A. Shonk, that Scribe 1 planned and oversaw many aspects of Auchinleck's production at the behest of the manuscript's commissioning patron ('A Study of the Auchinleck Manuscript: Bookmen and Bookmaking in the Early Fourteenth Century', *Speculum* 60 [1985], 71–91). More recently, M. Fisher has pushed Scribe 1's role a significant step further, arguing that Scribe 1's shaping of the manuscript extended to authorship of what Fisher terms 'derivative texts', which 'translate or assemble the words of numerous source texts, typically without acknowledging their textual indebtedness' (*Scribal Authorship and the Writing of History in Medieval England* [Columbus, 2012], p. 60).

[5] The number of scribal contributors to Auchinleck continues to be debated. For two recent installments in this debate, see A. Wiggins, 'Are Auchinleck Manuscript Scribes 1 and 6 the Same Scribe?: The Advantages of Whole-Data Analysis and Electronic Texts', *Medium Ævum* 73 (2004), 10-26; and R. Hanna's chapter in this volume. While Wiggins argues, largely on the grounds of scribal copying practices, that Scribes 1 and 6 were distinct contributors to the volume, Hanna asserts on palaeographical grounds that they were the same scribe. On the basis of the codicological evidence I consider here, I join Wiggins in treating them as different scribes.

but with two brief religious texts, the sorts of texts that more frequently appear elsewhere in the manuscript filling out space at the ends of booklets. Not only do the first two poems of the booklet, *Seuen Dedly Sinnes* and *Pater Noster*, defy scholarly expectations in their brevity and religious focus, but they also differ from the bulk of the religious material within the manuscript. These are no renegades from the first two booklets; they take an emphatically different form: both are non-narrative collections and marked as such on the page. Furthermore, as I will explore in this chapter, they serve a different function, guiding readers through increasingly sensitive and skilled modes of reading. The two final items in the booklet are even more idiosyncratic. *The Sayings of the Four Philosophers*, copied by Scribe 2, is the only macaronic poem – the only piece containing, indeed, Anglo-Norman verse of any sort – within the book. The list of names of Norman barons, *The Battle Abbey Roll*, copied by Scribe 4, stands out even more starkly as the manuscript's only list, with its text ruled in four columns.

To varying extents, the contributions of Scribes 2, 3, and 4 in booklet 3 elude the predominant organization and look of the manuscript. Their divergences have often prompted scholars to express perplexity over the booklet's unusual character.[6] Faced with its eccentricities, scholars have tended to set it aside as the exception to the rules imposed or upheld by Scribe 1, to treat it as an eruption of scribal incompetence or randomness in an otherwise explicable manuscript. Or they have attempted to make sense of it within Scribe 1's programme, with some going so far as to attribute its design to this master planner. Both perspectives slight the contributions of the booklet's scribes, and particularly those of Scribe 3, whose single Auchinleck stint fills most of the booklet. The former perspective shies away from allotting intelligent agency to these scribes on the implied or stated grounds that, of Auchinleck's scribes, only Scribe 1 has a knowable project. The latter perspective insists – in spite of the booklet's many divergences from Auchinleck's textual, decorative, and codicological programmes – that these scribes were working as

---

[6] M. Evans, for example, concedes that booklet 3's assortment of texts 'may well puzzle the reader' (*Rereading Middle English Romances: Manuscript Layout, Decoration, and the Rhetoric of Composite Structure* [Montreal, 1995], p. 86). R. Hanna remarks upon the exceptional nature of 'scribe 3's Booklet 3' in which 'the big items are buried' ('Reconsidering the Auchinleck Manuscript', in *New Directions in Later Medieval Manuscript Studies: Essays from the 1998 Harvard Conference*, ed. D. Pearsall (York, 2000), pp. 91–102 [p. 94]). D. Pearsall's summation of Scribe 3's contribution indicates no purpose behind – or any 'big items' central to – its design: it is the only stint to which he applies the catch-all term 'miscellaneous' ('Literary and Historical Significance of the Manuscript', in Pearsall-Cunningham, pp. vii–xi [p. ix]). Even as Bahr celebrates booklet 3's exceptional structure and probes its meaning, his conclusions regarding the production of Auchinleck do not fully reconcile these aspects of the booklet. Bahr suggests that 'Scribe 1 ... hangs over the booklet like a ghostly not-quite-author whose presence can be inferred but not proved', and that booklet 3's range and arrangement of contents render it a microcosm of Auchinleck. He sidesteps the problem of reconciling the booklet's strangeness with Scribe 1's oversight, suggesting that 'the many ways in which booklet 3 seems at odds with the rest of the manuscript ... press us to look more deeply into what ... we might call its *codicological unconscious*' (*Fragments and Assemblages*, p. 111).

helping hands to carry out Scribe 1's will and vision. I argue, instead, that booklet 3 – and Auchinleck more generally – was shaped by multiple scribal intelligences, and that Scribe 3 should be included in their number.

Rehabilitating Scribe 3's abilities and agency

One major obstacle to our acceptance of Scribe 3 as an independent and sophisticated literary agent is the enduring assumption of his linguistic incompetence. When Bahr took Scribe 3's eccentric orthography to exclude the possibility that he shaped his own stint and the booklet in which it survives, he followed Karl Brunner's much earlier assessment of the scribe as Norman and non-fluent in English.[7] Identifying this long-standing article of scholarly belief as 'the myth of the "Anglo-Norman scribe"', Cecily Clark has demonstrated that it is an untenable hypothesis.[8] According to Clark, our current knowledge of post-Conquest linguistic practices and developments in England indicates that Francophone monolingualism was never pervasive in England and that, even among the higher classes, where it can be assumed for the first few generations after the Conquest, it would not have persisted much, if at all, beyond the twelfth century.[9] Michael Benskin offers a more reasonable explanation for the orthographic eccentricities begetting the myth:

> We should think not of monoglot AN [Anglo-Norman] scribes making a mess of English, but rather of native English speakers whose written competence in the vernacular had been so far restricted to AN, and who were beginning to extend their written competence into English.[10]

Such scribes may have been prodigal in their orthographic practices, thereby upsetting the decidedly modern expectation that scribal competence be predicated on extremely economic orthography, but the systematic nature of their practices argues powerfully for their fluency in English.

Within Scribe 3's stint there is no evidence, orthographic or otherwise, to suggest that his command of English fell short of Scribe 1's. On the contrary, Scribe 3 demonstrates comfort with his English texts at the levels of individual words and

[7] See Bahr, *Fragments and Assemblages*, pp. 109–10. Brunner asserts in his edition of *Seven Sages* that Scribe 3 was 'obviously a French Norman ... not sure of the value of some peculiar English characters', and he cites the following practices as evidence: Scribe 3 'frequently uses ȝ instead of þ, as wiȝ for wiþ, ll. 22, 44, 61, etc., -eȝ for eþ (third pers. sing. and plur., pres.) 25, 94, 115, etc., ferȝe for ferþe 60, wroȝ for wroþ, 388, etc'.; see *The Seven Sages of Rome (Southern Version)*, ed. K. Brunner, EETS OS 191 (London, 1933), p. ix.

[8] C. Clark, 'The Myth of "the Anglo-Norman Scribe"', in *History of Englishes: New Methods and Interpretations in Historical Linguistics*, ed. M. Rissanen, O. Ihalainen, T. Nevalainen, and I. Taavitsainen (Berlin, 1992), pp. 117–29.

[9] Ibid., pp. 120–1.

[10] M. Benskin, 'On the Ignorance of Anglo-Norman Scribes', presented at the Conference on Multilingualism in Late Medieval Britain (Aberystwyth, 1997) and qtd in M. Laing, 'Confusion *wrs* Confounded: Litteral Substitution Sets in Early Middle English Writing Systems', *Neuphilologische Mitteilungen* 100 (1999), 251–70 (p. 261).

overall sense. The feature of his orthography that excites the most consternation in Brunner's and Bahr's accounts – the use of yogh where we would expect a thorn, as in *wiȝ* or *–eȝ* (present 3rd person singular) – occurs within a consistent pattern of usage: Scribe 3 only used the yogh to express the sound [θ/ð] where the [θ/ð] is syllable- or word-final. The coexistence of thorn and yogh in litteral substitution sets is not unique to Scribe 3 either. Margaret Laing notes, for example, that the writing system of the exemplar from which both surviving copies of *The Owl and the Nightingale* derive '[allows] occasional substitution of <ȝ> for <þ/ þ>' and that this practice can be observed in other South-West Midland writing systems.[11] Unless Scribe 3 was copying his entire stint from a single orthographically consistent exemplar, he could not have been a literatim copyist; all six of the texts he copied share consistent orthographic practices.[12] It is much more probable that Scribe 3 translated what he copied according to his own orthographic system. Far from indicating any linguistic difficulties on the part of Scribe 3, the internal consistencies of this system suggest that he understood and attended to the words he was copying sufficiently to replace spellings outside his repertoire with those within it. That Scribe 3 corrected occasional mistakes in spelling and syntax further substantiates this conclusion.[13]

In his strategies of visual presentation, Scribe 3 likewise exhibited alertness to the structure and content of the texts he copied. He adopted a series of systematic approaches to marking internal divisions within the first three texts of the six he copied. The first two non-narrative texts show a clear hierarchy of initials and paraphs that emphasize their structures and particularly accentuate that both are

---

[11] M. Laing, '*The Owl and the Nightingale*: Five New Readings and Further Notes', *Neuphilologische Mitteilungen* 108 (2007), 445–77 (p. 465, 465 n. 43). It is possible that the more localizable practice Laing identifies derives from a widespread association of these graphs and their associated phonetic range. M. Stenroos has observed in her study of the gradual loss of the graphs <þ> and <ȝ> that 'thorns and yoghs in Late Middle English texts seem to relate to each other in some kind of systematic way' and that '<þ> and <ȝ> belong to particularly large and complex substitution sets' ('A Middle English Mess of Fricative Spellings: Reflections on Thorn, Yogh and Their Rivals', in *To Make His Englissh Sweete upon His Tonge*, ed. M. Krygier and L. Sikorska [Frankfurt am Main, 2007], pp. 9–35 [pp. 11, 14]). Examining the extremely various Middle English spellings of the word *through* in *LALME*, Stenroos further observes that there is considerable overlap between the substitution sets for (th) and (gh): 'most notably, the spellings <ȝ>, <t> and <th> form part both of the (th) and (gh) sets' (p. 14).

[12] For an examination of Scribe 3's orthographic practices across his stint within Auchinleck, see *LALME* (Scribe 3's linguistic profile is designated LP 6500); and E. Runde, 'Reexamining Orthographic Practice in the Auchinleck Manuscript through Study of Complete Scribal Corpora', in *Variation and Change in English Grammar and Lexicon: Contemporary Approaches*, ed. R. Cloutier, A. M. Hamilton-Brehm, and W. Kretzschmar, Jr (Berlin, 2010), pp. 265–87.

[13] Scribe 3's stint contains multiple identifiable instances in which individual letters have been corrected – in *Sir Degare* (fol. 82va, line 704), *Seven Sages* (fol. 87vb, line 647; fol. 93vb, line 1700), and *Floris and Blauncheflur* (fol. 103ra, line 547) – as well as an insertion of a skipped word at the end of a line in *Seuen Dedly Sinnes* (fol. 70rb, line 67). On scribal corrections in Auchinleck, see also M. F. Vaughan's chapter in this volume.

collections. In the third text, *The Assumption of the Blessed Virgin*, Scribe 3 used paraphs as formal devices to mark stanzaic divisions throughout. The other three texts within Scribe 3's stint – *Sir Degare, The Seven Sages of Rome*, and *Floris and Blauncheflur* – share a narrative structure and a couplet form, allowing Scribe 3 the liberty to subdivide these texts interpretively (as opposed to formally). He adopted slightly different tactics of subdivision in each.[14] Here, his textual divisions nearly always accord with textual form and content. With just one exception, he marked only couplet-initial lines, and he employed paraphs and initials to indicate significant transitions in speech or narrative action.[15] Scribe 3 may well have varied his marking strategies in response to the content of the texts he was copying, but, if we take the differences in these strategies as evidence that he derived his subdivisions of these poems from different exemplars, we have to concede that the internally consistent orthographic system evident in his stint has to have been self-imposed. The combination of Scribe 3's generally systematic orthography and textually attuned subdivisions argues in favour of his intelligent scribal intervention as translating copyist or textually sensitive reader – and almost certainly as both at once.

Scribal oversight and independence in Auchinleck

The question of Scribe 3's agency in booklet 3 also depends upon an understanding of what independent scribal agency might look like in Auchinleck. When Bahr concluded that the only scribe who could possibly have overseen the compilation of booklet 3 was Scribe 1, he based that conclusion on problematic assumptions of Scribe 3's ineptitude and Scribe 4's dependence on another scribe for direction (as well as on an omission of Scribe 2's involvement in the booklet's production), and on the presumption of a temporally and qualitatively fixed relationship among Auchinleck's scribes.[16] A careful study of the booklet suggests that Scribe 1 did intervene in its production, but not in a straightforward managerial role. Rather,

[14] In *Sir Degare*, Scribe 3 initially relied on paraphs to mark narrative transitions, but abruptly switched to relying on initials to mark these transitions, shortly after having employed a number of paraphs to mark a significant dialogue rather than a narrative transition. In *Seven Sages*, he continued his use of initials to mark narrative transitions as well as embedded narratives and other structurally significant elements. And, in *Floris and Blauncheflur*, he returned to a technique closer to that of the opening of *Sir Degare*, in which frequent paraphs and relatively rare initials mark different levels of subdivision within the poem's narrative.

[15] The one exception to Scribe 3's marking of couplet-initial lines occurs in *Floris and Blauncheflur* (fol. 100vb, line 176).

[16] According to Bahr, 'The fact that Scribe 3 seems to have been uncomfortable or unfamiliar with texts in English makes it quite unlikely that he orchestrated a booklet of texts in that language for inclusion in a manuscript whose resolute Englishness is so remarkable. Scribe 4, too, is hardly likely to have gone rogue by copying so odd a text as the "Battle Abbey Roll" – quite the opposite of the anodyne filler that frequently concludes booklets, in Auchinleck and elsewhere – without receiving definite instruction from somebody; and it is hard to come up with another source of such a directive than Scribe 1 (possibly transmitting some set of desires from the patron)' (*Fragments and Assemblages*, pp. 110–11).

the evidence of the booklet attests to fluctuating levels of oversight on the part of Scribe 1 and to a significant degree of independence enjoyed by Scribe 3.

There is evidence elsewhere that the Auchinleck scribes operated with varying degrees of independence. We can enumerate the criteria by which oversight and independence can be ascertained in the work of the less prolific scribes. Writing on this subject with regard to the controversial Scribe 6, Alison Wiggins argues his distinctness from Scribe 1 and posits, on the grounds of quire structure, decoration, and the use of catchwords, that Scribe 6 worked with little or no supervision from Scribe 1.[17] Wiggins's reasons for distancing Scribe 6 from Scribe 1, though somewhat problematic, are still instructive:

> *Otuel* [i.e., Scribe 6's stint] is notable for its disunity and independence from the rest of the manuscript. It is unusual because it is headed by an enlarged capital. It is written on a quire constructed of ten folios whereas the other forty-six quires in the manuscript are of eight folios. There is also no catchword on the final folio of this quire whereas throughout most of the rest of the manuscript the editor Scribe 1 supplied catchwords consistently. That he did not add a catchword implies that Scribe 1 received the *Otuel* booklet pre-assembled and this, along with the visual differences and disunities, indicates that *Otuel* was copied independently. That is, it was copied without the direct supervision of the editor Scribe 1 and at an earlier stage, before Auchinleck and its design plan were conceived of.[18]

The ten-folio quire appears to be a distinguishing feature of the work attributed to Scribe 6, but the other characteristics Wiggins points to are far from unique. A consideration of these practices alongside those of Auchinleck's other scribes enables a fuller picture of the temporal conditions and scribal interactions driving divergences from the manuscript's dominant codicological and decorative programme.

Turning to the absence of a catchword at the end of the *Otuel a Kniȝt* quire, then, this omission is hardly remarkable in Auchinleck. Scribe 1 did have a consistent practice in regard to catchwords, but only within his own stints and at booklet boundaries. In only five observable instances did Scribe 1 add catchwords in the midst of another scribe's stint, and four of these instances link quires copied within Scribe 5's stint; the fifth links a quire copied by Scribe 3 to what was probably another quire copied by Scribe 3 (now lacking).[19] Only Scribe 5 seems to have been

---

[17] Wiggins, 'Are Auchinleck Manuscript Scribes 1 and 6 the Same Scribe?', p. 20. On Scribe 6, see, too, Hanna's chapter in this volume.

[18] Wiggins, 'Are Auchinleck Manuscript Scribes 1 and 6 the Same Scribe?', pp. 19–20.

[19] None of these five catchwords occur at a booklet boundary. Scribe 1's catchwords within Scribe 5's stint (fols. 167rb–201ra) survive on fols. 168v, 183v, 190v, and 198v. A leaf missing after fol. 175 would have been the final folio of the first complete quire copied in Scribe 5's hand. As this leaf would have marked the conclusion of a booklet as well as a quire, it is highly probable that it would have had a catchword in Scribe 1's hand as well. Scribe 1's catchword within Scribe 3's stint (fols. 70ra–104vb) is on fol. 99v. At least one quire has been lost between fols. 99 and 100, and all considerations point to the near certainty that Scribe 3 copied this lost quire. Scribe 3 was responsible for the preceding

working closely enough with Scribe 1 that Scribe 1 was in a position to join all of Scribe 5's quires with catchwords. Within longer stints by Scribes 2 and 3, Scribe 1 provided only one extant catchword.[20] The stint attributed to Scribe 6 almost certainly extended beyond the single surviving *Otuel* quire. Texts in Auchinleck are consistently copied by single scribes. Given that *Otuel a Kni3t* lacks an ending, having broken off at the end of the surviving quire, it is probable that the same scribe copied at least one other quire, now missing, in which he completed *Otuel*. Indeed, the gap in textual numeration between *Otuel* (numbered 'xxxvij' in the upper margin) and *Kyng Alisaunder* (numbered 'xliiij' in the upper margin) suggests that this scribe or a scribal colleague could have copied further items in one or more quires that have since been lost. In light of these considerations, the absence of a catchword at the end of the *Otuel* quire fits with Wiggins's argument that it was the work of a distinct Scribe 6, who copied all or part of a booklet of at least two quires that came into Scribe 1's hands as a unit. This level of pre-assembly is the rule rather than the exception for the scribes collaborating with Scribe 1. Only Scribe 5, and possibly Scribe 3, appear to have received further oversight.

Similarly, most of the Auchinleck scribes left space for enlarged initials at the beginning of one or more texts they copied. The typical format of the opening of a text in Auchinleck consists of a miniature placed proximate to a red title (itself placed late in the process wherever space allowed) and a two-line initial identical to those placed within texts. The miniatures presumably obviated the need in these cases for a large initial signalling a new text. What stands out in a survey of all of the larger initials in Auchinleck is the fact that they are to be found in the stints of five out of six scribes, including Scribe 1.[21] There could be several reasons for this:

---

quire and the beginning of the quire starting with fol. 100, and he has demonstrably copied part of *Seven Sages* and *Floris and Blauncheflur*, the two texts that would each have partially occupied this missing quire.

[20] Within Scribe 2's *Speculum Gy* stint in booklet 2, no catchword survives at the sole quire boundary within the stint, on fol. 46v. Scribe 2's *The Simonie* survives only within a single quire in which the final folio is lacking. Within Scribe 3's stint, there are four surviving quire boundaries where the quire-final verso is intact (fols. 76v–77r, 84v–84ʳr, 91v–92r, 99v), and only the last of these has a surviving catchword (see note 19 above).

[21] Scribe 4 is the only Auchinleck scribe who never left space for larger initials, but he left space for no initials whatsoever. Scribe 2, who never once left space to accommodate a miniature, left space at the openings of two of his three texts (*Speculum Gy* and *The Simonie*) for larger initials. In the third instance, where he copied *Four Philosophers* in booklet 3, Scribe 2 left almost no room for an initial, although he was working with tight space constraints here. In the three instances where it is possible to examine Scribe 3's practice, he twice left space for a larger initial (preceding *Seuen Dedly Sinnes*, which has no opening miniature, and *Sir Degare*, which very likely once did have an opening miniature) and once left space for a two-line initial preceding *Pater Noster*. This is an interesting case, though, because Scribe 3 actually left more space for the initial beginning the prayer proper, and this is the only initial in the text that is not two lines tall. Given the pre-eminence of this prayer, however, Scribe 3's emphasis on its beginning rather than the text's makes sense. Scribe 5 consistently left room for a larger initial, once preceded by space for a miniature (preceding *Reinbrun Gij Sone of Warwike*) and once to stand alone (preceding *Sir Beues of Hamtoun*). In two instances (preceding *The*

an auxiliary scribe, like Scribe 2, might have undertaken one or both of his larger stints before entering into collaboration on Auchinleck with Scribe 1; a scribe contributing only a text or two might forget or ignore some of Scribe 1's instructions or standard practices; or such instructions might not have been very specific. Scribe 1's participation in this phenomenon might also indicate that some or all of these formatting choices were made prior to the decision to include miniatures.[22]

Returning to the opening of *Otuel*, then, the presence of an unusually large initial at the opening of the text does not in itself argue for a divergence from Scribe 1's own practice. In fact, the nine-line excision preceding the opening lines of *Otuel* almost certainly indicates that the scribe left room for an opening miniature. Since it is highly unlikely that a scribe producing speculative piecework would have anticipated a buyer who could afford significant decoration, this scribe's allowances for a miniature strongly suggest he was copying *Otuel* for Auchinleck and working in concert, however distantly, with Scribe 1's overall decorative plan. It is possible that the *Otuel* quire was copied before Scribe 1 had finalized his decorative programme, but, if we accept the view of Scribe 6 as a distinct contributor, it is just as probable that Scribe 1's instructions focused primarily on leaving space for a miniature and made no specifications as to the size of the opening initial. As in the case of the catchwords, stylistic differences in *Otuel*'s opening initial accord with Wiggins's argument for a distinct Scribe 6 and further suggest that Scribe 6 was probably not working as closely with Scribe 1 as Scribe 5 was.[23] On the other hand, contrary to

Anonymous Short English Metrical Chronicle and *Sir Tristrem*), Scribe 1 also left space for a larger initial, and in one of these (*Tristrem*) he left space for a miniature.

[22] With the exception of the two initials that accompany miniatures, all of these larger initials occur at the beginnings of booklets. The consistently unusual decorations in this particular context (large initials and no miniatures open five of the nine booklets whose initial pages survive) might expose stages of the booklets' production that preceded the decision (or the funding) to incorporate a programme of miniatures. Taking booklets that Scribe 1 initiated himself, for example, he must have begun work on booklets 6 and 9 with the final decorative programme in mind, having left room for miniatures. In the case of the beginning of booklet 10, however, where he has left space for a large initial but no miniature, Scribe 1 appears to have begun copying the *Short Chronicle* either prior to embarking on this decorative programme or with a different final destination for it in mind. By the time it was handed off to an illuminator, though, it must have been Auchinleck-bound. The large initial at the beginning of the *Short Chronicle* was painted by the same artist responsible for the initial at the beginning of *Sir Beues* (and booklet 5). Details within this historiated initial confirm its production by the same artist that executed Auchinleck's miniatures. Indeed, the similarities between these two initials – and their execution by the same artist – may reinforce the codicological evidence that Scribes 1 and 5 (the latter of whom was responsible for *Sir Beues*) worked particularly closely. That these initials are placed at the openings of booklets without accompanying miniatures further suggests that they may have been working together at a relatively early stage in the manuscript's production.

[23] Wiggins remarks upon the style of *Otuel*'s large opening puzzle initial, stylistically unusual in the manuscript, suggesting that Scribe 6, like Scribe 2, had access to an artist other than the ones in the atelier executing Auchinleck's overall programme of decoration and illumination ('Are Auchinleck Manuscript Scribes 1 and 6 the Same Scribe?', p. 20). Based on differences in pigment and pen decoration, Scribe 2's and Scribe 6's initials do not appear to have been executed by the same artist, at least not at the same time.

Wiggins's claims, it would appear that Scribe 6 worked more closely to Scribe 1's programme than did Scribe 2.

With stints scattered across several booklets, Scribe 2 may have been involved in the project of producing Auchinleck over a longer period than were Scribes 3, 4, and 6.[24] Still, if he worked in direct contact or communication with Scribe 1, there is no manuscript evidence of this contact.[25] The texts, decoration, and layout of Scribe 2's stints reflect the likelihood that he worked with a greater measure of independence from the predominant aesthetic of Auchinleck than did the other scribes. All three of Scribe 2's texts tend towards didacticism, employing minimal narrative as a means to that end. Two of the three extant texts he copied for Auchinleck are multilingual – *Speculum Gy de Warewyke* incorporates Latin *sententiae*, and *Four Philosophers* is an Anglo-Norman/English macaronic poem – and these works incorporate more non-English material than the other four surviving multilingual texts in the manuscript.[26] Diverging visually from standard Auchinleck practice, Scribe 2 never left space for miniatures and copied two of his three texts – *Speculum Gy* and *The Simonie* – within page layouts accommodating fewer lines per page or column and with a larger script than elsewhere found in the manuscript. In booklet 3, Scribe 2's *Four Philosophers* submits to some of the strictures of Scribe 1's visual programme, but even here he left minimal space for decoration.[27]

[24] Scribe 5 also contributed to multiple booklets, having completed booklet 4 and initiated booklet 5.

[25] Arguing that Scribe 2 worked in more varied capacities than Scribe 1's other scribal colleagues, Wiggins has proposed two instances in which he might have interacted with Scribe 1, but there are problems with both of these scenarios. Specifically, she suggests that Scribe 2 served as intermediary between Scribes 1 and 6, relaying the former's instructions to the latter, and that Scribe 1 provided the ruling for *Four Philosophers* and passed booklet 3 from Scribe 3 to Scribe 2 (Wiggins, 'Are Auchinleck Manuscript Scribes 1 and 6 the Same Scribe?', p. 20). Scribe 2's connection with Scribe 6 is tenuous at best, and he could only have served as intermediary between Scribes 1 and 6 in temporally limited circumstances given that Scribe 6's stints suggest more oversight from Scribe 1 than Scribe 2's do. Wiggins's argument for direct contact between Scribes 1 and 2 in booklet 3 rests on an erroneous assertion, namely, that Scribe 1 provided the ruling for *Four Philosophers*. The ruling of the page is patently not Scribe 2's; he must compress his script to fit it within the ruled lines. It was almost certainly provided by Scribe 3, though, and not by Scribe 1. Scribe 3 did his own ruling, and he appears to have ruled by openings except across quire boundaries. Here I am in agreement with T. A. Shonk, 'A Study of the Auchinleck Manuscript: Investigations into the Processes of Book Making in the Fourteenth Century', unpublished PhD dissertation, University of Tennessee (Knoxville, 1981), p. 61.

[26] Among the other four, *The Disputisoun bitven þe Bodi and þe Soule* and *The Harrowing of Hell* employ Latin dialogue tags, and *Dauid þe King* (a meditation on Psalm 50) and *Pater Noster* interlineate Latin lines with their English translations or paraphrases.

[27] Scribe 2 reduced the size of his script to fit it within Scribe 3's ruling. Also, in contrast to his practice elsewhere, Scribe 2 did not provide his own paraphs in booklet 3; his guide marks are visible and the paraphs have been painted by the same paraphers working throughout the rest of the quire. On paraphing in Scribe 2's stints, see H. Marshall, 'What's in a Paraph? A New Methodology and Its Implications for the Auchinleck Manuscript', *Journal of the Early Book Society* 13 (2010), 39–62. There is, of course, no room available for a miniature at the beginning of *Four Philosophers*. Additionally,

Scribe 2's marked visual and textual divergences in his two booklet-initial stints may indicate that these booklet parts were pre-assembled with little or no reference to Scribe 1's planning. Helen Marshall has convincingly argued that Scribe 2 contributed the paraphs for *Speculum Gy* and *The Simonie* himself and even painted one of the initials in *Speculum Gy*.[28] On these grounds, she suggests that these two stints were probably completed before Scribe 2 began working with Scribe 1 on Auchinleck. As such, they testify to an 'improvisational' dimension of Auchinleck's production whereby preassembled texts – that is, texts copied and even partially decorated before their final destination was determined – might have been selected for inclusion in Auchinleck.[29] Certainly, Scribe 2 took a far greater measure of responsibility upon himself in producing these stints than the other auxiliary scribes typically did – with the possible exception of Scribe 3.

Scribes 1 and 3: convergences

Scribe 3's stint engaged differently with Scribe 1's practice and aesthetic over time. The single catchword added to Scribe 3's stint suggests that interventions by Scribe 1 were more sporadic than those in the stint of Scribe 5.[30] Early in his stint, Scribe 3 appears to have worked with a great deal of independence, fashioning a contribution to Auchinleck that stands apart in its appearance and content, like those of Scribe 2. Eventually, however, Scribe 1 may have communicated new stipulations regarding format or begun to exercise greater oversight. Changes in lineation across the quires of Scribe 3's stint bear this out, with the lineation in his final quires significantly closer to that of Scribe 1.[31] Similarly, these later quires more easily accommodate Auchinleck's predominant decorative programme.[32]

---

however, Scribe 2 left almost no space for the opening initial, which must extend upwards and outwards into the margin, even though he appears to have anticipated its inclusion, having not copied the first letter of the text himself.

[28] Marshall, 'What's in a Paraph?'.

[29] Ibid., p. 45. Marshall has proposed a production model for Auchinleck 'in which some booklets were "bespoke" while others – created in advance or, at least, created outside Scribe 1's planning – were incorporated into the codex as whole units or as the basis for booklets in which further scribal stints were added' (p. 45).

[30] As noted above, there is a single catchword in Scribe 1's hand on fol. 99v, at the end of quire 14.

[31] Quires 13, 14, and 16 (and possibly 15, if it had survived) are uniformly ruled for 44 lines per page, Scribe 1's own preferred line-count. Quires 11 and 12, the first two quires of the booklet, are not: quire 12 has consistently been ruled for two columns of 40 lines per page and the openings within quire 11 range from two columns of 33–38 lines per page. The fluctuations within quire 11 appear to be at least partially keyed to texts: *Seuen Dedly Sinnes* and *Pater Noster* have been copied in the range of 36–38 lines per page and the lowest line-counts are all employed in ruling for *Assumption*. It is possible that Scribe 3 judged the wider spacing appropriate to the poem's content or stanzaic form, but what is abundantly clear in Scribe 3's ruling of this quire is that he did not aspire here to the uniformity of Scribe 1's line-count. Seen in this light, his adoption in his later quires of Scribe 1's preferred line-count might suggest that Scribe 1 had stepped up his involvement.

[32] To the extent that losses within the booklet permit an assessment of the decorative programme, Scribe 3's policy of allowing space for an opening miniature appears to

When taken together, these observations shed some light on the circumstances in which Scribe 3 might have copied his stint, and they point to a shifting interaction between Scribes 1 and 3. Scribe 1's presence, in both his tangible interventions and the execution of his aesthetic, is felt most powerfully in the final three extant quires of the booklet. Here, Scribe 3 adhered closely to Scribe 1's preferred ruling format and to his visual programme. Here also, Scribe 3 copied texts whose length and content resemble those selected and privileged elsewhere by Scribe 1: *Sir Degare*, *Seven Sages*, and *Floris and Blauncheflur* align with the book's general tendency towards narrative, specifically romance narrative. Most of the scholars who find this booklet aberrant do so less on account of its contents as a whole than on account of the romances' placement at the centre rather than beginning of the booklet.[33] The confluence of codicological and textual shifts within the booklet suggests a means of accounting for its unusual structure: Scribe 1 was most likely exerting greater oversight over Scribe 3's stint by the time he was working on quires 13–16. Whether Scribe 3 was actually working in closer proximity to Scribe 1 at this point or was merely the recipient of more specific directives regarding page layout and text choice, his work in these later quires fits Auchinleck's visual and textual project nearly as seamlessly as does that of Scribe 5.

Scribes 2 and 3: divergences

Scribe 2's contributions to Auchinleck provide a key to understanding how Scribe 3 was operating earlier, when he began work on booklet 3. Particularly in quire 11, the texts Scribe 3 copied and the layout of the pages onto which he copied them resemble Scribe 2's stints more closely than those of Scribe 1. Here Scribe 3, like Scribe 2, left no room for miniatures, undertook some of his own rubrication, and ruled openings for far fewer lines per page than Scribe 1's typical forty-four. It seems possible that Scribe 3 executed most or all of his first quire under circumstances

have shifted over the course of his stint. As noted above, *Seuen Dedly Sinnes* begins with a large initial but without any space for a miniature. Though *Pater Noster* does have a framed miniature on its first folio, Scribe 3 does not appear to have planned for its inclusion, and his page layout limited its size and prevented its placement at the beginning of the new poem. While its atypical dimensions and location are in some senses quite appropriate to the text, itself atypical within Auchinleck, the miniature was squeezed into the upper margin of the page and thus was probably not anticipated by Scribe 3. The other four texts copied by Scribe 3 have all suffered some measure of loss at their openings, and *Sir Degare* is the only poem of the four that has not lost any lines of text at its beginning. The text commences on the eighth ruled line of fol. 78rb, and a rough excision has cut into this first line and removed all of the column above this line. Such excisions elsewhere in the manuscript indicate the removal of miniatures, and a miniature-hunter was probably the culprit here as well. The loss of whole leaves (or more) at the openings of the other three poems may also be the result of a miniature-hunter's zeal (again, this is a pattern observable elsewhere in Auchinleck). In any case, the small-scale excision at the opening of *Sir Degare* establishes that by the time Scribe 3 had begun to copy this poem he had almost certainly received instructions from Scribe 1 to leave space for a miniature at the opening of a new poem.

[33] See note 6 above.

similar to those in which Scribe 2 copied *Speculum Gy* and *The Simonie*, with relatively minimal direction from Scribe 1. If Scribes 2 and 3 were copying at Scribe 1's behest, he might have briefed them on rough page dimension and layout (or provided materials), but, in that case, the two scribes' *mises-en-page* express their own interpretations of what Scribe 1 had in mind. It is even conceivable, as Marshall has suggested in respect to Scribe 2, that both scribes provided Scribe 1 with material that they had copied in advance of his planning or direction.

Beyond its visual distinctiveness, the work of Scribes 2 and 3 generates points of textual disruption or redirection within Auchinleck. At these points, the narratives for which the manuscript is so famous give way to texts that call upon a reader's consciousness of his or her inner spiritual state or outer socio-political context. Between them, Scribes 2 and 3 copied the bulk of the manuscript's multilingual and non-narrative or minimally narrative works.[34] In the rare instances in which Scribe 1 copied such texts, they almost invariably occupy positions at the ends of booklets.[35] Scribes 2 and 3, on the other hand, gave such works pride of place at the beginnings of booklets. These two scribes were not necessarily collaborating – though it is certainly possible that they came into contact, given that quire 16 passed from Scribe 3 to Scribe 2 – but they do evince a common distance from the overall plan of Auchinleck in the texts they chose to copy and privilege.

The question of who selected these texts for inclusion remains open and compelling. Scribe 1 could have selected some or all of them after they were copied; he could have deputized both scribes to copy the bulk of the manuscript's overtly didactic material because they had access to the appropriate exemplars; or, again, he might have provided less specific instruction, perhaps enjoining them to provide some devotional texts – whether previously copied by them or available in exemplar – for inclusion within the manuscript. Scribe 2's *Speculum Gy* may be a more likely candidate for bespoke production than *The Simonie*. The latter is the sole (fragmentary) survival in the manuscript's final booklet, and its ruling in

---

[34] These include *Speculum Gy* (Latin/English, minimally narrative), *Seuen Dedly Sinnes* (non-narrative), *Pater Noster* (Latin/English, non-narrative), *Four Philosophers* (Anglo-Norman/English, minimally narrative), and *The Simonie* (minimally narrative). Scribe 4's sole contribution (the list of names of Norman barons) is also non-narrative – that is, a list rather than running text. It is worth noting that Scribe 1's two other scribal auxiliaries copied texts that fit comfortably within the manuscript's preoccupations: Scribe 5's *Reinbrun* and *Sir Beues* fit in with Scribe 1's Guy of Warwick material (*Reinbrun* being adapted from this tradition itself and *Sir Beues* belonging to an oft-associated tradition), and *Otuel*, attributed to Scribe 6, fits with Scribe 1's Charlemagne material, which it also follows in the manuscript.

[35] A generous round-up of these texts includes *The Desputisoun bitven þe Bodi and þe Soule* (Latin/English, minimally narrative), *The Harrowing of Hell* (Latin/English), *The Thrush and the Nightingale* (minimally narrative), *The Sayings of St Bernard* (non-narrative), *Dauid þe King* (Latin/English, non-narrative), *The Four Foes of Mankind* (non-narrative), and *Alphabetical Praise of Women* (non-narrative). On Scribe 1's selections, see S. Fein, 'The Fillers of the Auchinleck Manuscript and the Literary Culture of the West Midlands', in *Makers and Users of Medieval Books: Essays in Honour of A. S. G. Edwards*, ed. C. M. Meale and D. Pearsall (Cambridge, 2014), pp. 60–77.

a single column is a relative rarity in the manuscript. As for *Speculum Gy*, Guy of Warwick is undoubtedly a central figure in the manuscript (perhaps at the behest of the manuscript's patron), and his possible occasion-specific insertion into this text could argue for its deliberate inclusion in Auchinleck.[36]

Turning to Scribe 3's early stint, one can only speculate as to whether Scribe 1 (or the patron) might have requested *Seuen Dedly Sinnes* and *Pater Noster*. If they were included in response to the patron's wishes, the demand was probably couched in general rather than specific terms (e.g., 'Give me what the family and I need to prepare for confession'); the texts themselves are unique, but similar clusters of the fundamentals of lay piety survive in similarly mixed collections like, for example, Cambridge, University Library, MS Ff. 2. 38. *Seuen Dedly Sinnes* and *Pater Noster* offer early attestations of this kind of text rendered into English, and this earliness, along with these texts' brevity and singularity, argue for their having potentially been translated or adapted specifically for inclusion in Auchinleck (or, if Scribe 3 had produced them earlier, for some other purpose). It is even possible that Scribe 3 translated or adapted them himself. In any event, the specific form that these texts take most probably reflects the agency not of Scribe 1 but of Scribe 3, whether we go so far as to dub it authorial or confine it to the realm of selection, execution, and emendation.

Pedagogies of reading in Seuen Dedly Sinnes *and* Pater Noster

As I turn to the two texts that Scribe 3 probably copied – or even produced – under relatively independent circumstances, I think it important to stress their corresponding independence from our prevailing sense of what Auchinleck *is* as a manuscript. In asserting booklet 3's formal coherence, Bahr has suggested that these texts pick up 'the leitmotif of spiritual imitation that runs through what we might call Auchinleck's "religious overture"' in booklets 1 and 2.[37] Bahr sees all of these texts participating in the same spiritual project, but his point elides the differences of these texts and the potential significance of their more particular arrangements. With an eye to the idiosyncrasies of *Seuen Dedly Sinnes* and *Pater Noster*, my reading takes them on their own terms, probing the potential medieval reception of this particular node of texts. Scribe 3's divergent interventions in Auchinleck's third booklet find a literary parallel in the textual workings of the two poems in the vanguard of his stint. *Seuen Dedly Sinnes* and *Pater Noster* effect a productive kind of disruption for their audiences, placing a varied assemblage of collected materials within textual frameworks that goad readers to recognize and think about the many ways they read, and to read in ever more sophisticated ways. In the process,

---

[36] This possibility is suggested by J. H. Burrows, 'The Auchinleck Manuscript: Contexts, Texts and Audience', unpublished PhD dissertation, Washington University (St Louis MO, 1984), p. 23. She suggests that Scribe 2 emended Alcuin's *De Virtutibus et Vitiis Liber*, or a translation thereof, so as to incorporate Guy of Warwick in place of Guido of Tours, for whom Alcuin's text was written.

[37] Bahr, *Fragments and Assemblages*, p. 115. This assessment accords with his view that Scribe 1 assumed primary responsibility for planning booklet 3.

these poems cultivate readerly self-consciousness that is at once inwardly directed, morally deliberative, and imaginative.

Seuen Dedly Sinnes comprises a collection of lists, prayers, and meditations that point to its probable use for lay religious instruction and also necessitate different kinds of reading. The poem's textual framework takes up the mantle of a clerical instructor, sustained throughout the poem, expounding basic elements of the faith as well as the reasons and ways laypeople ought to learn them. The prefatory overview of its first section imagines a nearly universal audience for its penitentially needful contents – lists of the Seven Deadly Sins and Ten Commandments – asserting that 'children and wimmen and men / Of twelue winter elde and more, / … / Euerichone þai sscholden knowe' (lines 12–13, 15).[38] At the same time, these lines suggest that the lists' contents may already be widely known, and, in so doing, they call the preface's stated project into question. Though some readers may have learned the sins and commandments by reading this poem, its textual frame also offers guidance in reading itself. In addition to directing readers in what to read, *Seuen Dedly Sinnes* teaches an audience to read strategically and self-consciously.

The poem's textual frame guides users through three sections of collected materials, inviting them to read each with increasing sensitivity and skill. The first section presents its lists with terse economy, appropriate to the frame's focus on a practical internalization of their content. Here the reader reads in order to know. The second section of the poem, framing English translations of the Paternoster, Creed, and Ave Maria with the injunction to 'taken hede, / On Englissch to segge what hit were, / Als holi cherche ʒou wolde lere' (lines 18–20), promotes their repeated scrutiny and oral performance. Presenting these translations as visually distinct from their textual surroundings, the manuscript's layout enables readers to access them separately or en masse, without recourse to the poem's other sections.[39] They could be revisited, pondered and read repeatedly. The third and final section of the poem contains an account of Christ's Passion subdivided according to the hours of the divine office and punctuated by brief prayers. Employing paraphs for the first time in the text, Scribe 3 marked the transitions between the hours, emphasizing these temporal markers and increasing the likelihood that readers might move through the Passion narrative incrementally, even in tandem with the canonical hours.

Although this third part of the poem does not fulfill the function of an office such as one might encounter in a book of hours (the apparatus of Latin texts character-istic in hours is absent here), it does combine narrative and prayer to similar effect. Sylvia Huot, writing of books of hours as sites of 'polytextual reading', remarks that

---

[38] All quotations from *On þe Seuen Dedly Sinnes* are cited by line number from the online transcription in the Burnley-Wiggins facsimile.

[39] These prayers differ metrically from their framing text, written in octosyllabic couplets, and these metrical distinctions contribute to visual distinctions on the page. Furthermore, both the Paternoster and the Ave Maria terminate in 'Amen', which signals the conclusion of these discrete prayers, and two painted initials enhance the visibility of the Paternoster and the Creed.

they typically foster two kinds of reading: a visual kind that 'ignores the divisions into hours and moves through the episodes of the Virgin's life', and a textual kind that 'in effect uses the visual narrative as a springboard for more exploratory movement through a series of texts and passages'.[40] The text embedded in this poem attempts something similar without the benefit of actual images: passages keyed to the canonical hours recount a linear narrative of the Passion, while brief prayers interrupt the narrative's flow from one hour to the next. The poem's frame twice exhorts readers of this section to have or hold the Passion 'in minde' (lines 23, 162) so as to 'sturen out of dedli sinne' (line 27). The interpolated prayers provide an impetus for this prescribed internalization, drawing readers repeatedly into contemplative contact with the Passion. At the same time, for those reading and praying this cycle at the canonical hours, the Passion narrative follows real time in its movement through Scripture. For audiences reading in this manner, their own passage through time would progress in synchrony with that of the suffering Christ. This prayerful activity not only heightens the Passion's immediacy for its readers, but permits a kind of double narrative vision: the readers' experiences of their own time are overlaid with an awareness of scriptural time.

Following in the wake of *Seuen Dedly Sinnes* and its multifarious contents, *Pater Noster* by its very presence goads its audience to think about different ways of reading. This is not the first Paternoster in booklet 3 – *Seuen Dedly Sinnes* contains an English translation of the prayer as well – but *Pater Noster*'s presentation of the prayer demands that it be read differently, in ways more akin to the experience of the reader of the Passion narrative in *Seuen Dedly Sinnes*. *Pater Noster* asks that its audience approach the Paternoster in distinct increments:

> Seuen oreisouns þer beʒ inne
> Þat helpeʒ men out of dedli sinne
> And ʒif ʒe willeʒ a while dwelle,
> Al on Englissch ich wille ʒou telle
> Þe skile of hem alle seuene,
> Wiʒ help of Godes miʒt of heuene. (lines 21–6)[41]

As in the preceding poem, *Pater Noster*'s guiding framework encompasses a collection and mobilizes it against 'dedli sinne'. Here, however, the collected elements are canonical in their cohesion and sequence, deriving as they do from the fixed text of the Paternoster. The seven petitions of the prayer serve not only as an embedded authoritative text; they also stand as structural elements framing the heart of the poem, the 'skile of hem alle seuene'. *Pater Noster* does not purport to teach the Paternoster as a unitary and continuous text for memorization or

---

40 S. Huot, 'Polytextual Reading: The Meditative Reading of Real and Metaphorical Books', in *Orality and Literacy in the Middle Ages: Essays on a Conjunction and Its Consequences in Honour of D. H. Green*, ed. M. Chinca and C. Young (Turnhout, 2005), pp. 203–22 (p. 213). Huot defines 'polytextual reading' as a kind of learned reading whereby 'the reading of one text becomes a process of reading multiple "virtual" texts' (p. 203).

41 All quotations from *The Pater Noster Vndo on Englissch* are cited by line number from the online transcription in the Burnley-Wiggins facsimile.

recitation; rather, it uses it to structure more penetrating readings of the prayer as a richly significant text.[42]

In promoting this deep readerly engagement with text, *Pater Noster* invites the reader of English to participate in the learned and Latinate exegetical tradition. The poem teaches him or her to navigate textual multivalence and to read in the manner if not the language of clerks. The poem's structure and layout foreground the Latin Paternoster. Each of the seven petitions begins with a painted initial and the Latin line or lines of the Paternoster that correspond to it. Then follow corresponding English translations – notably distinct from the translation provided in *Seuen Dedly Sinnes*[43] – and explications of the Latin. As in the Passion section of *Seuen Dedly Sinnes*, the poem's structure compels an interrupted and (recalling Huot's formulation) polytextual reading. Rather than reading the prayer through, the reading audience is asked to read *into* it.

Conclusion: reframing Auchinleck's romances

If *Seuen Dedly Sinnes* encourages its readers to think not only of their sins but of how they are reading, *Pater Noster* capitalizes on such readerly self-consciousness to push readers into a complex relationship with text and with their own selves. *Pater*

---

[42] In doing so, this poem offers considerably more instruction than the Church required. All Christians were expected to know the Paternoster and be able to recite it. M. Hussey, treating some of the most sophisticated expositions of the Paternoster, observes the disjunction between the simplicity of what the Church had stipulated and the intricacy of what was produced, remarking, 'The subjects [i.e. articles of faith] were treated with a complexity that becomes paradoxical when we realize that the demands of the archbishops had been for frequent and, above all, simple expositions and exhortations in every church' ('The Petitions of the Paternoster in Mediæval English Literature', *Medium Ævum* 27 [1958], 8–16 [p. 8]). This essential, parochial, pedagogical goal finds humorous illustration in the later *A lytell geste how the plowman lerned his pater noster*, printed in 1510 by Wynkyn de Worde (*STC* 20034), in which a parish priest tricks a stingy plowman into learning the words of the prayer in the guise of the names of a string of debtors. See also 'How the Plowman Learned His Paternoster', in *The Oxford Book of Medieval English Verse*, ed. C. Sisam and K. Sisam (Oxford, 1970), pp. 514-21.

[43] The metrical English translation diverges almost completely from that provided in the other poem. The only exception occurs in the first petition, where the English translation is identical: 'Oure fader in heuene-riche, / Þi name be blessed euere iliche' (*Seuen Dedly Sinnes*, lines 79–80; *Pater Noster*, lines 29–30). This is also the one instance in *Pater Noster* where the English translation is out of sync with the Latin: the first petition, 'Pater noster, qui es in celis' (*Pater Noster*, line 27), corresponds to the first line of this couplet, while the second line corresponds to the second petition, 'Saunctificetur nomen tuum' (*Pater Noster*, line 51). Additionally, these are the only lines of the prayer in *Seuen Dedly Sinnes* that do not conform to the predominant metre of the poem's embedded prayers; instead, they make up an octosyllabic couplet. It is possible that the *Pater Noster*'s author began by copying from the translation in *Seuen Dedly Sinnes* only to realize the difficulties posed (not only the Latin/English correspondence but the metrical differences in the subsequent lines). This textual correspondence suggests that the *Pater Noster* might have been composed deliberately as a companion to *Seuen Dedly Sinnes*, in which case it may have been composed by someone close to this manuscript. If this were the case, Scribe 3's authorship would be a strong possibility.

Noster offers its readers 'skile', in the sense of a kind of hermeneutical knowledge, but, more importantly, it teaches them to develop the ability – 'skile' in our enduring sense of the word – to read hermeneutically. The poem invites readers to read the prayer as not only spiritually efficacious but also rich in sense and signification. Indeed, while the Paternoster situates this poem within extensive medieval exposritory and literary traditions structured around the interpretive and catechetical potential of the seven petitions of the Paternoster, Auchinleck's *Pater Noster* pursues a project out of keeping with those of most Paternoster tracts.[44] In other exposritions, the prayer's petitions provide a foundation on which a catechetically useful network of associations – including the Seven Deadly Sins, the Seven Gifts of the Holy Spirit, and the Beatitudes – can be erected. For all that such catechesis appears close at hand in *Seuen Dedly Sinnes*, however, Auchinleck's *Pater Noster* finds a different use for the matrix of the prayer, one that befits its manuscript context: the seven petitions serve here as sites of explication centred on the figurative richness of the prayer's language. *Pater Noster* encourages readers to read interpretively and, specifically, metaphorically.[45]

In doing so, *Pater Noster* erects associative frameworks that condition the ways in which its audience might read onward in the booklet – or in the manuscript as a whole. Most of the poem's metaphors make up the stuff of readers' lives, but, more to the point in their Auchinleck context, many of them make up the stuff of romance. For example, the poem's treatment of the sixth petition – 'Et dimitte nobis debita nostra, sicut & nos dimittimus debitoribus nostris' (line 124) – freights the concept of counsel, good and bad, with rich strata of meaning. *Pater Noster* focuses on the petition's second clause, which would probably have presented greater challenges to its reading audience, praying for God's forgiveness being more likely to strike many as a lighter (and more self-interested) burden to bear than forgiving those who had done them harm. The explication turns to diabolical metaphor to make a (self-interested) case for mercy and forgiveness:

---

[44] For extended discussions of these traditions in England, see Hussey, 'Petitions'; and F. G. A. M. Aarts, 'The Pater Noster in Medieval English Literature', *Papers on Language and Literature* 5 (1969), 3–16. It is worth noting that the septenary structure in Auchinleck's *Pater Noster* does not fit the most common septenary structure, that established already in the writing of Saint Augustine: 1. *Pater noster qui es in cœlis sanctificetur nomen tuum*, 2. *Adveniat regnum tuum*, 3. *Fiat voluntas tua sicut in cœlo et in terra*, 4. *Panem nostrum cotidianum da nobis hodie*, 5. *Et dimitte nobis debita nostra sicut nos dimittimus debitoribus nostris*, 6. *Et ne nos inducas in temptationem*, 7. *Sed libera nos a malo* (Hussey, 'Petitions', p. 8, drawing on Augustine's 'De Sermone in Monte', *PL* 34:1229–307). *Pater Noster* splits the first petition into two – 'Pater noster qui es in celis' (line 27) and 'Saunctificetur nomen tuum' (line 51) – and combines the sixth and seventh petitions above into one – 'Et ... / Set liber' (lines 147–8).

[45] The metaphors in *Pater Noster* are not unique to this poem. The later and longer *Speculum Vitae*, for example, deploys similar, and often more extensive, material in its explication of the prayer. Still, the pre-eminence of metaphorical analysis in Auchinleck's *Pater Noster*, to the exclusion of septenary catechetical materials, argues for the specificity of the poem's priorities. See *Speculum Vitae: A Reading Edition*, ed. R. Hanna, EETS OS 331, 2 vols. (Oxford, 2008).

> ӡif ani man þat is in londe
> Liueӡ in nyht oþer in onde
> Þourgh counseil of þe fendes red,
> He biddeӡ aӡenes his owene hed
> And makeӡ him heiere in erthe
> Þan Ihesu Crist þat more is werthe. (lines 131–6)[46]

There are several grave issues that arise from withholding forgiveness, most particularly that implied by the fourth line in this passage: the 'sicut' in the prayer renders God's forgiveness contingent on human forgiveness, implying that one who prays the Paternoster while having withheld forgiveness essentially prays that God likewise refuse forgiveness.[47] This passage expresses this spiritual risk in visceral terms, identifying action motivated by 'nyht' (wrath) and 'onde' (envy) as action taken by fiendish counsel. The self-evident wrongness of letting the devil tell you what to do conveys the spiritual harm of withholding forgiveness without resorting to an explication of the petition's conditional syntax. At the same time, this formulation permits the reader to imaginatively externalize sinful impulses towards wrath and envy as bad counsel to be repudiated. Here the passage obliquely acknowledges the Gift of the Holy Spirit most often associated with this petition, that of counsel.[48] The bad counsel of the fiend is presumably answered with the good counsel afforded by the Holy Spirit. The human agent occupies a position of judgement, weighing good and bad advice. The terms of this metaphor invite readers to imagine themselves in such evaluative positions, or, in other words, to understand their own moral choices through the idiom of a common romance scenario. At the same time, they encourage a different kind of polytextual reading from that prompted in *Seuen Dedly Sinnes*, one in which narrative scenarios, such as the receipt of (or action upon) bad counsel, might conceivably prompt rumination on the spiritual and ethical concerns raised here.

Ultimately, *Seuen Dedly Sinnes* and *Pater Noster* condition readings of their booklet in Auchinleck in much the same way that they condition readings of their own framed contents. The visual and textual frameworks of both poems lead the reader through their curated collections of text as they provoke an awareness of the processes and motivations informing the reader's experience. In their corresponding function as textual frames for the booklet as a whole – or, indeed, for a reader's experience of any other part of Auchinleck – these texts encourage readers to think about how and why they read different kinds of text. At the same time, they promote modes of reading that attend to textual layers – metaphors

---

[46] The explication goes on for eight more lines, but the losses to fol. 72a make it impossible to reconstruct the content of these lines.

[47] *Speculum Vitae* treats this idea at much greater length; see *Speculum Vitae*, ed. Hanna, I, pp. 100–05 (lines 2947–3106).

[48] See Hussey, 'Petitions'. It is worth noting that this is not the Gift aligned with the petition in *Speculum Vitae*. Instead it is knowledge, and, as its treatment of the petition implies, specifically self-knowledge.

and multivalences that enrich popular narratives, as well as explications of the Paternoster – and to how the reading of either sort of text may invest the other with meaning.

The foregoing reading begins to address the ways in which *Seuen Dedly Sinnes* and *Pater Noster* engage the rest of the booklet, and, indeed, the Auchinleck manuscript. Such a reading depends upon first recognizing the two poems' particularities. Scribe 3's opening pairing of two non-narrative texts begets a meaningful dialogue which also then resonates productively within the volume. This approach to the texts is necessarily grounded in the codicological circumstances under which the booklet may have taken shape, and it is specifically informed by the possibility that Scribe 3 copied these texts with relatively little oversight from Scribe 1. Our ideas of how and why Auchinleck came together necessarily condition our readings of its textual conjunctions and literary preoccupations. There is value – literary as well as codicological – in exploring the book's eccentricities, the apparently aberrant or even autonomous contributions that disrupt its broader coherences.

CHAPTER SIX

Absent Presence: Auchinleck and *Kyng Alisaunder**

Venetia Bridges

According to Chaucer's Monk, Alexander the Great's presence in the Auchinleck manuscript is unremarkable:

> The storie of Alisaunder is so commune
> That every wight that hath discrecioun
> Hath herd somewhat or al of his fortune.[1]

For the Monk, Alexander's story is an *exemplum* of 'false Fortune' despite his chivalric glories ('of knyghthod and of fredom flour').[2] The use of Alexander as an *exemplum* is indeed 'commune' in late-fourteenth-century literary culture, as shown by contemporary texts like John Gower's *Confessio Amantis*, in which Alexander (educated by Aristotle) is the perfect kingly ruler.[3] Gower's deployment of Alexander in this way is not an innovation, since the Macedonian is found as an *exemplum* throughout his medieval literary career.[4] Yet not all treatments of Alexander are equally didactic. The 'storie of Alisaunder' found in romance material is a multifaceted weaving together of ethical and philosophical reflection, battle prowess, and marvels both Oriental and magical.[5] As his legend develops from

---

* I am extremely grateful to Dr Aisling Byrne for her valuable comments on earlier drafts of this essay, and to the Danish Research Foundation for their support during its production (DNRF102).

[1] *Canterbury Tales*, VII 2631–3, in *The Riverside Chaucer*, p. 250.

[2] Ibid., VII 2669, 2642.

[3] John Gower, *Confessio Amantis*, ed. R. A. Peck, with Latin translations by A. Galloway, 3 vols. (Kalamazoo MI, 2004, 2006, 2013), III, 264–5 (Book 7, lines 1–22).

[4] See, for example, John of Salisbury, *Ioannis Saresberiensis: Policraticus I–IV*, ed. K. S. B. Keats-Rohan, CCCM 118 (Turnhout, 1993), p. 21 (Prologue to Book 1), dated 1159, which aligns Alexander with Caesar as an example of military skill. Gerald of Wales uses Alexander as both a positive and a negative *exemplum* in his preface to *De instructione principum* (Gerald of Wales, *Concerning the Instruction of Princes*, trans. J. Stevenson [London, 1858; rept 1991], pp. 7, 9).

[5] *Kyng Alisaunder* demonstrates these factors in Alexander's exchanges with Brahmins, his defeats of Darius and Porus, the wondrous animals and peoples he encounters in India, and his extraordinary conception via Nectanebus's magic. Although the medieval period increases the 'marvels of Alexander' narratives, they are found from late antiquity in the *Greek Alexander Romance*, a narrative collection of historical and legendary stories

late antiquity, the common feature in the accreted narratives is variety, making Alexander and his story a complex phenomenon, based in history yet depicted in fictive literature from an early date, and ethically ambivalent despite the conqueror's frequent extrapolation as an *exemplum*. The Monk's statement that Alexander is 'commune' is therefore accurate only up to a point. The Macedonian hero may well have been ubiquitous, but his 'fortune' was not a single one nor always easy to interpret from an exemplary standpoint. Before individual narratives and witnesses are considered, Alexander himself, a hero-villain who occupies indeterminate territory between history and fiction, makes contextualizing his narratives a difficult business.

The issue of contextualization is especially acute for the Alexander narrative in the Auchinleck manuscript (Edinburgh, NLS, MS Advocates 19. 2. 1), the late-thirteenth-century Middle English romance *Kyng Alisaunder* based on the c. 1175 Anglo-Norman *Roman de toute chevalerie* by Thomas of Kent.[6] Present in Auchinleck booklet 8, it is now largely lost because many relevant folios are missing, making it difficult to assess its immediate positioning in the manuscript. *Kyng Alisaunder* also raises questions beyond its local context because its place in Auchinleck's *compilatio* as a whole is difficult to understand. As Ralph Hanna has pointed out, its 'often substantial and learned historical interests … stand somewhat outside the usual concerns of the manuscript, with its profusion of later day English heroes'.[7] *Kyng Alisaunder* in Auchinleck is a challenge, then, on several levels: in terms of its poorly preserved text, its local role in booklet 8, and its impact on the manuscript as a whole. The challenge needs to be taken up, however, because the implicit questions raised by the presence of *Kyng Alisaunder* in Auchinleck relate closely to an important wider debate about the interpretation of works in their material contexts. This debate concerns the definition of multitext manuscripts using metanarratives identified within them. Derek Pearsall has warned that searching for these narratives (in Julia Boffey's terms 'governing principle[s]'[8]) risks finding 'subtle strategies of organisation that turn an apparent miscellany into a continuing thematic metanarrative', which in turn can 'overestimate the activity of the controlling or guiding

---

that is a key basis for European vernacular Alexander accounts. See *The Greek Alexander Romance*, trans. R. Stoneman (London, 1991), pp. 1–27.

[6] This is the accepted dating given by Smithers, in *Kyng Alisaunder*, ed. G. V. Smithers, 2 vols., EETS OS 227, 237 (Oxford, 1952, 1957), II, p. 59. Quotations from *Kyng Alisaunder*, cited in the text by line number, are taken from this edition. See also Thomas of Kent, *The Anglo-Norman 'Alexander' (Le Roman de toute chevalerie)*, ed. B. Foster and I. Short, 2 vols., ANTS 29–31 (London, 1976–77). Quotations from *Le Roman de toute chevalerie*, cited in the text by line number, are taken from the Foster and Short edition.

[7] R. Hanna, *London Literature, 1300–1380*, Cambridge Studies in Medieval Literature 57 (Cambridge, 2005), p. 105.

[8] Boffey's definition describes anthologies as opposed to miscellanies; she sees the latter as 'the fruit of more random incorporation' (J. Boffey, 'Short Texts in Manuscript Anthologies: The Minor Poems of John Lydgate in Two Fifteenth-Century Collections', in *The Whole Book: Cultural Perspectives on the Medieval Miscellany*, ed. S. G. Nichols and S. Wenzel [Ann Arbor, 1996], pp. 69–82 [p. 73]).

intelligence of the scribe-compiler'.[9] Pearsall's observation is timely, for it warns that perceived principles of organization can predetermine interpretations of individual texts and their witnesses (both anthologies and miscellanies). The corollary to his observation is that texts not supporting perceived metanarratives may often be jettisoned or ignored. This tendency may account for *Kyng Alisaunder*'s relative critical neglect as a part of the Auchinleck anthology: the romance does not fit easily into the manuscript's 'governing principle',[10] which is often defined as 'Englishness', both linguistic and national.[11] The fact that it diverges from Auchinleck's strong narrative of Englishness, however, does not make its concerns irrelevant, either at a local level in booklet 8 or as part of the manuscript more generally. The issues the text raises may be paralleled elsewhere in the collection.

This observation brings us back to the concept of variety already mentioned as characteristic of Alexander material. As well as being important potentially for *Kyng Alisaunder* and its history, variety – here meaning 'plural approaches or narratives' – may be a feature of Auchinleck that has been too little emphasized and too often overlooked in the justified critical aim of illuminating the manuscript's undeniable Englishness. I do not mean to deny that Englishness is a dominant concern in Auchinleck but rather to indicate that other, less obvious interests also play a part in its multiple identities – a stance that has begun to gain critical ground. The idea that both Auchinleck and Alexander need to be considered as multifaceted underlies my analysis of the nature and major preoccupations of *Kyng Alisaunder*, and also of its position within and impact upon Auchinleck.

Kyng Alisaunder: *textual troubles*

Although the poem has been the subject of scholarly interest focusing on large specific themes, such as the gender studies of David Salter and Christine Chism, and of manuscript studies, such as those of Simon Horobin and Alison Wiggins,[12] it has not received much attention in its own right (with some notable exceptions to be discussed below) or as part of Auchinleck. This may well be because *Kyng Alisaunder*'s ancient Greek hero and historical focus differentiate it from what scholars have perceived as the other Auchinleck romances' more definably English

---

[9] D. Pearsall, 'The Whole Book: Late Medieval English Manuscript Miscellanies and Their Modern Interpreters', in *Imagining the Book*, ed. S. Kelly and J. J. Thompson (Turnhout, 2005), pp. 17–29 (p. 18).

[10] Hanna, *London Literature*, p. 105; and Boffey, 'Short Texts', p. 3.

[11] See, for example, T. Turville-Petre, *England the Nation: Language, Literature, and National Identity, 1290–1340* (Oxford, 1996), esp. pp. 108–41.

[12] D. Salter, '"Born to Thraldom and Penance": Wives and Mothers in Middle English', in *Writing Gender and Genre in Medieval Literature: Approaches to Old and Middle English Texts*, ed. E. Treharne (Cambridge, 2002), pp. 41–59; C. Chism, 'Winning Women in Two Middle English Alexander Poems', in *Women and Medieval Epic: Gender, Genre, and the Limits of Masculinity*, ed. S. Poor and J. K. Schulman (New York, 2007), pp. 15–39; and S. Horobin and A. Wiggins, 'Reconsidering Lincoln's Inn MS 150', *Medium Ævum* 77 (2008), 30–53.

concerns.[13] The romance's textual situation in Auchinleck is also probably a factor, since it is a ghost text. Now mostly absent but leaving significant traces behind of its former presence, it is awkwardly just visible – or too invisible – making it seem less important than the manuscript's more complete works.

Although *Kyng Alisaunder* is far from being the only damaged text in the manuscript, it has suffered particularly badly from the loss of many folios.[14] In Auchinleck as it currently stands, a section from the end of *Kyng Alisaunder* survives on fols. 278ra and 279rb.[15] Several leaves originally from Auchinleck survive as fragments: London, University Library, MS 593, and St Andrews, University Library, MS PR 2065. A. 15 (MSS 1400, 1401).[16] The total number of lines found to date of Auchinleck's *Kyng Alisaunder* is thus about 704 (249 in Auchinleck, 307 in London 593, and 148 in St Andrews A. 15),[17] or about 9% of the poem as found in its longest witness, Oxford, Bodleian Library, MS Laud misc. 622.[18] These remnants match lines 6676–8021 of Laud misc. 622, although there are frequent gaps of 6–15 lines, mostly through textual loss from the bottoms of pages, and a longer gap of about 400 lines between lines 7388–760 (between where London 593 ends and Auchinleck begins).[19] In other words, what is preserved is not quite as fragmentary as is often implied,[20] since the extant text is a substantial, more-or-less continuous section of *Kyng Alisaunder*'s narrative that runs from Alexander's letter from Candace (queen of the Amazons) to his poisoning and death, including his conversations with the prophetical trees of the sun and

[13] On the 'English' characteristics of Auchinleck romances, see L. Olson, 'Romancing the Book: Manuscripts for "Euerich Inglische"', in K. Kerby-Fulton, M. Hilmo, and L. Olson, *Opening Up Middle English Manuscripts: Literary and Visual Approaches* (Ithaca NY, 2012), pp. 95–151, where she notes that 'tales of true social mobility' are popular among Middle English readers (p. 96). Hanna claims that 'the knight's normative at-home retirement, his achievement of his patrimony and of his position in a historicisable territorial succession, constitutes the unnarratable horizon of English romance' (*London Literature*, p. 131). None of these features are characteristic of *Kyng Alisaunder*.

[14] See the overview of the damage given in Burnley-Wiggins, at http://auchinleck.nls.uk/editorial/physical.html#damage.

[15] See *Kyng Alisaunder*, ed. Smithers, II, 4–5. I count 412, however, based on Smithers's edition (he gives 410).

[16] See Burnley-Wiggins, at http://auchinleck.nls.uk/mss/alisaunder.html; and the overview of the leaves given in D. Pearsall, "Literary and Historical Significance of the Manuscript', in Pearsall-Cunningham, pp. vii–xi (p. vii).

[17] This total is based on a count made from the online facsimile checked against Smithers's edition. Burnley-Wiggins, however, count 259 lines in the current Auchinleck, at http://auchinleck.nls.uk/mss/heads/alisaunder_head.html.

[18] See Smithers's description of this manuscript in *Kyng Alisaunder*, ed. Smithers, II, 1–3.

[19] The extant lines are as follows (numbering from B): London 593: lines 6676–711, 6724–61, 6768–805, 6812–50, 7214–52, 7258–63, 7266–91, 7294–300, 7306–44, 7350–88; St Andrews A. 15: lines 6856–81, 6900–24, 6945–68, 6988–7012, 7032–56, 7170–94; Auchinleck: lines 7760–981, 7992–8021. Smithers's edition includes the St Andrews lines but not those in London 593.

[20] This is the word used of the text by Hanna, *London Literature*, p. 105.

moon and Porus's treachery.[21] It is probable therefore that the Auchinleck text was a complete version of the *Kyng Alisaunder* narrative. A comparison of the other two extant manuscripts, Laud misc. 622, and London, Lincoln's Inn, MS 150, both of which Smithers dates to the late fourteenth century,[22] demonstrates that all three manuscripts share much the same text. Where there are differences (generally of vocabulary), the texts of Auchinleck and B tend to agree against L.[23] Sometimes this agreement is more because L produces a garbled text (like 'God to amours' where both B and Auchinleck have 'honoure' [line 6994]) rather than because the other two positively agree, but there still appears to be a closer correlation between B and Auchinleck than between Auchinleck and L. This proposition is supported indirectly by Horobin and Wiggins's idea that L is a revised version of *Kyng Alisaunder*.[24] Although far from a perfect solution, this essay will therefore use B where necessary as representative of the text lost from Auchinleck.

Kyng Alisaunder: *issues of identity*

What are *Kyng Alisaunder*'s major concerns, the characteristic features of its literary and cultural identities? Hanna's observation that *Kyng Alisaunder* differs from other Auchinleck romances in its lack of 'later day English heroes' implicitly poses this question. Whereas Hanna sees knightly achievement of inheritance and the establishment of royal (national) justice as characteristic of *Sir Orfeo* and *Sir Beues of Hamtoun*,[25] *Kyng Alisaunder*'s narrative of conquests and marvels does not lend itself to such interpretations. Scholars such as Dieter Mehl and Nancy Mason Bradbury have rightly emphasized the romance's 'instructive character' and its interest in learning, or 'bookness'.[26] Mehl's idea that *Kyng Alisaunder* is 'instructive' views the romance less as an ethically didactic work than as one concerned with 'the passing on of culture and learning',[27] an observation clearly related to Bradbury's idea of 'bookness'. The nature of *Kyng Alisaunder*'s interest in culture and learning is

---

[21] The gap of about 400 lines includes Porus's death and Alexander's meeting with Candace as found in the text of Laud misc. 622.

[22] *Kyng Alisaunder*, ed. Smithers, II, 2, 3. Horobin and Wiggins consider L to be written in a hand of the first quarter of the fifteenth century, however ('Reconsidering Lincoln's Inn MS 150', p. 31).

[23] For example, both Auchinleck and B preserve the unusual word 'trigoldrye' (line 7006), where Lincoln's Inn 150 produces 'sygaldrye': see *Kyng Alisaunder*, ed. Smithers, II, 13.

[24] Horobin and Wiggins, 'Reconsidering Lincoln's Inn MS 150', pp. 34, 43, 45. Especially notable is the silent omission of 1,300 lines on Alexander's adventures in India (lines 4763–5979 in Laud misc. 622).

[25] Hanna, *London Literature*, pp. 130–1, 134.

[26] D. Mehl, *The Middle English Romances of the Thirteenth and Fourteenth Centuries* (London, 1969), pp. 227–39 (p. 228); and N. M. Bradbury, *Writing Aloud: Storytelling in Late Medieval England* (Urbana IL, 1998), pp. 133–74 (p. 136). The idea that Auchinleck may have been intended for children also emphasizes its instructive character. See Olson, 'Romancing the Book', pp. 109–16; and N. Clifton, '*Of Arthour and of Merlin* as Medieval Children's Literature', *Arthuriana* 13.2 (2003), 9–22.

[27] Mehl, *The Middle English Romances*, p. 232.

still mostly unstudied, but I suggest that it can be identified in a variety of contexts that help to define the text's narrative culture: historical writing, language inter-action, relationship with sources, and the unusual literary headpieces.

Although fictional elements such as Oriental marvels were added to Alexander's stories early in their existence, the basis of the narratives is the historical achieve-ments of Alexander the Great.[28] Interest in Alexander from a historical perspective is demonstrated in a passage that lists and describes Alexander authors:

> Salomon, þat al þe werlde þorou3-3ede,
> In sooth witnesse helde hym myde.
> Ysidre also, þat was so wijs,
> In his bokes telleþ þis.
> Maister Eustroge bereþ hym witnesse
> Of þe wondres, more and lesse.
> Seint Jerome, 3ee shullen ywyte,
> Hem haþ also in book ywrite,
> And Magestene þe gode clerk
> Haþ made þerof mychel werk.
> Denys, that was of gode memorie,
> It sheweþ al in his book of storie.
> And also Pompie, of Rome lorde,
> Dude it writen euery worde.
> Ne heldeþ me þerof no fynder –
> Her bokes ben my shewer
> And the liif of Alisaunder,
> Of whom flei3 so riche sklaunder.
> 3if 3ee willeth 3iue listnyng,
> Now 3ee shullen here gode thing. (lines 4771–90)

This passage, derived from the *Roman de toute chevalerie* (lines 4604–13), expands freely upon its source. Where the Anglo-Norman text contains brief mentions of 'Solin li alosez' (Solin the renowned), Jerome, and 'li bon Magastenes' (the skilled Megasthenes) as its 'autoritez', the *Kyng Alisaunder* poet presents a fuller picture, providing not only names of prior authors with their epithets, but also brief descrip-tions of some of their writings. The English poem concludes by claiming these authors' moral importance as the poet's 'shewer' and thus, by implication, aids for his presentation of a 'gode thing'. Such a list of intellectual heavyweights – Aristotle rubs shoulders with Solomon, 'Maister Eustroge', Saint Jerome, 'Magestene þe gode clerk', and Pompey – invokes a weighty tradition of broadly historical writing, or 'books of storie' (4782), and thus positions the text as strongly interested in that subject. This tradition also encompasses more fictional writing because the 'storie' many of these 'gode clerkes' describes is in fact about the 'many wondres' (line 4766) Alexander is soon to encounter in India, which occupy much of the remaining text in Laud misc.

---

[28] Hanna, *London Literature*, p. 105, and, more tellingly, where he sums up *Kyng Alisaunder* (somewhat unfairly) as 'straightforwardly historical and strikingly uncritical' (p. 118).

622.[29] The text here thus emphasizes the learned nature of every kind of historical writing, both in the diversity of the writers named (Aristotle, Jerome, Megasthenes) and in those authors' descriptions of, and juxtapositions with, the 'wondres' that follow. We see a conscious intellectualization of Alexander sources being developed far beyond the corresponding passage in the *Roman de toute chevalerie*,[30] irrespective of the different sorts of composition involved. The multifaceted 'storie' of *Kyng Alisaunder* is presented as learned and intellectual, confirming the idea that the romance author wishes to pass on a sense of culture and learning.[31]

A similarly learned approach is found in *Kyng Alisaunder*'s approach to the languages that are part of its identity. Christopher Baswell describes the romance as having a 'richly French-derived diction' and extrapolates from this observation an interesting question about languages and cultures interacting:

> Is [*Kyng Alisaunder*] fundamentally French but largely coded in a more accessible tongue that is nonetheless easily penetrated, at intense moments, by its genuine voice? Is the narrative universe of this Middle English poem still, in fact, French?[32]

Baswell's idea about the 'fundamentally French' cultural identity of the text has been countered somewhat by Thea Summerfield, who claims that the French-language moments in Auchinleck texts are often conscious choices that highlight aspects of character or plot, aimed at an audience not proficient in French but able to recognize limited words.[33] In this idea of French, or what she calls 'semi-French'[34] (easily understood stock phrases), Summerfield diverges from Baswell's implication that French is an unconscious presence in English texts. Despite these differences, both scholars highlight, to a greater or lesser extent, the inherent multilingualism of *Kyng Alisaunder*'s broad narrative and identity. This multilingualism is discussed in a passage that invokes Latin as well as French material:

> Þis bataile distincted is
> In þe Freinsshe, wel iwys.

---

[29] Although *Kyng Alisaunder* does not go to the fictional extremes of the widely circulated *Roman d'Alexandre*, which contains the famous stories of Alexander's aerial and submarine adventures, these 'wondres' demonstrate that its interest in history reflects more fictional, romance conceptions as well as more factual ones. Many of the marvels are cut in Lincoln's Inn 150, as observed by Horobin and Wiggins, 'Reconsidering Lincoln's Inn MS 150'.

[30] Although many of the epithets attached to the authors may be ascribed to the requirements of the verse, it is notable that they emphasize knowledge and learning.

[31] Mehl, *The Middle English Romances*, p. 232.

[32] C. Baswell, 'Multilingualism on the Page', in *Middle English*, ed. P. Strohm, Oxford Twenty-First Century Approaches to Literature (Oxford, 2007), pp. 38–50 (pp. 43–4).

[33] T. Summerfield, '"And she answered in hir language": Aspects of Multilingualism in the Auchinleck Manuscript', in *Multilingualism in Medieval Britain (c. 1066–1520): Sources and Analysis*, ed. J. A. Jefferson and A. Putter, with A. Hopkins (Turnhout, 2013), pp. 241–58.

[34] Ibid., pp. 249, 255. In Summerfield's reading, the 'Frenchness' of *Kyng Alisaunder* is part of a general tendency in Auchinleck romances to use 'semi-French' to 'highlight the social standing of legendary aristocratic courts, or typify and ridicule the enemy' (p. 256).

> Þerefore [I] habbe [hit] to coloure
> Borowed of þe Latyn a nature,
> Hou hiȝtten þe gentyl kniȝttes,
> Hou hii contened hem in fiȝttes,
> On Alisaunders half and Darries also. (lines 2195–201)

The word 'coloure' is reminiscent of the colours of rhetoric, and 'distincted' – here probably meaning 'elucidate, explain' rather than the more common 'separate' – is likewise derived from Latin scholastic terminology.[35] This passage on style and language is an explicit attempt by the narrator to highlight his literary awareness or bookishness, again suggesting his concern to set his poetics in an intellectual context. Like the romance's interest in historical authors, we also find a consciously learned approach to language, another important aspect of *Kyng Alisaunder*'s cultural identity.

Multilingualism and sources are related topics since the 'Freinsshe' and 'Latyn' mentioned here refer to texts composed in those languages: the *Roman de toute chevalerie* and the *Alexandreis*, respectively.[36] Bradbury underlines the importance of French and Latin material for *Kyng Alisaunder*'s poetics, and not just its narrative, in her claim that 'the high quality of the verse seems to derive primarily from the poet's acquaintance with literary tradition in French and Latin'.[37] The poet's enthusiasm for scholarly discussion of languages and sources would appear to support this conclusion because *Kyng Alisaunder* defines itself by means of literary traditions derived from these prestigious languages. Although the *Roman de toute chevalerie* is the romance's source, the impact of French material is not confined to this one text nor to French Alexander literature in general. Smithers suggests that the episode in which Alexander destroys the city of Thebes in *Kyng Alisaunder* 'probably implies a knowledge of the [c. 1150] *Roman de Thèbes* at least in outline', pointing to similar descriptive passages in both works.[38] A comparison of the texts shows that the *Kyng Alisaunder* poet had greater knowledge of the *Roman de Thèbes* than the word 'outline' suggests. Indeed, the Middle English text reproduces the thematic approach of the Anglo-Norman poem. Both works claim that Thebes's violent Oedipal history, specifically the pride born of incest characteristic of Eteocles and Polynices, is directly responsible for the city's destruction, a moral cause-and-effect connection wholly absent in the *Roman de toute chevalerie* and Statius's *Thebaid* (another likely source for *Kyng Alisaunder*). This correspondence is evident from a comparison of *Kyng Alisaunder* and the *Roman de Thèbes*:

Kyng Alisaunder:

> Hii hym telden hou Eddipus
> Had yslawe his fader Layus,

---

[35] *MED*, s.v. *distincten, distincted*; and Bradbury, *Writing Aloud*, p. 141.

[36] For brief, tantalizing references to *Kyng Alisaunder*'s use of the *Alexandreis*, see *Kyng Alisaunder*, ed. Smithers, II, 15, 22, 24.

[37] Bradbury, *Writing Aloud*, p. 173.

[38] *Kyng Alisaunder*, ed. Smithers, II, 24, referring to i, lines 2643–53, 2677, 2851–74. He also notes the inclusion of 'a detail proper to Troy as described in the *Roman de Troie*'.

And more woo atte last –
Hou he wedded his moder Jocast,
And in hir biȝate twynnes two
(None wers ne miȝtten go:
Þe first was Ethiocles,
Þat oþer was Pollymyces –
Of pride nas non hir yliche);
Hou hii stryueden for þe kyngriche,
Hou for hem were slayn in fiȝttes
Of Grece alle þe gode kniȝttes …
[Thebes] þat was cite of mest werþe,
Of alle þat weren in erþe.
For her synne and dede on-hende
Nou is it brouȝth out of mynde;
Þus ended Tebes cite. (lines 2857–68, 2887–91)

Roman de Thèbes:

De deux friers vous dirrai
et lor gestes acounterai.
Li un sot non Ethioclés
et li autres Polinicés.
Edypodés lez engendra
en la reïne Jocasta:
de sa miere lez ot a tort
quant son piere le rei ot mort.
Por le pechié dount sount crié
furent felon et esragié:
Thebes destruistrent lor cite
et en après tout le regné;
destruit en furent lour veisin
et il ambedui en la fin.

I shall tell you about two brothers and recount their deeds. The name of one was Eteocles and the other Polynices. Oedipus fathered them with queen Jocasta: he made them with his mother, a vile deed, when he had killed the king his father. Through the sin that created them they became cruel and violent: they destroyed Thebes their city and afterwards the whole kingdom. Their neighbours were brought down and finally the pair themselves.[39]

Although a moral interpretation of Thebes's destruction could have been derived independently, the thematic similarities suggest that the Middle English poet drew

---

[39] *Roman de Thèbes*, ed. G. R. de Lage (Paris, 1966), lines 19–32; translation mine. The relevant passage in the *Thebaid* is i.76–81 (see *Thebaid, Books 1–7*, ed. and trans. D. R. Shackleton Bailey, Loeb Classical Library 207 [Cambridge MA, 2003]), and in Thomas of Kent, *The Anglo-Norman 'Alexander'*, ed. Foster and Short, lines 2116–288.

on the Anglo-Norman *Roman de Thèbes* not simply for historical detail but for inspiration. His engagement with the French poem highlights his scholarly reading of the text. He not only picks out relevant and useful details, but also deals with them in an intellectual fashion, extrapolating upon themes. This kind of *amplificatio* suggests a literary and intellectual approach that expands from the *Roman de toute chevalerie* to a wider range of French texts.

A similar relationship is found between *Kyng Alisaunder* and the *Alexandreis*. A Latin epic in ten books probably composed in 1180, the *Alexandreis* was widely read throughout Europe in the thirteenth and fourteenth centuries, with over two hundred surviving manuscripts.[40] A comparison of the first battle between Alexander and Darius shows that the Middle English poem and the *Alexandreis* share material that is absent from the *Roman de toute chevalerie*, such as the scene of the Persian Negusar's dismemberment and death.[41] The Middle English description is a free adaptation, differing in minor characters and details, but there are lines that are direct translations, demonstrating the English poet's close engagement with the Latin. This close relationship is shown in Philotas's killing of Negusar:

Kyng Alisaunder:

> Philotas sei3 and vnderstood
> Hou Negussar fau3th as he were wood
> He smoot to hym and dude hym harme,
> For of he carf his ri3th arme. (lines 2287–90)

Alexandreis:

> Hunc ubi multimoda uastantem cede Pelasgos
> Intuitus, stricto celer aduolat ense Phylotas … sinistram,
> Quam sibi forte manum frontem pretenderat ante,
> Amputat.

But when Philotas beheld him [Negusar] wasting Greeks with varied carnage, he swiftly drew his blade … it cut away the left hand where he [Negusar] held it before his brow.[42]

The Latin text depicts Negusar's loss of both hands in brutal detail. Simplifying the Latin, the English author alters which hand is amputated. Smithers's idea that the *Alexandreis* is used 'arbitrarily' 'as material for decoration'[43] misses how the *Kyng*

---

[40] On the *Alexandreis*'s dating, see N. Adkin, 'The Date of Walter of Châtillon's *Alexandreis* Once Again', *Classica et Mediaevalia* 59 (2008), 201–11. For a list of the manuscripts, see Walter of Châtillon, *Galteri de Castellione Alexandreis*, ed. M. L. Colker (Padua, 1978), pp. xxxiii–xxxviii (hereafter cited as '*Alexandreis*, ed. Colker').

[41] The passages are *Kyng Alisaunder*, ed. Smithers, I, lines 2269–2314; and *Alexandreis*, ed. Colker, iii.90–118.

[42] *Alexandreis*, ed. Colker, iii.98–99, 102–4; and Walter of Châtillon, *The 'Alexandreis' of Walter of Châtillon: A Twelfth-Century Epic*, trans. D. Townsend (Philadelphia, 1996), p. 44 (lines 118–20, 124–5).

[43] *Kyng Alisaunder*, ed. Smithers, II, 22, 15.

Alisaunder poet draws on the Latin text for thematic emphasis, using 'decorative' details to vivify the carnage in a way that, despite its mention of 'le champ hydus' (line 1979), the *Roman de toute chevalerie* does not. This kind of *amplificatio* demonstrates a literary and learned approach to the *Alexandreis* similar to that seen with regard to the *Roman de Thèbes*.

The *Kyng Alisaunder* poet's use of French and Latin material, then, is thorough and scholarly, thematically astute and consciously integrated into the learned *translatio* of the narrative performed by the poet. This treatment again emphasizes the poem's characteristics of 'culture and learning' or 'bookness', elements likewise present in the intriguing headpieces – that is, introductory passages, often seasonal, that interrupt the narrative flow.[44] Most of these are either entirely new to *Kyng Alisaunder* or freely developed from odd lines in the *Roman de toute chevalerie*.[45] Many provide gnomic and thematic introductions to subsequent narratives, as John Scattergood and Louise Haywood have demonstrated.[46] For example, the following headpiece describes the sorrow of autumn and the folly of the lover:

> Whan nutte brouneþ on heselrys,
> Þe lefdy is of her lemman chys.
> Þe persone wereþ fow and grys –
> Ofte he setteþ his loue amys.
> Þe ribaude plaieþ at the dys;
> Swiþe selde þe fole is wys.
> Darrie in a verger is,
> Tofore hym many kniȝth of prys. (lines 3289–96)

This headpiece precedes a section in which Darius, ashamed of Alexander's previous victory over him, decides to attack the latter once again. Haywood interprets it as a gnomic underlining of Darius's own folly. Other headpieces perform similar roles. In providing gnomic or proverbial interpretations of the action, they emphasize a variety of learning that seems distinct from 'bookness'. But, descending ultimately from French and Latin literary traditions, the headpieces are not a Middle English innovation. Smithers identifies them as derived from Old French epics and medieval Latin love lyrics. Bradbury agrees, citing 'the humble minstrel remark' as an additional influence, while Scattergood adduces various kinds of medieval French lyrical genres, such as the *aubade*.[47] The headpieces invoke vernacular and proverbial wisdom, often considered to be orally based, but presented through a

---

[44] For a useful overview, see *Kyng Alisaunder*, ed. Smithers, II, 35–39.

[45] Bradbury, *Writing Aloud*, p. 151.

[46] J. Scattergood, 'Validating the High Life in *Of Arthour and of Merlin* and *Kyng Alisaunder*', *Essays in Criticism* 54 (2004), 323–50; and L. M. Haywood, 'Spring Song and Narrative Organization in the Medieval Alexander Legend', *Troianalexandrina* 4 (2004), 87–105.

[47] *Kyng Alisaunder*, ed. Smithers, II, 35–38; Bradbury, *Writing Aloud*, p. 154; and Scattergood, 'Validating the High Life', esp. pp. 342–44. Haywood's focus is on contemporary medieval French, Spanish, and Middle English rather than on inherited literary traditions.

poetics derived from literary traditions. So, once again, bookishness is prominent, and, interestingly, it comes from a wide spectrum of texts and genres.

Interpreting the headpieces as both gnomic and based on literary traditions makes sense of some examples that seem disjunct in their immediate narrative contexts.[48] One such, not discussed by Haywood or Scattergood, occurs after Darius's earlier defeat:

> In tyme of Maij þe niȝttyngale
> In wood makeþ mery gale.
> So don þe foules, grete and smale,
> Summe on hylles and summe in dale.
> Þe day daweþ, the kyng awakeþ;
> He and hise men her armes takeþ.
> Hii wendeþ to þe batailes stede,
> And fyndeþ nouȝth bot bodies dede. (lines 2543–50)

The incongruous juxtaposition of the joys of spring and the battlefield covered with corpses seems designed to point up the pathos of battle. However, because this lyric passage departs undeniably from the narrative, interrupting both style and tone, its gnomic wisdom becomes difficult to interpret. Is it simply to provide brief, contextually bizarre light relief, or is it there for a different purpose?[49] In the absence of a clear connection between the passage's sentential observations and the battle narrative, the 'bookness' of the literary forms behind its poetics comes to the fore as an explanation. Seemingly separate from the 'storie', this passage overtly displays the author's literary knowledge. It is a moment of poetic preening that briefly dominates the narrative. 'In tyme of Maij þe niȝttyngale' has close parallels to a medieval Latin lyric found in the eleventh-century *Cambridge Songs*, demonstrating the pervasive presence of such lyrics in literary cultures beyond the Latinate.[50] While there is no suggestion of a direct link between these lines in *Kyng Alisaunder* and the Latin lyric, the similarity shows that this kind of vernal Latin poetry was so ubiquitous that the romance poet is able to draw on its *topoi* to show off his bookishness. Some headpieces in *Kyng Alisaunder* thus function as display verse in which the generally gnomic character of their content is subordinate to the conscious invocation of literary traditions.

By calling on Latin and French texts in these different contexts, the *Kyng Alisaunder* poet proclaims his mastery of a wide range of imaginative literature across both vernacular and Latin spheres, from romance to epic to complex Latin lyrics originally composed in schools. Moving beyond a fundamentally ethical

---

[48] Bradbury, *Writing Aloud*, pp. 155–56. Scattergood also notes that 'some of them are more integrated into the narrative than others' ('Validating the High Life', p. 339).

[49] Scattergood advances the concept of 'pleasure' or 'refreshment' as the purpose of some headpieces ('Validating the High Life', pp. 335, 339, 346).

[50] The poem *Carmen Aestivum*, beginning 'Vestiunt silve tenera ramorum', depicts various birds rejoicing at the arrival of summer (lines 9–20), reminiscent of the 'small foules' of the Middle English passage (*The Oxford Book of Medieval Latin Verse*, ed. F. J. E. Raby [Oxford, 1959], pp. 174–5).

interpretation of Alexander's 'storie', *Kyng Alisaunder*'s emphasis on inherited literary cultures sets it apart from other Auchinleck romances. Part of this is no doubt due to the accumulated weight of Alexander literature. Yet the poet's deliberate invocation of a variety of literary genres and traditions is not fully the result of the looming bulk of his source material. It shows, rather, a conscious desire to create a learned romance drawn from different literary and linguistic traditions. The same cannot be said of a romance like *Horn Childe*, also found in Auchinleck, composed not long after *Kyng Alisaunder*, and probably likewise based on an Anglo-Norman source, the *Romance of Horn*.[51] Judith Weiss describes *Horn Childe* as 'clad in sparer and simpler dress' than the 'ornate' Anglo-Norman romance with its 'vividly realised, complex world and dramatically plausible characters and situations'.[52] The simplification found in the English *Horn Childe* contrasts sharply with the conscious invocation of learned cultures seen in *Kyng Alisaunder*. The difference between the two *Horn* poems in length alone shows this. The English *Horn Childe* has no space for the kind of non-narrative digressions used in *Kyng Alisaunder* to highlight its poet's literary pretensions.[53] The Alexander romance thus differs from some Auchinleck romance companions in terms of both subject matter and poetic treatment.

This observation also applies to *Of Arthour and of Merlin*, which appears earlier in Auchinleck and is perhaps composed by the *Kyng Alisaunder* poet.[54] Although it too is based on a French source (the prose *Lestoire de Merlin*) and contains seasonal headpieces,[55] it does not create a consciously learned narrative universe in the same manner. Instead, its *translatio* often involves redacting its source (especially Grail elements) to focus on the politics of Englishness[56] rather than expanding to

---

[51] The nature of the two poems' relationship is 'impossible to unravel totally', according to J. Weiss; see *The Birth of Romance in England: 'The Romance of Horn', 'The Folie Tristan', 'The Lai of Haveloc', and 'Amis and Amilun' – Four Twelfth-Century Romances in the French of England*, trans. J. Weiss, FRETS 4 (Tempe AZ, 2009), p. 5.

[52] Ibid., p. 5.

[53] *Horn Childe* is 1,136 lines long in the edition based on Auchinleck: *Horn Childe and Maiden Rimnild*, ed. M. Mills, Middle English Texts 20 (Heidelberg, 1988), although the loss of two folios means that around 326 lines are missing; see Burnley-Wiggins, at http://auchinleck.nls.uk/mss/horn.html. In contrast, *The Romance of Horn* in Weiss's edition is 5,240 lines long.

[54] See *Kyng Alisaunder*, ed. Smithers, II, 41, where Smithers suggests that *King Richard* and *The Seven Sages of Rome* may also share authorship with these two texts. M. Fisher, *Scribal Authorship and the Writing of History in Medieval England* (Columbus OH, 2012), pp. 156–65, argues for their commonality in terms of scribal process rather than traditional authorship.

[55] Scattergood claims that these mostly have equivalents in *Lestoire de Merlin*, meaning that they are not 'display verse' as they are on occasion in *Kyng Alisaunder* ('Validating the High Life', pp. 332–34). For *Lestoire de Merlin*, see *The Vulgate Version of the Arthurian Romances, Ed. from Manuscripts in the British Museum*, ed. H. O. Sommer, 8 vols. in 4 (Washington DC, 1908–16), II.

[56] See E. S. Sklar, 'Arthour and Merlin: The Englishing of Arthur', *Michigan Academician* 8 (1975), 49–57; and S. B. Calkin, 'Violence, Saracens, and English Identity in *Of Arthour and of Merlin*', *Arthuriana* 14 (2004), 17–36.

theorize its own poetics. Another contrast with *Kyng Alisaunder* lies in the Prologue to *Of Arthour*, which discusses the poet's use of English. In stating that 'euerich Inglische Inglische can' (line 24), it engages primarily with the politics rather than the stylistic ramifications of language.[57] These differences suggest that *Of Arthour's* concerns diverge from those of *Kyng Alisaunder*, potentially casting more doubt on the idea of common authorship. Whatever the facts of their authorship, *Of Arthour* highlights *Kyng Alisaunder's* unusual nature within the context of Auchinleck, displaying how the latter romance reaches beyond its subject matter to showcase its engagement with sources and linguistic *translatio*.

Kyng Alisaunder's focus on learning thus sets it in a different context from other Auchinleck romances. The poem's concerns are with issues of literary-cultural *translatio* that, while they may play a part in constructing political and national identities, in this instance move beyond them to suggest a transnational character. Its consistent interest in multilingual literary genres and traditions, found indeed in insular circles but also much more widely, places the romance, despite its English-language status, in an inter- or transnational context in which the large questions are essentially the same for all texts regardless of their local origins and languages: how should one transmit culture and learning, and how should one perform *translatio studii*? The answer may, of course, be a localized one, as Hanna's analysis of Auchinleck's *Sir Orfeo* and *Sir Beues of Hamtoun* demonstrates, but *Kyng Alisaunder's* response to this vast question shows that localism is not inevitable.[58] In its transnational *translatio*, the Alexander romance implicitly counters Auchinleck's strong narrative of Englishness. Making the claim that *Kyng Alisaunder* has a definable impact on Auchinleck's *compilatio* is, however, a large assumption given the compendious nature of the manuscript. The idea that critics sometimes overinterpret and overestimate the impact of individual texts, mentioned earlier, is relevant here. How important, essentially, are *Kyng Alisaunder* and its concerns within Auchinleck? This is a question that can be asked of the manuscript only by considering the romance within its compilatory context.

Kyng Alisaunder *in Auchinleck*

The idea that Auchinleck's *compilatio* is more varied than its dominant metanarrative of Englishness is supported by its booklet structure, which according to Pearsall is a sign that Auchinleck is 'not a whole planned from the outset'.[59] This structure allows for different individual themes to be identified at different moments, as J. C. Mordkoff claims.[60] *Kyng Alisaunder* is a key starting-point for identifying some of these themes

---

[57] The romance *Of Arthour* is cited from *Of Arthour and of Merlin*, ed. O. D. Macrae-Gibson, 2 vols., EETS OS 268, 279 (Oxford, 1973, 1979). On its Prologue, see the chapters by P. Butler and E. Runde in this volume.

[58] Hanna, *London Literature*, pp. 103–1, 134.

[59] D. Pearsall, 'Literary and Historical Significance of the Manuscript', in Pearsall-Cunningham, pp. vii–xi (p. ix).

[60] See J. C. Mordkoff, 'The Making of the Auchinleck Manuscript: The Scribes at Work', unpublished PhD dissertation, University of Connecticut (Storrs CT, 1981), pp. 14–15, in

since its concerns are demonstrably dissimilar from many of Auchinleck's other romances, and may therefore suggest other motives in the *compilatio*.

Kyng Alisaunder's structural position in the manuscript, like its text, is problematic given the loss of folios. The useful table printed in the Pearsall-Cunningham facsimile shows its position within the whole.[61] I replicate it here, adding an extra column on booklets:

Gatherings	Item nos.	Texts	Scribe	Booklet
1–6	1–9	Religious poems (incl. *The King of Tars*)	1	1
7–10	10	*Speculum Gy de Warewyke*	2	2
	11–13	Religious poems (incl. *Amis and Amiloun*)	1	
11–16	14–19	Miscellaneous	3	3
	20	*The Sayings of the Four Philosophers*	2	
	21	*The Battle Abbey Roll*	4	
17(?)–25	22–3	*Guy of Warwick* and continuation	1	4
	24	*Reinbrun Gij Sone of Warwike*	5	
26–36	25	*Sir Beues of Hamtoun*	5	5
	26–9	*Of Arthour and of Merlin* plus 3 fillers	1	
37	30–31	*Lay le Freine, Roland and Vernagu*	1	6
38– [?]	32	*Otuel a Kniȝt* (and other poems?)	6	7
[?]–41	33–6	*Kyng Alisaunder* plus 3 fillers	1	8
42–4	37–9	*Sir Tristrem* and *Sir Orfeo* plus 1 filler	1	9
45–7	40–2	*Short Chronicle* and *Horn Childe and Maiden Rimnild* plus 1 filler	1	10
48– [?]	43	*King Richard*	1	11
52	44	*The Simonie*	2	12

Kyng Alisaunder occupies the eighth booklet. Mordkoff suggests that it may have been the only large item present in this section, but the fact that the folios at the beginning of the text are lost makes this unknowable.[62] The loss of folios also means that booklet 7 now only contains *Otuel a Kniȝt*. As the Pearsall-Cunningham table indicates, it may have held other poems. Both these factors need to be borne in mind when considering *Kyng Alisaunder*'s place in Auchinleck.

---

which she considers eleven of the twelve booklets to be 'unified in content', the exception being booklet 3 (p. 15). The same idea is found more circumspectly in the Pearsall-Cunningham facsimile, where Pearsall considers the individual fascicles to have 'some integrity of contents' ('Literary and Historical Significance', p. ix).

[61] Pearsall, 'Literary and Historical Significance', p. ix. The righthand column, 'Booklets', is not in the original table, but is derived from information in Mordkoff, 'The Making of the Auchinleck Manuscript', pp. 12–15. Due to the lost folios, several booklets, including *Kyng Alisaunder*'s (booklet 8), are incomplete, making observations about their structure difficult.

[62] Mordkoff, 'The Making of the Auchinleck Manuscript', p. 15.

The idea that there is thematic unity in individual booklets has led Mordkoff to suggest that booklets 6 and 7, containing *Lay le Freine, Roland and Vernagu* and *Otuel a Kniȝt*, 'largely concern French heroes',[63] an observation locating this section's identity in a different kind of nationalism. This notion may provide a context for *Kyng Alisaunder*'s subject matter and potentially also for its French 'narrative universe' as envisaged by Baswell. However, this 'French' section of Auchinleck turns out to contain a variety of different themes that cannot be characterized in such an implicitly nationalistic way. *Lay le Freine*, although set in the 'west cuntré' (line 29), is a tale of mistaken identity and 'mervailes' (line 16) that locates itself within the literary culture of the Breton lay, as its prologue makes clear (lines 1–22).[64] Although the next two, very different poems, *Roland and Vernagu* and *Otuel a Kniȝt*, are both Matter of France romances involving Charlemagne, their engagement with the broad theme of Christians versus Saracens makes their conceptualization and setting more universal than national or regional. The fact that the themes of 'mervailes' and Saracen-Christian conflict are found elsewhere in Auchinleck, for example in *Of Arthour and of Merlin* (a romance set in Britain), makes a separate nationalistic identity based on 'French heroes' for booklets 6 and 7 untenable.[65] Useful as it would undoubtedly be to see these booklets as providing a clear narrative of 'Frenchness' to contextualize *Kyng Alisaunder*'s non-insular subject matter and general concerns, this does not appear to be the case. It is tempting to identify *Kyng Alisaunder*, with Mordkoff, in this context simply as Auchinleck's 'bow to antiquity'[66] – thus, by implication, a text out of place physically and thematically in the manuscript.

Yet such a reading ignores the manuscript's plurality, *Kyng Alisaunder*'s learned and international focus, and the fundamental, though inconvenient, fact of the text's quondam presence in Auchinleck. The texts that follow *Kyng Alisaunder* in booklet 8 may help to elucidate the romance's position. Pearsall-Cunningham characterize these texts as 'fillers'. Although this term technically describes their function, it also implies that they are not relevant to Auchinleck's *compilatio*.[67] In contrast, Hanna suggests they are important as inherited (rather than new) items in Auchinleck, 'remains from a regional literary culture of the late thirteenth century, communicated by trilingual miscellanies copied far from London'.[68] The emphasis

---

[63] Ibid., p. 14.

[64] *Lay le Freine*, in *The Middle English Breton Lays*, ed. A. Laskaya and E. Salisbury (Kalamazoo MI, 1995), pp. 61– 87 (p. 68). *Lay le Freine*'s prologue is also attached to versions of *Sir Orfeo*, although not in Auchinleck.

[65] *Of Arthour and Merlin* follows *Sir Beues of Hamtoun* in booklet 5. The 'mervailes' include the stories of Merlin's and Arthur's births. See *Of Arthour and of Merlin*, ed. Macrae-Gibson, i.

[66] Mordkoff, 'The Making of the Auchinleck Manuscript', p. 15.

[67] Pearsall, 'Literary and Historical Significance', p. ix.

[68] R. Hanna, 'Reconsidering the Auchinleck Manuscript', in *Later Medieval Manuscript Studies: Essays from the 1998 Harvard Conference*, ed. D. Pearsall (York, 2000), pp. 91–102 (p. 100). On the fillers in Auchinleck, see also S. Fein, 'The Fillers of the Auchinleck Manuscript and the Literary Culture of the West Midlands', in *Makers and Users of*

Hanna places on these 'fillers' chimes with the interests of *Kyng Alisaunder*: multilingual, 'antique' rather than new or 'original', and not part of any narrative with obvious nationalistic resonances. They may therefore be useful in considering the romance's impact within the immediate context of booklet 8.

The three 'filler' texts that follow *Kyng Alisaunder* in Auchinleck are *The Thrush and the Nightingale*, *The Sayings of St Bernard*, and *Dauid þe King* (a metrical version of Psalm 50 including Latin quotation). Their position in booklet 8 suggests that, in structural terms at least, they are a unified group, although booklets themselves do not necessarily have an inherent thematic unity, as we have seen. *The Thrush and the Nightingale* is a debate poem concerning the vices and virtues of women; only 74 lines are extant because the next five folios are lost.[69] Debates on the nature of women have a long scholastic history and a wide circulation, as much-read texts like Walter Map's *Dissuasio Valerii ad Ruffinum* demonstrate, so the subject matter alone suggests that *The Thrush and the Nightingale*, despite its generic relationship with vernacular works like *The Owl and the Nightingale*, derives ultimately from a 'learned' context akin to that evoked by *Kyng Alisaunder*.[70] Although it is obviously a very different work from *Kyng Alisaunder* in terms of style and subject matter, there are some interesting connections between the two works. First, the unusual and mostly seasonal headpieces characteristic of *Kyng Alisaunder* find a parallel in the opening of *The Thrush and the Nightingale*:

> L .... wiþ loue ....
> Wiþ blosme & wiþ briddes roun;
> Þe notes of þe hasel springeþ,
> Þe dewes derken in þe dale,
> Þe notes of þe niȝtingale;
> Þis foules miri singeþ. (lines 1–6)[71]

This opening locates the often gnomic sentiments that follow – 'For þai bitraien eueri man / Þat mest bileueþ hem on' (lines 19–20) – alongside a traditional invocation of springtime and love. The invocation is common in medieval lyric poetry in French and Latin as well as English, as shown above, but its presence here in a debate poem is another reminder of the shared intellectual and multilingual context that lies behind both *The Thrush and the Nightingale* and *Kyng Alisaunder*.

Medieval Books: Essays in Honour of A. S. G. Edwards, ed. C. M. Meale and D. Pearsall (Cambridge, 2014), pp. 60–77.

[69] See the details given in Burnley-Wiggins, at http://auchinleck.nls.uk/mss/heads/thrush_head.html.

[70] Walter Map, *De nugis curialium – Courtiers' Trifles*, ed. and trans. M. R. James, rev. C. N. L. Brooke and R. A. B. Mynors (Oxford, 1983), pp. 288–313.

[71] All quotations from *The Thrush and the Nightingale* and *The Sayings of St Bernard* are cited by line number from the online transcriptions of the poems found in the Burnley-Wiggins facsimile. The first line of *Thrush* is damaged. The poem is also preserved in Oxford, Bodleian Library, MS Digby 86, fols. 136vb–138rb, where the equivalent line reads 'Somer is comen with loue to toune'. On Auchinleck and the other versions of these two poems, see Fein, 'The Fillers', pp. 68–71.

Further, the collocation of sentential wisdom and seasonality already demonstrated in *Kyng Alisaunder* is likewise found here, another factor indirectly connecting the two works.

A plural context is also suggested by an intriguing reference to Alexander within *The Thrush and the Nightingale*:

> [The Thrush:]
> 'Þei þai ben fair & briȝt in hewe,
> Þai ben fals fikel vntrewe
> & worcheþ wo in ich lond.
> King Alisaunder meneþ him of hem;
> In þe world nis non so crafti men
> No non so riche of lond'. (lines 43–8)

It is common for Alexander to be used as an *exemplum* (as in the works of John of Salisbury and Gerald of Wales), so this mention probably does not refer directly to *Kyng Alisaunder* but instead alludes to well-known Alexander stories in general circulation.[72] Yet the brief moment wherein the poem gestures towards these stories evokes them for the reader. Multilingual, multicultural Alexander literature, derived from antiquity, becomes a presence behind the text of the poem. This Alexander literature – combining ancient and medieval texts, blurring fiction and history – does not promote a single dominant cultural narrative. One of the most highly investigated aspects of Alexander texts, in fact, is the conqueror's multivalence and, hence, the difficulty of local interpretation.[73] Its presence here, however momentary, again demonstrates the plural literary culture shared by *The Thrush and the Nightingale* and *Kyng Alisaunder*, a literary culture focused on multilingualism and inheritance rather than on innovative Englishness.

In contrast, the text that now follows *The Thrush and the Nightingale*, *The Sayings of St Bernard*, appears to have little shared literary heritage with *Kyng Alisaunder*. Focusing not on any romance theme or lyric tradition, it commends the reader to Christ as it reminds him or her of human mortality. However, the terms in which this reminder is expressed resemble those of the general gnomic wisdom of many of *Kyng Alisaunder*'s headpieces:

> Where ben men biforn ous were,
> Þat houndes ladden & haukes bere
> & hadden feld & wode,
> Þe riche leuedis in her bour
> Þat werd gold in her tresour
> Wiþ her briȝt rode? (lines 1–6)

---

[72] See the references to Alexander in Chaucer's *Monk's Tale* and Gower's *Confessio Amantis* discussed above (p. 88).

[73] On Alexander's general ambiguity, see L. Harf-Lancner, 'Alexandre le Grand dans les romans français du moyen âge: un héros de la démesure', *Mélanges de l'école française de Rome: Moyen Âge* 112 (2000), 51–63 (pp. 52, 53).

Moreover, a theme of loss is not the only commonality between *The Sayings of St Bernard* and *Kyng Alisaunder*'s headpieces. The terms in which human mortality are expressed evoke tropes of chivalric romance (hounds and hawks, beautiful and noble women) as well as *Kyng Alisaunder*'s gnomic warnings, as this comparison demonstrates:

> It fareþ wiþ man so dooþ wiþ floure –
> Bot a stirte ne may it dure;
> He glyt away so dooþ þe[ss]ure.
> Fair is lefdy in boure,
> And also kni3th in armoure. (lines 4312–16)

Such sentiments are, of course, familiar to readers of medieval literature, yet to find them paralleled stylistically to this extent between two unrelated and contrasting texts (in terms of subject matter) is worth noting. In this instance, the literary culture shared by the two works is not, as with *The Thrush and the Nightingale*, one that can be demonstrably traced to a plural, multilingual context. Instead, it derives from wisdom literature found in a wide range of contexts like Old English poetry and biblical books. Despite this difference, the shared focus of parts of *Kyng Alisaunder* and of *The Sayings of St Bernard* suggests that the latter is appropriately positioned in proximity to the romance – and also in proximity to *The Thrush and the Nightingale*, given both poets' concern for generic wisdom. This shared theme is also demonstrated in an explicitly Christian sense by the final text in booklet 8, *Dauid þe King*, a metrical version of Psalm 50 that asks God for forgiveness and reminds the reader of sin and death.

Booklet 8's 'fillers', then, are appropriate companions for *Kyng Alisaunder*, as they highlight several themes that are also prominent in that romance. Literary traditions, both linguistic and cultural, are present alongside – and are part of – a concern for intellectual history and gnomic wisdom. The 'fillers' do not create a restrictive thematic unity in this section of Auchinleck; rather, some of their preoccupations overlap with those of *Kyng Alisaunder*, creating a varied narrative that prioritizes different aspects of learning.

Conclusion

If we accept that many of Auchinleck's texts, especially the romances, focus on aspects related to English identity, the interests of *Kyng Alisaunder* and booklet 8 represent a departure (or series of departures) from the manuscript's more frequent compilatory preoccupations. Seeing booklet 8's identity (and also that of the whole extant manuscript) as fluid and varied, as focused on priorities rather than dominant narratives, may allow sections that seem incongruous to be understood as part of Auchinleck's wider anthologizing *compilatio*. For example, booklet 3's contents, described by Pearsall-Cunningham and also by Mordkoff as 'miscellaneous',[74] may contribute to some of the themes identified in booklet 8. In a

---

[74] Pearsall, 'Literary and Historical Significance', p. ix; and Mordkoff, 'The Making of the Auchinleck Manuscript', p. 15.

broad sense, its combination of romance, piety, and philosophical wisdom (*Floris and Blauncheflur, The Pater Noster Vndo on Englissch,* and *The Sayings of the Four Philosophers*) is reminiscent of booklet 8, even if booklet 8's dominant interest in learning does not appear to be present. The idea of wisdom (both sentential and explicitly theological) present in booklet 8 also connects it to some of the religious works in booklets 1 and 2, although this is a very general observation that pertains less to *Kyng Alisaunder* itself.

In conclusion, *Kyng Alisaunder* does seem to 'stand outside the usual concerns of the manuscript' in its poetic interest in 'culture and learning'.[75] Yet, within booklet 8, its preoccupation with multilingual literary and intellectual cultures, along with proverbial wisdom, is paralleled by texts often overlooked as mere 'fillers', but which are just as much a part of Auchinleck's *compilatio* as the longer and more high-profile romances. Despite the distinct character of booklet 8, some of its themes are found elsewhere in the manuscript, although perhaps not in an especially marked fashion. In this sense, *Kyng Alisaunder* is both unusual (in its interest in literary and intellectual cultures) and 'commune' (in its contributing to a set of themes found elsewhere in Auchinleck). Above all, it underscores the literary-cultural plurality of the manuscript's *compilatio*, a feature that the text's own delight in varied languages and cultures also highlights. *Kyng Alisaunder* is thus an important challenge to Auchinleck as a witness to nationalistic concerns, a challenge whose individual impact is increased by the shared themes of booklet 8's texts. Despite its ghostly near-absence in Auchinleck as it now stands, the romance still continues to make its presence felt.

---

[75] Hanna, *London Literature*, p. 105; and Mehl, *The Middle English Romances*, p. 232.

CHAPTER SEVEN

Sir Tristrem, a Few Fragments, and the Northern Identity of the Auchinleck Manuscript

Ann Higgins

THERE is little mystery about the history and ownership of Edinburgh, NLS, MS Advocates 19. 2. 1, commonly known as the Auchinleck manuscript, from the early eighteenth century onwards – that is, from around 1740, the year in which Alexander Boswell, Lord Auchinleck, wrote his name on a paper flyleaf of the book. That, however, leaves us with a period of approximately four hundred years during which the book apparently lay in a kind of limbo from the 1330s, when it was copied and put together in London, until it fell into Boswell's hands. In general, the assumption has been that the Auchinleck manuscript's original ownership was as London-based as its production. Laura Hibbard Loomis's argument for Chaucer's familiarity with some of the romances found in the book depends on that premise.[1] Ralph Hanna's discussion of the Northern affinities of some of its texts in *London Literature, 1300–1380* likewise assumes that, although the manuscript's first owner had close ties to the North, he was living in London at the time he commissioned the manuscript, and that he stayed there after he took delivery of it.[2] In this chapter I take the question of those Northern affinities considerably further than Hanna allows. I argue not only that the book's first owner had ties to northern England, but that, in terms of its owner and its earliest readers, the Auchinleck manuscript is a Northern book, copied and compiled in London for a regional client who brought the manuscript home with him on its completion.[3]

---

[1] L. H. Loomis, 'Chaucer and the Auchinleck MS: "Thopas" and "Guy of Warwick"', in *Essays and Studies in Honor of Carleton Brown* (New York, 1940), pp. 111–28, and 'Chaucer and the Breton Lays of the Auchinleck MS', *Studies in Philology* 38 (1941), 14–33. In the former, Loomis argues that Chaucer's *Franklin's, Wife of Bath's*, and *Merchant's Tales* owe a debt to the Auchinleck romances *Sir Degare, Lay le Freine*, and *Sir Orfeo*; her argument in the latter depends on correspondences she identifies between lines and phrases from *Sir Thopas* and the Auchinleck *Guy of Warwick*.

[2] R. Hanna, *London Literature 1300–1380*, Cambridge Studies in Medieval Literature 57 (Cambridge, 2005), pp. 44–147.

[3] 'Northern' here has a somewhat flexible meaning – I mean by it the area of England that lies roughly north of a line drawn from Chester on the west coast and passing a little south of Lincoln on its way to a corresponding point on the east coast. A more accurate term for the geographic idea here might be 'Northerly'.

Location and identity

Even those scholars who take the presence of Northern texts in the manuscript as evidence that the book's patron came from the north of England assume that he had by then settled in London. That assumption has the advantage that it restricts the grounds for determination of the book's identity to the hard evidence provided by the manuscript itself. It is, after all, hard to quarrel with such facts as the dialect of the book's texts; its affinities of layout and copying style with other large books produced in London in the same period; and the resemblances between Auchinleck's miniatures and the illuminations produced by the London-affiliated artists of the Queen Mary Psalter.[4] It is also hard to argue with the lack of any concrete evidence regarding the book's owners during the four hundred years that passed before it fell into the Laird of Auchinleck's hands around 1740. On the other hand, these criteria offer no place for what is perhaps the most important factor in a bespoke manuscript's identity – that is, the person who commissioned it and imagined it even before it existed. Insofar as the book is the product of the scribes who ruled its pages, copied its texts and numbered its items, of the artists who decorated its pages, of the stitchers who assembled its booklets, and of the binder who bound them into a codex, Auchinleck is without question a London book. However, insofar as it is the product of the person who thought of it, brought that idea to a bookmaker and commissioned its production, it is, I would argue, something else entirely.

The question of whether the Auchinleck manuscript is simply and entirely a London book pertains to fundamental issues relating to the way we identify and localize books that were produced in the pre-print era. It hardly needs stating here that every manuscript is an individual handmade copy of a text rendered unique by the inevitable scribal variations, no matter how tiny, that it contains. Examine a medieval English manuscript and its texts, compare and contrast it with others from the same period, and, bit by bit, you will move towards at least some understanding of when and where it was made and, very often, of the kind of English spoken by its scribe or scribes. These are the criteria that, for instance, allow us to identify London, BL, MS Harley 2253 as a West Midlands manuscript, and to recognize London, BL, MS Cotton Nero A. x as a product of the Northwest. However, these criteria are confined to the beginning of the manuscript's life, privileging the scribe who copied its texts and assembled its pages over the patron who commissioned the project and took delivery of the book once the work was done. Production-end identification centres on the tangible evidence left by the hand that copied the text onto the page; patron-centred identification involves a certain amount of speculation and risk, even if its end result largely confirms an identification derived from the production end of the equation.

---

[4] In L. Dennison, "'Liber Horn", "Liber Custumarum" and Other Manuscripts of the Queen Mary Workshop', in *Medieval Art, Architecture and Archaeology in London,* ed. L. Grant, British Archaeological Association Conference Transactions 10 (London, 1990), pp. 118–34 (p. 133 n. 70), Dennison notes the stylistic affinities between Auchinleck's illuminations and those found in 'Liber Custumarum', whose decorations she ascribes to a subsidiary workshop of the central Queen Mary group.

The evolution of commercial book production in late medieval England opened a gap between the person who produced a book and the person who owned that book. This gap resembles in some ways that existing between a publisher and a purchaser today.[5] In the world of commercial manuscript production, the relationship between scribe and client is both financially driven and clearly demarcated. Furthermore, as book production in the pre-print era became more commercialized, it became more geographically centralized, because the independent scribes who carried out this kind of work tended to congregate in the metropolitan areas where their skills were most in demand.[6] The result of this centralization was that, unless you could call on scribal services whenever you needed them, perhaps because you were a scribe yourself, perhaps because you were sufficiently wealthy to employ a personal secretary, your best – indeed your only – option was to find someone to do the work for you in one of England's larger cities.[7] Perhaps you would provide the exemplars yourself; perhaps you would hand over a list of preferred texts. Either way, your scribe would, like most of his colleagues, modify the language of the texts he copied to accord, to some extent, with his own dialectal practice.

Scholars have reason to be grateful for those modifications, as they allow us not only to identify regional variations of medieval English, but also to trace the movements of scribes from city to city, and identify with some certainty where an individual manuscript was most likely copied and assembled. However, they have another effect: they centre the identity of the book firmly in the circumstances of its production rather than in the mind of the person conceiving of it and later enjoying

---

[5] I must emphasize here that, when I use the term 'commercial book production', I refer not simply to books copied in return for pay, but specifically to manuscripts produced without the scribe's having a direct personal connection with the text he copied or the person who commissioned him to copy it. A monk copying the Gospels in a monastic scriptorium, a petty landowner's steward making a personal copy of Marie's *Lanval*, a nobleman's secretary working on a collection of miscellaneous secular and religious texts for his lord, a legal scribe in Westminster picking up some work on the side copying poems and treatises for favoured clients – all of those men, even if they were paid for their work, had a personal connection to that work that contributed to the book's identity. This seems true of Andrew Horn's relationship with the scribe who copied at his behest both the Anglo-Norman *Mirror of Justices* (Cambridge, Corpus Christi College, MS 258) and *Quadripartitus*, Book I (Cambridge, Corpus Christi College, MS 70). When we try to determine the provenance of manuscripts such as these 'non-commercial' ones, we are on fairly firm ground when we assume that the internal evidence provided by a manuscript and its texts offers insight on the regional affiliations of not only its scribe but also its first owners and readers, and we identify the manuscript accordingly.

[6] See, for instance, A. I. Doyle and M. B. Parkes, 'The Production of Copies of the *Canterbury Tales* and the *Confessio Amantis* in the Early Fifteenth Century', in *Medieval Scribes, Manuscripts and Libraries: Essays Presented to N. R. Ker*, ed. M. B. Parkes and A. G. Watson (London, 1978), pp. 163–210.

[7] It is, of course, unlikely that anyone, no matter how enthusiastic, would travel a significant distance simply to buy a book. Book production in the pre-print era was labour-intensive and, as a consequence, relatively expensive. Anyone who could afford to commission a book of Auchinleck's size and expense would probably have had other reasons – commercial, governmental, or both – to travel to London on occasion.

it. If a manuscript's scribe and owner are closely associated with each other (or are even one and the same person), inferences drawn about place and language can reasonably be applied to the patron as well as to the scribe. In cases of commercial copying, however, the unavoidable gap between a manuscript's scribe and its owner calls into question any certainty we may wish to have about the book's true home, requiring us to consider very carefully any evidence that suggests that the finished book ended up, and perhaps was always intended for, somewhere far from the place where it was made.

Even though there are no actual records of Auchinleck's post-production presence in London, the assumption prevails that the reason the manuscript was copied in London was that its owner was a resident of that city and that it therefore remained in that city for at least some decades following its production. In *London Literature*, for instance, Hanna observes that 'Northern influence is pervasive in Auchinleck and appears scattered throughout', and he notes that Maldwyn Mills 'demonstrates that a substantial group of Auchinleck poems, large and small, may have been imported from a centre like York'.[8] That word 'imported' is, however, key, for Hanna finds the manuscript to be appropriative in its relationship with regional cultures as it joins the products of those cultures to 'local London writings' and combines these varied regional contents into a newly London entity. In this reading of the totality of the manuscript, the presence of Northern elements is thus an assertion less of the strength of regional cultures than of London's developing cultural hegemony, and so, Hanna observes, 'the entire Auchinleck manuscript might be seen as a self-conscious heralding of a new centre'.[9] That scenario pays due tribute to the circumstances of the manuscript's production, but it wholly ignores its patron, except insofar as consideration of his contribution to the book serves a London-centred view of its identity. While Hanna reminds us that York served as the kingdom's 'second capital' during Edward I's Scottish campaign and for at least a couple of decades afterwards, he sees the resultant patterns of 'inter-regional cultural exchange' as largely the product of individuals who kept their Northern connections despite having settled in London.[10] In this reading of the situation, Auchinleck's handful of Northern texts acquires a nostalgic value, reminding the book's owner of the ancestral lands he fondly remembers but to which (in contrast to the heroes of several of the book's romances) he is unlikely to return.

In the absence of hard evidence to the contrary, it is difficult at first to argue with that scenario, especially since Auchinleck's Northern texts are far outnumbered by the many whose dialect indicates that they originated in the South. I would argue, though, that the origins of Auchinleck's texts are less important to this question than the fate of those texts following their inclusion in the manuscript. Given that the book was produced in England's capital, at a time of increasing interest in English-language works, a surprising number of Auchinleck's texts are found

---

[8] Hanna, *London Literature*, p. 126, citing *Horn Childe and Maiden Rimnild*, ed. M. Mills, Middle English Texts 20 (Heidelberg, 1988), p. 81.

[9] Ibid., p. 130.

[10] Ibid., p. 126.

nowhere else. Nineteen of Auchinleck's forty-four surviving texts appear there in unique copies, and a further four are in unique versions.[11] In the case of another three texts, the Auchinleck copy is the most recent that survives, although one or two earlier versions or witnesses are extant.[12] Attention is most often paid to the manuscript's eight unique romances, and deservedly so, but the significance of the fifteen other unique works should not be overlooked. Thirteen of them are religious or moral works, including six saints' lives or legends. Put those six saints' lives together with the romances, and we have at least fourteen works from the two most popular vernacular genres in late medieval England that apparently drew the attention of no one in early-fourteenth-century London other than Auchinleck's owner and the scribe he commissioned to copy them.

Sir Tristrem*'s afterlife and its implications*

In 2005, Rhiannon Purdie made a convincing case that the primary target of Chaucer's burlesque in *Sir Thopas* was *written*, rather than oral, tail-rhyme romance, and, specifically, the practice found in some manuscripts of using brackets to set off the tail rhymes.[13] If Chaucer's mockery were to make a point, his London audience must have been aware both of a critical mass of written popular romance and of the different formats used to copy examples of the genre, even if they felt that those who were still enjoying them in the third quarter of the fourteenth century signalled thereby their lack of sophistication. Given the apparent popularity of metrical romance in early-fourteenth-century London, it seems strange indeed that so few of Auchinleck's examples of the genre are found in later copies, if the manuscript itself were a London possession, or if the exemplars for its works were owned by its copyist or easily available to him.

In some cases, this neglect may be explained by an individual text's limited regional interest. For instance, in addition to the traces of Northern English found in its language, the geography of *Horn Childe and Maiden Rimnild* ties that romance closely to northern Yorkshire. As Mills has observed, 'nothing like the specificity of the Yorkshire place-names is to be found in the scenes set in Wales, or in southern England'.[14] Likewise, the assertively Northern dialect of *The Four Foes*

---

[11] The unique texts are: *Seynt Mergrete, Seynt Katerine, St Patrick's Purgatory, The Clerk Who Would See the Virgin, Life of St Mary Magdalene, On þe Seuen Dedly Sinnes: The Pater Noster Vndo on Englissch, The Assumption of the Blessed Virgin,* stanzaic *Guy of Warwick, Reinbrun Gij Sone of Warwike, The Wenche þat Loued a King, Of Arthour and of Merlin, Lay le Freine, Roland and Vernagu, Otuel a Kniȝt, Sir Tristrem, The Four Foes of Mankind, Horn Childe and Maiden Rimnild,* and *Alphabetical Praise of Women.* Found there in unique versions are *The Disputisoun bitven þe Bodi and þe Soule, The Sayings of the Four Philosophers, A Penniworþ of Witte,* and *Dauid þe King.*

[12] *Floris and Blauncheflur, Hou Our Leuedi Saute Was Ferst Founde,* and *The Thrush and the Nightingale.*

[13] R. Purdie, 'The Implications of Manuscript Layout in Chaucer's *Tale of Sir Thopas*', *Forum for Modern Language Studies* 41 (2005), 263–74.

[14] *Horn Childe,* ed. Mills, p. 41.

of Mankind might have discouraged London readers. Angus McIntosh notes that the Auchinleck scribe was surprisingly careful to preserve its Northern forms, to the extent that the poem would have seemed linguistically alien to a contemporary London reader.[15]

A more compelling argument is offered by the fate of *Sir Tristrem*, the tail-rhyme version of the story of Tristan and Iseult that bears the item number 'li' in the Auchinleck manuscript.[16] Joan Tasker Grimbert describes the story of Tristan and Iseult as 'one of the founding myths of Western culture', and she notes its viral transmission throughout Western and Northern Europe 'and well beyond, for there are even early versions in Czech and Byelorussian'.[17] Thus it is hardly surprising that we should find some version of this story in the Auchinleck manuscript, a book anchored by romances.[18] What *is* puzzling is that no other witness to *Sir Tristrem* exists, even though it was the only English-language Tristan narrative that we know of until Thomas Malory reworked the Old French prose *Roman de Tristan* into his *Book of Sir Tristram de Lyones* over a hundred years later.[19]

The lack of contemporary attention given to *Sir Tristrem* is even more perplexing when we consider that the romance was copied into the manuscript in London, England's capital and the country's developing centre of commercial book production. Few critics still accept Loomis's view that Auchinleck was Chaucer's source for *Guy of Warwick, Sir Orfeo, Lay Le Freine, Sir Degare*, and *Horn Childe*, and Fred Porcheddu and Purdie argued convincingly against it in 2001 and 2006.[20]

---

[15] A. McIntosh, 'The Middle English Poem *The Four Foes of Mankind*', *Neuphilologische Mitteilungen* 79 (1978), 137–44.

[16] *Sir Tristrem* is the thirty-seventh of forty-four texts in the manuscript as it survives today. However, each item bears a number in the hand of Scribe 1, who appears to have been in charge of the project. These numbers indicate that at least sixteen items are now lost – the first item in the extant manuscript bears the number 'vi', and the last has the number 'lx'. *Sir Tristrem*'s number is 'li'.

[17] J. T. Grimbert, ed., *Tristan and Isolde: A Casebook* (London, 1995), p. xiii. The Tristan legend first appeared in the twelfth-century Anglo-Norman verse romances composed by Beroul and Thomas of Britain. From there, it spread across medieval Europe until, by the fifteenth century, versions could be found in the vernacular literatures of France, Italy, Spain, Germany, Britain, and also Ireland, where it was reworked into the stories of Diarmuid and Gráinne and of Deirdre and the Sons of Uisneach.

[18] Who knows how many romances were originally in the book in addition to the eighteen that survive?

[19] R. C. Norris, *Malory's Library: The Sources of the Morte Darthur* (Cambridge, 2008), pp. 95–113. The prose *Roman de Tristan* is Malory's primary source, but he also incorporates details from other versions, including material that may possibly derive from *Sir Tristrem*; see P. Hardman, 'Malory and Middle English Verse Romance: The Case of *Sir Tristrem*', in *Arthurian Studies in Honour of P. J. C. Field*, ed. E. Archibald and D. F. Johnson (Cambridge, 2004), pp. 215–22. Norris finds that the parallels Hardman identifies between *Sir Tristrem* and Malory 'are interesting, but alone they do not show that he knew this English poem' (pp. 103–4, citing Hardman, pp. 220-2).

[20] Loomis, 'Chaucer and the Auchinleck MS' and 'Chaucer and the Breton Lays' (see note 1 above). F. Porcheddu, 'Edited Text and Medieval Artifact: The Auchinleck Bookshop and "Charlemagne and Roland" Theories, Fifty Years Later', *Philological Quarterly* 80 (2001),

On the other hand, Loomis's theory has never quite disappeared from the popular narrative of the manuscript, doubtless because it is, as Derek Pearsall has observed, so 'irresistibly romantic'.[21] As recently as 2002, Brian Murdoch and J. A. Tasioulas cited Loomis's argument in the introduction to their edition of *The Apocryphal Lives of Adam and Eve*. While they note that it is 'an unprovable view', their very citation of it grants it some credibility, especially since they include no mention or citation of Porcheddu's well-argued challenge.[22] In any case, if Auchinleck stayed in the capital long enough that it could have been at all possible (as Loomis argues) for Chaucer to have become familiar with its *Guy of Warwick*, *Sir Orfeo, Lay Le Freine*, *Sir Degare*, and *Horn Childe*, it is strange indeed that neither he nor anyone else noticed that this manuscript also contained a version of the famous and tragic story of Tristan, even though that version immediately precedes *Sir Orfeo* in booklet 9 of the codex.

This neglect cannot have been because the legend had gone out of fashion – records of romances owned by members of the English court in the fourteenth century include frequent references to *Tristan*. These were, of course, copies of the French, not the English, *Tristan*, but they attest to a continuing level of interest in the story among the elite at a time when English was beginning to recover its status as a literary vernacular in England.[23] Nor does it seem that the story lacked appeal for more general audiences. The existence of fourteenth-century misericords in Lincoln and Chester Cathedrals depicting scenes from the Tristan story argues that the story had gained a place in popular culture. In her 2009 discussion of these and other misericords depicting scenes from Middle English romance, Jennifer Fellows

465–503, sums up many of the problems with Loomis's arguments: on one hand, she ignores the possibility that many correspondences she cites are explicable on the grounds that they reflect stock phrases; on the other, she assumes that writers work in a wholly textual universe, so that the discovery of a text that in any way resembles a later text serves as proof positive of its use by the later author. These difficulties are compounded by the fact that in neither case is Loomis working from the actual manuscript sources, but draws her inferences instead from the evidence provided by edited texts, at least some of which are the product of editors' manipulation of several witnesses. Purdie, 'The Implications', offers an even stronger challenge to Loomis's argument for Auchinleck as a source for Chaucer's knowledge of tail-rhyme romance, pointing out that the mockery of graphic tail-rhyme layout is a feature of early manuscripts of *Sir Thopas* (including Hengwrt and Ellesmere, the two manuscripts most closely associated with the poet himself), which implies that his specific target here is the manuscript tradition of Middle English verse romance and its unsophisticated readers, rather than the romance genre itself. Since none of Auchinleck's tail-rhyme romances use the graphic format, it seems unlikely that this particular manuscript was Chaucer's source, no matter the correspondences identified by Loomis.

[21] D. Pearsall, 'Literary and Historical Significance of the Manuscript', in Pearsall-Cunningham, pp. vii–xi (p. ix).

[22] *The Apocryphal Lives of Adam and Eve, Edited from the Auchinleck MS and from Trinity College, Oxford MS 57*, ed. B. Murdoch and J. A. Tasioulas, Exeter Medieval Texts and Studies (Exeter, 2002), p. 3.

[23] See R. Field, 'Romance in England, 1066–1400', in *The Cambridge History of Medieval English Literature*, ed. D. Wallace (Cambridge, 1999), pp. 152–76.

argues that the appearance of romance motifs in misericords is worth our attention.[24] Not only can they tell us which details from some romances seem to have
appealed to their contemporary audiences, but they also tell us something about
the dissemination of those texts. The Lincoln and Chester misericords discussed by
Fellows both depict the same scene from the Tristan story: the tryst beneath the tree.
In the case of the Chester misericord, the carver seems to include some details from
other parts of the story, but the tryst remains the main focus. In this scene, Tristan
and Iseult meet under a tree, unaware that King Mark is hiding among its branches.
Before they can betray themselves, the lovers see him reflected in a pool at their feet.
As in the case of the romances depicted in the other misericords Fellows discusses,
the Lincoln and Chester carvers could have used scenes from *Tristan* only if they
were familiar with the story, indicating that, by the fourteenth century, the legend
had found an audience at all levels of English society, even among those who knew
no language other than English.

Interest in *Tristan* was not confined to fans of romance in England. The love
story's tragic end also suggested that it could be used as a moral lesson. Several
illustrations of details from the story of Tristan and Iseult appear in the early-
fourteenth-century didactic manuscript London, BL, MS Additional 11619. Tony
Hunt includes a list of that manuscript's texts in his 1987 article on the illustrations, and notes that Additional 11619 'is a monastic book designed for edification,
combining religious and theological texts with didactic *exempla* such as the Fables
of Aesop or the *Disciplina clericalis* of Petrus Alfonso'.[25] These illustrations do not
accompany a copy of the romance in the manuscript, nor are they directly relevant
to any one of its texts. As Hunt concludes, the context suggests that they serve
something of the same purpose as the didactic texts and Aesopic fables included in
the book. That is, they serve as a negative *exemplum* of the 'vicissitudes of earthly
love', an argument Hunt has previously made about the text they appear to illustrate, Thomas's *Tristan*.[26] The illustrations would have had no point were the book's
readers unable to recognize and interpret the allusion correctly, and so, like the
misericords, they argue that people in fourteenth-century England, high and low,
knew Tristan and his tragic story very well indeed.

Although *Sir Tristrem* apparently failed to draw the attention of London readers
around the time it was copied into Auchinleck, matters were different north of the
capital. An intriguing detail of the Chester misericord discussed by Fellows is its
depiction of a little 'dog lapping the water beneath the tree'. As Fellows notes, this
'could be an allusion to another incident, occurring only in [*Sir Tristrem*], where
Iseult's little dog laps up the remains of the love potion that irrevocably binds Tristan

[24] See J. Fellows, 'The Representations of Middle English Romances on English Misericords',
    in *Profane Imagery in Marginal Arts of the Middle Ages*, ed. E. C. Block and M. Jones
    (Turnhout, 2009), pp. 123–41.

[25] T. Hunt, 'The Tristan Illustrations in MS London BL Add. 11619', in *Rewards and
    Punishments in the Arthurian Romances and Lyric Poetry of Medieval France*, ed. P. V.
    Davies and A. J. Kennedy (Cambridge, 1987), pp. 45–60.

[26] Ibid., p. 45, citing T. Hunt, 'The Significance of Thomas's *Tristan*', *Reading Medieval
    Studies* 7 (1981), 41–61.

and Iseult to each other'.[27] That misericord dates approximately from 1390. About forty years earlier, in the prologue to his *Chronicle*, Robert Mannyng of Brunne described problems relating to the transmission of a work called 'Tristrem'.[28] On one hand, we have (of course) no hard evidence that he is speaking of the Auchinleck *Sir Tristrem*, and, even if he were, that would simply argue that he was familiar with *a* copy of the romance, not necessarily the Auchinleck copy or its exemplar; on the other, his words bear an intriguing relationship to the *actual* copy of *Sir Tristrem* that appears in Auchinleck (see Table 1).

Mannyng wrote his *Chronicle* between the years 1327 and 1338 in the Gilbertine priories of Sempringham and Sixhills – both located northeast of Lincoln near the Lincolnshire town of Market Rasen. Mannyng begins the passage excerpted, in Table 1, by listing all the complex and 'strange' verse forms and rhyming schemes he could have used were it not for the need for simplicity in this work. He then cites a work he calls 'Sir Tristrem' and says that he hears 'no man so say' it as Thomas made it. Is Mannyng speaking of our romance, and, if he is, is he speaking of the text as it appears in Auchinleck? As Joyce Coleman points out, the Auchinleck *Sir Tristrem*

> employs every one of the four varieties of strange rhyme mentioned by Mannyng. ... [I]t is in tail rhyme (*couwee*); its rhymes interlace (*enterlace*); and it is in stanzas (*baston*). It can also be labeled *strangere* ... because it qualifies as unusual or recondite.[29]

At lines 100–3, Mannyng speaks of some corruption of the text, as he says 'þat of som copple, som is away'. The Auchinleck text of *Sir Tristrem* has five missing lines that were afterwards inserted in the same hand as the original inscription. However, it is also missing two couplets, one each in stanzas 8 and 80, and neither of those omissions is corrected by the copyist. If by 'som copple' Mannyng means 'couplets', the omissions he speaks of would match the deficiencies found in the Auchinleck inscription.

Admittedly, this offers no definitive proof that Mannyng had seen the Auchinleck *Sir Tristrem* itself, since it can be argued that a corrector who spotted missing lines would surely have also noticed missing couplets, unless they were missing from the exemplar as well and therefore could not be supplied. It is worth remembering, though, that, when a copyist is scanning a completed copy and comparing it from time to time with the exemplar, a line missing from a couplet is easily apparent because of the broken rhyme. A missing couplet, however, offers no such clue,

---

[27] Fellows, 'The Representation', p. 137, referring to *Sir Tristrem*, lines 1673–6.

[28] Robert Mannyng of Brunne, *The Chronicle*, ed. I. Sullens, Medieval and Renaissance Texts and Studies (Binghamton NY, 1996).

[29] J. Coleman, 'Strange Rhyme: Prose and Nationhood in Robert Mannyng's *Story of England*', *Speculum* 78 (2003), 1214–38 (p. 1221). Coleman notes that 'Studies of tail-rhyme generally confine that term to the basic pattern of *aabccbddbeeb* characteristic of the popular Middle English romances' (p. 1221 n. 30). As she points out, however, '*Sir Tristrem*'s eleven-line stanzas scan in a demanding *abababababcbc* pattern; the standard metre has three stresses, but the first *c* line qualifies as a tag, with only one. Thus it is in tail rhyme' (p. 1221).

Table 1   Robert Mannyng's *Chronicle* and *Sir Tristrem*: comparative passages

I present here the relevant passage from Robert Mannyng's *Chronicle*, together with stanzas 8 and 80 of the Auchinleck *Sir Tristrem*. Stanza 7 is included for the purpose of comparison because it has the full complement of eleven lines required by the form. In the Auchinleck *Sir Tristrem*, stanzas 8 and 80 lack couplets at lines 80–1 and 874–5.

Chronicle, lines 85–108 *(significant words in bold)*	*Sir Tristrem (stanzas 7, 8, 80)*

If it were made in **ryme couwee**,　85	7
or in **strangere** or **enterlace**,	Glad a man was he,
þat rede Inglis it ere inowe	Þe tournament dede crie,
þat couthe not haf coppled a kowe;	Þat maidens miȝt him se
þat othere in **couwee** or in **baston**,	And ouer hem walles to lye.　　70
som suld haf ben fordon,　90	Þai asked, who was fre,
so þat fele men þat it herde	To win þe maistrie:
suld not witte howe þat it ferde.	Þai seyd, þat best was he,
I see in song, in sedgying tale	Þe child of Ermonie,
of Erceldoun & of Kendale:	In tour;　　75
Non þam says as þai þam wroght,　95	For þi chosen was he
& in þer saying it semes noght.	To maiden Blauncheflour
þat may þou here in **sir Tristrem**,	
ouer gestes it has þe steem	8
Ouer alle þat is or was,	Þe maiden of heiȝe kinne
if men it sayd as mayd Thomas.　100	Sche cald hir maisters þre:
Bot I here it no man so say	*(line missing)*　　80
þat **of som copple, som is away**.	*(line missing)*
So þare fayre saying here beforn	'Bot giue it be þurch ginne,
is þare trauayle nere forlorn;	A selly man is he;
þai sayd it for pride & nobleye　105	Þurch min hert wiþ inne
þat non were suylk as þei,	Ywounded haþ he me　　85
And alle þat þai wild ouerwhere,	So sone:
alle þat ilk wille now forfare.	Of bale bot he me blinne,
	Mine liif days ben al done!'
	80
	On his brest adoun　　870
	Of his nose ran þe blod.
	Tristrem swerd was boun,
	And ner þe douke he stode.
	(line missing)
	(line missing)　　875
	Wiþ þat was comen to toun
	Rohand wiþhelp ful gode
	And gayn.
	Al þat oȝain hem stode,
	Wiȝtly were þai slayn.　　880

especially when, as in both instances here, the stanza crosses a folio, distracting the reader from the fact that the number of lines is incomplete.[30] Regarding the corrupted transmission that Mannyng speaks of, Robert William Kelton makes the intriguing suggestion that the Auchinleck scribe was working from an exemplar in which the poem was written out in prose. If that were indeed the case, line and stanza breaks were presumably marked in some way, but errors would have been unavoidable. Kelton finds a pattern of erasures and corrections that, he argues, is exactly what one would expect if the Auchinleck scribe were working from an exemplar laid out in this way and were unfamiliar with the oddities of the poem's form.[31] Since *Sir Tristrem* is, as George Saintsbury noted, the earliest example of this stanzaic form in Middle English metrical romance, and only one other usage of that form is known, one cannot fault the Auchinleck scribe for having difficulty in transcribing it.[32] Thus, I suggest, it is not altogether impossible that Robert Mannyng, a man interested in popular works in the English vernacular, may have seen the Auchinleck manuscript at some point between its copying in London around 1330 and Mannyng's completion of his *Chronicle* in 1338.

The details of Mannyng's life are somewhat uncertain, however. His own remarks in *Handlyng Synne* and the *Chronicle* indicate that he was living in either the Gilbertine mother house in Sempringham or its sister house at Sixhills from at least 1303 until his death, which occurred soon after he had completed the *Chronicle* in 1338. Thus, if Mannyng read *Sir Tristrem* in the Auchinleck manuscript, noticing the copyist's errors as he did so, this would locate the manuscript in Lincolnshire sometime before 1338. Nor is Mannyng's the only more northerly allusion to *Sir Tristrem* to be found within a decade of its being copied into the Auchinleck manuscript in London. Around the year 1340, the Yorkshireman Laurence Minot modified one of his series of eleven poems on the military campaigns of Edward III.[33] The poem in question, sixth in the series, deals with the siege of Tournai in 1340. In writing these poems, Minot employed a variety of styles drawn from Middle English romance. Some of the poems are in couplets, some stanzaic, and he even employs alliterative verse. The style of Poem VI is particularly interesting. Each of the first six stanzas has eight lines whose structure is (except for a slight variation in the rhyme scheme) identical to the first eight lines of each of *Sir Tristrem*'s eleven-line stanzas, and the last three stanzas have eleven lines each and follow *Sir Tristrem*'s bob-line stanza in full. In other words, the three stanzas preserve the only parallel that we have to the unusual verse form found in *Sir Tristrem*.

---

[30] See *Sir Tristrem* in the Burnley-Wiggins facsimile. Citations of the poem, by line number, are from this transcription.

[31] 'A Critical Edition of *Sir Tristrem* edited from the Auchinleck Manuscript', ed. R. W. Kelton, unpublished PhD dissertation, The Ohio State University (Columbus OH, 1974), p. 26.

[32] G. Saintsbury, *A History of English Prosody from the Twelfth Century to the Present Day*, 3 vols. (New York, 1906), I, 94–5.

[33] Laurence Minot, 'Poem VI', in *The Poems of Laurence Minot, 1333–1352*, ed. R. H. Osberg (Kalamazoo MI, 1996), pp. 48–50.

Minot's poems are preserved in a single manuscript, London, BL, MS Cotton Galba E. 9, which dates from the beginning of the fifteenth century, but the last of Minot's poems were composed about fifty years before that. The poems describe campaigns that occurred between 1333 and 1352. Although they are grouped in the manuscript, internal evidence suggests that some were composed on an ongoing basis, close in time to the events described.[34] This is especially true in the case of Poem VI, which deals with the siege of Tournai. Edward III began the siege on 1 August 1340. At first, there was good reason to think Tournai would fall to the English forces. Eventually, however, as the stalemate continued and Edward ran short of money and supplies, he agreed to the Truce of Esplechin and withdrew the siege. As McIntosh points out, the failure of Edward's siege suggests an explanation for Minot's shift from an eight-line stanza to the eleven lines incorporating a bob that we find in the final three stanzas.[35] The first eight lines of the seventh stanza (lines 49–56) appear to be have been the original final stanza, completed while the siege was still under way and looking (in its eighth line) towards Edward's presumed success. In autumn 1340, however, Edward abandoned the siege, and, as McIntosh notes, Minot's addition of a bob and two lines to stanza 7, and then two more stanzas, rather skillfully solved the problem of the original argument having been overtaken by events.

McIntosh does not imply that Minot was the author of *Sir Tristrem*. Aside from its stanza form, *Sir Tristrem* has nothing in common with any of Minot's works and was composed at least two decades earlier. McIntosh suggests, rather, that the reason for

> the structural similarities of the stanzas in them, similarities which cannot
> be matched in any third poem that has survived from either England or
> Scotland, may be that they both spring from a single locally restricted
> tradition in which this verse-form was current in the earlier part of the
> fourteenth century.[36]

In a general sense, this may be so. However, the argument assumes that, when Minot used the far more standard eight-line stanza for the first part of the poem, he chose not to use the bob-line stanza that the tradition made available to him and yet subsequently reverted to that stanza. This hypothesis seems rather strained. The principle of Occam's razor urges us to consider instead the possibility that, between writing the first seven stanzas and then discovering that he needed to both modify the poem and develop a bridge to that modification, Minot had encountered the eleven-line bob-stanza in the only work from that period where it survives: *Sir Tristrem*. It is interesting – and perhaps significant – that Minot's poem is the only

---

[34] Osberg, 'Introduction', in Minot, *The Poems*, ed. Osberg, pp. i–viii.

[35] A. McIntosh, 'Is *Sir Tristrem* an English or a Scottish Poem?', in *In Other Words: Transcultural Studies in Philology, Translation and Lexicography Presented to Hans Heinrich Meier on the Occasion of His Sixty-Fifth Birthday*, ed. J. L. Mackenzie and R. Todd (Dordrecht, 1989), pp. 85–95.

[36] Ibid., p. 92.

instance we have other than *Sir Tristrem* of this eleven-line form, and that Minot's poem was composed in Yorkshire less than a decade after the only text that now survives of *Sir Tristrem* was copied into the Auchinleck manuscript.

A further indication of a contemporary association between the Middle English *Sir Tristrem* and the North of England is perhaps to be found in a brief passage from *Castleford's Chronicle*. Written in a northern Yorkshire dialect and associated with the village of Castleford near Wakefield, *Castleford's Chronicle* is a lengthy account in couplets – twelve books and nearly 40,000 lines – of the history of Britain from the mythological arrival of Brutus to the deposition of Edward II.[37] Although its only surviving manuscript dates from the fifteenth century, the *Chronicle*'s terminus with the reign of Edward II suggests that it was completed in 1327 or shortly thereafter. Several references to English heroes of romance are inserted into the chronicle, including Guy of Warwick and Bevis of Hampton. From the perspective of my argument here, the most interesting of those references comes in Book IX and involves Tristan, or 'Tristreme' as is written in the *Chronicle*. The passage immediately follows an account of tribute paid by Northumbria to Ireland in the ninth century:

> Now, quiles Adulf diademe bare,
> Cessede þe strife fore euermar
> Þoru Rolande son, a knight, Tristreme,
> Þat trauailde for Kyng Mark, his heme,
> Northumbre broght of sorow and site,
> Of seruage to be claimede quite. (Book IX, lines 28,788–93)

Apart from *Sir Tristrem* itself, this is the only text in which Tristan's father is identified as Roland (other versions of the Tristan story name his father variously as Rivalen, Kanelangres, or Meliadus). As Caroline Eckhardt notes, the other details in this brief account (particularly the shift of the field of action from southern England and, especially, from Cornwall to Northumbria) do not accord with those traditionally found in the story of Tristan.[38] However, the association of Tristan (through his father) with the Charlemagne cycle in both *Sir Tristrem* and *Castleford's Chronicle*, but (as far as we can tell) nowhere else, suggests that this may have been a Northern tradition. Similarly, while the *Chronicle*'s relocation of the Irish tribute episode to Northumbria has no analogy anywhere else in the Tristan tradition, it is worth remembering that, in *Sir Tristrem*, Tristan's uncle Mark is king not just of Cornwall but of all England, and that Tristan 'faught for Inglond', not merely for Cornwall, when he challenged the Irish champion Morholt and freed his country from the tribute owed to the Irish king.

---

[37] *Castleford's Chronicle, or, The Boke of Brut*, ed. C. D. Eckhardt, 2 vols., EETS OS 305, 306 (Oxford, 1996). Citations, given by line number, are from this edition.

[38] C. D. Eckhardt and B. A. Meer, 'Constructing a Medieval Genealogy: Roland the Father of Tristan in *Castleford's Chronicle*', *Modern Language Notes* 15 (2000), 1085–111. As Eckhardt and Meer note, Tristan's presence (however brief) in *Castleford's Chronicle* is especially interesting because no mention of him is to be found in any of the other medieval chronicles of British history.

A few fragments and some speculation

My argument thus far has relied on an admittedly speculative interpretation of the lack of any London reference to an English-language version of the Tristan story in the century following the inscription of *Sir Tristrem* into the Auchinleck manuscript, and also on the existence of several direct and indirect allusions to *Sir Tristrem* in more northerly parts of the country during the same period. I will now consider more concrete traces of the book – that is, the physical evidence deposited by the manuscript between its creation in the 1330s and its arrival at the Advocates Library in Edinburgh in 1744.

Few though they are, those traces of physical evidence have all been found far to the north of London. The manuscript itself (as we have it today) was apparently already in Edinburgh when Lord Auchinleck found it. The most frequently cited additional fragments of the book are the Tullideph folios, found by David Laing in the early 1830s and by G. H. Bushnell in 1946, in the bindings of student notebooks that had belonged to Thomas Tullideph (or Tullidelph), co-founder and first Principal of the University of St Andrews.[39] The fragments found by Laing consist of one bifolium containing 352 lines from *The Life of Adam and Eve*, originally the eighth item in the book, and another bifolium containing 351 discontinuous lines of *King Richard*, numbered 'lvi' by the scribe who apparently collated the contents of the original codex. The fragment found by Bushnell is the immediately adjacent bifolium of *King Richard* and, because its 349 lines of text are continuous, it is clear that it was originally the central bifolium of the quire. Since Tullideph was a student at St Leonard's College around 1717, that discovery pushes Auchinleck's presence in Edinburgh back a couple of decades earlier than Boswell's ownership.

More telling evidence is provided, however, by another group of fragments: the St Andrews and London folios from the Auchinleck *Kyng Alisaunder*.[40] The St Andrews fragments were found in 1946 by Neil Ker and Bushnell in the binding of a 1543 Paris edition of Horace that was part of John Scot of Scotstarvet's gift to the University of St Andrews Library. Some years later, in 1963, Winifred A. Myers donated a fourteenth-century bifolium containing part of the Auchinleck copy of

---

[39] Thomas Tullideph was a student at St Leonard's College before 1720, and later a founder of St Andrew's University (formed by the union of St Leonard's and St Salvator's Colleges). The fragments are now held by the University of Edinburgh (Edinburgh, University Library, MS 218) and the University of St Andrews (St Andrews, University Library, PR 2065. R. 4). See G. V. Smithers, 'Two Newly Discovered Fragments from the Auchinleck MS', *Medium Ævum* 18 (1949), 1–11 (p. 3), for a discussion of the St Andrews fragments and a chart of their position in the manuscript relative to the Edinburgh fragments.

[40] The St Andrews fragments – University Library, PR 2065. A. 15 (MS 1400) and PR 2065. A. 15 (MS 1401) – consist of two horizontal strips cut from the same bifolium and trimmed on the right-hand side, thus losing a full column from each bifolium in addition to the truncation at the foot. PR 2065. A. 15 (MS 1400) includes lines 6856–65, 6900–9, 6924, 6945–54, 6988–97, 7032–41 and 7070–9 and 7180–94 of *Kyng Alisaunder*. PR 2065 A. 15 (MS 1401) includes lines 6866–80, 6910–24, 6967, 6998–7012, 7042–56 and 7180–94 of *Kyng Alisaunder*.

Kyng Alisaunder to the University of London Library.[41] Investigation of the Myers bifolium revealed it to have been immediately adjacent to the Scotstarvet fragments when both were still bound into the manuscript. No direct information regarding its provenance is available beyond G. V. Smithers's remark in an article about the fragment that Myers's 'source was a Scots one of unknown identity'.[42] As we will see, however, the information we have about the Scotstarvet fragments, or, at least, about their hiding place, allows us to draw some inferences about the Myers bifolium.[43]

In 1620, John Scot of Scotstarvet endowed a Chair of Humanity at St Leonard's College in Edinburgh (the precursor of the University of St Andrews) and backed his endowment with a gift of the books necessary for a basic classical library, including the Paris volume of Horace noted above. To be more precise, the Horace volume did not come directly from Scot himself, but was the contribution of John Sandilands of Eastbarns to the endowment; nonetheless, the records indicate that the Horace gift was made at the time of the original endowment, or soon thereafter.[44] The binding is not contemporary with the book itself but is consistent with David Pearson's descriptions of bookbinding styles from the late sixteenth or early seventeenth century, and there is no indication that it was rebound after its arrival at St Andrews.[45] The binding includes no information about its maker. It is reasonable, however, to assume that Sandilands purchased the book in Edinburgh or, at least, had it bound there. Not only was Edinburgh near his home, but, since Sandilands was an advocate, at least some of his employment must have brought him from time to time to that city.[46]

The Scotstarvet fragments consist of two strips from the central bifolium of a quire. The binder trimmed the bifolium vertically on the left-hand side and then

[41] The London fragment (University Library, MS 593) is an imperfect bifolium missing a strip cut from the bottom. It includes lines 6675–712, 6724–61, 6768–806, 6811–50, 7214–52, 7306–44 and 7350–89 of *Kyng Alisaunder*.

[42] G. V. Smithers, 'Another Fragment of the Auchinleck MS', in *Medieval Literature and Civilization Studies in Memory of G. N. Garmonsway*, ed. D. A. Pearsall and R. A. Waldron (London, 1969), pp. 192–209 (p. 192).

[43] To avoid confusion, in the rest of this discussion I will use the term 'Scotstarvet fragments' when speaking of the fragments discovered in the Scotstarvet volume (St Andrews, University Library, PR 2065. A. 15 [MSS 1400, 1401]), and the term 'Myers fragment' to identify the fragment donated by Myers (London, University Library, MS 593).

[44] See R. V. Pringle, 'An Early Humanity Class Library: The Gift of Sir John Scot and Friends to St Leonard's College (1620)', *The Bibliotheck* 7 (1974), 33–55, for a full discussion of the Scotstarvet endowment and a list of the books donated by Scot and his associates. I am grateful to Elizabeth Henderson, Rare Books Librarian of the University of St Andrews, for providing me with information about the Scotstarvet bequest and with copies of the correspondence between N. R. Ker, G. H. Bushnell, and G. V. Smithers regarding the fragments (University Library, PR 2065. A. 15).

[45] See D. Pearson, *English Bookbinding Styles 1450–1800* (London, 2005). These observations were made by Elizabeth Henderson in response to my enquiries concerning the binding of the volume in which the fragments were found.

[46] Eastbarns is a village in the parish of the town of Dunbar, located approximately thirty miles east of Edinburgh, and J. Sandilands was admitted to the Society of Advocates in 1613.

cut it into narrow horizontal strips that he stitched into place under the end papers of the volume in which they were found more than three hundred years later.[47] The light colour of the vellum and the relative sharpness of the ink suggest that the binder used this bifolium very soon after he tore it out of its quire, as it does not seem to have been lying around for very long, darkening from exposure to air. It is clear from the text contained in the folios of the Myers fragment that they are from the Auchinleck *Kyng Alisaunder* and immediately precede and follow the Scotstarvet bifolium.[48] In other words, if we imagine our bookbinder tearing out the bifolium which he used to bind the Scotstarvet volume of Horace, the next bifolium available to him would have been the one that Myers donated some 350 years later to the University of London Library, and that she apparently said she obtained in Scotland.

A comparison of the Myers bifolium with the Scotstarvet fragments yields some intriguing results. The Myers bifolium is, like the Scotstarvet bifolium, imperfect, since here, too, a binder's knife has trimmed enough off the bottom to lose about six lines of text from each column. Otherwise, the bifolium is complete and supplies approximately 266 lines of missing text, coming immediately before and immediately after the Scotstarvet text. It seems hardly likely that two wholly unconnected bookbinders would have obtained one each of two consecutive bifolia from the Auchinleck manuscript and then trimmed each of them in much the same way. The more reasonable possibility is that both the Scotstarvet and the Myers fragments ultimately came from the same source: the bookbinder who rebound Sandilands's Horace before he donated it to St Andrews.

However, this likelihood raises another question, one prompted by a comparison of the condition of the Scotstarvet and Myers fragments.[49] The Myers fragment has nothing of the freshness of the Scotstarvet bifolium. It is noticeably darker in colour, and the text is rubbed and worn on the recto side of the first leaf and on the verso side of the second, perhaps a little more so in the case of the first leaf than of the second. I infer from this that the Myers bifolium spent some time lying folded and unused on a binder's scrap-shelf between the time when it was taken out of the quire and Myers's acquisition of it in the mid-twentieth century. According to Pearson, the use of manuscript waste for end-leaves and paste-downs dwindled in the course of the seventeenth century, and had almost died out by its end. The preservation of the Myers fragment in one piece, except for the strip taken from the bottom, certainly suggests that no immediate use was made of it by the binder.[50]

---

[47] G. H. Bushnell describes the discovery of the fragments in a letter to G. V. Smithers dated 23 March 1948 (St Andrews, University Library, PR 2065. A. 15).

[48] The text included in the Myers fragment is as follows: lines 6675–712, 6724–61, 6768–806, 6811–50, 7214–52, 7306–44, and 7350–89. As may be seen, the text contained in the Scotstarvet fragment belongs in the middle of the Myers bifolium, between line 6850 and line 7214.

[49] This comparison is made possible by consulting digital images in the Burnley-Wiggins facsimile, at http://auchinleck.nls.uk/mss/alisaunder.html

[50] Pearson, *English Bookbinding*, pp. 31–8. Pearson's discussion is confined to the practices of binders in England. It is reasonable, however, to assume that the practice in Scotland followed a similar path. This point applies primarily to books containing textual matter.

The possibility that the same bookshop was responsible for the preservation, however inadvertent, not only of the Scotstarvet and Myers fragments of *Kyng Alisaunder*, but also, a century later, of the Tullideph fragments of *Adam and Eve* and *King Richard*, is intriguing. Nor is it entirely unlikely. In 1719, Tullideph's brother David was apprenticed as a mercer and bookbinder to the Edinburgh bookseller James McEuen. While that date comes a couple of years after Thomas's purchase of his notebooks, the very fact of David's apprenticeship indicates that the Tullideph family already had some acquaintance with McEuen, a bookseller who was deeply embedded in the bookselling and and publishing trade in Edinburgh.[51] It is reasonable to suppose, therefore, that the young student Thomas Tullideph patronized McEuen's shop while he was enrolled at St Leonard's College. The NLS's *Scottish Book Trade Index* makes very clear how closely entwined and even incestuous that trade was in the sixteenth, seventeenth, and eighteenth centuries. The same names recur again and again in the records of multiple establishments, reminding us not only of how vibrant the book trade was in Edinburgh, but also that it was a business very much dominated by family connections, in which companies formed, dissolved and formed again, in varying combinations of familial and professional partnership.[52] While McEuen operated about a century too late to have had anything to do with the binding of the Scotstarvet Horace, it is well within the bounds of possibility that the tradesman who did that work was one of his direct predecessors in the profession; that the Auchinleck manuscript and its attendant fragments came into McEuen's possession as a result of that connection; and that one of his apprentices tore a quire out of it when he was binding some blank notebooks for Thomas Tullideph.

The hard physical evidence thus strongly suggests that the Auchinleck manuscript was already in Edinburgh by the time Sandilands's copy of Horace was rebound in the early seventeenth century and donated to the University of St Andrews. That gift totaled more than a hundred volumes, many of which are now missing from the library shelves. It is tempting to think that some of those missing volumes were bound in the same shop and at the same time as the Horace volume, and that the binder used other scraps of Auchinleck to reinforce their boards. Certainly, there are enough leaves missing from the manuscript as we have it today to have contributed to the bindings of quite a few books, and to prompt us to hope that more fragments are waiting to be discovered. In the meantime, however, we must make do with what we have: a sizeable but still incomplete manuscript in Edinburgh; some fragments in Edinburgh, St Andrews, and London; and forty-four

---

As Pearson notes, the use of manuscript waste for stationery bindings (account books, notebooks, etc.) continued into the nineteenth century, explaining the discovery of several leaves from the Auchinleck manuscript in the early-eighteenth-century bindings of Thomas Tullideph's notebooks.

[51] See the *Scottish Book Trade Index*, at http://www.nls.uk/catalogues/scottish-book-trade-index, for evidence of J. McEuen's associations with a number of significant figures in the Scottish printing and publishing industry in the seventeenth century.

[52] The *Scottish Book Trade Index* contains records of all those involved in the book trade in Scotland from the early seventeenth century up to 1850, and it is 1,550 pages long.

texts – some complete, some imperfect, some merely scraps. And, making do with what we have, we can come to the following conclusions – some founded on the rock of physical evidence, some resting on the shifting sand of speculation, but all, I argue, worth our consideration if we are ever to come close to understanding what the Auchinleck manuscript really is.

By the early 1600s, the Auchinleck manuscript was already in the hands of a Scottish bookbinder, valued only for the raw material it provided him as he reinforced the covers of more treasured volumes. The survival of the book's original numbering indicates that the fragments that have so far been discovered come from items 'viii', 'xxxiii', 'xliiii' (8, 33, 44) of the original manuscript.[53] Items 'i'–'v', 'xxxviii'–'xlii', 'xlvii'–'l', 'lvii'–'lix' (1–5, 38–42, 47–50, 57–9) are still missing (without taking into account the possibility that several additional items followed item 'lx', the last one currently extant) and were probably put to the same use. A very conservative estimate of the amount of missing material involved would be at least seventy leaves, and a glance at the item numbers of the missing or damaged items suggests that the bookbinder generally tore leaves out from either end of the book, occasionally reaching further into the manuscript as the stitching loosened. While the binder who supplied Tullideph's notebooks used entire bifolia to make their covers (as was the common practice when binding everyday items of that type), the craftsman who rebound the Scotstarvet Horace about a hundred years earlier cut his pieces of waste into narrow strips and may sometimes have made one bifolium reinforce the bindings of two or more volumes. If we assume for a moment that the manuscript's heyday as a recyclable resource came to an end with the shelving of the Myers fragment some time in the early 1600s, it is possible that the book was being used for scrap by some Edinburgh bookbinder from the mid-1560s onwards. Where it was before then is a mystery that can be approached only through speculation.

In 1948, Bushnell engaged in such speculation when he made the intriguing suggestion in a letter to Smithers that 'the early history of the Auchinleck manuscript should probably be sought in the Balcarres Library before the days of the great Bibliotheca Lindesiana'. He went on to say, 'My theory is that the Lady Balcarres, who is well-known to have sold many MSS. and books to tradesmen, disposed of the so-called Auchinleck MS. to the junk merchant, Thomas Tullideph'.[54] Unfortunately, the dates do not fit, since the Lady Balcarres in question was the wife of Alexander Lindsay (1752–1825), 6th Earl of Balcarres, and it was not until near the end of the eighteenth century that, according to her grandson, 'the greater portion of the library was literally thrown away and dispersed – torn up, I believe, for grocers, as useless

[53] The Tullideph fragments came from items 'viii' and 'xxxiii'; the Scotstarvet/Myers fragments came from item 'xliiii'.

[54] G. H. Bushnell letter to G. V. Smithers, 7 June 1948 (St Andrews, University Library, PR 2065. A. 15). Bushnell implies that this Tullideph was a relative of Principal Thomas Tullideph; however, it seems more likely that they were one and the same, since Tullideph's commonplace book from his student days includes marginal notes in his hand of various commercial transactions. There is a gap of approximately six years between Tullideph's graduation from St Leonard's and his taking orders in 1727, and he appears to have spent that time as a merchant or grocer.

trash, by her orders or by her permission'.[55] On the other hand, the Lindsay library was begun in about 1580 by Lindsay's great-great-great-grandfather John Lindsay, Lord Menmuir, and developed by his heir David Lindsay into what was considered to be the best library of his time in Scotland.[56] Lord Menmuir and his successors were far more interested in the ancient classics than in vernacular literature, unless the vernacular papers related to the Lindsay family. One could perhaps imagine that, if a manuscript like Auchinleck had somehow made its way into the Lindsay library in its early years, a bookbinder working there a decade or so later on the various volumes of Horace, Ovid, Juvenal, and so on might have been made free to use its folios, and even have been allowed to take a few quires away with him. We do not know how or where Lord Auchinleck obtained the Auchinleck manuscript, but the nobility and gentry of Scotland formed a small social circle, and it may well have been that a later Lindsay gave it to him in 1740, having little interest in this non-classical volume that had already lost a number of its leaves. The fact that Lord Auchinleck himself was primarily interested in the classics may likewise explain why he left no records of the manuscript, and why he passed it on four years later, apparently with little fanfare, to the Advocates Library, to be discovered there by later scholars.

The physical evidence therefore indicates that the Auchinleck manuscript was in Edinburgh at least as early as the last decades of the sixteenth century, and the textual evidence invites us to infer that the book's first owner was a resident of one of England's more northerly counties – perhaps a Yorkshireman or a native of Lincolnshire. How the book made its way in the course of three hundred years from northern England to Scotland remains a mystery, but the intertwined history of England and Scotland suggests some possible answers. As is the case in England, many of Scotland's prominent families derive their ancestry from Normans who first settled in northern England on land granted them by William following the Battle of Hastings. For instance, Robert Bruce's distant ancestor Robert de Brus (d. 1142) held large estates in Yorkshire as vassal to Henry I, and the Lindsays of Balcarres derive their name from Lindsey in Lincolnshire, where their Norman ancestors lived before they moved to Scotland in the twelfth century as vassals of the future King David I. In time of peace and in time of war, the Scottish lowlands and England's Northern regions were the stage for interactions of various kinds between members of the two rival but closely connected nations. It is not too fanciful to imagine that one of those interactions (peaceful or otherwise) may have resulted in some Scottish knight's or petty nobleman's bringing a large and somewhat interesting book home with him to Edinburgh. And there it sat, neglected, on a shelf until, one day, an itinerant bookbinder started tearing leaves out of it as he began to renew the binding on a more treasured volume and thus inadvertently preserved a few more fragments of the corpus of Middle English romance for posterity.

---

[55] Alexander William Lindsay, 8th Earl of Balcarres, qtd by N. Barker, *Bibliotheca Lindesiana* (London, 1978), p. 26.

[56] Interestingly, David Lindsay was a friend and correspondent of both Drummond of Hawthornden and Scot of Scotstarvet.

CHAPTER EIGHT

The Invention of *King Richard**

Marisa Libbon

O N those rare occasions when we talk or write about the text we have
come to refer to as *Richard Coer de Lion*,[1] the Middle English romance
depicting England's late-twelfth-century crusader-king Richard I, we often begin
with particular details about it to pique the interests and jog the memories of our
listeners or readers. First, Richard's mother is an Eastern princess and perhaps
a fairy, who, when made to watch the Eucharist's elevation, shoots up through
the church roof, never to be heard from again. Next, Richard twice cannibalizes
Saracens while on crusade, once with plausible deniability and the second time
with full knowledge. And, finally, the earliest extant copy of the romance survives
in the Auchinleck manuscript (Edinburgh, NLS, MS Advocates 19. 2. 1), a book
probably produced in London between 1331 and 1340, and known today for its large
number of the earliest or only copies of texts that significantly comprise our corpus

---

* For Joseph J. Duggan.

[1] The standard edition is *Der mittelenglische Versroman über Richard Löwenherz*, ed. K.
Brunner, Wiener Beiträge zur englischen Philologie 42 (Vienna, 1913) (hereafter cited as
'*Löwenherz*, ed. K. Brunner'). *Richard Coer de Lion* survives in seven manuscripts dated
from the fourteenth to the early sixteenth centuries, and one independent fragment. The
record of witnesses in the *NIMEV* is listed under 'Richard Coer de Lion', no. 1979, and
in the *DIMEV* under no. 3231. On possible dates and provenances, see G. Guddat-Figge,
Catalogue of Manuscripts Containing Middle English Romances (Munich, 1976). Wynkyn
de Worde printed editions in 1509 (*STC* 21007) and 1528 (*STC* 21008). According to the
Stationers' Register, the licence was transferred in 1568–69 to Thomas Purfoote; see H.
Cooper, *The English Romance in Time : Transforming Motifs from Geoffrey of Monmouth
to the Death of Shakespeare* (Oxford, 2004), p. 425; and *Löwenherz*, ed. Brunner, p. 1. On
the independent fragment, which has been dated to the first quarter of the fifteenth
century, see N. Davis, 'Another Fragment of "Richard Coer de Lion"', *Notes and Queries*
16 (1969), 447–52. When Davis examined the fragment, its shelfmark was Badminton,
Duke of Beaufort, MS 704. 1. 16, and it is still listed as such in the *NIMEV* and the
DIMEV. However, the fragment is now on deposit in the Gloucestershire Archives as
Gloucester, Gloucestershire Archives, MS D2700/V/1 No. 8. To my knowledge, this is
the first time the fragment's new location and shelfmark have been cited in print. I am
grateful to Elaine Milsom at the Badminton Estate Office and to Andrew Parry at the
Gloucestershire Archives for their assistance in locating this fragment.

of Middle English romance (a seemingly cold, hard, scholarly fact self-consciously deployed amid the sensationalism).[2]

Beyond the many, many obvious problems to which fairy mothers and cannibalism give rise, this 'common knowledge' that has come to at once emblematize, advertise, and contextualize *Richard Coer de Lion* presents an additional difficulty, made more acute when one sits down to write about the earliest extant copy of the romance: none of these things we think we know about *Richard Coer de Lion* are true of its inscription in the Auchinleck manuscript. Rather, Auchinleck's *Richard Coer de Lion* – or *King Richard* as it is titled in the manuscript and as I will refer to it here – makes no mention of a fairy mother, beginning instead with a Prologue, the fall of Jerusalem, and Richard's preparations for sea travel to Acre. It does not now and probably never did contain scenes of cannibalism. And it is only partially preserved in the Auchinleck manuscript proper.[3] Of the little more than a thousand lines of *King Richard* that survive, roughly seven hundred occur as almost-consecutive fragments that were recovered, remarkably, in various eighteenth-century Scottish notebooks and bindings, now held in multiple libraries.[4] The *King Richard* material that today survives as item 43 between Auchinleck's boards consists of a single bifolium, fols. 326r–v and 327r–v, comprising the first and the last leaves of a quire that once contained the recovered fragments.[5] Although a full couplet, which declares Richard conqueror of Acre and offers a satisfying conclusion to the narrative, occupies the leaf's final two ruled lines on fol. 327vb, the bottom margin

---

[2] On Auchinleck's dating see T. Turville-Petre, *England the Nation: Language, Literature, and National Identity, 1290–1340* (Oxford, 1996), p. 111; and H. Cooper, 'Lancelot, Roger Mortimer, and the Date of the Auchinleck Manuscript', in *Studies in Late Medieval and Early Renaissance Texts in Honour of John Scattergood*, ed. A. M. D'Arcy and A. J. Fletcher (Dublin, 2005), pp. 91–9 (p. 95). On Auchinleck's provenance and production see L. H. Loomis, 'The Auchinleck Manuscript and a Possible London Bookshop of 1330–1340', *PMLA* 57 (1942), 595–627; T. A. Shonk, 'A Study of the Auchinleck Manuscript: Bookmen and Bookmaking in the Early Fourteenth Century', *Speculum* 60 (1985), 71–91; and R. Hanna, 'Reconsidering the Auchinleck Manuscript', in *New Directions in Later Medieval Manuscript Studies: Essays from the 1998 Harvard Conference*, ed. D. Pearsall (York, 2000), 91–102.

[3] My arguments for the absence of the cannibalism episodes in a group of manuscripts, including Auchinleck, as well as a discussion of the complex response to the episodes in the manuscripts that preserve them, form part of my book in progress, *Richard I and the Idea of England*.

[4] Discovered by N. R. Ker and others, the fragments are now Edinburgh, University Library, MS 218, and St Andrews, University Library, MS PR 2065. R. 4. See G. V. Smithers, 'Two Newly-Discovered Fragments from the Auchinleck MS', *Medium Ævum* 18 (1949), 1–11 (pp. 1–3); and D. Pearsall, 'Literary and Historical Significance of the Manuscript', in Pearsall-Cunningham, pp. vii–xi (p. vii). The Edinburgh fragments have been edited in 'Kleine publicationen aus der Auchinleck-hs. III', ed. E. Kölbing, *Englische Studien* 8 (1885), 115–19.

[5] A miniature depicting a scene from the romance, but with no known visual analogues or precedents, occurs at the top of fol. 326ra, under the rubricated title 'King Richard' and immediately preceding the text. Auchinleck appears to have at one time contained at least nineteen miniatures; this is one of four that survive and the only illumination to accompany any manuscript copy of *Richard Coer de Lion*.

contains a hanging catchword, 'þe sarraȝins seyȝe þai', which is seemingly related to Richard's preceding siege of Acre and thus perhaps evinces significant loss at the text's end.[6] Our expectations for what *Richard Coer de Lion* is about and what it should contain derive mostly from Karl Brunner's 1913 edition of the romance, which instantiated through Brunner's editorial methods a complex idea of narrative completeness,[7] and which, in the absence of any more recent, collated, or diplomatic published editions, has remained the most accessible and by far the most accessed monument of *Richard Coer de Lion*'s text and transmission.[8]

That a discussion of what Auchinleck's earliest copy of the romance is, was, or might have been necessitates first describing what it is *not* – and, moreover, distinguishing it from the narrative inscribed in Brunner's edition and enshrined in much of the scholarship that has proceeded from it – may seem initially an unorthodox way to begin this essay. In fact, we can trace this unorthodoxy back to *King Richard* itself. For there, in its thirty-two-line Prologue – of which the first twenty-four tail-rhymed lines are unique to Auchinleck – what *King Richard* is comes into relief against a rendering of what it professes *not* to be vis-à-vis the 'established' literary canon: an old French romance about an old French hero. After the first six lines give thanks for Richard and 'his stori', the Prologue abruptly begins to sketch a storytelling universe where, in part:

> Romaunce make folk of Fraunce
> Of kniȝtes þat were in destaunce
> Þat dyed þurth dint of sward:
> Of Rouland & of Oliuer
> & of þe oþer dusseper,
> Of Alisander & Charlmeyn
> & Ector þe gret werrer
> & of Danys le fiz Oger,
> Of Arthour & of Gaweyn.
> As þis romaunce of Frenys wrouȝt,
> Þat mani lewed no knowe nouȝt,

---

[6] A. J. Bliss, 'Notes on the Auchinleck Manuscript', *Speculum* 26 (1951), 652–8 (p. 656). Following the catchword, Bliss estimates the loss of three quires vis-à-vis Brunner's 'complete' edition. However, as far as I've discovered, the catchword does not correspond to any line in Brunner's edition or its variants, troubling our impulse to supplement 'the rest' of *King Richard* with Brunner's edition.

[7] *Löwenherz*, ed. Brunner, pp. 11–14, 23. Brunner's edition is a composite of one late-fifteenth-century copy preserved in Cambridge, Gonville and Caius College, MS 175/96 – the longest extant copy, but far removed from Brunner's hypothetical ur-text – and a sixteenth-century printed edition.

[8] For a recent edition of the copy preserved in London, British Library, MS Additional 31042, see '*Richard Coeur de Lion*: An Edition from the London Thornton Manuscript', ed. M. C. Figueredo, unpublished PhD dissertation, University of York (York, 2010). Four other manuscript copies also have been edited diplomatically; see 'An Edition of the Middle English Romance: *Richard Coeur de Lion*', ed. P. Schellekens, unpublished PhD dissertation, University of Durham (Durham, 1989).

> In gest as-so we seyn;
> Þis lewed no can Freyns non;
> Among an hundred vnneþe on,
> In lede is nouȝt to leyn. (lines 4, 10–24)[9]

This relentless attention to 'Frenys' knights and the 'romaunce[s]' that render them at once dead and canonized evinces a preoccupation not with fairies or Saracens, but with things made mundane only by comparison: books and their relationship to identity. Here, the terms of that preoccupation expressly reflect the fourteenth-century milieu of Auchinleck's own production, bookended by, on one side, the late-thirteenth-century Barons War, as well as a coup that ended in 1327 with the regicide of Edward II, and, on the other, a budding crisis with France that would bloom into the Hundred Years War and require England to unite under Edward III.[10]

The intensifying opposition between England and France comes to complete, if seemingly simple, fruition in the Prologue to *King Richard*,[11] where, in these fifteen lines at its heart, Englishness is evoked as capacious in its absence, while Frenchness is carefully circumscribed. 'Frenys' is made to mean here both a language and a 'folk' – distinct from, or perhaps encompassing, Anglo-Norman,[12] and rejected by the surrounding (English)men whose 'lewedness' figures them as insurgent and bookishly demanding. Their linguistic inability to access French texts most immediately precipitates the call for new and better English ones, as the Prologue continues:

> Noþeles, wiþ gode chere
> Fele of hem wald yhere
> Noble gestes, ich vnderstond,
> Of douȝti kniȝtes of Inglond.
> Þerfore now ichil ȝou rede
> Of a king douhti of dede,
> King Richard, þe werrour best
> Þat men findeþ in ani gest. (lines 25–32)

---

[9] All citations of *King Richard* are from the transcription in Burnley-Wiggins. Lines 25 ff. are in rhymed couplets; see R. Purdie, *Anglicising Romance: Tail-Rhyme and Genre in Medieval English Literature*, Studies in Medieval Romance 9 (Cambridge, 2008), pp. 8–9, 93–125.

[10] M. Prestwich, *The Three Edwards: War and State in England, 1272–1377*, 2nd edn (London, 2003), pp. 146–218; and Turville-Petre, *England the Nation*, pp. 109–12.

[11] What the Prologue accomplishes has been variously interpreted as speaking to a monolingual audience; registering a shift in the hierarchy of languages; and presaging the literal and ideological beating the French take from the English within *King Richard*. See J. J. Thompson, 'The *Cursor Mundi*, the "Inglis tong", and "Romance"', in *Readings in Medieval English Romance*, ed. C. M. Meale (Cambridge, 1994), pp. 99–120 (pp. 114–15); Purdie, *Anglicising Romance*, pp. 100–1; and E. Salter, *Fourteenth-Century English Poetry* (Oxford, 1983), pp. 27–8.

[12] The project of differentiating 'English' from Norman identity was underway in England from the mid-twelfth century; see J. Gillingham, 'Foundations of a Disunited Kingdom', in *Uniting the Kingdom? The Making of British History*, ed. A. Grant and K. J. Stringer (New York, 1995), pp. 48–64 (p. 54).

The impulse to inscribe English romances and thus English heroes in response to the equally imprecise declaration that 'Romaunce make folk of Fraunce' troubles the carefully policed boundary between Englishness and Frenchness the Prologue appears to construct. French folk make romances, but their collective identity has been, the line implies, reciprocally made or formed by these romances – a realization that impels the following train of thought about French knights and English readers. This recognition ultimately compels the Prologue's 'I' to write a similarly generative English romance about an English knight – a romance that aims, crucially, to replace rather than reside among those old 'French' romances it fundamentally emulates.

It is precisely this productive tension between displacing Frenchness and instrumentalizing its cultural production that both contextualizes and characterizes *King Richard* in the Auchinleck manuscript. Even as we are told about the death of French romance knights 'thruth dint of sward', they are resurrected by name: Charlemagne, Roland, Oliver, the Twelve Peers, Arthur, Gawain, and the others. Instead of urging us to forget their stories, the Prologue prompts us to remember them through the uninterrupted list of their names that triggers the *inventio* of their textual bodies in our minds.[13] With these heroes and their stories freshly reconstituted there, we readers turn from the Prologue to the story of *King Richard*, where, as I will show, the old French texts and their heroes are translated – that is, moved from French to English and from the Matter of France to the Matter of England – in order to invent Richard I as a romance hero and to reimagine his late-twelfth-century reign as a site of England's own invention.

Behind Auchinleck's Richard I material stands not a single lost Anglo-Norman romance about Richard I, as has been long rumoured,[14] but a network of stories about Charlemagne and Roland that had been circulating widely in England – indeed, contained partially within Auchinleck itself – since at least the second quarter of the twelfth century, when the earliest extant copy of the Anglo-Norman *Chanson de Roland* was written down in Oxford, Bodleian Library, MS Digby 23.[15] I say 'Richard I material' because, in addition to Auchinleck's item 43 (*King*

---

[13] Auchinleck embodies this tension and trigger in its *ordinatio*; see Hanna, 'Reconsidering the Auchinleck Manuscript', pp. 97–8.

[14] L. H. Loomis, *Medieval Romance in England: A Study of the Sources and Analogues of the Non-Cyclic Metrical Romances* (New York, 1960), p. 147. The examples and line numbers Loomis cites to support her hypothesis, which has been widely repeated but neither bolstered nor challenged, refer to Brunner's edition. Cf. J. Finlayson, '*Richard, Coer de Lyon*: Romance, History or Something in Between?', *Studies in Philology* 87 (1990), 156–80 (p. 161).

[15] On the *Chanson de Roland* and the Oxford copy's date, see *Oxford Version*, ed. I. Short, in *La Chanson de Roland – The Song of Roland: The French Corpus*, ed. J. J. Duggan *et al.*, 3 vols. (Turnhout, 2005), I, I/11–338 (p. 19). However, Short dates the composition of the version of *Roland* transmitted in the Digby manuscript to the late eleventh century (I, 39–50). Auchinleck contains two Charlemagne romances: *Roland and Vernagu* and *Otuel a Kniȝt* (items 31, 32). The question of why Charlemagne romances survive in a manuscript seemingly bent on asserting English identity has been raised in T. H. Crofts and R. A. Rouse, 'Middle English Popular Romance and National Identity', in *A*

Richard), Auchinleck holds a copy of the so-called *Anonymous Short English Metrical Chronicle* (item 40), which contains over a hundred unique lines on the reign of Richard I (lines 2038–188).[16] The two texts are related but distinct: they share phrases, lines, and scenes at certain points,[17] but the *Short Chronicle*'s material is necessarily briefer, and, although it is as ostensibly anti-French as *King Richard*, it offers fundamentally different descriptions of and attention to certain events. Both texts begin their narratives about Richard with his preparations for crusade and setting sail for the East, and both texts exploit the contemporaneously documented discord between Richard and the French king Philip Augustus as the English and the French travel together.[18] Where *King Richard* defers Richard's arrival at Acre, detailing his conquering of Messina and Cyprus en route, and concludes with his strangely spectacular landing at and siege of Acre (during which he slings loaded beehives over the city walls), the *Short Chronicle* proceeds straight from England to the waters outside Acre. There, while aboard his ship, Richard constructs apparently grotesque windmills and a tower from which he launches the beehives.[19] The French and English armies then proceed to Jerusalem's outskirts, where a quarrel over whether Richard or Philip will take credit for the crusade's (limited) successes provokes Richard's precipitous return to England. Both *King Richard* and the *Short Chronicle* are copied in the hand of Scribe 1, who was responsible for over 70% of Auchinleck's contents and who was, at least, the manuscript's editor and, at most, something more proximate to an author – a hypothesis that the (by turns) unique, earliest, and expanded Richard I material he inscribes would seem to support.[20]

Companion to Medieval Popular Romance, ed. R. L. Radulescu and C. J. Rushton, Studies in Medieval Romance (Cambridge, 2009), 79–95 (pp. 86–95).

[16] All citations of the Auchinleck *Short Chronicle* are from the transcription in Burnley-Wiggins. Unique material from each of the text's seven manuscripts is appended to the standard edition: *An Anonymous Short English Metrical Chronicle*, ed. E. Zettl, EETS OS 196 (London, 1935), pp. 46–91.

[17] Zettl offers a side-by-side comparison of the bee episodes (*Anonymous Short English Metrical Chronicle*, ed. Zettl, p. xcvi).

[18] The standard biography of Richard I is J. Gillingham, *Richard I* (New Haven, 2002), pp. 222–53 (for Philip's propaganda campaign). On the events of the Third Crusade, see C. Tyerman, *God's War: A New History of the Crusades* (Cambridge MA, 2006), pp. 431–74; and Gillingham, *Richard I*, pp. 123–221.

[19] On the bees as English signifiers (in Brunner's edition) see G. Heng, *Empire of Magic: Medieval Romance and the Politics of Cultural Fantasy* (New York, 2003), pp. 101–2.

[20] See Hanna, 'Reconsidering the Auchinleck Manuscript', p. 93; Shonk, 'A Study', pp. 72–4; and R. Hanna, *London Literature, 1300–1380*, Cambridge Studies in Medieval Literature 57 (Cambridge, 2005), pp. 104–5. Zettl hypothesizes that material in the *Short Chronicle* was 'borrowed' from *King Richard* (*Anonymous Short English Metrical Chronicle*, ed. Zettl, pp. xcv–xcvii). Other theories have been advanced recently, including by M. Fisher, *Scribal Authorship and the Writing of History in Medieval England* (Columbus OH, 2012), pp. 158–67, who argues that Scribe 1 had multiple exemplars of *King Richard* to hand, but also engaged in significant 'scribal authorship'. Smithers suggests common (though not scribal) authorship for several of Auchinleck's texts, including *King Richard*, though he does not provide proof: *Kyng Alisaunder*, ed. G. V. Smithers, 2 vols., EETS

For besides Scribe 1's access to, facility with, and apparent interest in stories about Richard, there are dispersed across his work in *King Richard* and the *Short Chronicle* narrative and verbatim echoes of Charlemagne material that survives in what is perhaps an unexpected place: the Old Norse *Karlamagnús saga* (*Kms*), an extensive ten-branch prose cycle constructed and translated from Latin and Anglo-Norman *chansons de geste* about Charlemagne, Roland, and other 'kni3ts' named in Auchinleck's unique Prologue to *King Richard*.[21] The saga's transmission history is complex, but the saga-cycle began to be compiled at the behest of Hákon Hákonarson IV, who reigned over Norway from 1217 to 1263 and was an Anglophile, demanding copies of texts fashionable in Henry III's court.[22] The earliest extant textual evidence of *Kms* is a fragment dated to the second half of the thirteenth century that contains material associated with the Norse *Chanson de Roland*, used as the eighth branch of *Kms*. But much of what survives in *Kms* provides a 'prequel' to the *Chanson de Roland*, including, especially, an account of 'Charlemagne's Sin': the incestuous affair that produced Roland. The circulation in England of 'Charlemagne's Sin' and other Charlemagne stories now extant only in *Kms* is verified, first, by the Oxford *Roland*, which gestures obliquely but pointedly to the affair as if its reader already knows or could easily discover the lurid details,[23] and, subsequently, by the various vitae of Saint Giles, Charlemagne's confessor, that circulated, for instance, in copies of the *Legenda aurea*, which survives in hundreds of vernacular translations and over a thousand manuscripts, as well as in the *South English Legendary*, which survives in at least fifty-two copies.[24] Most likely, Anglo-Norman and a few Latin exemplars came to Norse and Icelandic scribes from Britain independently or in groups, and were then translated and assembled before

---

OS 227, 237 (1952, 1957), II, p. 41. How many, if any, lost Middle English copies precede Auchinleck's is an open question, but one whose answer does not alter my present argument.

[21] In some cases, *Kms* is the only witness to otherwise lost *chansons de geste*. It survives in five manuscripts (following recent work of Lacroix) and five fragments, though monastic library and antiquarian records indicate many more copies existed. See *La Saga de Charlemagne: Traduction française des dix branches de la Karlamagnús saga norroise*, trans. D. W. Lacroix (Paris, 2000), pp. 19–21; and S. Steingrímsson, 'Árni Magnússon', in *The Manuscripts of Iceland*, ed. G. Sigurðsson and V. Ólason (Reykjavik, 2004), pp. 85–99. Since Unger's first edition of *Kms*, several additional early fragments have been found. Nevertheless, the manuscript sigla Unger assigned remain standard. See *Karlamagnús saga ok Kappa Hans*, ed. C. R. Unger (Christiania, 1860), pp. xxxvi–xxxix.

[22] *La Saga de Charlemagne*, trans. Lacroix, p. 9. All citations of *Kms* will refer to Lacroix's edition, which is the most recent and contains all extant branches.

[23] *Chanson de Roland*, I, lines 2095–8, in *Oxford Version*, ed. Short, and Short's accompanying note (I, I/308).

[24] Jacobus de Voragine, *The Golden Legend*, trans. W. G. Ryan, 2 vols. (Princeton, 1993), I, pp. xiii–xviii; *The South English Legendary*, ed. C. D'Evelyn and A. J. Mill, 3 vols., EETS OS 235, 236, 244 (London, 1956–9), III, 1–3; and R. Hanna, 'Middle English Verse from a Bodleian Binding', *Bodleian Library Record* 17 (2002), 488–92. On Giles's long popularity in England, see E. Duffy, *The Stripping of the Altars: Traditional Religion in England 1400–1580* (New Haven, 1992), pp. 155, 178.

1300 into something resembling a unified prose cycle, which was continuously revised and recopied.[25]

The Charlemagne material in *Kms* related to Auchinleck's Richard material occurs in two places in the Norse saga: branch i, or the 'Life of Charlemagne', which comprises an abridged life and includes a brief account of Charlemagne's war against the Saxons; and branch v, or 'Guitaclin the Saxon', a fifty-five chapter narrative of the same war, derived from a different source from branch i.[26] That two distinct versions of Charlemagne's Saxon war survive in *Kms* attests to the suspected piecemeal compilation of *Kms* and, more particularly for my purposes here, to the Saxon war story's wider circulation in England before it reached – in multiple copies, iterations, and instances – the North. Indeed, the stories about the Saxon war in *Kms* probably have a Continental relative in the late-twelfth-century *Chanson des Saisnes* ascribed to Jean Bodel. However, the contents of *Kms* branch v, where Roland plays a significant role, much more closely reflect Auchinleck's Richard material than does Bodel's work.[27] Moreover, branch v preserves traces of a specifically English provenance, including an early reference to Roland's horn Oliphant and the Norse translator's fragmentary comments about his Anglo-Norman source.[28]

---

[25] See A. C. Rejhon, *Cân Rolant: The Medieval Welsh Version of the Song of Roland* (Berkeley, 1984), pp. 68–74. Rejhon's insightful work on the processes by which the Welsh Charlemagne materials were collected and managed offers a useful parallel for the production of *Kms*. See also P. Foote, *The Pseudo-Turpin Chronicle in Iceland: A Contribution to the Study of the Karlamagnús saga* (London, 1959), p. 47. For a detailed discussion of the *Kms* translation process and its cultural implications, see Sif Rikhardsdottir, *Medieval Translations and Cultural Discourse: The Movement of Texts in England, France and Scandinavia* (Cambridge, 2012), pp. 53–75.

[26] The Saxon war appears in branches i and v of the 'A' manuscript (Copenhagen, University Library, MS Arnamagnæan 180 c fol.), thought closest to the 'original' thirteenth-century compilation. When branch v appears in other manuscripts, it does so alone, suggesting later redactors aimed to eliminate repetition; see *La Saga de Charlemagne*, trans. Lacroix, pp. 520–1.

[27] Jehan Bodel, *La Chanson des Saisnes*, ed. A. Brasseur, 2 vols. (Geneva, 1989), I, ix–x. As Lacroix rightly stipulates, while the material in *Kms* and Bodel is proximate, no absolute proof of a common source exists (*La Saga de Charlemagne*, trans. Lacroix, p. 521). Leach argues that branch v derives from an account predating Bodel's; see H. G. Leach, *Angevin Britain and Scandanavia* (Cambridge MA, 1921), p. 248. In Bodel's version, the war occurs after Roncevaux, excluding Roland from the narrative.

[28] Although exemplars are sometimes referred to as occurring in 'Old French', it is widely accepted that internal manuscript evidence supports specifically Anglo-Norman sources behind most branches, esp. branches i and v. See P. Skårup, 'Contenu, Sources, Rédactions', in *Karlamagnús saga: Branches I, III, VII, et IX*, ed. K. Togeby et al. (Copenhagen, 1980), pp. 333–55 (p. 334), where he also summarizes scenarios for copying and translation; and *Karlamagnús saga: The Saga of Charlemagne and His Heroes*, trans. C. B. Hieatt, 3 vols. (Toronto, 1975), I, 23. For a list of probable sources, see E. F. Halvorsen, *The Norse Version of the Chanson de Roland*, Bibliotheca Arnamagnæana (Copenhagen, 1959), pp. 64–6. On branch v's date and provenance, see P. Aebischer, *Des annales carolingiennes à Doon de Mayence: nouveau recueil d'études sur l'épique française médiévale* (Geneva, 1975), p. 227; *Karlamagnús saga*, trans. Hieatt, III, 8–12; and *La Saga de Charlemagne*, trans. Lacroix, p. 522.

At the height of the mid-twentieth century's resurgent interest in Auchinleck, born largely of Laura Hibbard Loomis's work on the manuscript's production and contents, Ronald Walpole suggested that an Anglo-Norman exemplar lay behind Auchinleck's own Charlemagne material, including *Roland and Vernagu*, for which Scribe 1 is responsible.[29] The most immediate source for Scribe 1's material on the Saxon war might, too, be an Anglo-Norman one, especially since original translations and complicated interpolations from Anglo-Norman exemplars occur in his hand.[30] Yet the possibility that Scribe 1 had one or more Old Norse sources to hand has become increasingly convincing. The evidence includes close likenesses between episodes extant in *Kms* and Auchinleck's Richard I material. Additionally, Ralph Hanna posits that a scene unique to Scribe 1's *Sir Beues of Hamtoun* may have been adapted from a Scandinavian source.[31]

The episodes in which Charlemagne's words, actions, and ingenuity are most obviously translated into the character of Richard contribute to a dramatic setpiece in both *King Richard* and the *Short Chronicle*, and also in all later extant copies of *Richard Coer de Lion*: Richard's strange and spectacular siege of Acre.[32] In the *Short Chronicle*, Richard ascends the throne and immediately begins preparations for his journey to Acre, charging ships and then building on his own ship a castle with high towers from which the English can spy on their enemies (lines 2051–4). This scene closely recalls Charlemagne's preparations for war in branch v of *Kms*. There, Charlemagne and his men build a great ship, upon which they have mounted castles with towers, to cross the Rhine. They also fit the ship with a statue of Charlemagne, fashioned and dressed in his exact likeness, but made hollow so that a man could stand inside, shake the statue's beard and shout at the enemy as the ship sails towards the Saxon shore: an ingenious 'trick'.[33] The French place the statue on one of the ship's towers and turn it towards the Saxons. The man inside yells insults at the Saxons, who assail the statue with stones and other objects, but nothing harms what appears to them to be the real Charlemagne. Distressed and afraid, the Saxons discuss

[29] Loomis, 'The Auchinleck Manuscript'; and R. N. Walpole, 'The Source MS of Charlemagne and Roland and the Auchinleck Bookshop', *Modern Language Notes* 60 (1945), 22–6 (p. 23).

[30] Fisher, *Scribal Authorship*, pp. 153–4.

[31] Hanna, *London Literature*, pp. 135, 147 n. 45. On Northern affiliations for the Auchinleck *Sir Tristrem*, see also A. McIntosh, 'Is *Sir Tristrem* an English or a Scottish Poem?', in *In Other Words: Transcultural Studies in Philology, Translation, and Lexicology Presented to Hans Heinrich Meier on the Occasion of His Sixty-Fifth Birthday*, ed. J. Mackenzie and R. Todd (Dordrecht, 1989), pp. 85–95; and A. Higgins's chapter in this volume.

[32] That the popularity of this scene in some (not necessarily written) forms predates Auchinleck is suggested by uncaptioned pen sketches associated with at least two versions of it in Oxford, Christ Church, MS 92, a book made for the young Edward III between 1325 and 1327. Hanna discovered and identified the sketches (*London Literature*, pp. 116–23).

[33] *La Saga de Charlemagne*, trans. Lacroix, p. 578: 'Autre astuce de fabrication'.

the situation among themselves and then cry out that this 'is no man, but a devil whom weapons will not bite'.[34]

After Richard similarly constructs his castle aboard ship, fitting it with a stone-throwing windmill, the *Short Chronicle* specifies how the view from this castle affords Richard the opportunity to 'seye in priuete / What Sarraȝines dede in þe cite' (lines 2055–6). Richard and his men then 'make a queynter þing, / Windemilles in schippes houend on water', that is a 'Wel griseliche þing ariȝt to sen' (lines 2008–9, 2114). When

> Þe Sarraȝins seye þat mervaile,
> Þai no durst abide to ȝif batayle.
> Þai seyden hem ichon among,
> 'Lordinges, to dyen it wer strong,
> For þis is þe deuel of helle
> Þat wil ous euerichon aquelle'. (lines 2115–20)

Like Charlemagne, Richard's enemies perceive him as 'no man, but a devil' because of this theatrical and psychological warfare. And, similar to shifts in perspective found in *Kms*, readers in Auchinleck are first positioned with Richard aboard ship, and then are repositioned, suddenly, with the Saracens behind Acre's walls. At the correlating moment in *King Richard*, Richard sets up a 'gin' – that is, a similarly ingenious contraption called a 'Robinett' – 'Þat cast into Acres hard stones' (lines 1011–14), eliciting verbal protests from its victims similar to the Saxons' distress in the *Short Chronicle*. When he slings loaded beehives over the city walls in the summer heat, the Saracens declare, in an echo of the Saxons' lament about Charlemagne's perplexing imperviousness, 'King Richard is ful fel, / When his fleyȝen bite so wel' (lines 1009–10).

In the least fantastic but most compelling moment of correspondence among the texts, while on his way to Acre in *King Richard*, Richard rallies his men against the emperor of Cyprus by vowing upon Saint Denis ('bi seyn Denis' [lines 370–1]) that the English will be victorious. Charlemagne swears an almost identical oath in branch v of *Kms* ('par Saint-Denis en France') that the French will conquer Saxony.[35] In *chansons de geste* and romances, Charlemagne swears by Saint Denis almost as frequently as he tugs his beard in worry, and Auchinleck's unique copy of *Otuel a Kniȝt* (item 32) introduces Charlemagne as 'born in seint Denys / Nouȝt bote a litel fram Parys' (lines 11–12).[36] In *King Richard*, when Richard (in Charlemagne's image) prays to Saint Denis to ensure English victory, the moment quietly embodies the

---

[34] *La Saga de Charlemagne*, trans. Lacroix, pp. 577–8: 'Les païens dirent alors: "Ce n'est pas un homme, mais un diable sur lequel les armes ne mordent pas"'.

[35] *La Saga de Charlemagne*, trans. Lacroix, p. 584. These textual associations between Richard and Charlemagne arguably enact an association that the historical Richard himself had in mind. See J. J. Duggan, 'La France des Plantagenêts dans les versions rimées de la *Chanson de Roland*', in *Les Chansons de geste: Actes du XVIe Congrès International de la Société Rencesvals, pour l'étude des épopées romanes, Granada, 21–25 juillet 2003*, ed. C. Alvar and J. Paredes (Granada, 2005), 205–14.

[36] All citations of *Otuel a Kniȝt* are from the transcription in Burnley-Wiggins.

processes of *inventio* and *translatio* behind Richard's own romance invention. Here the English king invokes the French saint to spur the English army, and the moment simultaneously evokes for the romance's reader both the spectre of Charlemagne and his inscription in Auchinleck.

The success of these textual inventions and translations depends upon a readership for Auchinleck different from the type we have tended to imagine, and distinct from the 'lewed' Englishman drawn in the Prologue to *King Richard*.[37] Elsewhere, in fact, Auchinleck itself projects an alternate reception: a reader who resembles Scribe 1 in his physical proximity to books and linguistic access to a wide range of stories.[38] The manuscript's *Short Chronicle* contains a unique set of lines in which Lancelot builds Nottingham Castle with underground caves and chambers, where he and Guinevere can steal away from Arthur. As Helen Cooper explains, this strange anecdote expressly recalls the recent, much-spoken-of events of 1330, when Edward III's mother Isabella of France and her lover Roger Mortimer barricaded themselves in Nottingham Castle against Edward and his men. In addition to suggesting that Scribe 1's interests are topical as well as historical and literary, these implicit associations between Isabella and Guinevere, Mortimer and Lancelot, and Edward and Arthur presume a particular kind of reader since, according to Cooper, Auchinleck's reference to the affair between Guinevere and Lancelot is the first trace of this story in English and a reader's knowledge of it is assumed.[39]

Scribe 1's complex textual inventions of Richard and Edward pointedly assert that French romance can 'make', at least partially, the folk of England, for, instead of excising the French canon, Auchinleck reinvents it as England's rightful inheritance and reinvests that inheritance in its own English corpus. We might read this tactic as preservative and practical rather than abrupt and incursive, for the invention, translation and reinvention of Frenchness that occurs across the Richard material – and, indeed, at all levels of the manuscript's production – constructively harnesses the contemporary cultural milieu into which Auchinleck is deployed. By the early fourteenth century, French stories, broadly construed, and the books that contained them had long been implicitly constitutive of England's identity. But the real and present fourteenth-century difficulty of what to do when your own cultural identity cannot be cleanly distinguished from that of your (renewed) enemy – when you read and write and tell the same stories about the past – resides everywhere in Auchinleck. To this problem, the manuscript proposes at least one possible working solution: a clearly planted flag in the cultural field.

Auchinleck's proposition that the old French canon and England's collective identity are inextricable rather than opposed – an idea implicitly rendered in

---

[37] Turville-Petre, *England the Nation*, p. 109; however, cf. Hanna, *London Literature*, pp. 111–16.

[38] A picture of precisely such an audience emerges from recent scholarship. See L. Olson, 'Romancing the Book: Manuscripts for "Euerich Inglische"', in K. Kerby-Fulton, M. Hilmo, and L. Olson, *Opening Up Middle English Manuscripts* (Ithaca NY, 2012), pp. 95–151 (pp. 97–106); and A. Bahr, *Fragments and Assemblages: Forming Compilations of Medieval London* (Chicago, 2013), p. 135.

[39] Cooper, 'Lancelot', pp. 95–8.

Richard's textual form – is in fact codified in *King Richard* when Richard, made partly of Charlemagne's textual body, cries out that England's enemies have 'despised our naciouns' (line 264), a declaration that at once unites his men around him and conjures a unified English body. This is one of the earliest usages, perhaps even the earliest usage, of 'nacioun' in its modern sense,[40] and significantly – in what may be the text's most potent instrumentalization of Frenchness – it is the traitorous French alliance with the Greeks or 'Griffons' of Messina that provokes England's articulation as a nation here. Having declared it as such, Richard and his men defeat their Christian enemies and proceed to Acre, where they are, likewise, stunningly victorious.

The Third Crusade was an enterprise to which most of Auchinleck's early-fourteenth-century readers would have been related through ancestral participation, and the siege of Acre, especially, would have made a good and frequently told war story.[41] For fourteenth-century England, which was first on the edge of and then fully immersed in war with France (with the Barons War still within living memory), *King Richard*'s rescription of England's victories at Messina, Cyprus, and Acre – arguably the few clear successes of the Third Crusade – would have offered a powerful *exemplum* of an England not under the thumb of France culturally or martially,[42] but rather unified under its king. Auchinleck's *King Richard*, then, intervenes not only in fourteenth-century England's extant literary canon, but also – as a historically retrospective romance – in the account(s) of England's past contained in both the textual record and the collective memory, allowing its readers to reimagine the present moment by presenting them with an invented, and expediently positive, precedent. Since Brunner's early-twentieth-century edition of *Richard Coer de Lion*, we have read the Auchinleck *King Richard* mainly for its fairies and cannibals, and we have been sorely disappointed by an imperfect ending that we imagine evinces their loss. The copy's so-called 'imperfect' ending coincides with England's victory at Acre and concludes with the lines:

> Þat day so Richard sped þer
> Þat he was holden conquerer,
> For better he sped þat day ar none
> Þan þe oþer in seuen 3er hadde done. (lines 1043–6)

Perhaps, like us, this is as far as *King Richard*'s contemporary reader would have been able to read, but, by this point, he had gained a nation.

---

[40] The *OED* lists this as the earliest attested usage, c. 1330, of *nation*: '1 (a): a large aggregate of communities and individuals united by factors such as common descent, language, culture, history, or occupation of the same territory, so as to form a distinct people. Now also: such a people forming a political state; a political state. (In early usage also in *pl.*: a country.)'

[41] N. Paul, *To Follow in Their Footsteps: The Crusades and Family Memory in the High Middle Ages* (Ithaca NY, 2012), pp. 11–12; and C. Tyerman, *England and the Crusades, 1095–1588* (Chicago, 1988), pp. 65–70.

[42] Turville-Petre, *England the Nation*, pp. 8–9.

CHAPTER NINE

Auchinleck and Chaucer

Helen Phillips

T HIS paper is not about whether Chaucer knew the Auchinleck manuscript.[1] It asks what looking from Auchinleck to Chaucer might reveal about Chaucer, and perhaps about Auchinleck.

Compilation analogies

Chaucer's *Canterbury Tales* is among other things a manuscript anthology. For both its frame story, with exchanges between pilgrim narrators and listeners, and its sequencing of items, his inspirations surely included manuscript compilation as much as real-life pilgrims' storytelling and chatting or literary tale-collections. The Auchinleck manuscript (Edinburgh, NLS, MS Advocates 19. 2. 1), and also London, British Library, MS Harley 2253, prefigure Chaucer's *Tales* in several aspects of their compilation.[2] Two such aspects become in Chaucer's hands highly creative. One is their use of narrator/listener passages on the borders of items: headlinks and endlinks containing formulaic appeals, 'Listeth lordes … And I wol telle' (VII 712–13), with variants, including (in Auchinleck) copious prayers. In Auchinleck, these formulae appear fairly regularly between items (where openings or endings survive), contributing a sense, albeit limited, of unity of tone to junctures between texts. The 'I' who speaks and the 'ye' who are asked to listen are never individualized, contributing further regularity to these passages. Between his own anthology's items, Chaucer creates a dramatized framework of individualized narrators and listeners. Consequently, the narrator/listener relationship becomes two-way and introduces responses from the listeners. When combative, such responses can intensify contrastive sequencing of tales.

---

[1] Chaucer's direct knowledge of the Auchinleck manuscript has been a matter of speculation ever since L. H. Loomis proposed that Chaucer did know it and its romance contents ('Chaucer and the Auchinleck MS: "Thopas" and Guy of Warwick"', in *Essays and Studies in Honor of Carleton Brown* [New York, 1940], pp. 111–28). For a recent study framed in this manner, see C. Cannon, "Chaucer and the Auchinleck Manuscript Revisited," *Chaucer Review* 46 (2011), 131– 46.

[2] On comparisons with other story collections and other aspects of manuscript compilation and construction, see M. F. Vaughan, 'Chaucer's *Canterbury Tales* and the Auchinleck MS: Analogous Collections?', *Archiv* 242 (2005), 259–74.

A second compilatorial element Chaucer's *Tales* shares with Auchinleck and Harley is subtle juxtapositioning, which offers readers the option of perceiving parallels and contrasts between items. This differs from the obvious thematic or generic grouping basic to the Vernon manuscript's design and frequent in Auchinleck: for example, two saints' lives or three Guy of Warwick romances together; *On þe Seuen Dedly Sinnes* with *The Pater Noster Vndo on Englissch*; or eschatological subjects in items 'xi' and 'xii'. Carter Revard shows 'oppositional thematics and metanarratives' informing subtle sequencing in Harley; Susanna Fein finds its compiler offering audiences diptych-like or longer combinations, whose effect is 'a progressive entertainment', actual or imagined.[3] The 'act of compilation builds meaning without making an authoritative comment', a description that captures exactly a technique central to Chaucer's distinctive management of structures and his self-presentation as author.[4]

Though Auchinleck's losses limit investigations, booklets 9 and 10 provide examples of such sequencing, offering interesting implicit links to any reader who chooses to pick them up. Thus *Horn Childe and Maiden Rimnild*, which starts by promising to teach its listeners 'Stories … / Of our elders þat were / Whilom in þis lond' (lines 4–6), complements *The Anonymous Short English Metrical Chronicle*. This Auchinleck tail-rhyme *Horn* contains, according to Maldwyn Mills, 'its own, highly distinctive' versions of history, a vision of insular history.[5] Rosalind Field further characterizes it as derived 'more from Insular writing than Insular history', a significant testimony to the place of literary culture in patriotic English historical consciousness that Auchinleck's famous headlinks about the 'use of English' also convey.[6] Additionally, demonstrations of women's faithfulness and man/woman devotion link two romances and a Breton lay – *Horn Childe and Maiden Rimnild*, *Sir Tristrem*, *Sir Orfeo* – with the *Alphabetical Praise of Women*. The comparison in Auchinleck's *Horn* of its lovers' devotion to that of Tristan and Iseult (lines 310–11) strengthens this implicit thread.

Associating praise for women with Mary, the *Alphabetical Praise* links back to earlier items in praise of Mary and female saints' lives. The *Short Chronicle* includes praise of Edward I as a chivalric king whose ideal was a crusade (never realized) and the Auchinleck text expands the account of Richard I's crusading, drawing on the romance *King Richard*. The *Short Chronicle* thus similarly connects widely: with crusades material prominent throughout Auchinleck, in *Roland and Vernagu*, *Otuel a Kniȝt*, *The King of Tars*, *King Richard*, and *Horn*'s fighting with Saracens.

---

[3] C. Revard, 'Oppositional Thematics and Metanarratives in MS Harley 2253, Quires 1–6', in *Essays in Manuscript Geography: Vernacular Manuscripts of the English West Midlands from the Conquest to the Sixteenth Century*, ed. W. Scase, Medieval Texts and Cultures of Northern Europe 10 (Turnhout, 2007), pp. 95–112; and S. Fein, 'Compilation and Purpose in MS Harley 2253', ibid., pp. 67–95 (esp. p. 71).

[4] Fein, 'Compilation and Purpose', p. 78.

[5] *Horn Childe and Maiden Rimnild*, ed. M. Mills, Middle English Texts 20 (Heidelberg, 1988), p. 11.

[6] R. Field, 'Romance as History, History as Romance', in *Romance in Medieval England*, ed. M. Mills, J. Fellows, and C. M. Meale (Cambridge, 1991), pp. 163–74 (p. 171).

Chaucer's own 'oppositional thematics and metanarratives' are ubiquitous, running across tales of varied subject and genre. The *Wife of Bath's* and *Friar's Tales* share encounters with shape-shifters reproving arrogant thugs; the *Wife's*, *Friar's*, and *Summoner's Tales* celebrate lower-class people standing up to those who abuse power. The *Second Nun's* and *Canon's Yeoman's Tales* present spiritual versus worldly gold and transformation. The fact that Chaucer's reader can perceive simultaneous forces of rapprochement and opposition, parallels and disparities, between items puts a restless, stimulating experience of inquiry, intellectual and aesthetic, at the heart of the *Canterbury Tales*'s design, quite other than the overt organization of human diversity within a large work of art constructed by Dante or Boccaccio. Like many Chaucerian strategies, it evades overt authorial and narratorial direction or monologism. Juxtaposition is the presiding structural principle of the *Book of the Duchess*, the *House of Fame*, and the *Parliament of Fowls*, their major vehicle for generation of meaning. Like the *Canterbury Tales*, these texts become for modern readers less disconcertingly abrupt, disparate, and resistant to reading if their designs are read in the light of the juxtapositions in many manuscript miscellanies: of genres, sources, cultural backgrounds, and moods. Many contain within their boards sacred and secular, humour and education – *mélanges* of complaint, lyric, debate, treatise, next-world journey, classical tale, courtly fancy, allegories – whether (apparently) fortuitously assembled together or subtly sequenced as often in Auchinleck and Harley.

That sophisticated aesthetic offered to the beholder exemplifies a medieval principle of design and exposition familiar in visual art.[7] Arnold Hauser half a century ago identified juxtaposition as central to Gothic aesthetics. It appears also, of course, in Thomist thesis and antithesis, and Revard, invoking an earlier philosopher, talks of Harley's *sic et non* juxtaposition.[8] Hauser, reflecting his period's perception of the medieval and his own Marxist analysis, derived it from collective, rather than individual, perceptions of art production in the Middle Ages. One could, however, add that some significant juxtapositional structures are highly individual, like Langland's progressive, parallel realizations of the Dowel triad, and that Chaucer's retreat from authorial ownership, not least by such designs which defer to the reader's perceptions of design and meaning, may in part reflect a career in a world of patronage and prince-pleasing. Hauser adds, using words which, like Fein's above, aptly describe Chaucer's dream poetry and the *Canterbury Tales*: 'The beholder is, as it were, led through the stages and subtleties of a journey which is … not a one-sided, unified representation, dominated by a single view'.[9] Reading the last sections of the *Tales* illustrates that. The penultimate tale, the Manciple's, foregrounds a multifaceted exploration of language that runs implicitly through all the tales. Its end, asking for restraint of all speech except about God (IX 329–31),

---

[7] H. Phillips, '*The Book of the Duchess*: Structure and Consolation', *Chaucer Review* 16 (1981), 107–18.

[8] A. Hauser, *The Sociology of Art*, trans. K. J. Northcott (Chicago, 1982); and Revard, 'Oppositional Thematics', p. 96.

[9] Hauser, *The Sociology of Art*, p. 3.

prefigures the profound but mind-dizzying rejection of fiction by the *Parson's Tale* and the rejection of all worldly literature by the *Retraction*.[10]

Fictional interruption – by the Knight of the Monk, the Host of *Sir Thopas*, and perhaps (or perhaps not) the Franklin of the Squire – is another device by which Chaucer's management of his concatenation of items seems to build creatively on the contemporary experience of reading in manuscripts: familiarity with lost endings; fragments, variants, and centos; missing leaves; lacunae from exemplars (such as those evident ironically now in some of Chaucer's own compositions: in the *Romaunt of the Rose* copied into Glasgow, University Library, MS V. 3. 7; and the *Book of the Duchess* in Oxford, Bodleian Library, MSS Fairfax 16, Tanner 346, and Bodley 638).

Fictional interruption, a dynamic way of admitting chance and incompleteness into the artistic canvas, and of demonstrating the ease with which control over design can be deposed, is also a device that enacts a dismissal of whatever offends a receiver of an utterance. The *Monk's Tale* and *Sir Thopas* empty princes and chivalry of glory, but their recital plus their interruption and their curtailment enact both a potential subversion and its disarming (we should not assume that all effects with possible roots or parallels in manuscript structures will be calming ones, remote from the world of power, deference, and political prudence). Fictional interruption creates a space for expression of disapproval *within* Chaucer's work. It performs self-censorship, but only after a certain line of writing has been opened up, allowing the multiplicity, disparities, and relativistic tendencies of his collection to happen. Interruption can be re-energizing and it facilitates redirection without overt authorial control. It avoids length once a mode has been sufficiently displayed. It avoids conclusion.

Some other interruptions do not produce incomplete items: the Miller hijacking the Host's hierarchical plan for the sequencing, the Host silencing the Parson, the Summoner interrupting the Friar, and the Friar attempting to silence the Wife (explicitly denounced by the Summoner as an attempt to 'entremette' [interpose] his own view and 'lette oure disport' [hinder the entertainment] [III 834, 839]). They do coincide with moments where Chaucer introduces into the textual world of his anthology voices that might be considered controversial, calling for suppression: a peasant demanding to speak, a suspected Lollard proposing to 'prechen' or gloss the gospel (II 1177), an exposure of clerical financial abuses, a woman assuming the right to debate authorities.

In contrast, Auchinleck's miscellany is only a miscellany within uncontested outlooks. It seems to issue from the viewpoint of Parson and Knight. On the surface at least, its political world seems establishment in outlook and relatively consistent: chivalry, English history through kings and baronial dynasties, crusading, faith-fulness, devotion to Mary and mainly female saints, and clear pastoral teaching, stimulated by frequently reinforced apprehension about sin, penitence, and the next world. The narrator/listener formula so regularly interposed here adopts one

---

[10] All references to Chaucer are from *The Riverside Chaucer*. Citations from the *Canterbury Tales* are given by fragment and line number.

voice, and the listeners are constructed as those who will be told and taught things he considers they need to know. Robert Mannyng's preface to *Handlyng Synne* explains the need to provide good English texts to discourage uneducated laypeople from being attracted to highly popular other 'talys' and 'rymys', 'In gamys and festys & at þe ale' (lines 43–52), which often offer wanton material that can lead to folly, bad behaviour, and deadly sin.[11] Here and in Auchinleck, calls for English literature might also have been a mission to provide suitable English literature, to impose *this* kind of vision of English writings and not *that*: the unpoliced literary culture of pub and festival. Far from there being a shortage of literature for those who knew no French and Latin, there was, from some viewpoints, too much. Does Auchinleck enshrine a Golden Treasury anthology or something like an approved syllabus?

Analogies with many manuscripts' discordant juxtapositions and the possibilities of lacunae, suspensions, and inclusions of unconnected items remind us that not all medieval aesthetic experiences or large-scale literary volumes point towards a Dantesque ideal of unified and unifying vision. Manuscripts, their construction, and their frequent containment of diverse or incomplete elements make it possible, Míċeál Vaughan suggests, to think of the *Tales* as a frame from which parts could be taken at will, indeed perhaps being collated with a conscious refraining from a single imposed unity or conclusion.[12] Yet we could also see Chaucer creating a daring miscellany within which contradictory impulses and multiple human levels of discourse can eternally confront and illuminate each other, a single book animated unceasingly by cross-currents and internal debates of one kind of text with another. The *Retraction* taken together with its Hengwrt and Ellesmere rubrics directs the reader's attention back to this/the 'book' created by a 'makere' who is also compiler, but it then adopts again the precautionary device, used first after the Miller's interruption, of inviting displeased listeners and readers to adjudicate what should and should not have been included (X 1081–91). God's own judgement is assumed, with humility and prayer, to be against all literature on worldly subjects.

In a world where reading experience, in manuscripts, meant familiarity with chance, incompleteness, and unlooked for juxtapositions, in contrast to the modern book, to elevate interruption to a fictional device suggests Chaucer's sense that significance could hang from it. Critics have found signification in it. Barry Windeatt sees Chaucer's interruptions as constructing a central and characteristic aesthetic where 'plans and patterns are recurrently not allowed to pursue their course to the conclusion'.[13] Richard Pearson's study of interruption in Chaucer and in William Morris's *Kelmscott Chaucer* draws on both ideological and psychological approaches to interruption. Invoking business psychology – where interruption has been seen positively, as stimulating productivity and energy, making multitasking and sifting relevant information easier – he also associates interruption with

---

[11] *Robert of Brunne's Handlyng Synne*, ed. F. J. Furnivall, 2 vols., EETS OS 119, 123 (London, 1901, 1903), I, 2–3.

[12] Vaughan, 'The *Canterbury Tales*', pp. 265–6.

[13] B. Windeatt, 'Literary Structures in Chaucer', in *The Cambridge Companion to Chaucer*, ed. P. Boitani and J. Mann (Cambridge, 2003), pp. 214–32 (p. 226).

national or historical cultural discontinuity and psychological crises of discontinuity.[14] Pearson sees Morris's book design, especially his elaborate woodblock borders, as interrupting Chaucer, in the reader's experience, in the interests of an ideological desire to distance the medieval text from the humanity-destroying pressures of capitalist production. Morris's socialist vision of separate worlds, present and past, from which to attack Victorian capitalism, imposed an imprisoning, static aesthetic on the *Canterbury Tales*.[15] The opposite, of course, holds for Chaucer's own use of juxtapositional design and interruption, since these appeal to the reader's mind, moving dynamically with an endless creative restlessness between items, to articulate both design and significance: an eternal *mouvance*.

'Herkeneþ lordinges'

Chaucer's 'Listeth, lordes in good entent' mimics the narrator/listener formulaic lexicon that, with its variants ('Alle herkneþ to me nou', 'Leste3, and 3e sschollen here, iwis', etc.) is often labeled 'minstrel'. I shall use instead '*listeth* formula' for shorthand because several different effects are embedded in it: minstrel performance, preacher-like teaching, prayer, and also mnemonic aid signalling each new subsection, for example, during the *Pater Noster*. Using 'I', 'ye', and, often in Auchinleck, 'we', a merging of narrator and audience found particularly there in connection with sin and prayer, the formula constructs its listeners anonymously, generically, and inclusively: as 'alle', 'bope eld & 3ing', 'men and wimmen'. Even 'lordes' or 'lordynges' as a term of address was a polite convention not denoting specifically lordly class personages present in the room (though it may be a form of address implying a lower-class speaker, occasionally ingratiating).[16] The relatively regular appearance of *listeth* formulae in Auchinleck raises its own critical questions. Were these expressions of engagement between narrator and listeners ready-mades, provided for the use of reciters as blueprints for how to introduce and sign off their text in performance? Or were they for readers? Fein observes that such 'minstrel' openings, forming 'a continuous and conscious feature' of Harley, make 'many texts *look* like they are being orally delivered'.[17] Even commoner in Auchinleck, with its plethora of tail-rhyme items (and *listeth* formulae appear statistically more often in tail rhyme than in other metres), do they indicate actual oral performance as the norm, with the written version functioning as transcriptions, or aides-mémoires? Whereas Fein suggests an artistry of seeming orality – which is neither simply oral nor written, providing a reader with pleasurable mental imagination of a performance – running through the book, Karl Reichl's analysis of *listeth* formulae leads him to assert that popular romances certainly, and maybe others, 'should and can'

---

[14] R. Pearson, 'William Morris Interrupted Interrupting Chaucer', in *Chaucer's Poetry: Words, Authority and Ethics*, ed. C. Carney and F. M. McCormack (Dublin, 2013), pp. 158–84.

[15] Ibid. p. 170.

[16] *MED*, s.v. *lord*, 13.

[17] Fein, 'Compilation and Purpose', p. 89 n. 55.

be appreciated as orally performed narratives, though by the late Middle Ages there may have been 'an intensive interaction' with provision for an increasingly literate public.[18] The 1830s saw a similar framing rhetoric for introducing stories. Dickens's story-collection *Sketches by Boz* uses a sliding, multivalent, unstable 'we' and 'us'. Both periods saw literature widening out to audiences with patchy literacy. Fourteenth-century English provision of quality literature and didactic material, like the 1830s access to cheaper print and journalism, takes written narratives to audiences more used to orality.

The conundrums of the heritage of *listeth* formulae emerge particularly sharply with the prayers that are so often an element in them in Auchinleck. When opening and closing items, Auchinleck authors use prayer (spoken by a narrator's voice and involving his listeners) more often and more strikingly than the so-called minstrel requests for audience attention. The narrative voice's call to 'harken' can become a call for spiritual receptiveness, not just listening: for example, 'Let hit in 30ure hertes be leid … And 3e sscholle here hit ytold' (*Seuen Dedly Sinnes*, lines 30, 32). Prayer was a fairly routine sign-off for medieval texts and for scribal stints of copying. Several Auchinleck initial and final prayers, however, contribute intensity to the *listeth* formula. Though some may not be original to the Auchinleck compiler or its scribes, and neither narrator nor listeners are individualized, the wording sometimes voices concern for its hearers: 'Ich beseche 30u alle þat han yherd', begins the longish prayer-conclusion to the *Life of St Mary Magdalene*, which also asks them to pray for him who translated for them the text from Latin, because 'alle men Latin no conne nou3t' (lines 666, 670). The melding here of prayer with other familiar tropes of the *listeth* formula – the audience as listeners ('3ou all þat han yherd') and as a generalized totality of humanity ('alle' repeated) – is also united with the Auchinleck agenda of providing English texts for English speakers. The pastoral tone sounds warmly engaged, too, at the end of *Floris and Blauncheflur*: 'bote' came after 'bale' for the hero and heroine; may our Lord grant it to us 'And ich schal helpe 30u þerto' (line 862). Where are this speaker and such help positioned? Is his forthcoming spiritual help going to be extratextual or disseminated further on during Auchinleck's anthology? The next item, *The Sayings of the Four Philosophers*, a composite of well-known 'complaint of the times' rhymes, has appended to it a comparatively lengthy prayer, a mini-sermon that urges its listeners to act with 'love', the word warmly reiterated, as the chief way 'þe deuel to shende' (line 95). In contrast, for all their psychological acuteness and occasional grand beauty, the prayers, brief or longer, on the borders of Chaucer's tales, even from clerics, show no such fervent, paternal affection for the audience (though those of the two female religious reach great heights in address to Mary). Several Auchinleck prayers draw out spiritual or didactic themes from the item they begin or end, for example, in the headlinks to *Speculum Gy de Warewyke* and *Hou Our Leuedi Saute Was Ferst Founde*, where Mary is drawn in as one of the listeners to whom the piece will be

---

[18] K. Reichl, 'Orality and Performance', in *A Companion to Medieval Popular Romance*, ed. R. L. Radulescu and C. J. Rushton, Studies in Medieval Romance (Cambridge, 2009), pp. 132–49 (esp. p. 149).

told by the narrator, or with the Auchinleck *Short Chronicle* closing with a prayer for Edward III.

Chaucer's Marian prayer-prologues are more powerful and complex headlink prayers with learned intertextuality. Yet, because prayer was a regular sign-off for a text, the briefer prayers that end most tales are minor critical puzzles. Where are they on a scale from verbal formulae devoid of illocutionary force – that is, perfunctory – to words that are to be read as issuing sincerely from the individual pilgrim narrator's subjectivity? In fact, Chaucer takes some minimal care to make many even short ones seem worded for the occasion: the Knight's one-liner specifies 'God save al this faire compaignye' (I 3108), and the Man of Law's prayer introduces themes of governance and 'joye after wo' reminiscent of his tale (II 1160–2).

Whereas prayer in Auchinleck's headlinks and endlinks is regularly entangled in the other *listeth* formulae, like requesting an audience to harken, Chaucer keeps the prayer on the borders of his tales mostly discrete, as prayer. Some sound briskly routine: 'This tale is doon, and God save al the rowte' (I 3854). Others foreground the issue of sincerity. Thus the speech-act force of a concluding prayer blessing the listeners disappears when the narrator simultaneously curses one of them, 'God save yow alle, save this cursed Frere!' (III 1707), or the Reeve combines prayer and smug triumph in revenge (I 4322–4), or the Friar, whose lengthy prayer begins (unusually for Chaucer, but like many in Auchinleck) with a formulaic address, 'Lordynges …':

> Waketh and preyeth Jhesu for his grace
> So kepe us fro the temptour Sathanas.
> Herketh this word! (III 1645, 1654–6)

And ends:

> And prayeth that thise somonours hem repente
> Of hir mysdedes, er that the feend hem hente. (III 1663–4)

Prayers in both these manuscript anthologies are often hinges, concluding an item but also addressing the audience within a link and consequently not completely belonging to the discourse of either item or link. They are vehicles for some of the most discourse-jolting moments in Chaucer: the Wife's prayer for unsubmissive husbands' early deaths (III 1261–4), the Shipman's prayer for plenty of sex, lifelong 'taillynge' (VII 434), and the Pardoner's unsettling ricocheting between a concluding prayer that names Christ's true pardon (VI 916–18) and the immediately following sales pitch for false pardons to the Host. Chaucer's concluding prayers join with another inherited concluding trope – the declaring of a message deduced from the item – and Chaucer uses both, sometimes together, to offer readers multiple, competing, or distracting ways of interpreting some tales (the *Clerk's, Nun's Priest's, Wife's,* and *Canon's Yeoman's Tales*), not to speak of the sometimes bizarrely idiosyncratic readings voiced by pilgrims during the ensuing link.

The critical question of where (at those junctures closing the *Pardoner's Tale*) fictional discourse ends – shifting into prayer as a sincere speech act, and out again – mimics the shifting between false and true pardons. The slide within the

Pardoner's Prologue, his *Tale*, and the endlink passages, from fiction to prayer, and from falsehood to sincerity, curiously also raises, *in malo* and *in micro*, questions presented at the end of Chaucer's manuscript anthology: between the final point of the fiction, of the whole 'book of The Tales of Caunterbury', and prayer in the *Retraction*. The *Retraction* represents an elaborately significant development of the routine sign-off of compositions and scribal stints with prayer, and also of the difficulties of deciding how to relate the discourse of prayer, and a turn to prayer, with the many discourses of human literary artistry.

Chaucer mismetring tail rhyme

Chaucer's targeting of tail rhyme might have been for its being old-fashioned or even provincial in some way, but the clearest attack is on the English metrical traditions it represented: a wrong direction for modern(ist), late-fourteenth-century English narrative metre. While the *Sir Thopas* parody inheres quite a lot in phrases, even more features are designed to mangle its metre. Tail rhyme, four-stress couplet rhyme, and alliterative verse, the established narrative metres of Chaucer's day (and continuing to flourish after), use stress rhythm. To Chaucer is due, of course, a virtuoso achievement in a refined and flexible syllabic metre, especially iambic pentameter. Tail-rhyme stanzas, like those abounding in Auchinleck, are not clumsy. Chaucer makes them sound clumsy.

Frequent fillers from the start ('in good entent', 'verayment', etc.) create an impression of incompetent laboriousness in metre and rhyme. Overusing rhyme words which were subject to variable stress (French dissyllabic loans and English words in *-ing*) makes the reader repeatedly feel forced to devote attention to where to put the stress. Overuse of final *-e* has the same effect. This last device also suggests a further possible reason for Chaucer's attack on tail rhyme: regionalism.

Does Chaucer's yoking in *Troilus and Criseyde* of 'diversite' to fears of the mismetring of his own verse (V, 1793–6) indicate awareness of the differing regional rates at which organic final *-e* was ceasing to be pronounced, and the attendant problems for syllabic English prosody? His iambic pentameter and rhyme-royal stanza do use irregular positioning and numbers of unstressed syllables, but for particular artistic effects in specific places – not as a regular element – as in the strongly stress-timed lines traditional to earlier English verse. Often Chaucer contrives wording in *Sir Thopas* that means the stress pattern can only be obtained with strain or that there is a jumble of strong and weak stresses:

> Men speken of romances of prys,
> Of Horn child and of Ypotys,
> Of Beves and sir Gy. (VII 897–9)

Even allowing for fluid, contemporary scribal spelling possibilities, the metrical problems these words pose seem in-built.

The introduction of a bob at VII, line 793, after creating this environment of metrical struggle, further renders the stanza pitfall-ridden to readers. Bobs are in themselves a useful, emphatic vehicle – a device that delightfully, like the tango, puts the brakes on momentarily for the reader, suddenly foregrounding the artifice of fitting statements to metre: art displaying art. Amid the bathos, however, of much of *Sir Thopas*, and the regular efforts needed by a reader to produce the right stress pattern, the halt that the bob starts bringing into the stanzas seems like a stumble, not a moment of exquisite suspension or even rhetorical magnificence it might achieve in other writers' hands, in drama, narrative, and lyric.[19]

Marina Tarlinskaja's statistics show that Chaucer already in the *Book of the Duchess* (dated in the mid-1370s at the latest) writes vastly more regularly eight-syllable four-stress lines (84%) than other English writers before him.[20] She points out that earlier poets' octosyllables combine four stresses (unlike the often greater number of stresses in alliterative verse lines) together with toleration of more than one unstressed syllable between stresses. Kristin Lynn Cole suggests that Chaucer at first used this combination, though with more frequent strictly octosyllabic lines than any prede-cessor, as 'a refiguration of the received tradition prior to his development of iambic pentameter', but abandoned it almost entirely for the pentameter.[21] It is relevant to this development, I think, that that the scribe of the Fairfax 16 text of the *Book of the Duchess* often inserts a fairly mechanical midline virgule, as if still expecting a midline caesura, as in alliterative lines and often in traditional octosyllabics, whereas the punctuation in Tanner 346 responds sensitively to the moving pauses in Chaucer's octosyllabic lines. As to why the iambic pentameter came to attract him more, we might hypothesize a combination of influences: Latin, French, and Italian models; greater spaciousness available for effects using variations in syllable length and stress; and the option of signalling beginnings and shaping verse paragraphs (important for a narrative poet like Chaucer) by marking their first lines with a reversed iambic foot.[22] Perhaps also relevant in relation to Chaucer's apparent mockery of traditional tail rhyme, which combines four- and three-stress lines, is Tarlinskaja's suggestion that because four-stress lines come readily to human language, they are popular and therefore unattractive to innovative writers.[23] Writing in an English form rooted also in the strong-stress contrasts that characterize English particularly, Chaucer would be yoking his career to the past English heritage of prosody, rather than breaking, avant-garde-like, with the sounds of that heritage, while experimenting with lines and stanzas that might, among other things, rival contemporary poetry in France and Italy.

If both tail-rhyme and stress-timed metre represented a threat, that was perhaps sharpened because they were core forms at the centre of an established and powerful canon of English narrative – socially powerful and nationally powerful,

---

[19] See A. Putter, 'Metres and Stanza Forms of Popular Romance', in *A Companion to Medieval Popular Romance*, ed. R. L. Radulescu and C. J. Rushton, Studies in Medieval Romance (Cambridge, 2009), pp. 111–31.

[20] M. Tarlinskaja, 'Meter and Rhythm of Pre-Chaucerian Rhymed Verse', *Linguistics: An Interdisciplinary Journal of the Language Sciences* 121 (1974), 65–87 (pp. 74–6).

[21] K. L. Cole, 'Chaucer's Metrical Landscape', in *Chaucer's Poetry: Words, Authority, Ethics*, ed. C. Carney and F. M. McCormack (Dublin, 2013), pp. 92–106 (p. 98).

[22] Ibid., pp. 98–102 (esp. p. 98 n. 27).

[23] Tarlinskaja, 'Meter and Rhythm', p. 124.

with claims to occupy already the role of national narrative. Tail-rhyme romances, which comprise half the extant English romances and are found only in English, became 'a unique English form, inextricably linked with the romance genre itself in a way that no other verse form does'.[24] Its national status seems confirmed by its frequency in Auchinleck, which arguably enshrines a vernacular canon, drawing often on earlier collections and literary culture, represented today especially by Harley and by Oxford, Bodleian Library MS Digby 86. Chaucer seems not to have wanted to include many of its genres in his own anthology of contemporary types of verse. The kinds of moralistic and eschatological pieces Fein shows forming a major component of Auchinleck and its predecessors are absent from the *Canterbury Tales*, even though some of these visits to and visitants from the next world might have fitted well within a pilgrimage frame.[25] Apart from his antifraternal, miniature revelation of hell prefaced to the *Summoner's Tale*, Chaucer's focus remains on humans still on this side, teetering on the edge of the eschatological abyss – and on the earthly conduct that might imperil them – in the *Friar's*, *Pardoner's*, and *Parson's Tales*. Even the *Summoner's Tale* fiend's description of infernal practices concentrates on how fiends enter human beings. Chaucer's universe is a persistently human-centred, a *this-world*-centred look at eschatology.

That Chaucer's apprehension about anxiety of influence was focused especially on metre is suggested not only by his tail-rhyme parody but also by his dealings with lyrics. The glorious heritage of English lyrics, showcased by Harley and Digby, is represented in Chaucer's work only in mockery. His main lyrics lamenting mutability are the *Complaint of Mars* and *Fortune*, premised on classical and Continental inter-textualities, and in ballade stanzas, not the grimly terrifying energies of *The Four Foes of Mankind* (Auchinleck), *Were Beth They Biforen Us Weren?* (Digby), or *Nou Skrnketh Rose ant Lylie Flour* (Harley). Interestingly, however, Chaucer's *Lak of Stedfastnesse* includes echoes of the widely known 'complaint of the times' mode, of which Auchinleck's *Sayings of the Four Philosophers* is a fine example. Possibly in that instance, couching a description of what was currently wrong with English governance and order, addressed to the king, seemed safer if done in manifestly traditional (i.e., unspecific) style.

Chaucer's surviving lyrics, displaying mastery of the ballade, roundel, complaint, and envoy, represent a different ideal of what lyric writing in English might achieve from the rich and diverse lyrics preserved in Harley or Digby. His ambitions in these centre on creating in English beauties and metrical subtleties analogous to those of contemporary French masters – the ballades and complaints of Guillaume de Machaut, Jean Froissart, Eustache Deschamps, and Oton de Graunson. They were co-workers, in several French and English princely courts, in the creation of a modern, at times avant-garde court literature: modern masters with strong mutual admiration.

[24] R. Purdie, *Anglicising Romance: Tail-Rhyme Romance and Genre in Medieval English Literature*, Studies in Medieval Romance 9 (Cambridge, 2008), p. 1.

[25] S. Fein, 'The Fillers of the Auchinleck Manuscript and the Literary Culture of the West Midlands', in *Makers and Users of Medieval Books: Essays in Honour of A. S. G. Edwards*, ed. C. M. Meale and D. Pearsall (Cambridge, 2014), pp. 60–77 (pp. 66–9).

When Chaucer introduces references to vernacular lyrics, it tends to be with a laugh: the Pardoner's 'Com hider, love, to me!' (I 672), Malkyn and John's dawnsong (I 4236–40); Nicholas's untraced 'Kynges Noote' (alongside his 'Angelus ad virginem' containing potentially daring bawdy parallels to the seduction) (I 3216–17); and Absolon's little serenade song (I 3698–707). Chanteleer may sing 'Mi lief is faren in londe!' (VII 2879), but Chaucer doesn't – though he laughs more than once in Chantecleer's tale at the dunghill cock's lyric taste.[26]

If there is anxiety of influence (and therefore implicitly a compliment to a power of established writings) in these laughs at a heritage of English forms, whether tail rhyme or lyrics, then the ridiculous Thopas's own call for minstrels to accompany his ritual knightly arming seemingly underlines where that influence lies. He wants *geste*, tales, 'game and glee' (VII 840; cf. VII 846; significantly perhaps an ancient English alliterative poetic formula), in what is a *mise-en-abîme* of the old-established romances that *Sir Thopas* mockingly represents: the taste of chivalric man. The stanza on Thopas's literary tastes (VII 845–50) is appropriately scarred by linguistic features and pitfall variants likely to make the reader stumble in arriving at a realization of the metre.

If Chaucer did know Auchinleck, 'romances ... / Of popes and cardinales' (VII 848–9) might refer to its sensational pious romance *The Legend of Pope Gregory*. This minstrel moment in *Sir Thopas* also shares with the opening of *Sir Beues of Hamtoun* the terms 'rowne' and 'murier than a niȝtingale' (VII 834, 835; cf. Auchinleck *Beues*, lines 1–4), a bob (as in *Sir Tristrem*) and two popular romance formulae: 'game and glee' (VII 840), an alliterative phrase going back to Old English alliterative verse; and the trope of calling up 'myrie men' (VII 839), in the sense of a lord's retainers.[27] The first line of Auchinleck's *Sir Tristrem* mentions Thomas of Erceldoune, and *Sir Thopas* includes the elf queen. Another Auchinleck item, *Kyng Alisaunder*, perhaps prompted the motif of adulterous seduction engineered by a lustful intellectual by claiming supernatural powers, transferred to the 'ful subtile and ful queynte' (I 3275) clerk Nicholas in the *Miller's Tale*.

Chivalry

Thopas is 'fair and gent', a 'doghty swayn', a 'knight auntrous' of 'roial chivalry', superior to romance heroes Horn, Bevis, Guy, Percival, and others.[28] Chauntecleer

---

[26] D. Pearsall shows further possible echoes in the *Nun's Priest's Tale*, VII, lines 2874–9, 'trewely she hath the herte in hold ... loken in every lyth', in *A Variorum Edition of The Works of Geoffrey Chaucer: Volume II: The Canterbury Tales, Part Nine: The Nun's Priest's Tale*, ed. D. Pearsall (Norman OK, 1984), pp. 154–5. See additionally the serious citation of the 'newe Frenshe song' 'Jay tout perdu mon temps' in the *Parson's Tale* X 248, and *Fortune*, line 7.

[27] The merry men perhaps recalls Robin Hood and 'greenwood balladry' (J. A. Burrow, Notes to *Sir Thopas*, in *The Riverside Chaucer*, pp. 921–2, note to VII 839), but it is worth noting in this context that summoning up merry men was also a heroic romance formula, often marking a military and tragic crisis. See H. Phillips, 'Merry, Merry Men and Greenwood: A History of Some Meanings', in *Images of Robin Hood: Medieval to Modern*, ed. L. Potter and J. Colhoun (Newark NJ, 2008), pp. 83–101.

[28] See *Sir Thopas*, VII 715, 724, 909, 902, 898–9, 916.

is another parody of the chivalric, military hero celebrated in the romance tradition, a hero of love and heraldic chivalric magnificence, whose adventure is compared with those of Lancelot de Lake, Roland, Troy, and Richard I.[29]

Why did Chaucer not make his *magnum opus* a mighty romance on one of the great subjects, showing off chivalric, and, perhaps especially *British* chivalric, glories: Arthur, Grail, Charlemagne, antique chivalry, or English heroes like King Richard, Bevis, or Guy? Apart from the possibility that he died before he could, would such an enterprise have entailed subscription to militaristic, aristocratic, and often precisely dynastic ambitions associated with the policies and regional power bases held by the magnates whom Richard II (whose servant Chaucer was for much of his career) sought to counter by alternative policies? These included centralizing, pacific, and French-friendly policies, together with a new court culture, artistically closer to Bohemia, Gascony, and Paris than to Edward III's cult of chivalry, Arthurian self-projection, and cultivation of his baronage.[30] Omitting the linear-stranded romances of battle, foreign enemies, and happy-ever-after young lovers, abundant in Auchinleck, Chaucer's *Canterbury Tales* (and also *Troilus*) produce compactly plotted romance narratives, extended not into linear hero-adventure but into philosophy, personal relationship crises, moral and religious symbolic patterns.

Chaucer's romance-writing centres on love relationships, not chivalry, for knights of Venus, not Bellona (whom Richard II's critics saw as finding favour in royal circles).[31] We can link it to a growing late medieval English taste for such themes, which Michael Johnston labels the development of gentry romance.[32] *Sir Thopas* provides Chaucer's only classic chivalric romance and hero. In having him booed off the stage, is Chaucer also brushing aside those 'romances of prys'? Humphrey de Bohun commissioned a manuscript of *William of Palerne* around 1350.[33] Guy of Warwick romances served a dynastic image over several generations. Thorlac Turville-Petre suggests that Auchinleck's crusading preoccupations indicate patronage from a dynasty like the Beauchamps or the Percys with a long crusading history.[34] In contrast, Chaucer's known celebrations of great patrons' affairs are neither dynastic nor historical romances – though it may be significant that the Monk suggests Saint Edward, one of Richard II's favoured saintly alter-egos, as his possible contribution (VII 1970). This mention is perhaps another example, like interrupted proposals and tales, of Chaucer bringing a theme into his text without

---

[29] Parodic chivalry is evoked at *Nun's Priest's Tale*, VII 4100–10, 4331–9.

[30] See J. Vale, *Edward III and the Cult of Chivalry: Chivalric Society and Its Context, 1270–1350* (Woodbridge, 1982).

[31] On evidence for Richard's literary tastes see V. J. Scattergood, 'Literary Culture at the Court of Richard II', in *English Court Culture*, ed. V. J. Scattergood and J. W. Sherborne (London, 1983), pp. 29–43; and P. J. Eberle, 'Richard II and the Literary Arts', in *Richard III*, ed. A. Goodman and J. Gillespie (Oxford, 1999), pp. 233–53.

[32] M. Johnston, *Romance and the Gentry in Late Medieval England* (Oxford, 2014).

[33] A. Doyle, 'English Books In and Out of Court', in *English Court Culture*, ed. V. J. Scattergood and J. W. Sherborne (London, 1983), pp. 161–81.

[34] T. Turville-Petre, *England the Nation: Language, Literature, and National Identity, 1290–1340* (Oxford, 1996), p. 136.

pursuing it in full. Those roads not taken in his compilation, yet flagged up there (another is the Host's invitation to the Monk as most appropriate successor to the Knight), thicken the many strands of the structure offered for reader interpretation. Instead, Chaucer's compositions in response to mighty patrons were dream *dits amoureux*, creating in the prologues to the *Book of the Duchess* and the *Legend of Good Women* English equivalents to *dits* by Machaut and Froissart that are worthy to stand beside their French analogues. The English literature enshrined by Auchinleck might have posed challenges not only for alternative ambitions of modernity and metre, but also for Chaucer as, above all, a narrative artist. Romances were not just *a* narrative form but *the* narrative form, with tail-rhyme romances having become the dominant national mode.

The romances represented in Auchinleck may have appeared not so much outdated as threateningly well established, as a national narrative canon, and not so much provincial as associated with regional power and the entrenched interests (entrenched also in literary culture) of great dynasties. Auchinleck draws on a long-established, respected corpus and conception of what represented English literature, with significant roots in Western thirteenth-century writing and book production. John Scattergood shows how Harley's contents often evince an English regionalism, resistant to the royal or centralizing encroachments of its day,[35] marking a national literature that is *also* regionally rooted and cultivated. This existing representation of taste and literary heritage ('romances of prys') might have appeared alien to the late medieval political climate Chaucer worked in, with Richard II's policies of forging more centralist administration and personal support, aimed (unsuccessfully) at countering baronial power. And alien, too, from the geography of the imagination discernible in Chaucer's writing, centred on London and points south and east – Kent, France, Brittany, Flanders, northern Italy, Rome, Syria, and Asia – and extending out from London into England only golden-triangle-wise, to Oxford and Cambridge and in a few, often commercially significant, directions: East Anglia, Bath, Dartmouth, Holderness, plus long-ago realms such as Northumbria, Athens, King Arthur's court, and Apollo's palace.

Poppets

Two people get called a 'poppet' in the *Tales*: Alisoun ('popelote', I 3254) and Chaucer in the *Sir Thopas* headlink ('popet', VII 701). Here is another of those places in his writings where Chaucer puts himself – writes himself – somewhat in a woman's place: pushed around, pretty, teased, vulnerable to getting embraced. Both characters are clothed in verbal formulae that abound in Auchinleck's Golden Treasury. What E. Talbot Donaldson seminally labeled the 'idiom of popular poetry' is abundant in the *Alphabetical Praise of Women*.[36] If tail rhyme became

---

[35] J. Scattergood, 'Authority and Resistance: The Political Verse', in *Studies in the Harley Manuscript: The Scribes, Contents and Social Contexts of British Library MS Harley 2253*, ed. S. Fein (Kalamazoo MI, 2000), pp. 163– 201 (pp. 168–9).

[36] E. T. Donaldson, 'Idiom of Popular Poetry in the Miller's Tale', in E. T. Donaldson, *Speaking of Chaucer* (London, 1970), pp. 13–29.

a source for an especially 'poetic', lyric glitter that later romance writers could exploit,[37] such conventions illuminate further Chaucer's use of vocabulary familiar from tail-rhyme texts – 'hende', 'rose on ris', 'tretis', 'childe', 'lemman', and others – in *Sir Thopas* and the *Miller's Tale*. Does its use for Thopas and Absolon show him gendering tail rhyme as feminine and/or emasculating? Moreover, Alisoun's description resembles Auchinleck's *Alphabetical Praise* in exhibiting the same laudatory/misogynist, appreciative/contemptuous masculine appreciation (Oliver Pickering and Fein point to its coarsening of the French original's refinement and respect).[38] It contains many terms associated with Alisoun and her suitors: even harp, fiddle, and psaltery cannot praise the lady enough (lines 67, 236); her breath and kiss are sweet as 'piment' and 'meþ' (lines 170–1); she is a fine apple stored up: 'fin mele / In hord' (lines 195–6). Beside the Auchinleck poem's comparison of a woman to a 'paruink' (line 144), Alisoun is like 'a prymerole, a piggesnye' (I 3268). It also ventures beyond conventional flower comparisons: the 'woderof þat springeþ on heþ / Is non so swete in his odour' as woman's breath (lines 167–8). Chaucer's assessment of Alisoun as suitable for a yeoman to marry or 'any lorde to leggen in his bedde' (I 3269) is class snobbery – with even a touch of the insulting, if mythic, *droit de seigneur* over serfs' daughters – but it also resembles *Alphabetical Praise*'s repeated appreciation of women as deliciously fit for men 'O niȝt in armes for to wende' (line 13) and as 'Loueliche to leggen under line' (line 191). They 'swetely lol [men] in her harm / Wel oft' (lines 316–17). Women's love makes men happy who would otherwise 'spille', lie and 'dwine hem selue to dede' (line 29–30), as Nicholas threatens he will 'spille' (I 3278). Besides solacing men, woman are sweet, fragrant, and like flowers, spices, and delicious drinks; their breath and kisses from their mouths are sweet as flowers and spices (lines 166–83). And Chaucer makes mouths, sweet breath, sweet flavours, smells, drinks, and kissing linked motifs in his tale.

Sir Thopas is more deeply interesting as a document of Chaucer's authorial identity than as a document of his humour or attack on tail-rhyme romances. Chaucer uses the so-called minstrel formula when his role as storyteller is enacted: 'Listeth lords ... / And I wol telle' (VII 712–13). This moment when he dramatizes himself as author, and specifically a narrative author, is (typically of his explorations of authorship) marked by intensity, elusiveness, intertextuality, and passivity. As when the *House of Fame*'s eagle picks him up, chides him for numbed brain and emptiness of original material for making poetry, this self-representation as author places Chaucer in the position of being bullied, and by his own avian character.[39] The Host sweeps his narrative 'minstrel' performance off the stage, judges his poetry 'drasty' (the lowest, dregs, faecal) (VII 930). When, in the *House*

---

[37] Purdie, *Anglicising Romance*, pp. 5–6.

[38] All quotations from *Alphabetical Praise of Women* are cited by line number from the online transcription in the Burnley-Wiggins facsimile. See O. Pickering, 'Stanzaic Verse in the Auchinleck Manuscript: The *Alphabetical Praise of Women*', in *Studies in Late Medieval and Early Renaissance Texts in Honour of John Scattergood*', ed. A. M. D'Arcy and A. J. Fletcher (Dublin, 2005), pp. 287–304; and Fein, 'The Fillers', pp. 71–2.

[39] He is both bullied about his subject matter and given new orders in the *Legend of Good Women*, G 238–316, and pushed around literally by Scipioun in the *Parliament of Fowls*,

of Fame, some nameless 'oon' suddenly questions what he is doing there, implicitly his ambitions for his art, Chaucer's answer is self-emptying: not seeking fame but hoping to receive, from outside himself, material for poetry. The encounter has a surrealist, uncanny, elvish air, not belonging entirely in either a fictional plane or a textual, like the uncanniness in Chaucer's self-presentation through the tropes of tail rhyme. In *Sir Thopas*, the narrative purporting to represent England's superlative narrative poet is an external ready-made thing, 'lerned long agoon'. The garb he cloaks himself in as narrator is the so-called 'minstrel' formula. It is supremely textual. Chaucer does not make 'Minstrel' this speaker's profession, like 'Prioress' or 'Miller'. Other pilgrims wear clothes and accoutrements that denote social and occupational identity. It is the tail rhyme, which Chaucer renders rigid and dead through caricature of its metre and diction, that decks and identifies this speaker. The verbal formula, collaged here, is an empty raiment cloaking a speaker who, hailed by Harry Bailly, has no identity ('What man artow?', VII 695), does not look at anyone or make conversation with anyone (VII 704). The garment of 'Listeth lordes' leaves the speaker's subject position empty – a ringwraith or, more comically, a 'popet', a puppet or doll.

A parodic narrative like *Sir Thopas* is metafictional as well as intertextual: Simon Dentith writes that it 'draws attention to the conventions that constitute narrative writing'.[40] Like Marcel Duchamps's parodic Mona Lisa, Chaucer's piece confirms its pretext(s) as classic and iconic. Parody does not destroy its target. *Sir Thopas* does not aim a thumping blow in the chest of tail rhyme any more than does Chaucer's minstrel-address conjure a figure of a minstrel, or any other narrative persona. *Sir Thopas*'s parody of English romance does not confirm Chaucer's adoption of a persona. Indeed, parody typically dislodges our readerly sense of authorship: the text is so obviously a network of allusions. As John Traugott says of Swift's parody, the array of voices and personas argues against the notion of a consistent persona.[41]

That evasive voice of all Chaucer's writing has its characteristic virtuosity in a polysemic and intertextual inhabiting of multiple genres and registers. His parody is only a small but showy, almost emblematic, exhibition of that. Robert Phiddian says 'the chief value of perceiving parody as a sort of erasure lies in the sense that notion captures of simultaneously recalling and displacing the pretexts'.[42] That simultaneous recalling and displacement aptly leads us to the fact that *Sir Thopas* stems as much from the power of sophistication as that of parody. It has the qualities Faye Hammill sees as key to sophistication: a combination of modernism and nostalgia (recalling and displacing), detachment, urbanity, camp, dandyism, superiority, absolute absorption of and in a style, and also an engagement with what it shuns predicated on apprehension of ever becoming like it. Hammill also

---

120, 154, again to provide externally the materials for supplying poetry, which – again –
he cannot supply out of his own, interior, head.

[40] S. Dentith, *Parody*, The New Critical Idiom (London, 2000), p. 15.

[41] J. Traugott, 'A Tale of a Tub', in *Modern Essays on Eighteenth-Century Literature*, ed. L. Damrosch, Jr (New York, 1988), pp. 3–45 (pp. 18–19).

[42] R. Phiddian, *Swift's Parody* (Cambridge, 1995), p. 13.

historically links sophistication as an ideal to a rising middle class that appropriates aristocratic markers of distinction, changing these to an 'elite quality ... in manners and conversation', not just in birth.[43]

Chaucer's *Sir Thopas* identity is as a ventriloquist's dummy. Wrapped in and built from words and formulae recognizably from past writings, *Sir Thopas* embodies that dummy – not the figure of Sir Thopas (although he is doll-like and dressed in gaudy clothes) but the text. It is the text *Sir Thopas* that is the puppet. The dummy is the verbal structure – the parody *Sir Thopas* – verbally representing both the writing of romance and the writer of romance.

The Host calls this figure a 'popet', meaning primarily 'doll' or 'darling' (again, effeminizing). But it also captures that self-representation through raiment, a verbal carapace, a failure of full subject position. The puppet – popet – poet. We might say that the adopted style of *Sir Thopas*, adopted out of material like some contents of Auchinleck, acts like the Punch-and-Judy man's swazzle, presenting the professional delivery, uttering the performance of the professional story-deliverer, but deflecting away from the unseen deliverer of it all: an apparent voice that is a thing, a contraption, artificial, distorting, deflecting, and deferring, rendering both performance and invisibility.

---

[43] F. Hammill, *Sophistication: A Literary and Cultural History* (Liverpool, 2010), p. 210.

CHAPTER TEN

Endings in the Auchinleck Manuscript

Siobhain Bly Calkin

W HEN one consults either the digital or the print facsimile of the Auchinleck manuscript (Edinburgh, NLS, MS Advocates 19. 2. 1), one of the codicological notes encountered most frequently is 'Ends imperfect'. This statement is true, first, of the whole manuscript. The last item in the codex as it exists today, *The Simonie*, itself ends imperfect, and, as David Burnley and Alison Wiggins note, 'has the original item number *lx* (60)', a designation which indicates further 'imperfection' in the completeness of the reading experience one can have with the manuscript today.[1] Since only forty-three manuscript items survive, the numbering here indicates that at least seventeen items have been lost and we cannot know, because *The Simonie* ends imperfect, whether more items originally followed that poem and have also been lost.[2] While the manuscript itself 'ends imperfect', so do a number of its extant texts. Burnley and Wiggins note that 'Frequently, the first leaf of a new text (where the miniature was positioned) has been cut out or, in some cases, just the miniature itself has been excised, ... resulting in a series of lacunae throughout the manuscript'.[3] The excision of one text's beginning often means the loss of the previous text's ending, as happens, for example, with *Seynt Katerine*. This saint's life

---

[1] Burnley-Wiggins, at http://auchinleck.nls.uk/editorial/physical.html#damage.

[2] The number of items in the manuscript is forty-three if, like Burnley-Wiggins, one accepts the scribal numeration of the couplet and stanzaic *Guy of Warwick* as one item (item number 'xxviii'). The manuscript contains forty-four items if, like Pearsall-Cunningham, one counts *Guy of Warwick* as two separate texts (D. Pearsall, 'Contents of the Manuscript', in Pearsall-Cunningham, pp. xix–xxiv [pp. xxii]). I follow the scribal numeration as I consider notions of ending in Auchinleck. It is clear from the original numeration that Scribe 1 did not consider the text of *Guy of Warwick* to have ended when the metre changed at fol. 146vb. As A. Wiggins notes, 'there are none of the usual visual markers (title, miniature, new item number) which would signal the start of a new text' at this point ('Imagining the Compiler: *Guy of Warwick* and the Compilation of the Auchinleck Manuscript', in *Imagining the Book*, ed. S. Kelly and J. J. Thompson [Turnhout, 2005], pp. 61–73 [p. 71]). The identification of seventeen missing items should also be qualified by noting that 'These calculations are ... only approximate as they rely upon the accuracy of the item numbering of the lost leaves and do not take account of the scribe's sometimes erratic numbering' (Burnley-Wiggins, at http://auchinleck.nls.uk/editorial/physical.html#damage).

[3] Burnley-Wiggins, at http://auchinleck.nls.uk/editorial/physical.html#damage.

immediately precedes *St Patrick's Purgatory*, and that text's imperfect beginning is attributed by I. C. Cunningham to 'a desire for the miniature' and the excision of a folio containing it which would also have contained the terminal lines of *Seynt Katerine*.[4] In other places, entire gatherings that would have included a text's ending have been lost, as is the case for *King Richard*. For twenty-five items, however, we do have what one might call 'perfect' endings, namely original terminations preserved in the manuscript as it exists today. These items are: *The Life of Adam and Eve*, *Seynt Mergrete*, *St Patrick's Purgatory*, *The Desputisoun bitven þe Bodi and þe Soule*, *The Clerk Who Would See the Virgin*, *Life of St Mary Magdalene*, *Nativity and Early Life of Mary*, *On þe Seuen Dedly Sinnes*, *The Assumption of the Blessed Virgin*, *Floris and Blauncheflur*, *The Sayings of the Four Philosophers*, *The Battle Abbey Roll*, *Guy of Warwick*, *Sir Beues of Hamtoun*, *Of Arthour and of Merlin*, *A Penniworþ of Witte*, *Hou Our Leuedi Saute Was Ferst Founde*, *Roland and Vernagu*, *Kyng Alisaunder*, *The Sayings of St Bernard*, *Dauid þe King*, *Sir Orfeo*, *The Four Foes of Mankind*, *Anonymous Short English Metrical Chronicle*, and *Alphabetical Praise of Women*.

The variety of texts that end 'perfectly' is clear from these titles, and includes, among other genres, lengthy romances (e.g., *Sir Beues*), hagiographic texts (e.g., *Seynt Mergrete*), brief religious instructional pieces (e.g., *Seuen Dedly Sinnes*), a chronicle (*Short Chronicle*), a version of *The Battle Abbey Roll*, and guides to spiritual life (e.g., *The Desputisoun bitven þe Bodi and þe Soule*). There is also, however, a surprising amount of variety among the 'perfect' endings themselves. Some items are very clearly completed interpretationally and materially, such as *Floris and Blauncheflur*:

> Nou is þis tale browt to þende
> Of Florice and of his lemma[n] hende,
> How after bale hem com bote;
> So wil oure louerd þat ous mote,
> Amen sigge3 also,
> And ich schal helpe 3ou þerto.
> E X P L I C I T. (lines 857–63)[5]

In this 'perfect' ending, not only does a narrator state that the tale is ended and provide a brief recapitulation of it, but the text also includes a rubricated 'explicit' that spans the width of a full column in the *mise-en-page* and is followed by almost half a column of blank space – visual attributes that signal a clear termination.[6]

---

[4] The excision of a folio is discernible from the stub labeled 'fol. 24a' by I. C. Cunningham, 'Physical Description', in Pearsall-Cunningham, pp. xi–xiv (p. xii), and 'stub 024_a' in the Burnley-Wiggins facsimile. Regarding incomplete beginnings, I. C. Cunningham writes, 'The folios on which begin items 1, 3, 6 [*St Patrick's Purgatory*], 8, 9, 11, 12, 16, 18, 19, 22, 23, 28, 31, 33, 35, 38, and 42 are wholly or partly lost, and the removal may in many cases be ascribed to a desire for the miniature' ('Script and Ornament', in Pearsall-Cunningham, pp. xv–xvi [p. xv]). Miniatures remain at fols. 7r, 72r, 167r, 256v, and 326r.

[5] All transcriptions are those of Burnley-Wiggins and follow their line numbering.

[6] A. Bahr, *Fragments and Assemblages: Forming Compilations of Medieval London* (Chicago, 2013), notes that this explicit is 'unusually florid and conspicuous', and 'more eye-catching

Auchinleck's 'perfect' endings, however, also include texts such as *Nativity and Early Life of Mary*, which ends with six lines recounting Joseph's response when he discovers his wife Mary is pregnant:

> He þouȝt he wald oway flen
> þat no man schuld it wite.
> A niȝt as he awayward was
> an angel to him cam
> & bad him bileuen al þat diol
> þat he to him nam. (lines 308–10)[7]

These lines do not straightforwardly signal the text's conclusion. Although the rhyme is completed ('cam'/'nam'), it does not seem to communicate a definitively concluded narrative action since no resolution of the interaction between Joseph and Mary is provided.[8] Moreover, there is no statement of conclusion, unlike the situation at the end of *Floris and Blauncheflur*, where one finds multiple statements of conclusion ('Nou is þis tale browt to þende', 'Amen siggeȝ also', and 'EXPLICIT'). The last six lines of *Nativity* are, however, the only material copied on fol. 69v and are followed by blank space and a catchword that 'indicates no material has been lost from the manuscript'.[9] The extant text is thus codicologically 'perfect', but interpretationally problematic. Burnley and Wiggins state that the text was 'Apparently copied from a fragment or abandoned with only six lines on f[ol]. 69v', while Derek Pearsall identifies the text as 'fragmentary' before suggesting that there may have been a plan to insert fillers on the remainder of fol. 69v, but he does not state whether (or how many) more lines of *Nativity* might have been included before such fillers.[10] Both sets of editors indicate that something is wrong with this ending, and Pearsall implies that the scribe left space in order to address the matter later by including more text, a well-attested scribal response to problematic textual gaps, as Stephen Partridge and Daniel Wakelin have demonstrated.[11] No Auchinleck

---

than most' that remain. He argues that its exceptionality may 'have inclined a reader to mark visually the generic transition … between *Floris and Blauncheflur* and "Four Philosophers"' (pp. 139–40).

[7] Burnley-Wiggins describe the metrical layout thus: 'Long-line couplets, written as quatrains, but marked by paraphs as eight-line stanzas in the MS' (at http://auchinleck. nls.uk/mss/heads/nativity_head.html). Their line numbering marks the couplets and facilitates comparison with other versions of the poem rather than signalling the number of lines on folios. It should be noted, however, that the paraph marking at the end of the text is not as regular as it is at the beginning, and that, if it does indeed mark stanzas, on fol. 69r the stanzas marked by paraphs are, respectively, 32, 12, and 28 lines.

[8] Other versions of this narrative do not end at this point, and indeed often continue for many more lines. See *The South English Nativity of Mary and Christ*, ed. O. S. Pickering, Middle English Texts 1 (Heidelberg, 1975), pp. 9–30, for a discussion of the various versions and manuscripts.

[9] Burnley-Wiggins, at http://auchinleck.nls.uk/mss/heads/nativity_head.html.

[10] Burnley-Wiggins, at http://auchinleck.nls.uk/mss/heads/nativity_head.html; and Pearsall, 'Contents', p. xxi.

[11] S. Partridge, 'Minding the Gaps: Interpreting the Manuscript Evidence of the *Cook's Tale*

editor, however, states that *Nativity* 'ends imperfect'; the codicological evidence makes such an assertion impossible. Readers of the manuscript, both medieval and modern, are thus left to ponder this termination as a 'perfect' ending.

As these two examples show, the 'perfect' endings of Auchinleck beg the question: what constitutes a complete, or achieved, ending for readers, and how do texts in the Auchinleck manuscript accomplish this? Moreover, what issues might the manuscript's 'perfect' endings engage for the manuscript's readers, both modern and medieval? This essay attempts to answer such questions by considering what makes for a good ending in modern and medieval estimations, what closing devices the 'perfect' endings of Auchinleck employ, and how those devices are used to different effect within the same manuscript. Auchinleck affords an opportunity to examine texts that embrace and deploy, as well as sometimes defy, traditional medieval methods of concluding texts. The manuscript reminds us that texts that seem to stress cessation merit literary study alongside texts that refuse closure,[12] and that medieval definitions of a good ending were diverse and wide-ranging, perhaps more so than current critical concepts of aesthetically meritorious endings.

Various modern theorists have discussed the importance of ending a text well. Frank Kermode writes, 'Men, like poets, rush "into the middest," *in medias res*, when they are born; they also die *in mediis rebus*, and to make sense of their span they need fictive concords with origins and ends, such as give meaning to lives and to poems'.[13] According to Kermode, 'we use fictions to enable the end to confer organization and form on ... temporal structure'.[14] Textual endings are thus fictions that provide a desired sense of conceptual and formal closure for readers. They craft in the reader what Barbara Herrnstein Smith calls 'a sense of appropriate cessation'.[15] As Kermode and Smith suggest, however, readers in the past century have tended to value more highly endings that provide a sense of conclusion that is neither too definite nor too easy.[16]

---

and the *Squire's Tale*', in *The English Medieval Book: Studies in Memory of Jeremy Griffiths*, ed. A. S. G. Edwards, V. Gillespie, and R. Hanna (London 2000), pp. 51–85; and D. Wakelin, 'When Scribes Won't Write: Gaps in Middle English Books', *Studies in the Age of Chaucer* 36 (2014), 249–78. Wakelin describes one sort of textual gap as 'occur[ring] when a scribe thinks that there is text missing from his exemplar and so leaves a space in order to slot in what's missing later' (p. 250). Wakelin's article focuses on much smaller gaps in manuscripts (words or lines left blank), while Partridge discusses the much larger gaps sometimes left by scribes in response to Chaucer's *Cook's Tale*.

[12] I use the term *closure* to mean the 'resol[ution of] a work and its issues', and an ending that 'confirm[s] ... expectations ... established by the structure of [a work], ... is usually distinctly gratifying ... [and is] experienced as integral: coherent, complete, and stable'. The two definitions are drawn, respectively, from S. Knight, 'Chaucer and the Sociology of Literature', *Studies in the Age of Chaucer* 2 (1980), 15–51 (p. 27), and B. H. Smith, *Poetic Closure: A Study of How Poems End* (Chicago, 1968), p. 2.

[13] F. Kermode, *The Sense of an Ending: Studies in the Theory of Fiction* (Oxford, 1966), p. 7.

[14] Ibid., p. 45.

[15] Smith, *Poetic Closure*, p. 36.

[16] Kermode, *The Sense of an Ending*, pp. 178–80; and Smith, *Poetic Closure*, pp. 237–60.

This readerly desire may explain why so many studies of endings in Middle English texts draw attention to the ways in which these texts resist closure. Stephen Knight, for example, writes:

> Closure, in the sense of a climax of plot and meaning together, is not an inherent feature of 'high' medieval texts. ... The structural fissures that a modern aesthetic finds in such texts were not problematic because they replicated a world view expecting no organic grasp of the physical world from humans and their art.[17]

Arthur Bahr, in a recent study focused on fragments and assemblages, discusses the ways in which medieval compilations, 'in their strange juxtapositions, suggestive fragmentation, and complex literary effects, ... press us to reread, to continue rather than conclude'.[18] Other scholars have likewise identified a resistance to closure in late medieval texts and have expressly challenged a perceived critical tendency among non-medievalists to identify 'open-ended form as a modern development'.[19] The best example of this work is Rosemarie McGerr's *Chaucer's Open Books: Resistance to Closure in Medieval Discourse*. McGerr's study is particularly interesting because, even as it emphasizes Chaucer's subversion of medieval traditions of closure, it points out the variety of such traditions available to medieval writers. McGerr and others, however, tend to study endings in Chaucer's works or those of the *Gawain* poet. There has been less discussion of the endings found in Middle English romances not written by these authors, or in Middle English saints' lives, biblical narratives, and didactic poems, texts generally considered to exhibit less artistic innovation or subversion of traditional structures and devices. Even when the endings of such texts are discussed, as in Bahr's fascinating study of booklet 3 in Auchinleck, efforts to argue the aesthetic value of these texts again emphasize openness and resistance to closure resembling that found in Chaucer's writings. For example, Bahr focuses on how

> the selection and arrangement of texts in manuscripts ... can produce those "metaphorical potentialities," discontinuities and excesses, multiple and shifting meanings, resistance to paraphrase, and openness to rereading that have deservedly become resurgent objects of critical value.[20]

Accordingly, Bahr concludes his discussion of booklet 3 by emphasizing the ways in which the Auchinleck manuscript 'frustrates even wily efforts to impose closure'.[21]

Ending a text well in late medieval England, as these scholars have shown, often involves the creation of conclusions that undercut cessation, either by promoting

---

[17] Knight, 'Chaucer and the Sociology of Literature', p. 27.

[18] Bahr, *Fragments and Assemblages*, p. 256.

[19] R. McGerr, *Chaucer's Open Books: Resistance to Closure in Medieval Discourse* (Gainesville FL, 1998), p. 4.

[20] Bahr, *Fragments and Assemblages*, p. 10. Bahr here cites D. Pearsall, 'Towards a Poetics of Chaucerian Narrative', in *Drama, Narrative and Poetry in the Canterbury Tales*, ed. W. Harding (Toulouse, 2003), pp. 99–112 (pp. 99–100).

[21] Ibid, p. 151.

re-reading and alternative interpretations, or by 'emphasiz[ing] the self-delusion of accepting the end of any text as truly conclusive'.[22] However, many ideas about good endings circulated in late medieval England, and some emphasized cessation instead of re-reading and resistance to closure. Sometimes ending texts well meant finishing them in a decisive and traditional manner, as the conclusion of the Auchinleck *Floris and Blauncheflur* shows with its multiple statements of completion. Endings of this nature also elicited authorial and scribal investments, in the sense that writers wrote such endings for their texts and subsequent writers copied them, thereby signalling their aesthetic agreement that the matter copied provided 'a sense of appropriate cessation'.[23] (When such a sense was not clear, as in *Nativity* or, more famously, Chaucer's *Cook's Tale*, a gap could well be left to denote aesthetic incompleteness.) Texts that emphasize closure and cessation must be considered alongside their more 'open' and subversive fellows if we wish to explore fully what made for a good ending in the estimation of medieval readers. Moreover, endings displaying many different types of aesthetic engagements, occasionally simultaneously, are found alongside each other in medieval manuscripts. This essay therefore attempts to broaden scholarly discussion of what makes a good ending in Middle English texts by considering various traditional medieval directives about endings and then examining their deployment in the 'perfect' endings of Auchinleck, a manuscript containing nothing by Chaucer or the *Gawain* poet but yet displaying for consideration a wide variety of genres, texts, and endings.

Auchinleck items that end 'perfect' engage medieval ideas about concluding a text promulgated both in theoretical treatises from the Latinate tradition and in the practices of vernacular writers. In the twelfth century, Matthew of Vendôme defines a conclusion as 'the termination according to the rules of meter and involving uniformity of the subject-matter'.[24] In other words, a good ending fits with what has gone before in both its metrical format and its subject. Matthew then identifies

---

[22] McGerr, *Chaucer's Open Books*, p. 41

[23] I use the term 'writer' here to signal the continuity of the creative and productive process across a spectrum of authorial/scribal activity that is often presented as definitively divided between author and scribe. In so doing, I wish to communicate my sense of the aesthetic investments and activities of medieval scribes as creative and authorial in a variety of ways, even when they are not the first 'makers' of the text they copy. For a full discussion of the scribe-author continuum, scribal authorship, and multiple arguments in favour of it (including a prolonged study of the possible creative and production processes underlying Auchinleck's *Short Chronicle*), see M. Fisher, *Scribal Authorship and the Writing of History in Medieval England* (Columbus OH, 2012). For an equally provocative discussion of 'literary scribes', see S. Fein, 'Literary Scribes: The Harley Scribe and Robert Thornton as Case Studies', in *Insular Books: Vernacular Manuscript Miscellanies in Late Medieval Britain*, ed. M. Connolly and R. Radulescu, Proceedings of the British Academy 201 (Oxford, 2015), pp. 61-79.

[24] Matthew of Vendôme, *Ars versificatoria (The Art of the Versemaker)*, trans. R. P. Parr (Milwaukee, 1981), p. 105. The Latin reads: 'Conclusio est, prout hic accipitur, tenorem propositi complectens legitima metri terminatio' (Matthew of Vendôme, *Ars versificatoria*, in *Les arts poétiques du XIIe et du XIIIe siècle: Recherches et documents sur la technique littéraire du moyen âge*, ed. E. Faral [Paris, 1958], pp. 106-93 [p. 191]).

recapitulation of meaning, emendation, a plea for indulgence, a demonstration of pride, an expression of thanks, and praise of God as appropriate ways of ending a work.[25] Geoffrey of Vinsauf, writing in the early thirteenth century, says, 'Let the end, like a herald of the completed course, send [the poem] away with honor'.[26] His words suggest that the ideal ending is both an announcement of what has come before ('the completed course'), and a ceremonial marking of the occasion of ending that communicates the importance and value of the poem. Elsewhere Geoffrey offers practical instruction for how such an ending may be accomplished, suggesting that 'the ending of the matter is to be handled three ways: either from the body of the matter, or from a proverb, or from an exemplum'.[27] John of Garland, also writing in the thirteenth century, lists 'an awkward ending' – namely, 'a conclusion inappropriate to its work' – as one of six vices to avoid in a poem.[28] He advises deriving an ending either 'from the body of the matter, by way of recapitulation', or 'purely from the poet's pleasure', and, like Geoffrey, he notes that endings can be crafted out of examples or proverbs.[29]

While these precepts describe Latin rather than vernacular writings, many are exemplified in Middle English texts. For example, recapitulations of narrated events frequently appear at the ends of texts, as do prayers praising God or his Mother and articulations of artistic pride in the composition or copying of a text. Vernacular writers also employed ways of ending a text not noted by the Latin theoreticians. These include simple statements that the end of the text has been reached as well as generic conventions, such as a dreamer's awakening from a dream vision, or a romance hero's return to his community, reunion with family, and death.[30] Late medieval theory and practice thus identify a number of ideas about what makes for a good ending, namely: that it may be important and signalled as such; that it

---

[25] Matthew of Vendôme, *Ars versificatoria*, trans. Parr, pp. 105–6; for the Latin, see Matthew of Vendôme, *Arts poétiques*, ed. Faral, pp. 191–3.

[26] Geoffrey of Vinsauf, *Poetria nova*, ed. and trans. E. Gallo, in *The 'Poetria nova' and Its Sources in Early Rhetorical Doctrine* (The Hague, 1971), pp. 13–132 (p. 19). The Latin reads: 'Finis, quasi praeco / Cursus expleti, sub honore licentiet illam' (p. 18 [lines 73–4]).

[27] Geoffrey of Vinsauf, *Documentum de modo et arte dictandi et versificandi (Instruction in the Method and Art of Speaking and Versifying)*, trans. R. P. Parr (Milwaukee, 1968), p. 95. The Latin reads: 'Finis igitur materiae tripliciter sumenda est vel a corpore materiae, vel a proverbio, vel ab exemplo' (Geoffrey of Vinsauf, *Documentum de modo et arte dictandi et versificandi*, in *Les arts poétiques du XIIe et du XIIIe siècle: Recherches et documents sur la technique littéraire du moyen âge*, ed. E. Faral [Paris, 1958], pp. 263–320 [p. 319]).

[28] John of Garland, *The 'Parisiana Poetria' of John of Garland*, ed. and trans. T. Lawler (New Haven, 1974), pp. 85, 89. The Latin reads: 'finis infelix', defining this as 'inconueniens operis conclusio' (pp. 84, 88).

[29] John of Garland, *The 'Parisiana Poetria'*, ed. Lawler, p. 89–91. The Latin reads: 'ad quod uitandum finis siue conclusio aliquando sumi debet a corpore materie per recapitulationem precedencium … aliquando a licencia, vt aput Virgilium in Bucolicis' (p. 88). For precepts about how to close a text, see pp. 90–1.

[30] On medieval practices for ending a text, including generic conventions, see McGerr, *Chaucer's Open Books*, pp. 27–8. Regarding the romance genre's practice of depicting the hero's reunion with family and death as an ending, see as well A. C. Spearing, *Readings in Medieval Poetry* (Cambridge, 1987), pp. 112–13.

engage the material it concludes; that it may be crafted through a variety of formal devices and generic traditions; and that, even though it may involve resistance to closure, it may also, conversely, emphasize conclusion through (for example) statements of ending, a hero's demise, or the termination of a metre.

The 'perfect' endings in Auchinleck in many ways exemplify medieval precepts and practices. Their importance is frequently marked visually by the inclusion of separate 'explicit' statements and by paraph marks or elaborate capitals, as can be seen in the endings of *Seynt Mergrete* (fol. 21ra) and the *Alphabetical Praise of Women* (fol. 325vb). Endings often engage their preceding matter by summarizing the events narrated, thereby enacting John of Garland's advice about deriving a conclusion 'from the body of the matter, by way of recapitulation'. An ending of this sort appears, for example, in *Guy of Warwick* (fol. 167ra–b), which begins its final stanza by reminding its audience:

> Now haue ȝe herd lordinges of Gij
> Þat in his time was so hardi
> & holden hende & fre,
> & euer he loued treuþe & riȝt
> & serued God wiþ al his miȝt. (lines 10500–4)

Other endings exhibit some of the other concluding devices described by theorists. For example, *Sir Orfeo* and *Seynt Mergrete* include in their endings the demonstration of artistic pride endorsed by Matthew of Vendôme. *Sir Orfeo*'s ending includes lines communicating both the artistic tradition to which the text belongs and multiple judgements of the text's aesthetic quality (lines 599, 602):

> Harpours in Bretaine after þan
> Herd hou þis meruaile bigan
> & made herof a lay of gode likeing
> & nempned it after þe king;
> Þat lay 'Orfeo' is yhote;
> Gode is þe lay, swete is þe note. (lines 597–602)

Seynt Mergrete's penultimate stanza, meanwhile, identifies a human source for the narrative, makes a claim for the text's wide circulation and fame, and advertises the pleasure to be derived from hearing the text:

> Teodosious þe kniȝt,
> he lete writen hir liif
> Þat is now ouer al þe world
> name-couþe & riif:
> Hou sche þoled hir passioun
> stille wiþouten striif,
> Þat mirþe is of to here
> to maiden & to wiif. (lines 405–8)[31]

---

[31] Burnley-Wiggins number the lines to signal the 'monorhymed, long-lined quatrains' (at http://auchinleck.nls.uk/mss/heads/mergrete_head.html).

Prayer is another traditional concluding device, and eighteen of Auchinleck's twenty-five ended texts terminate with this form of the 'praise of God' advised by Matthew of Vendôme. Generic conventions of closure also appear, such as the romance narrations of death that end *Kyng Alisaunder* and *Guy of Warwick*. Simple statements that the end has been reached also turn up, as in *Floris and Blauncheflur* ('Nou is þis tale browt to þende', line 857) and *Sir Beues* ('Þus endeþ Beues of Hamtoun', line 4443). In many ways, then, the 'perfect' endings in Auchinleck illustrate models of closure promulgated by medieval theorists and/or repeated across many medieval texts. Such endings are often traditional and conservative, and employ prescribed modes of cessation. They do not challenge readers' expectations, but they do provide aesthetic pleasure. Certainly, they seem to have pleased the scribes who wrote Auchinleck and presented its texts, with their endings, to readers.

What constitutes that aesthetic pleasure is not to be discerned, however, from the mere identification of traditional modes of ending a text. Aesthetic pleasure lies, in part, in the experience of discerning how, and to what end, a text employs the conventions and 'horizons of expectation' it invokes.[32] Such readings are necessarily subjective, but they often provide fodder for thought, even when engaged in by modern readers. The remainder of this essay considers in greater detail some of the 'perfect' endings found in Auchinleck, examining the devices employed, the different ways the same devices are deployed in the manuscript, and the issues engaged by specific endings. Such study shows both the rich variety of issues traditional devices can engage as well as the coexistence of many such devices with some very open-ended textual conclusions in Auchinleck.

The *Life of St Mary Magdalene* and the *Alphabetical Praise of Women*, like many medieval texts, conclude with prayers. They show the many issues a prayer can address, and the portrait of text and audience it can help to create. My point here is not to argue that these two texts are 'original' in relation to other versions that exist[33] but merely to examine how, in the endings preserved in Auchinleck, they deploy a

---

[32] This notion of aesthetic pleasure draws on H. R. Jauss, *Toward an Aesthetic of Reception*, trans. T. Bahti (Minneapolis, 1982), esp. pp. 22–8, 144–8.

[33] Both texts are designated 'unique copies', but both exist in other versions. Narratives of the life of Mary Magdalene existed in a number of late medieval collections and languages, while *Alphabetical Praise of Women* is closely related to a similar Anglo-Norman text generally considered its source and extant today only in London, British Library, MS Harley 2253 (*ABC a femmes*). I may here somewhat overstate the non-originality of Auchinleck's *Alphabetical Praise* since, as O. Pickering notes, this Middle English text exists only in this version, demonstrates a 'novel stanza form', and exhibits some marked differences from the Anglo-Norman poem. Pickering himself, however, makes a strong case for understanding the Auchinleck manuscript not as a unique or innovative compilation but rather as a conservative preserver of 'antique' content. See O. Pickering, 'Stanzaic Verse in the Auchinleck Manuscript: *The Alphabetical Praise of Women*', in *Studies in Late Medieval and Early Renaissance Texts in Honour of John Scattergood*, ed. A. M. D'Arcy and A. J. Fletcher (Dublin, 2005), pp. 287–304 (p. 291); and also S. Fein, 'The Fillers of the Auchinleck Manuscript and the Literary Culture of the West Midlands', in *Makers and Users of Medieval Books: Essays in Honour of A. S. G. Edwards*, ed. C. M. Meale and D. Pearsall (Cambridge, 2014), pp. 60–77 (pp. 71–73).

traditional device in ways that craft distinctive relationships with the audience and also draw the audience's attention to specific issues for consideration. Both achievements create an aesthetically pleasing 'sense of cessation' for readers. Certainly, Scribe 1, who copied these texts and has been shown to be the driving editorial force behind the production of Auchinleck (and, if one accepts Fisher's argument, the creator of some texts), inscribed these endings and thereby demonstrated his aesthetic sense that they merited presentation and preservation for readers.[34]

After relating the death of Mary Magdalene, the Auchinleck life of the saint concludes thus:

> ⸿ Ich biseche ȝou alle þat han yherd
> Of þe Maudelain hou it ferd
> Þat ȝe biseche al for him
> Þat þis stori in Jnglisse rim
> Out of Latin haþ ywrouȝt,
> For alle men Latin no conne nouȝt:
> Þat Ihesu Crist for his holy grace
> He ȝiue ous al miȝt & space
> Þurth schrift þat he make ous clene
> As was Marie þe Maudelene;
> Þat we mot to þat ioie wende
> Þat euer schal lest wiþouten ende.
> Amen, amen, sigge al we,
> God it ous graunt [par charite.] Amen. (lines 666–79)

Here, the traditional closing prayer is used to engage the audience directly and make the experience of the text communal, active, political, and religious. The use of the second person in 'ȝou alle' draws readers into direct relationship with the narrator while also implying an audience of more than one. The sense of a wide audience is further conveyed in the reference to all who have heard the text – a model of reception that may be formulaic but expands the reach of the text beyond those able to read it to those who merely have the ability to listen. The third line, with its

---

[34] Regarding Scribe 1's formative role in Auchinleck's compilation see T. A. Shonk's foundational article, 'A Study of the Auchinleck Manuscript: Bookmen and Bookmaking in the Early Fourteenth Century', *Speculum* 60 (1985), 71–91. R. Hanna summarizes the findings thus: 'It's difficult to see Auchinleck as anything other than scribe 1's book. Not only did he copy more than four times as much as all his colleagues combined, but, as Timothy Shonk … insists, he provided every catchword at a booklet boundary, as well as every surviving text title but one and all the numeration assigned to texts' ('Reconsidering the Auchinleck Manuscript', in *New Directions in Later Medieval Manuscript Studies: Essays from the 1998 Harvard Conference*, ed. D. Pearsall [York, 2000], pp. 91–102 [p. 93]). For an argument that Scribe 1 was responsible for composing the Auchinleck *Short Chronicle* and for ideas about the mixture of compositional and compilational practices involved in the production of Auchinleck, see Fisher, *Scribal Authorship*, pp. 146–87. Fisher's argument raises a number of questions about the creation of Auchinleck's unique texts when such texts are simultaneously embedded in a network of previously composed yet different versions.

request for prayer from the audience, makes the experience of concluding this text ideally an active and participatory one for audience members, while the description of the narrator provided in 'him / Þat þis stori in Jnglisse rim / Out of Latin haþ ywrouȝt' draws readers' attention to the multilingual artistic effort involved in the production of the poem. This statement can be seen as an assertion of pride, one of the closing devices identified by Matthew of Vendôme, in that it brings the artist to mind rather than allowing him to remain unacknowledged in the background. The next line ('For alle men Latin no conne nouȝt') represents the poem as a deliberate political act designed to make religious information accessible to a vernacular audience, and it continues the manuscript's well-studied foregrounding of English language and cultural identity.[35] The ensuing lines then turn from the earthliness of language politics to spiritual concerns, and shift from the 'Ich-ȝou' of the ending's beginning to the first-person plural pronouns 'ous' and 'we'. The repeated use of these pronouns crafts a sense of Christian unity between readers and writer, while line 674 reminds the audience of the content of the tale narrated and its emphasis on the 'schrift' that makes all Christians 'clene'. The last four lines continue turning the audience's perspective outwards, away from the here-and-now moment of reading/hearing the text to a shared Christian eternity. In one use of a traditional closing device, then, we find artistic self-reflection, the engagement of religious and socio-political concerns addressed elsewhere in the manuscript, the interpellation of an active and numerous audience, and the melding of one prescribed closing device – prayer – with two others: textual recapitulation (lines 674–5) and assertion of artistic pride (lines 667–9).

A concluding prayer also terminates the *Alphabetical Praise of Women*:

> Leuedi, þat ert flour of al þing,
> Þat al godenes haþ in wold,
> For þe loue of þat tiding,
> Þat Gabriel wiþ mouþe þe told,
> Þat Jesu, þat is heuen-king,
> In þi bodi liȝten he wold,
> ȝif hem al gode ending,
> Þat honour wiman ȝing & old
> In word & dede:
> Þe child, þat our leuedi bare,
> Graunt hem heuen to mede. Amen.
> Explicit. (lines 320–31)

The prayer that ends a text praising women unsurprisingly makes its appeal to the Mother of God first. Describing Mary, the conclusion emphasizes the source of her power as her body and its physical bearing of Jesus ('In þi bodi liȝten he wold'). Even when the poem moves to address Christ briefly, it invokes him as 'Þe child,

---

[35] See, for example, T. Turville-Petre, *England the Nation: Language, Literature, and National Identity, 1290–1340* (Oxford, 1996); and S. B. Calkin, *Saracens and the Making of English Identity: The Auchinleck Manuscript* (New York, 2005).

þat our leuedi bare'. The conclusion's emphasis on Mary's body is apt because the *Alphabetical Praise* often roots its defence of women in appreciation of their physical bodies. The poem includes lines expressing straightforward physical appreciation of women's bodies (e.g., 'Is non so swete in his reles, / So is a cosse of womannes mouþe', lines 181–2) as well as lines yoking together religious evocation and more corporeal references (e.g., '[Women] ben birddes of Godes sond, / Loueliche to leggen vnder line', lines 190–1). Physical maternity is also singled out for praise:

> Of hem it springeþ day & niȝt
> Swete morseles, þis lond to fede,
> Frout þat is so michel o miȝt
> Men y-armed stef on stede
> & strong. (lines 115–19)

Women's childbearing provides sustenance to others, since they produce 'Swete morseles' that 'fede' a land. These sons, like the one that 'In [Mary's] bodi liȝten ... wold', nourish others, albeit through their martial fortitude rather than through their eucharistic consumption. Mary's own childbearing is also frequently referenced in the poem's allusions to her (lines 21, 55, 87, 91–2, 111–14, 153–65), and it is worth noting that these allusions tend to emphasize her physical bearing of Jesus more than, for example, her mourning at the cross or her virginity. The concluding prayer thus crafts its entreaty to Mary in terms that signal the importance accorded by the text to her physical body and, particularly, to the childbearing experience that links her to mothers everywhere.

The *Alphabetical Praise*'s concluding prayer also requests a 'gode ending' for 'hem ... / Þat honour wiman ȝing & old / In word & dede'. The prayer thus emphasizes multiple application and inclusiveness by requesting salvation for any composers and copiers of a poem praising women; for those who have heard or read such a work and acted upon its message; and for others who may already naturally do what the poem advises. The linking of narrator, audience, and larger world is here accomplished not by a use of pronouns but rather by a recapitulation of the poem's oft-repeated message. The text then signs off definitively with 'amen' and 'explicit'. The prayer as a whole develops the poem's focus on women's bodies, childbearing, and Mary's physical maternity, and it advocates on behalf of those who, like the poem's narrator, 'honour wiman'. This ending – and the text it concludes – engages a broader manuscript interest in women, as seen in Auchinleck's tales of the Virgin Mary and her miracles, its lives of female saints (Margaret, Katherine, Anne, Mary Magdalene), its shorter narratives involving women (*The Wenche Þat Loued a King, A Penniworþ of Witte*), and its romances that assign substantial and/or formative roles to women (*Sir Beues, Horn Childe and Maiden Rimnild, Lay le Freine, Guy of Warwick*).[36]

While prayers are used to bring closure to poems of various genres, the death of the hero has been identified by A. C. Spearing as one of the most common ways

---

[36] On the manuscript's apparent efforts to appeal to women readers, see Pickering, 'Stanzaic Verse', p. 295; and Turville-Petre, *England the Nation*, p. 135.

of providing and strengthening the sense of closure in medieval romances.[37] This device is obviously not exclusive to romances – the endings of saints' lives, for example, also involve death – but there is no denying that, in many romances, death serves as the occasion around which to craft a conclusion. Concluding deaths can be deployed to different effects, however, evoking and emphasizing for readers issues quite particular to the romance they finish. Two examples from Auchinleck illustrate this: the endings of *Sir Beues* and *Kyng Alisaunder*. The last lines of *Sir Beues* read:

> To his stable Beues gan fare;
> Arondel a fond þar ded
> Þat euer hadde be gode at nede;
> Þarfore him was swiþe wo,
> Into chaumber he gan go
> & seȝ Iosian drawe to dede.
> Him was wo a moste nede,
> And er her body began to colde
> In is armes he gan hire folde,
> And þar hii deide boþe ifere.
> Here sone ne wolde in non manere
> Þat hii in erþe beried were.
> Of sein Lauarauns he let arere
> A faire chapel of marbel fin
> Þat was ikast wiþ queint engin;
> Of gold he made an hiȝ cornere
> And leide hem þarin boþe ifere.
> An hous he made of riligioun
> For to singe for sire Beuoun
> And ek for Iosian þe fre
> God on here saules haue pite
> & also for Arondel,
> ȝif men for eni hors bidde schel.
> Þus endeþ Beues of Hamtoun
> God ȝeue vs alle is benesoun.
> amen. (lines 4420–45)

The multiple deaths described here build ending onto ending, and they conclude the adventures of Bevis, Josian, and Arondel while reminding readers of the ways in which the fates of these three characters have been intertwined throughout the narrative. The role of Arondel has always been one of this romance's most distinctive features, and the conclusion signals both the horse's centrality and the oddness of his role ('ȝif men for eni hors bidde schel'). The final embrace of Josian and Bevis reminds readers of the heroine's strong role in Auchinleck, where she occasionally becomes the protagonist of some very involved independent

---

[37] Spearing, *Readings in Medieval Poetry*, pp. 112–13.

adventures. The reference to Bevis and Josian's son and his construction of a marble chapel also engages the larger narrative. The genealogical continuity of Bevis's lineage is a focus of the narrative, from the opening depiction of Bevis's parents' marriage to the establishment of Bevis's sons as kings of Ermony and England. Guy's actions here assure readers of the continuity of Bevis's family, its wealth, and its Christian puissance. These actions also constitute the only depicted Christianization of the territory of Mombraunt. Bevis and Guy 'ma[k]e Cristen [a]l þe londe of Ermony … wiþ dent of swerd' (lines 3841–3), but the Auchinleck *Bevis* is never explicitly said to Christianize his own realm.[38] Guy's building of this burial chapel, however, makes Bevis a permanent Christian presence in Mombraunt, and the action implies an ongoing Christian incursion into Saracen lands, something repeatedly depicted in the romance. The fact that Bevis's final resting place is in the Saracen world also reminds readers that this Matter of England hero has never been 'at home' in England. Repeatedly attacked, dispossessed, and banished while there, Bevis eventually cedes his English earldom to his uncle (lines 4399–400) and settles in Mombraunt. The romance's concluding death scene thus engages many of the text's key elements before relying on two formal devices – a statement of ending and a brief prayer – to bid the reader farewell.

The Auchinleck *Kyng Alisaunder* is another romance that uses the hero's death to conclude its narrative. The ending, which is one of the manuscript item's few surviving bits, demonstrates how a romance hero's death may signal textual concerns very different from those of *Sir Beues*. The last twelve lines read thus:

> Þo þe king was bidelue
> Jch douke went to himselue
> & maden wo & contek anouȝ
> Jch of hem neiȝe oþer slouȝ
> For to haue þe kinges quide,
> Michel bataile was hem midde.
> Þus it farþ in þe midlerd
> Among þe lewed & lerd:
> When þat heued is yfalle
> Acombred beþ þe membres alle.
> Þus endeþ Alisaunder þe king
> God ous graunt his blisseing. amen
> Explicit. (lines 7999–8011)

Rather than ending right at the hero's death, this text briefly recounts ensuing events and then offers a pointed reflection on the political scene they represent. The 'wo & contek' that follow Alexander's death become the occasion for a proverbial observation about socio-political structures:

---

[38] Bevis, Terry, Miles, and Guy slay all the Saracens who come with Yvor to fight against Bevis in their final battle (lines 4067–76), but Ermony, not Mombraunt, is the site of this slaughter (line 3938).

Þus it farþ in þe midlerd
Among þe lewed & lerd:
When þat heued is yfalle
Acombred beþ þe membres alle. (lines 8005–8)

The image of a polity without a leader as a headless body evokes a widespread
medieval political metaphor – found, for example, in John of Salisbury's *Policraticus*.
It reminds readers of Alexander's associations with medieval texts providing
precepts for princes (e.g., the pseudo-Aristotelian *Secreta secretorum*). With the
non-romance associations of Alexander thus evoked, the audience is invited to
reflect upon the romance and consider how it might likewise function as political
commentary. This ending combines the death of the romance hero with a proverbial
statement (a closing device endorsed by both Geoffrey of Vinsauf and John of
Garland), provoking reconsideration of the text and reflection upon the reader's
own world experiences. The proverb's pointed allusion to 'midlerd' thwarts a sense
of closure by pointing out that princes' deaths and subsequent power struggles are
recurring events as likely to be experienced by readers as by characters in a romance.
Kyng Alisaunder's ending thus uses traditional devices – proverb, statement of
ending, prayer, romance hero's death – to embrace both cessation (Alexander's end)
and continuation (the ongoing pertinence of the depicted events to socio-political
structures). It both asserts and refuses closure.

The Auchinleck endings discussed above employ a number of traditional
medieval closing devices that tend to emphasize cessation, using them to distinctive
effect. I wish to conclude, however, by considering two 'perfect' endings that
neither deploy typical closing devices nor emphasize clear cessation: those of
Roland and Vernagu and *Of Arthour and of Merlin*. These examples show how, in
late medieval codices, endings that employ traditional concluding devices and
emphasize cessation coexist alongside others that do not. Both texts also convey a
distinctive sense of an aesthetically desirable romance ending perhaps attributable
to the co-ordinating scribe of Auchinleck.

In *Roland and Vernagu*, copied by Scribe 1, the narrative of Roland's battle is not
concluded by prayer, statement of ending, or hero's death, but rather by continued
narrative. The text ends with the following lines:

⁊ & al þe folk of þe lond
For onour of Roulond
Þonked God, old & ȝong,
& ȝede a procesioun
Wiþ croice & gomfaynoun
& *salue* miri song,
Boþe widowe & wiif in place
Þus þonked Godes grace,
Alle þo þat speke wiþ tong.
To Otuel also ȝern,
Þat was a Sarraȝin stern,
Ful sone þis word sprong. (lines 869–80)

The romance closes with a brief narrative recounting what people do to celebrate Roland's victory and how this victory is communicated to the Saracen knight Otuel. The final lines propound a model of more narrative as an appropriate ending for *Roland and Vernagu*. No formal literary device ends the romance, and nothing physically signals conclusion in the manuscript. One finds, instead, a catchword leading the reader to the beginning of a new text, *Otuel a Kniȝt*. As Wiggins has shown, this text was not produced by Scribe 1 but instead 'was copied independently ... without the direct supervision of the editor Scribe 1 and at an earlier stage, before Auchinleck and its design plan were conceived of'.[39] Scribe 1, however, integrates this text into the manuscript by assigning it an item number and including an ending for *Roland and Vernagu* (whether structured so by him or an exemplar) that sets the stage for Otuel's story. The next romance, *Otuel*, is clearly identified by a new item number in Auchinleck, but, otherwise, the manuscript presentation suggests that *Roland and Vernagu*'s appropriate ending is *more* narrative, indeed, even a separate item or sequel. This model in many ways fits the narrative dilation characteristic of the romance genre. It also fits conventions employed in Middle English manuscripts that contain Charlemagne romances. Marianne Ailes and Phillipa Hardman note that Middle English manuscripts containing Charlemagne romances present 'evidence of purposeful juxtaposition to create meaningful pairings', and that readers often find 'two Charlemagne romances set together in a diptych-like arrangement'.[40] Auchinleck effectively creates such a diptych out of *Roland and Vernagu* and *Otuel a Kniȝt*. Ailes and Hardman further suggest, however, that the diptych-like layout they identify may 'reflect[] the practice of insular French-language manuscripts containing epic texts', and certainly evokes 'a feature of epic style: its resistance to closure through allusion to further action beyond the end of the narration, as seen, for example, in the final lines of *La chanson de Roland, Fierabras*, or *Girart de Vienne*'.[41] In other words, Scribe 1's decision to follow one Charlemagne romance with another immediately afterwards may reflect manuscript traditions surrounding such texts in late medieval England, and certainly accords with a traditional resistance to closure found in French *chansons de geste*. In *Roland and Vernagu*, he employs generic and manuscript traditions of *not* ending a text – of resistance to closure – to end a Matter of France romance. He thereby shows an aesthetic appreciation of resistance to closure as strong as his appreciation for the definitive markings of closure in other Auchinleck texts.

The same valorization of more narrative as an appropriate conclusion to a text might also be seen to influence Scribe 1's presentation of *Guy of Warwick*. As

---

[39] A. Wiggins, 'Are Auchinleck Scribes 1 and 6 the Same Scribe?: The Advantages of Whole-Data Analysis and Electronic Texts', *Medium Ævum* 73 (2004), 10–26 (p. 20).

[40] M. Ailes and P. Hardman, 'Texts in Conversation: Charlemagne Epics and Romances in Insular Plural-Text Codices', in *Insular Books: Vernacular Manuscript Miscellanies in Late Medieval Britain*, ed. M. Connolly and R. Radulescu, Proceedings of the British Academy 201 (Oxford, 2015) pp. 31–47. I am grateful to Phillipa Hardman for generously sharing this essay with me before its publication.

[41] Ailes and Hardman, 'Texts in Conversation', pp. 39, 44.

Wiggins notes, Scribe 1 seems to have chosen to continue the couplet-rhymed *Guy of Warwick* by waiting for a version of Guy's adventures as a pilgrim to come into his hands[42] and makes no attempt to unify the two sections metrically. He seems not to share Matthew of Vendôme's belief that a good conclusion is a 'termination according to the rules of meter'. Instead, he simply continues the couplet *Guy's* narrative with the stanzaic *Guy*, joining the two physically and signalling their unity – and the stanzaic *Guy's* role as fitting conclusion – through his attribution of just one item number ('xxviii') to the composite text. Here, an entire lengthy text becomes the conclusion for the couplet *Guy*, much as *Otuel* works in many ways to conclude *Roland and Vernagu*. Clearly, more story is an appropriate type of ending in this scribe's work, with some of his texts evincing a marked deferral of closure, while others (*Alphabetical Praise of Women, Life of St Mary Magdalene, Kyng Alisaunder*) use traditional closing devices and emphasize cessation more firmly.

If the most radical deferral (maybe even refusal) of closure in Auchinleck does not belong to *Nativity* (discussed above), then it most likely belongs to another text copied by Scribe 1: *Of Arthour and of Merlin*. This text ends 'perfect', but it does so in a manner that thoroughly problematizes the expectations of 'appropriate cessation' constructed by other manuscript items. In the romance *Of Arthour*, a reader finds what might be called 'completed non-conclusion', an ending wherein the manuscript's visual cues indicate very clearly that the text has ended and that the scribe neither anticipates nor sees any need for further additions to make sense of it, yet the words themselves seem to refute the visual 'sense of cessation'. *Of Arthour* ends, after approximately 9,700 lines, with the following passage:

> Arthour cleued king Maulas
> & Ban ato girt king Ridras,
> Bohort biheue[de]d king Dorilan
> & ich of þe oþer slouȝ a paien þan.
> Þe oþer paiens flowe swiþe
> & our went oȝain biliue
> Into þe cite of Carohaise,
> Wiþ her feren hem made at aise;
> Þai maden gret blis & fest
> & after ȝeden hem to rest. (lines 9754–63)

There is no formal closing device: no prayer, no proverb, no hero's death, no amen, no 'explicit'. More narrative might be expected to provide some closure, as it does in *Roland and Vernagu*, but the depiction of the Christian party led by Arthur feasting and then 'ȝed[ing] hem to rest' simply does not wrap up the events depicted in the text. There is no indication that this battle has been decisive: the Saracens have just fled, as they have many times before only to reappear later and restart more conflict. Moreover, this battle occurs in Leodegan's kingdom, not Arthur's. The last vision of Arthur's kingdom is of efforts to rescue an aristocratic woman who has been abducted and abused by Saracens.

---

[42] Wiggins, 'Imagining the Compiler', pp. 61–73.

In contrast, the Old French *Lestoire de Merlin*, upon which this text is based, continues for much longer, recounting Arthur's return to England, the decisive expulsion of the Saracens from Britain, and the adventures of Arthur and his knights overseas. The French narrative provides a much more expected sense of cessation for a reader. *Of Arthour*, however, breaks off with no decisive resolution of the Saracen-Christian conflict. Unlike *Nativity*, though, *Of Arthour* does not strike a reader (or editor) as fragmentary both because it is long and because a battle terminated with a celebratory feast serves as an ending of sorts. The text's relationship to its Old French source thus seems more one of idiosyncratic abridgement than of fragmentation.[43]

Nonetheless, the ending would make more sense if the manuscript had here a lacuna, an excised miniature, or a missing folio. But there is nothing to indicate loss. The next item begins immediately below these lines, in the same column, on fol. 256vb (Figure 1). Scribe 1 may not have chosen to end his poem thus – an exemplar may merely have broken off at this point – but he makes no effort to conclude the tale more decisively – that is, by adding an account of a final rout of the Saracens or a couplet resolving the conflict. Moreover, Scribe 1 does not leave any space on the folio after the termination of *Of Arthour*. Instead, he inserts the next item (*The Wenche þat Loued a King*) immediately below the ending of *Of Arthour*, within the same column. Unlike the page left near-empty at the termination of *Nativity*, Scribe 1 indicates that, here, he sees no need to leave space to insert an ending should one come to hand later. With the next item's inception (marked by one of the few remaining miniatures in the manuscript), Scribe 1 signals that *Of Arthour* has ended in an entirely acceptable fashion. Ironically, *Of Arthour* opens with 'Ihesus Crist Heuen-king / Al ous graunt gode ending' (lines 1–2). If these lines had appeared at the end, or had even been recopied there, one would find a less thought-provoking close to this Arthurian text. As it is, however, the reader is left to engage with a puzzling ending endorsed by Scribe 1.[44]

This ending elicits a number of questions. First, is *Of Arthour* simply too long and involved to be continued? Is 9,700 lines long enough, in the context of a large manuscript, that no more narrative is to be desired? *Guy of Warwick*, a longer text, terminates at line 10,511, yet adding even 800 lines would not likely accommodate a narrative completion of the Auchinleck *Of Arthour* along the lines of *Lestoire*. The question of what counts as 'too long' is one that only individual readers can answer, and responses might well vary synchronically within a given period as well as diachronically across periods. Perhaps, however, we are expected to draw on knowledge of the Arthurian tradition to fill in the ending for ourselves, either by knowing that Arthur does triumph and unify his realm in other texts, or by

---

[43] For discussion of the abridging tendencies in this text see *Of Arthour and of Merlin*, ed. O. D. Macrae-Gibson, 2 vols., EETS OS 268, 279 (Oxford, 1973, 1979), II, 7–14. For *Lestoire de Merlin*, see *The Vulgate Version of the Arthurian Romances, Ed. from Manuscripts in the British Museum*, ed. H. O. Sommer, 8 vols. in 4 (Washington DC, 1908–16), II.

[44] Of this ending, the poem's most recent editor writes, 'one would have expected some formula of conclusion to be cobbled up. I cannot suggest any really satisfactory explanation' (*Of Arthour and of Merlin*, ed. Macrae-Gibson, II, 161).

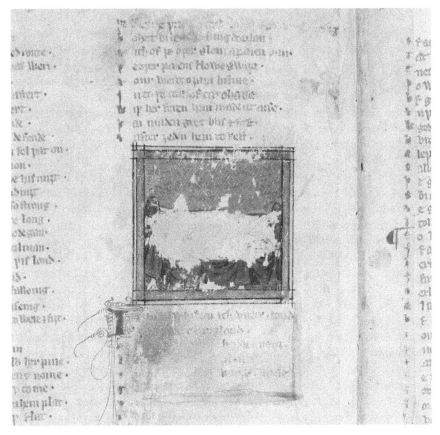

Fig. 1 End of *Of Arthour and of Merlin* and beginning of *The Wenche Þat Loued a King*. Auchinleck manuscript (Edinburgh, NLS, MS Advocates 19. 2. 1), fol. 256vb. Reproduced by permission of the National Library of Scotland.

knowing that in the end Arthur's realm falls apart, riven by conflict and destruction. In some ways, reflecting on the larger tradition supplies readers with a 'choose-your-own-adventure' conclusion: one may select the happy ending and think of the heyday of Arthur's kingship and the Round Table, when all these conflicts are resolved; or one may choose the tragic ending and reflect upon the final doom of Arthur's court. A third method might be to fall back on rhetorical precepts identifying the ending as something in harmony with the text as a whole. In other words, one may consider the ways in which this final vision of momentary victory engages thematic concerns advanced elsewhere in *Of Arthour*. As the ending replays twenty-three earlier moments of battle cessation, it appropriately continues the image advanced in the preceding narrative of an English king continually embroiled in conflict and war. The Prologue to *Of Arthour*, with its references to conquest and linguistic conflict in England, advances a similar vision of the English king's realm at the time of the text's production. All told, the 'completed non-conclusion' of *Of*

Arthour gives rise to a number of reflections that may each provide closure, albeit of different sorts. In all cases, the onus is on the reader to provide the information that most satisfyingly rounds out his/her appreciation of the preceding text. This ending may reflect exigencies of manuscript production and scribal practice rather than artistic intentionality, but there is no denying that it is as provocative as any ending crafted by a writer deliberately eschewing closure.

The ending of *Of Arthour* seems an appropriate place to conclude this essay because it returns us to the questions outlined in my opening about what counts as a 'perfect' ending for readers medieval and modern. It also raises an interesting query relative to the many 'imperfect' endings in Auchinleck. Had the miniature that opens *The Wenche þat Loued a King* been deemed worthy of excision over the centuries following Auchinleck's compilation, and had that excision been accomplished by the removal of an entire folio, as was often the case in Auchinleck, then we would, I suggest, have no sense of the Arthurian text's original 'perfect' ending. It seems unlikely that scholars would have any idea, had the final folio been lost, that *Of Arthour* concludes in the manner it does, given that the only analogous text for comparison is the Old French source text,[45] and given that so many 'perfect' endings in Auchinleck differ so markedly from this one. *Of Arthour* thus serves as a signal reminder of medieval writers' abilities to surprise us even when, as in the case of Auchinleck's Scribe 1, we possess a not-insignificant corpus of their work.

Although they often come from the pen of the same scribe, the 'perfect' endings in Auchinleck are many and varied. They range from deployments of traditional concluding devices (emphasizing termination, marking it decisively) to completed non-conclusions (demanding as much readerly engagement as the open-ended texts most discussed by scholars). Auchinleck's 'perfect' endings include that found in *Kyng Alisaunder*, which uses multiple traditional ending devices both to embrace cessation and to remind readers of the never-ending repetition of certain political situations. They also include the ending of the *Alphabetical Praise of Women*, which uses a traditional concluding prayer to venerate the Virgin Mary as childbearer and to encourage, one last time, the honouring of women that is the poem's focus. The endings of all Auchinleck texts deserve consideration because they show aesthetic choices both to embrace and to refuse traditional ending devices, both to strive for definitive cessation and to thwart any such sense. The endings remind us that aesthetic evaluations of what constituted a good ending in fourteenth-century England, even those evaluations made by the same scribe, were fiercely heterogeneous, perhaps more so than those of scholars today. Whether evoking or avoiding traditions of termination, however, all of Auchinleck's 'perfect' endings invite us to consider what makes their texts distinctive. They hint at what Middle English writers considered important about the texts they penned and the audiences they envisioned. In sum, Auchinleck's endings call us to reflect broadly on what makes for a 'perfect' ending in medieval estimations of the aesthetic and in our own.

---

[45] All other extant Middle English versions of *Of Arthour* break off much earlier, the longest stretching only to about 2,500 lines. See *Of Arthour and of Merlin*, ed. Macrae-Gibson, I, 4–168.

CHAPTER ELEVEN

Paraphs, Piecework, and Presentation: The Production Methods of Auchinleck Revisited

Timothy A. Shonk

I N the years since a probative version of this paper was presented at the LOMERS Conference in London, in July 2008, two important studies in palaeography and in codicological methodology have appeared that may change the way scholars approach the study of manuscript production and of the communities of scribes and artisans who completed those manuscripts in the fourteenth century. The landmark work of Linne Mooney and Estelle Stubbs in their identification of the scribes engaged in the London Guildhall and in the production of literary manuscripts will undoubtedly shape the future of manuscript studies.[1] Having identified by name those scribes producing the works of Chaucer, Gower, and Langland while employed in the Guildhall, Mooney and Stubbs demonstrate a fascinating connection between the clerks in the city and the production of literary manuscripts. To be sure, their study has some qualifications: the clerks copied the works of authors with whom they were often familiar; they worked some fifty years or more after the production of the Auchinleck manuscript (Edinburgh, NLS, MS Advocates 19. 2. 1); they appear to have been acquainted with one another; and they seem to have had an agenda larger than the mere copying of these poets' texts – that is, 'the preservation and dissemination of literature written in English' as part of a broad political aim.[2] Whether similar evidence will appear of clerks' involvement in manuscripts produced decades earlier, like Auchinleck, remains to be seen. And I would add one final caution: we must not be too eager to lay all, or even most, literary manuscript production at the feet of this type of scribe. To do so would be to ignore the evidence, produced by such scholars as C. Paul Christianson, of the stationers, scribes, and other artisans engaged in the production of manuscripts in the London area.[3]

The second study is one that promises a new direction for codicological studies. Helen Marshall has studied the paraphs in the work of Scribe 2 in Auchinleck,

---

[1] L. R. Mooney and E. Stubbs, *Scribes in the City: London Guildhall Clerks and the Dissemination of Middle English Literature, 1375-1425* (York, 2013).

[2] Ibid., p. 137.

[3] C. P. Christianson, *A Directory of London Stationers and Book Artisans 1300–1500* (New York, 1990).

and she has found some evidence suggestive of the existence of this parapher's work – perhaps Auchinleck Scribe 2 himself – in another manuscript: London, BL, MS Egerton 1993.[4] While a possible connection between these two manuscripts is intriguing in itself, both the methodology employed and the larger implications of studying the common, largely ignored, paraph suggest means for identifying book craftsmen other than scribes. Marshall's precise, concrete methodology in her analysis of paraphers' work argues that we may be able to identify a parapher's work with the same confidence now applied to identifying a particular scribe's idiosyncratic letter forms. Such work – especially when combined with other methodologies like Alison Wiggins's 'whole-data analysis' – seems a promising avenue for future investigation.[5]

My study provides an analysis of the work of the four independent paraphers in Auchinleck – if we accept Marshall's persuasive work on the paraphs in Scribe 2's two works in which he begins a new booklet or completes a booklet alone. The work of these paraphers is scattered throughout the manuscript. The appearance and disappearance of these decorators at various times confirm the piecework production for the manuscript that I detailed in an earlier study.[6] Moreover, this analysis sheds some light on a possible order for the copying of some of the booklets, and suggests that the troublesome third booklet is a late addition to the contents of Auchinleck.

With regards to the Auchinleck manuscript, some key overviews have remained constant. We have moved away from the supposition of Laura Hibbard Loomis that book producers in London were following the model of the monastic scriptoria in keeping shops full of redactors, scribes, artisans, and exemplars.[7] More recent work by Christianson has shown, for example, that many of the book 'shops' in Pater Noster Row and other nearby places each occupied approximately 100–200 square feet, and that 'ownership or rental by stationers of properties large enough to have sizeable workroom is not directly indicated in surviving records'.[8] Even by the end of the fifteenth century, as Kathleen Scott demonstrates, artists 'worked in different shops, to which scribes, stationers, and monastic houses brought their books for decoration'.[9] My own earlier study of the Auchinleck manuscript bears out these assertions in demonstrating that a scribe, or scribe/stationer, assumed a bespoke order to produce the codex, organizing the work of additional scribes and planning

---

[4] H. Marshall, 'What's in a Paraph? A New Methodology and Its Implications for the Auchinleck Manuscript', *Journal of the Early Book Society* 13 (2010), 39–62 (pp. 46–9).

[5] See A. Wiggins, 'Are Auchinleck Scribes 1 and 6 the Same Scribe?: The Advantages of Whole-Data Analysis and Electronic Texts', *Medium Ævum* 7 (2004), 1–10. On the number of scribes, see note 30 below.

[6] T. A. Shonk, 'A Study of the Auchinleck Manuscript: Bookmen and Bookmaking in the Early Fourteenth Century', *Speculum* 60 (1985), 71–91.

[7] [7] L. H. Loomis, 'The Auchinleck Manuscript and a Possible London Bookshop of 1330–1340', *PMLA* 57 (1942), 595–627.

[8] Christianson, *A Directory of London Stationers*, p. 29.

[9] K. L. Scott, 'A Mid-Fifteenth-Century English Illuminating Shop and Its Customers', *Journal of the Warburg and Courtauld Institutes* 31 (1968), 170–96 (p. 194).

the layout and decoration of the manuscript's final appearance. Furthermore, the problem fits of gatherings and some infelicitous moments in the scheme of the rubrication and decoration – those 'messy' moments Ralph Hanna describes[10] – appear to support the view that these craftsmen were working in only a loose association.

Scholars of the last few decades have also brought about an evolution in the way we look at these codices. In her 1980 article, Pamela Robinson described a type of book production based upon the compiling of independent, self-contained booklets into a larger text.[11] Some of her conclusions were later challenged by Hanna, who offered a different perspective on booklet production, one that seems especially useful in our consideration of Auchinleck: booklets may also be seen from the perspective of the producer rather than from that of an owner or assembler.[12] In Hanna's view, booklet production of an entire codex allows the assembler to delay until the final moments decisions regarding the text's order and layout, and allows for the introduction of pieces that may not have become available for copying until the major project had already been undertaken.[13] In short, as Hanna concludes, for some instances of manuscripts compiled from booklets, 'rather than conceiving of the booklet as a basic unit, the producer began to conceive of the unit as a whole codex'.[14]

Auchinleck does seem to have been produced in booklet form. As Derek Pearsall describes the text, it is composed of twelve booklets.[15] Clearly, as he further notes, the writing of the texts was not assigned to the scribes gathering by gathering (with Scribe 1 copying some three-fourths of the text), as would have been 'the swiftest production procedure; maybe the organisation was not very sophisticated'.[16] Rather, the scribes worked to copy complete texts, *Reinbrun Gij Sone of Warwike* being the debatable exception. With these noteworthy views of the Auchinleck production methods firmly in mind, we can safely assume that the manuscript was a professional production, a bespoke book organized around romance-heavy booklets copied under the direction of the dominant Scribe 1 with the assistance of other scribes and artisans when conditions demanded or when exemplars became available in relative profusion.

---

[10] R. Hanna, 'Reconsidering the Auchinleck Manuscript', in *New Directions in Later Medieval Manuscript Studies: Essays from the 1998 Harvard Conference*, ed. D. Pearsall (York, 2000), pp. 91–102 (p. 92).

[11] P. R. Robinson, 'A Study of Some Aspects of the Transmission of English Verse Texts in Late Medieval Manuscripts', unpublished B Litt thesis, University of Oxford (Oxford, 1972). Her ten features for identifying booklets are summarized in P. R. Robinson, 'The "Booklet," A Self-Contained Unit of Composite Manuscripts', *Codicologica* 3 (1980), 49–69.

[12] R. Hanna, *Pursuing History: Middle English Manuscripts and Their Texts* (Stanford 1996), pp. 21–34.

[13] A similar problem with exemplar availability is at work in London, BL, MS Harley 7333; see T. A. Shonk, 'BL MS Harley 7333: The "Publication" of Chaucer in the Rural Areas', *Essays in Medieval Studies* 15 (1998), 81–9.

[14] Hanna, *Pursuing History*, p. 25.

[15] Pearsall, 'Literary and Historical Significance of the Manuscript', in Pearsall-Cunningham, pp. vii–xi (p. ix).

[16] Ibid., p. ix.

What has not been so intensively studied as the layout of the texts, the organization of the booklets, and the relationship of the Auchinleck texts to those found in other manuscripts is the decoration of the manuscript in general, and the paraphs in particular. There seems to be general agreement that the miniatures of Auchinleck are in the style of those who produced the Queen Mary Psalter, work amounting to some two dozen manuscripts of the early fourteenth century.[17] Because of the very different types of texts found in Auchinleck and the Psalter, the identification of this style is based primarily upon similarities in the figures in Auchinleck miniatures to those in the Queen Mary Psalter. The miniatures that survive appear to be by the same hand. The majority of Auchinleck items were probably once preceded by miniatures, although an exact number is impossible to assign owing to the lost gatherings and the stub pages that suggest some sort of decoration has been lost. Almost all the capitals that open some pieces and mark segments within pieces also seem to have been done by one hand, though not necessarily the hand of the miniature artist. Recent work by Wiggins, for example, argues that the large initial at the head of *The Simonie* is by the same artist who did most of the text capitals throughout the manuscript, and that the capitals preceding *Sir Beues of Hamtoun* and the *Anonymous Short English Metrical Chronicle* are done by one who may well have produced the miniatures of the text.[18] Whether the artists at work here are those associated with the Queen Mary Psalter, with the 'Subsidiary Queen Mary Artist'[19] or merely those working in the style of those artists is beyond the scope of this paper (though the last case seems the most likely possibility). As Lynda Dennison concludes in her study of *Liber Horn* and other manuscripts and their relation to the Queen Mary Psalter workshops, 'It can be stated with confidence that the style practiced in the capital was that of the Queen Mary workshop.'[20] And that style, sustained by independent artists, is reflected throughout the folios of the Auchinleck.

The focus of this paper, however, is not upon these prominent decorations, but upon a marker often overlooked or treated dismissively by students of the manuscript: the paraph. Indeed, aside from the work of Joel Fredell[21] and of Marshall noted above, I know of no other work dedicated to the study of the paraph. The paraph remains a largely ignored mark within manuscripts. The paraphs, of course, were used to indicate textual divisions of lesser importance than those marked by the 2- to 4-line capitals; they were used most often in Auchinleck to mark the

[17] See L. Dennison, '"Liber Horn", "Liber Custumarum" and Other Manuscripts in the Queen Mary Psalter Workshops', in *Medieval Art, Architecture and Archaeology in London*, ed. L. Grant, British Archaeological Association Conference Transactions 10 (London, 1990), pp. 118–34; L. F. Sandler, *Gothic Manuscripts, 1285–1385*, 2 vols. (London, 1986); and Hanna, 'Reconsidering the Auchinleck Manuscript', p. 96.

[18] Wiggins, 'Are Auchinleck Manuscript Scribes 1 and 6 the Same Scribe?', p. 11 n. 43.

[19] See L. Dennison, 'An Illuminator of the Queen Mary Psalter Group: The Ancient 6 Master', *The Antiquaries Journal* 16, pt 2 (1986), 287–314.

[20] Dennison, '"Liber Horn"', p. 129.

[21] J. Fredell, 'The Lowly Paraph: Transmitting Manuscript Design in the *Canterbury Tales*', *Studies in the Age of Chaucer* 22 (2000), 213–80.

beginnings of stanzas, minor narrative shifts, and the like. While most scholars indicate that more than one artist affixed the paraphs, the resulting descriptions of their work usually remain rather vague, including my own in an earlier article.[22] I. C. Cunningham, for example, devotes only two sentences to the paraphs in his description of the ornamentation of the codex, including a suggestion that Scribe 2 may have inserted his own paraph marks,[23] though this identification is problematic, as I have argued elsewhere.[24] The paraph designs that signify different artists change almost always at the beginning of a gathering, rather than at the beginning of a new text. But, as is often the case with medieval manuscripts, those cases that demand the 'almost always' qualifier can be the most illuminating.

As Malcolm Parkes has shown in a landmark study, the layout and design of the leaves of manuscript collections derive from the centuries preceding Auchinleck.[25] Tracing the evolution of literary manuscript layout to the scholastic *lectio* reading and the need for quick reference to textual subdivisions, Parkes finds the *paragraphi* first introduced in the twelfth century. Parkes defines it as a scribal mark of parallel double lines used, in the thirteenth century, to guide the rubricator and denote running titles – an 'ancient practice' that had been neglected – within a text.[26] It was also in the thirteenth century, Parkes concludes, that the organized book trade in Paris began catering to the needs of students for quick reference and attempting to therefore bring some uniformity to the texts. As these marks of *ordinatio* came to find their way into literary texts, an author began to organize his work for publication, 'and if he did not do so then a scribe would, for inside many a scribe there lurked a compiler trying to get out'.[27] Following the tradition, Auchinleck Scribe 1 inserted running titles but reduced the mark for the paraph to a single diagonal stroke. Scribe 6, on the other hand, used the two parallel strokes as guidemarks.

The Auchinleck paraphs, however, offer much more for our understanding of Auchinleck's production methods. They signify the work of four independent artisans as well as paraphs done by Scribe 2, who would make for a fifth, though not independent, parapher within the codex. The artists' paraphs are distinguished primarily by the shape of the body of the paraph, but also by the aspect of the paraph in relation to the line of script it precedes.

The most active of these artists I deem the *upcurl artist* (Figure 1). His paraphs tend to have a sharp curve upward on the bottom horizontal, and their bodies frequently angle back and to the left from the line of text.

The second most active parapher I call the *flat artist* (Figure 2). In contrast to the upcurl artist, this decorator brings the bottom horizontal line more parallel to the

---

[22] Shonk, 'A Study', pp. 77–80.

[23] I. C. Cunningham, 'Script and Ornament', in Pearsall-Cunningham, pp. xv–xvi (p. xv).

[24] Shonk, 'A Study', p. 79.

[25] M. Parkes, 'The Influence of *Ordinatio* and *Compilatio* on the Development of the Book', in *Medieval Learning and Literature: Essays Presented to Richard William Hunt*, ed. J. J. G. Alexander and M. T. Gibson (Oxford, 1976), pp. 115–41.

[26] Ibid., p. 119.

[27] Ibid., p. 138.

Fig. 1 Upcurl paraph, fol. 38rb. Auchinleck manuscript (Edinburgh, NLS, MS Advocates 19. 2. 1). Reproduced by permission of the National Library of Scotland.

line of script, and his upper horizontal lines tend to intrude more deeply into the text area than those of the first artist. In addition, these paraphs often angle down and to the right in respect to the text line.

The third most productive artist I call the *long-descender artist* (Figure 3). His paraphs are characterized by the long vertical line on the right of the paraph that curls back to the left at its end. My identification of this long-descender artist is the most difficult of the four because the paraph's body shape nearly matches that of the flat artist. I distinguish the two types of paraphs for two reasons. First, it is difficult to see why an artist would at times and for several gatherings suddenly make long descenders on his paraphs – especially when both forms appear within one booklet (booklet 3) and when such descenders break the uniform appearance of the paraphs. Second, the long-descender artist inserts only red paraphs. The flat artist paints both red and blue paraphs; the long descender never occurs on blue paraphs.

The fourth artist's paraphs are the most distinctive – and debatable – of the group. Narrower in body than those of all the other artists, his paraphs display a distinctive wave in the upper horizontal, hence my term *wavy-top artist*. He produces nearly all the paraphs in Scribe 2's work, the exception being the single leaf of *The Sayings of the Four Philosophers*, where the typical wavy-top red paraph is not present (fol. 105r). Moreover, he inserts only red paraphs. The details of Marshall's analysis show some distinct differences among these consistently red wavy-top paraphs,[28] which are found in the booklets begun by Scribe 2 (booklets 2 and 12); in booklet 3 (three red paraphs in Scribe 3's stint and one leaf copied by Scribe 2 to help fill the booklet); and in booklets 4 and 5 (one gathering each). In these instances of the wavy-top paraph, Marshall distinguishes two paraphers: *wavy top 'b'* (occurring only within two of Scribe 2's stints) (Figure 4) and *wavy top 'a'* (Figure 5). She notes an upcurl on the bottom stroke of the paraphs by 'a', and the absence of a bottom stroke in those of 'b'; the primarily straight descender used by 'a' and the left-angling descender used by 'b'; and the longer top strokes and descenders drawn by 'a'. Marshall argues that Scribe 2 (the wavy top 'b' parapher) inserted his own paraphs. It seems entirely

---

[28] Marshall, 'What's in a Paraph', p. 42.

Fig. 2 Flat paraph, fol. 30rb. Auchinleck manuscript (Edinburgh, NLS, MS
Advocates 19. 2. 1). 256vb. Reproduced by permission of the National Library
of Scotland.

Fig. 3 Long-descender paraph, fol. 66rb. Auchinleck manuscript (Edinburgh,
NLS, MS Advocates 19. 2. 1). Reproduced by permission of the National Library
of Scotland.

Fig. 4 Wavy-top 'b' paraph, fol. 39rb (Scribe 2 stint). Auchinleck manuscript
(Edinburgh, NLS, MS Advocates 19. 2. 1). Reproduced by permission of the
National Library of Scotland.

Fig. 5 Wavy-top 'a' paraph, fol. 77rb. Auchinleck manuscript (Edinburgh, NLS, MS Advocates 19. 2. 1). Reproduced by permission of the National Library of Scotland.

possible that Scribe 2 copied the beginning of booklet 2 and all of booklet 12 (the last booklet), before the final planning for Auchinleck was completed, perhaps even before its copying was begun. Still, the identification of a separate parapher outside the booklets begun by Scribe 2 raises difficulties.[29] For example, why would not Scribe 2 insert his own paraphs in his second stint, comprising a single leaf? Why would a separate parapher appear to insert red paraphs in only two gatherings and three single paraphs in another? Still, even if one accepts Marshall's contention – I do, and there is ample evidence to do so – there remain four independent paraphers at work in the manuscript aside from the putative scribe/parapher embodied by Scribe 2, whose work in the booklets he begins may have preceded the planning and assembling of the codex.

The work of the four independent artists is distributed quite unevenly in the codex (see Appendix). The upcurl paraphs, in either red or blue, appear in some thirty-seven of the forty-seven surviving (in whole or in part) gatherings; the flat paraphs in fourteen; the long-descender paraphs in nine; and the wavy-top red 'a' and 'b' in six. The upcurl artist appears in every booklet but the final one (the work of Scribe 2 solely) and in every stint written by Scribe 1. Of the thirty-two gatherings in which Scribe 1's work appears, we find the upcurl parapher in twenty-eight.

The dominance of one parapher in the leaves suggests to me that the work of the decoration may have proceeded in much the same way the copying did. That is, the paraphs indicate that one artist, the upcurl parapher, dominated this aspect of the codex, his work appearing in some three-fourths of the extant gatherings. The other artists appear and disappear throughout the codex, suggesting the sort of piecework done in the copying rather than artists working in close collaboration on an entire text, a gathering at a time, in one location. For example, the work of the two wavy-top artists, who made only red paraphs, appears only in the work of Scribes 2, 3, and 5, never in the texts copied by Scribe 1 (the sole piece copied by

---

[29] Marshall designates him the *wavy-top 'a' parapher* ('What's in a Paraph?', p. 42); see Figure 5.

Scribe 4, *The Battle Abbey Roll*, has no paraphs at all in its two-plus leaves).[30] The upcurl red paraphs are found only in gatherings written by Scribes 1, 5, and 6, never in any gatherings copied by Scribes 2 or 3. One last example will suffice to show the intermittent work of these artists: in the work of Scribe 2, the paraphs are nearly always red; blue paraphs appear only in his brief stint on fol. 105r. As a rule, the paraphs alternate red and blue throughout the texts. Furthermore, the wavy-top 'b' red paraphs end with the conclusion of Scribe 2's first stint in mid-gathering, evidence that the paraphs were in place before the gathering was completed.

To be sure, other oddities occur. For example, upcurl red paraphs never appear in the text unless the alternating blue paraphs are also in the upcurl design. This correspondence has led to my surmise that these leaves were done by a single hand. On fol. 78r, the second leaf of a gathering, the last column ends a poem, and the paraphs are all blue (rather than alternating red and blue). On fol. 79r, the red/blue pattern picks up again from the first leaf (fol. 77r). On fol. 150v, at the bottom of the right column, a long-descender red paraph appears even though it is not the red paraph that occurs regularly throughout the gathering. The hesitant line of the descender, however, gives me pause in identifying it as an extraordinary appearance of the artist who draws these paraphs. Perhaps it is a later addition. In gathering 25, there are two places in which the wavy-top red paraphs lack their descenders, probably because the descender would have run into the red flourishes of the capitals at those points. If so, these incidents suggest the capital letter work was done prior to the paraphing work.

Thus it would appear that one hand inserted most of the paraphs in the places marked by the scribes in the text, just as one scribe wrote most of the text. That artist performs most of his work in those leaves copied by the major scribe, a tantalizing suggestion that he may have been a preferred artist for the scribe who organized and oversaw the work of the manuscript. Given the environment in which scribes and artists appear to have worked individually in their own shops, as Scott has described it, it would seem natural that some alliances would form. A scribe/stationer would have at hand a particular artist to whom he went when work was to be done and when that artist was not preoccupied with other work. To expedite the work or to continue the work when this preferred artist was otherwise engaged, the scribe/stationer enlisted other artists to assist with the timely completion of the work.

Indeed, the placement of the paraphs seems to have been among the last bits of work performed on the manuscript. On fol. 117ra, for example, a blue paraph covers the spray decoration of the capital. On fol. 225ra, the usual long descender on the red paraph has been aborted, it seems, to avoid overlapping the sprays of

---

[30] There has been considerable disagreement over the number of scribes at work in the manuscript. Cunningham accepts the view of A. J. Bliss, 'Notes on the Auchinleck Manuscript', *Speculum* 26 (1951), 652–8 (p. 653), as did I, in Shonk, 'A Study', p. 73. Robinson, 'Some Aspects', pp. 128–31, argues that Scribes 6 and 1 are the same figures, 'persuasively' according to Hanna, 'Reconsidering the Auchinleck Manuscript', p. 92. Wiggins's recent analysis provides a compelling argument that these are separate scribes ('Are Auchinleck Manuscript Scribes 1 and 6 the Same Scribe?'). But see, too, Hanna's chapter in this volume.

the capital below it. Other instances in which the paraph signs overlap and cover the sprays of the capitals appear on fols. 134vb, 239va, 260ra, and 307va, to cite a few instances from throughout the manuscript. If the evidence of the overlapping colours demonstrates that the paraphs were among the last items inserted into the manuscript, we can establish a more definite sequence of the work: the leaves were copied and marked for miniatures, capitals, and paraphs by the scribes. The leaves were then sent to the artists, the capital letters being done first, the paraphs being done afterwards. It remains unclear to me at what point the miniatures may have been painted. Some instances, however, indicate that the capitals were placed after the miniatures. On fol. 326ra, at the beginning of *King Richard*, the upper sprays of the opening capital appear to curl around the lower left corner of the miniature's border, avoiding even the ruling for the border, but one spray intrudes into the miniature, covering the paint of the illustration. On fols. 259rb and 279va, moreover, the opening capitals have no ascending sprays, perhaps because they would have overlapped the miniature. Of course, it is also possible that the capital artist simply restrained the sprays at points where they might intrude into a miniature space, but this assumption would seem to argue some very precise planning.

One last curiosity in the decoration seems to secure this sequence. On fol. 157rb, a red capital, not the usual blue, has been inserted over a paraph. Assuming that this capital was inserted either at the time the leaves were being finished off or soon after, we see that someone has corrected an error in the decoration scheme. This person does not appear to be the one who inserted the other capitals: the colour scheme is wrong, and the capital lacks the usual sprays that accompany almost all the other capitals in the text.

Although we now have a clearer sense of the sequence in which the artwork was done, another question arises: in what manner and in what order did the leaves arrive in the hands of the artists? It does not appear that the artists were presented with the complete text at one time. If that were the case, one would assume that – as Pearsall has argued would have been the most logical distribution of material for the work of the scribes – the gatherings would have been distributed more evenly among the various artists for reasons of speed and efficiency. But the evidence suggests otherwise. Moreover, the work of the paraphers appears in bunches, often running through several gatherings (in the case of at least two of the artists), and then abruptly terminating, with new artists taking up the paraphs in succeeding gatherings.

The one exception occurs in the opening leaves of gathering 8. At the end of Scribe 2's *Speculum Gy de Warewyke*, on the remaining stub of fol. 48r, the wavy-top, all-red paraphs end; and with the beginning of *Amis and Amiloun*, the red/blue alternating pattern of the paraphs returns, with the red paraphs changing shape in mid-gathering to those of the upcurl artist (on fol. 49r, following the stub page). The suggestion of this instance is that Scribe 2 had finished the *Speculum Gy de Warewyke*, and Scribe 1 began *Amis and Amiloun* on the second leaf of the gathering to avoid a waste of vellum or to avoid a gathering cut to two leaves. The *Speculum Gy de Warewyke*, therefore, may well have been completed prior to Scribe 1's final conception of the layout of the manuscript, or Scribe 2 may have been at work on this piece as Scribe 1 attended to other works. The shift in the paraph shapes indicates quite clearly that gathering 8 was not done by the same artist at the same time. At any rate, except for this unusual occurrence, the evidence makes certain that the paraphers were working predominantly gathering by gathering. The shift in paraph shapes in mid-gathering at the beginning of *Amis and Amiloun*, one of the major romances of the codex, suggests it was decorated after *Speculum Gy de Warewyke*.

In the last gathering of booklet 2, another change in the paraph shapes occurs: the red paraphs shift to the long-descender design, its first appearance in the book. The *Life of St Mary Magdalene* begins on the leaf of the preceding gathering, where *Amis and Amiloun* ends. Undoubtedly, it was added at this point to fill the remaining verso. But the shift in the paraph shapes in the following gathering as the *Life of St Mary Magdalene* continues demonstrates that the final gathering of *Amis and Amiloun* was finished by one decorater, with the final gathering decorated in part by a different parapher.

It is possible, then, that the paraphs indicate for us that the manuscript was coming to the artists in booklets or scribal stints, rather than as a complete text, lacking only the decoration before being returned to the organizing scribe, who put the booklets into their final order and presented the text to its buyer. The evidence for this hypothesis is not always easy to see. The four paraph styles manifest themselves throughout the manuscript, and a number of different paraph forms appear within a single booklet, rather than a single paraph style or pair of styles (alternating red/blue). A closer look, however, suggests that the patterns of the paraphs' occurrences support the view that the copied leaves were sent to the decorators in booklet form, perhaps as soon as the booklet was completed or as soon as the major poems within booklets were completed by the minor scribes, and returned to Scribe 1, who occasionally inserted filler pieces to complete gatherings begun by other scribes.

For example, in the latter half of the manuscript, in booklet 5, seven full gatherings copied by Scribe 1 follow successfully after the ending of *Sir Beues*, by Scribe 5 (his only stint), in the first leaves of gathering 29. This lengthy stint by Scribe 1 completes booklet 5 and continues through five of the next six booklets, broken only by the single ten-leaf booklet 7 (*Otuel a Kni3t*) copied by Scribe 6. Noteworthy in this lengthy segment of Scribe 1's work, whether copied sequentially or not, is the profusion of romance material: *Of Arthour and of Merlin, Lay le Freine, Kyng Alisaunder, Sir Tristrem, Sir Orfeo, Horn Childe and Maiden Rimnild,* and *King Richard* – the very kinds of poems likely to be circulating or available in booklet form. In terms of the paraphs, the consistency of the hands is of paramount interest in this segment: they belong to the upcurl and long-descender paraphers, the same two who finished booklet 2. While booklets 2 and 3 evidence three paraphers, this segment by Scribe 1 shows a consistency of paraph forms throughout.

In booklet 5, this series of booklets of primarily romance material continues, after the beginning of *Guy of Warwick* in booklet 4. In the last five of the eleven gatherings comprising booklet 5, all copied by Scribe 1, the long-descender red paraph occurs accompanied by the upcurl blue. In short, a single pair of artists decorated these five gatherings. The long-descender artist did not appear in booklet 4. Moreover, the wavy-top red seen in the last complete gathering by Scribe 5 disappears. The following gathering – beginning on fol. 199r and reverting to the copying of Scribe 1, who begins *Of Arthour and of Merlin* on fol. 201r – returns to the red and blue upcurls. Again, the wavy-top red never appears in the work of the major scribe. Except for the single gathering in which the wavy-top red appears in this booklet and except for the long-descender reds in the final four gatherings, the remainder of the paraphs are inserted by the upcurl artist.

In this segment, furthermore, another pattern reveals the probability that the artists were decorating the leaves in a piecemeal manner, perhaps in units smaller than complete booklets. Scribe 5's stint began in the preceding booklet as he copied *Reinbrun*, starting on fol. 167r, the penultimate leaf of gathering 24 in booklet 4. As the work of Scribe 5 continues into the last gathering of this booklet to complete *Reinbrun*, the distinct wavy-top red 'a' makes an appearance. The wavy-top red 'a' also makes its appearance in the last full gathering (28) Scribe 5 copied in the succeeding booklet 5, providing a suggestive bookend stint by this artist. Thus in Scribe 5's complete gatherings, in his only appearance in the manuscript, his work is decorated by the wavy-top and upcurl artists. The paraph shapes change with his first full gathering in booklet 4, where, prior to Scribe 5's arrival, the paraphs were all done by the flat artist and the upcurl artist. The paraph shapes change again at the end of his last full gathering, shifting to a series of gatherings all done by the upcurl artist. The wavy-top 'a' artist never appears again in the remaining eight gatherings of booklet 5. It seems likely, then, that Scribe 5's work was completed and sent to the decorators at a time different from when the rest of the booklet was sent on. Thus, while the content is clearly organized into booklets, the decorator's work may have proceeded on groupings sometimes smaller than a full booklet. The different times at which the pieces went to the decorators may indicate either that Scribe 1 was copying other texts while Scribe 5 finished *Sir Beues* or that the exemplar for *Amis and Amiloun* was unavailable for copying when Scribe 5 returned his leaves.

In succeeding booklets 6, 9, and 11, all copied by Scribe 1, only upcurl reds and blues appear. These booklets also contain some of the romance materials mentioned above. In my view, at least two of these three booklets were thus sent to the artists and the paraphs inserted in one batch. Because at least three gatherings are lost from booklet 11, it is difficult to assume that it arrived in the artists' hands at the same time as booklets 6 and 9 (a similar problem appears in booklet 8, where the two surviving gatherings are decorated by the long-descender red paraph and the upcurl blue, suggesting a stint by two paraphers, but too much text is missing for certainty). We must recall that these booklets are heavily weighted with romance material: *Lay le Freine, Roland and Vernagu, Kyng Alisaunder, Sir Tristrem*, and *Sir Orfeo*. Again, these booklets of romance material seem to have been conceived, copied by the scribes, and decorated by the paraphers, at least, in one sequential activity.

Finally, booklet 10, a three-gathering booklet solely by Scribe 1, shows a combination of two paraph styles: upcurl reds and blues in the first gathering, and flat reds and blues in the last two gatherings. Of particular interest here is that the manuscript shows the same combination (upcurls and flats in succeeding gatherings) in booklet 1. This mirror pattern leads me to speculate that these two booklets might have gone to the artists at the same, or nearly the same, time. It is noteworthy that the flat red never appears in the second half of the manuscript (i.e., after gathering 24) except in this booklet 10, and that the paraphs frequently show in both early and late gatherings an unusually long upper horizontal on the paraph body that extends farther into the text than is seen in most of the paraph shapes (see, for example, fols. 10r and 314r). It seems possible also to include booklet 4 with this grouping. Booklets 1, 4 (to the first full gathering by Scribe 5), and 10 are the only booklets completed solely by the flat and upcurl paraphers.

The suggestion of these groupings of the paraphers' work is that the leaves were decorated as they came to the artists as complete booklets or as completed stints by the scribes, sometimes comprising a unit smaller than a booklet. The upcurl artist alone remains a constant throughout this lengthy stretch of Scribe 1's work, and is the single parapher whose work appears in every booklet but for the last, a booklet copied solely by Scribe 2 . If my hypothesis about the similarities between booklets 1 and 10 has merit, the groupings of the paraphs also suggest that the copying and decorating of the manuscript were not done in the order in which the pieces now occur.

The earlier booklet 3, as it now exists, is more problematic because the shapes of several paraphers appear within it. In fact, booklets 2 and 3 are the only booklets showing the work of more than two paraphers, aside from the anomaly in booklet 4, where the wavy-top red parapher appears in the final gathering for one stint. In booklet 3, written by Scribe 3, one of two possibilities arises. Either Scribe 3 was initially unaware of the decorating scheme for the larger codex, or most of his gatherings were completed before the final form of the manuscript was conceived by Scribe 1. This booklet 3, copied almost exclusively by Scribe 3 (Scribe 4's only stint, *The Battle Abbey Roll*, appears in the last leaves of the gathering), defies the very consistent decorating plan from the outset, opening with a 10-line initial capital (fol. 70ra) for *On þe Seuen Dedly Sinnes* that is not inset into the text, as is the historiated initial for *Sir Beues* (fol. 176ra) or the filled lombard for *The Simonie* (fol. 328ra), for example. Moreover, no space was allowed for a title (Scribe 1 squeezing in 'sinnes' and what appears to be the item number above the left column rather than centred, perhaps to avoid covering the spray from the initial). On fol. 72r, a miniature for *The Pater Noster Vndo on Englissch* was squeezed in between the columns, again with no space allowed for it by the scribe. Furthermore, in Scribe 3's second and third gatherings, only one paraph appears at all.

In the first gathering of the booklet (a collection of relatively short, religiously oriented pieces), the paraphs are by the flat artist. In the second gathering, *Sir Degare* begins on the second leaf. The paraphs change shape at the beginning of this gathering to the distinct wavy-top red and the upcurl blue. *Sir Degare* ends on the first leaf of the succeeding gathering of the booklet. Surprisingly, the last five leaves of this poem show no paraphs at all, and no places for the paraphs were marked by the scribe. The following gatherings, 13 and 14, evidence only one paraph in their sixteen leaves. Gathering 15 is missing, but, in gathering 16, at which point *Floris and Blauncheflur* is in progress (with nearly 400 lines lost at its opening), paraphs once again appear regularly in the forms of the long-descender red and the upcurl blue – coincidentally the same pair that decorated the last gathering of the preceding booklet 2, the other booklet also showing frequent and sudden shifts in the paraph shapes. Perhaps this final poem by Scribe 3, a romance, was decorated later than his earlier pieces and brought into conformity with the larger presentation scheme. But there is another possible explanation. Perhaps booklets 2 and 3, those that show three and four paraphers with frequent shifts in their work at the beginnings of gatherings, were conceived originally as a separate unit or inserted late as a 'bridge unit' between the predominantly religious material and the centrepiece romances. If the manuscript were nearing its completion, the teamwork of the independent paraphers could quickly complete the gatherings.

While I still insist that the manuscript was conceived as a whole at some early point in its production by the organizer, Scribe 1, the evidence here supports Hanna's view of booklets as a production method. One might question, of course, whether it seems plausible that booklets would be allotted to decorators for such brief and specialized work. Yet, as Scott has shown in her analysis of a fifteenth-century decorating shop, 'the organizing of labour in an illuminating shop was apparently of a highly divided and mobile nature'.[31] In one of the texts Scott examined, Oxford, Bodleian Library, MS Bodley 283, a text in which only two border decorations were inserted, two artists were employed, and there appears to have been a distinction between greater and lesser artists.[32] As in Scott's description, Auchinleck seems to have been decorated by a group of greater and lesser artists whose 'attachments to a shop must have been rather free and easy',[33] and who entered and exited the manuscript when needed or when other artists were occupied. In his discussion of the shifting identifications of the assignments of hands of the 'Queen Mary Group', Hanna offers a useful suggestion for resolving the argument: the problems 'might better be explained by considering the books as dispersed piecework among whatever hands happened to be available and capable of specific tasks'.[34]

And yet further information about the sequence of decorating and the order in which the gatherings may have been completed is not everything that a close study of the paraphs yields. In his interesting book *Rereading Middle English Romance*, Murray Evans argues that decoration patterns may assist us in defining what the medieval writers and audience perceived as 'romance', a term that eludes precise definition even today.[35] In an effort to determine whether manuscripts presented a different layout and decoration pattern for romances and poems with romance materials (for example, lays), Evans studied several aspects of romance-heavy manuscripts: titles, incipits, opening initials, and the extent of decoration, among other items. While his review of the Auchinleck manuscript was handicapped by the large number of missing leaves at the openings and closings of poems and by the excised miniatures that may have also removed titles or incipits, Evans's analysis of the decoration of manuscripts with groups of romances draws a number of conclusions, the most pertinent for my

[31] Scott, 'A Mid-Fifteenth-Century English Illuminating Shop', p. 194.

[32] Ibid., p. 194.

[33] Ibid., p. 195.

[34] R. Hanna, *London Literature, 1300–1380*, Cambridge Studies in Medieval Literature 57 (Cambridge, 2005), p. 81.

[35] M. J. Evans, *Rereading Middle English Manuscripts: Manuscript Layout, Decoration, and the Rhetoric of Composite Structure* (Montreal, 1995).

purposes being that 'romances are more decorated than nonromances' in Evans's group of fifteen prominent manuscripts featuring romances.[36]

At first glance, this conclusion seems to offer little of use for our study of Auchinleck. It is extensively decorated throughout, and even minor poems (for example, *The Wench Þat Loued a King*) appear to have been preceded by a miniature, an instance seeming to defy the notion that romances were distinguished by opening illustrations and larger, more ornate capitals. And yet the paraphs – to be more precise, the numbers of paraphs in relation to the capitals marking major segments of the narrative in romances – offer some suggestive, though inconclusive, evidence about the layout and decoration of the manuscript.

A review of Auchinleck shows that virtually every kind of poem in the piece has paraphs and capitals as part of the decorative scheme (*The Battle Abbey Roll* being an exception, as a piece of non-poetry). When we look at the major elements of the manuscript – that is, the lengthy romances (longer than ten leaves) – we often see more pervasive use of filled lombard capitals with their flourishes and less use of paraphs for section markers. Nearly all students of the manuscript point to *Guy of Warwick*, for instance, as one of the manuscript's prestige items. In my review of the couplet segment of *Guy*, I found more capitals than paraphs used to denote major sections (approximately 130 capitals to 123 paraphs). *Guy* in couplets runs for some thirty-eight leaves, yielding an average of about three capitals per leaf. In other segments of the manuscript containing legends, hagiographies, and other non-romance poems, the average appears to be about one capital per page. The paraph is used more heavily in these minor poems, many of which are in stanza form, most notably because the paraphs are used to mark stanza beginnings. The use of the paraph to mark stanzas also means that the capitals appear much less frequently in the stanzaic *Guy of Warwick*, as one might expect. To be sure, placing a 2- or 3-line capital at every stanza opening, whether it occurs every four lines or every twelve, would have been time-consuming (i.e., expensive) and led to unpleasantly busy pages.

In *Sir Beues*, a romance in a mixed style (the opening 400-plus lines in 6-line tail-rhyme stanzas, the remaining nearly 4,000 lines in couplets), we find a pattern similar to that of the couplet *Guy*: the capitals occur at least as frequently as paraphs in the couplet segment, perhaps slightly more frequently. *Sir Beues* also opens with a historiated initial, a device often used in other manuscripts to distinguish romances from other pieces.[37] In *Lay le Freine,* the distribution of paraphs and capitals follows virtually the same pattern – roughly even. In the early couplet romance *Sir Degare*, though it is less than ten leaves in length, capitals outnumber the paraphs five to one, with all the paraphs coming in the first three leaves. And, in the remaining pages and fragments of *King Richard*, I find that the capital is favoured almost two to one for designating divisions within the text.

Still, the pattern of this distribution is not as clear as these few examples seem to show. In the couplet lines of *Of Arthour and of Merlin*, a romance of some fifty-five

---

[36] Ibid., p. 50.

[37] See, for example, the Thornton manuscript (Lincoln, Cathedral Library, MS 91), cited by H. Hudson, 'Middle English Popular Romances: The Manuscript Evidence', *Manuscripta* 28 (1984), 67–78 (p. 70, n. 8). The historiated initial opening *Sir Beues* appears on the cover of this volume.

leaves, the paraphs far outnumber the capitals. I would note, however, that no paraphs appear on the first leaf of the work (fol. 201rb), and a number of leaves appear with no paraphs at all, some leaves with a capital or two and no paraphs. *Sir Tristrem*, a stanzaic romance, has, as one would expect, far more paraphs than capitals. But again, I would point out that it begins with a large 11-line capital, the largest in the text (fol. 281ra). On the other hand, in the couplet romance *Floris and Blauncheflur*, albeit not a major romance (only about five leaves in length and copied by the curious Scribe 3), the paraphs far outnumber the capitals. Moreover, in other non-romance poems, capitals dominate, though there are logical explanations for many of them (for example, *Alphabetical Praise of Women* and *Dauid þe King*, a translation of Psalm 50). The booklet containing *Otuel a Kniȝt* is surprisingly free of capitals, having only three in its ten-leaf surviving gathering after the filled initial and border work that begins the piece (fol. 268ra). Perhaps this piece, the only one copied by Scribe 6 in the manuscript, was completed as a stock piece before the final plan of the manuscript was conceived, or perhaps it simply provides counter-evidence to the idea that the romances were to be presented with numerous flourished capitals throughout the texts.

Thus, we can draw no definitive conclusions about this pattern of distribution. The evidence presented here is further obscured, of course, by the absence of certain exemplars for pieces, exemplars that might have dictated many elements of presentation. We can, however, offer some tentative hypotheses. It would seem that the paraph – obviously a marker of less prestige and decorative value than capitals with flourishes – was used, as a general rule, with less frequency in the prestige items of the manuscript. Moreover, that the dominance of capitals in marking narrative sections falls largely within the romance items – though I concede that the pattern is not consistent – suggests that the manuscript's organizer felt it appropriate to highlight these texts in a less workaday fashion than a series of paraphs would accomplish. As Harriet Hudson argues, 'It is partly because [the gentry] sought to display and enhance their gentility that they owned manuscripts of romances in the first place.'[38] If this is indeed the case, it may well be that the organizing scribe of Auchinleck sought some means of decorating the romances to 'enhance their gentility', and called for the more artful and pleasing capital letters, including the huge opening capital and the historiated initial, to highlight these items.

This study of the paraphs largely affirms what we have suspected or surmised with little hard evidence for the production process, as opposed to the organizing process. Admittedly, my analysis contains a good deal of conjecture, and yet this conjecture seems in keeping with what we assume must have been the process. Further work is needed to substantiate all this. For example, it would be very instructive to know how the texts came to the copyists and whether or not the booklet divisions reflect, in the main, the decorative collaborations or piecemeal work in other booklets. It would also be most valuable to look for the work of these paraphers among other manuscripts of the period, to determine whether evidence exists to show they were working in one shop or were indeed independent

[38] Hudson, 'Middle English Popular Romances', p. 78.

craftsmen available to work on other texts. Clearly, as I have shown, the work of paraphers can be identified by the shapes and aspects of their forms. The next stage in the study of this form would be to build upon the work of Mooney and Stubbs, Wiggins, and Marshall to determine if these forms can be found in other contemporary manuscripts. Marshall has identified a manuscript written by Scribe 2 that has paraphs similar, though not definitively so, to those in his work in Auchinleck. Identifying the work of a parapher in other manuscripts would add greatly to our understanding of the communities of bookmakers and the transmission and circulation of these texts in the early fourteenth century.

To be sure, the Auchinleck manuscript is big and messy, and yet it remains one of the most important and most extensively, if not sumptuously, decorated manuscripts of secular literature of its time. Its selection of materials alone places it in a rather exclusive category in the manuscript tradition, for, as Ian Doyle insists, manuscripts containing vernacular texts 'were only a small proportion of the production and dissemination of literature, and scholars cannot afford to forget or neglect this'.[39] The extensive system of decoration within the manuscript makes it even more noteworthy, though not necessarily unique. Hanna makes clear that some features of the decoration of Auchinleck (for example, the offset initial letter of each line in separate columns, often slashed with red) denote 'textual presentation developed very early on in Anglo-Norman books [that] … has simply carried over into English. In essence, format follows content'.[40]

While Auchinleck is distinctive yet imitative, innovative yet traditional, it remains one of the most important books of the fourteenth century. Its patterns of decoration comprise a critical part of its importance, revealing much about the methods of book production in the first half of the century: independent scribes and artists, perhaps peripatetic individuals, collaborated (albeit often in an intermittent fashion) to produce a bespoke text order undertaken by a scribe/stationer. The text was prepared in production booklets and sometimes sent to the decorators in even smaller pieces. The content itself may not have been fully determined at the time of the original agreement, and some texts may have existed in small booklets before the complete work took its form. Such a circumstance would explain the troublesome work of Scribe 3, who left no room for the sorts of miniatures and titles that appear consistently throughout the codex. But, soon afterwards, the image of the final text began to take place in Scribe 1's mind, and the extant decoration reflects that image. The means of *ordinatio* for the compilation does not merely subordinate certain aspects and highlight others, such as the romances; rather, as Evans suggests,[41] it also unifies the book, providing a single collection of some of the most desired pieces for the prosperous owner, and providing for us today critical evidence for the state of Middle English literature, its readers, and the methods of production and presentation of that literature.

---

[39] A. I. Doyle, 'Recent Directions in Manuscript Study', in *New Directions in Later Medieval Manuscript Studie: Essays from the 1998 Harvard Conference*, ed. D. Pearsall (York, 2000), pp. 1–14 (p. 3).

[40] Hanna, 'Reconsidering the Auchinleck Manuscript', p. 98.

[41] Evans, *Rereading Middle English Manuscripts*, p. 4.

APPENDIX

Paraph distribution by gathering and booklet[42]

Booklet	Gathering	Scribe	Red	Blue
1	1	1	flat	upcurl
	2	1	flat	flat
	3	1	flat	upcurl
	4	1	flat	flat
	5	1	flat	flat
	6	1	upcurl	upcurl
2	7	2	wavy-top 'b'	—
	8	2/1	wavy-top 'b'/upcurl	upcurl
	9	1	upcurl	upcurl
	10	1	long-descender	upcurl
3	11	3	flat	flat
	12	3	wavy-top 'a'	upcurl
	13	3	—	only one upcurl
	14	3	—	—
	15	3	(missing)	(missing)
	16	3/2/4	long-descender	upcurl
4	17	1	upcurl	upcurl
	18	1	flat	upcurl
	19	1	flat	upcurl
	20	1	upcurl	upcurl
	21	1	flat	upcurl
	22	1	flat	upcurl
	23	1	flat	upcurl
	24	1/5	flat	flat
	25	5	wavy-top 'a'	upcurl
5	26	5	upcurl	upcurl
	27	5	upcurl	upcurl
	28	5	wavy-top 'a'	upcurl
	29	5/1	upcurl	upcurl
	30	1	upcurl	upcurl
	31	1	upcurl	upcurl
	32	1	long-descender	upcurl
	33	1	long-descender	upcurl
	34	1	long-descender	upcurl
	35	1	long-descender	upcurl
	36	1	long-descender	upcurl
6	37	1	upcurl	upcurl
7	38–?	6	upcurl	upcurl
8	39 (and others missing)			
	40 (Alisaunder fragments)		long-descender	upcurl
	?–41	1	long-descender	upcurl

[42] Booklet divisions follow those given in Pearsall, 'Literary and Historical Significance', p. ix; gathering divisions follow I. C. Cunningham, 'Physical Description', in Pearsall-Cunningham, pp. xi–xiv (pp. xii–xiii). The paraph identifications are my own.

9	42	1	upcurl	upcurl
	43	1	upcurl	upcurl
	44	1	upcurl	upcurl
10	45	1	upcurl	upcurl
	46	1	flat	flat
	47	1	flat	flat
11	48–?	1	upcurl	upcurl
	49–51 (*missing*)			
12	52	2	wavy-top 'b'	—

CHAPTER TWELVE

Scribal Corrections in the Auchinleck Manuscript

Míceál F. Vaughan

W HILE there is general agreement that Scribe 1 served in a final, compilational role in the construction of the Auchinleck manuscript (Edinburgh, NLS, MS Advocates 19. 2. 1), we have not (so far) succeeded in making entirely clear the chronological order in which the various booklets (or fascicles) came together and how they came to be arranged as they now stand in Auchinleck.[1] Even if we set aside the continuing dispute over whether there were six (A. J. Bliss, Derek Pearsall and Ian Cunningham, Alison Wiggins),[2] five (Eugen Kölbing, Malcolm Parkes, Ralph Hanna)[3] or four (Pamela Robinson)[4] scribes at work on the collection, we are unable to describe a firm sequence for the production of the twelve booklets that now comprise the manuscript: we do not know exactly how the contributions of the various scribes fit together into a fully convincing chronology. And, while the catchwords and item numbers attest to the present (i.e., final), compiled order of the fascicles, which we now (following Timothy Shonk)[5] confidently attribute to

---

[1] The numbering of scribes follows the two facsimiles (Pearsall-Cunningham, Burnley-Wiggins). An alphabetic order used by P. R. Robinson (with adjustments to the number of scribes) may more satisfactorily present the probable chronological order of the scribes' work on the manuscript; see P. R. Robinson, 'A Study of Some Aspects of the Transmission of English Verse in Late Mediaeval Manuscripts', unpublished B Litt thesis, University of Oxford (Oxford, 1972), pp. 120–38. She letters and lists the scribes 'in the order in which they worked on the manuscript' (p. 129).

[2] In addition to the introductions to the two facsimiles listed in note 1, see A. J. Bliss, 'Notes on the Auchinleck Manuscript', *Speculum* 26 (1951), 652–8; and A. Wiggins, 'Are Auchinleck Manuscript Scribes 1 and 6 the Same Scribe?: The Advantages of Whole-Data Analysis and Electronic Texts', *Medium Ævum* 73 (2004), 10–26.

[3] E. Kölbing, 'Vier romanzen-handschriften', *Englische Studien* 7 (1884), 177–201. The opinion of Malcolm Parkes is reported by P. R. Robinson, 'A Study', pp. 130–1, and accepted by R. Hanna, 'Reconsidering the Auchinleck Manuscript', in *New Directions in Later Medieval Manuscript Studies: Essays from the 1998 Harvard Conference*, ed. D. Pearsall (York, 2000), pp. 91–102 (pp. 92–3). See also R. Hanna's chapter in this volume.

[4] Robinson, 'A Study', pp. 128–31.

[5] T. A. Shonk, 'A Study of the Auchinleck Manuscript: Bookmen and Bookmaking in the Early Fourteenth Century', *Speculum* 60 (1985), 71–91; Shonk's view (p. 84) that the catchword at the bottom of fol. 99v is by Scribe 1 is persuasive.

Scribe 1 (Robinson's Scribe D),[6] that order certainly cannot correspond to, or even clearly reveal, the earlier stages of the manuscript's composition and arrangement. As Wiggins quite properly notes: 'Clues as to how the fascicles were organised and arranged during the various stages of production are not easily found or interpreted as no regular system of signatures has survived in the manuscript.'[7] And it is not just the absence of signatures that is an obstacle to identifying the 'stages of production': the composition of booklets in which two (or more) scribes participated works against any simple, linear sequence of production.

If the old idea of a 'London workshop'[8] has become no longer entirely tenable, how do the irregularities in the serial composition of the constituent booklets make sense? Scribe 3, for instance, clearly preceded Scribe 2 (in booklet 3) and Scribe 2 preceded Scribe 1 (in booklet 2). And, of course, if the final ordering of the quires (with their catchwords) and the titles were the work of Scribe 1, then he succeeded all of the other scribes, and not simply in those booklets where his texts appear after those of Scribe 2 (in booklet 2) and Scribe 5 (in booklet 5), but also in booklet 4, where Scribe 5's *Reinbrun Gij Sone of Warwike* followed his stanzaic *Guy of Warwick*.

It is, however, less demonstrable that Scribe 1 had a decisive role in the *earlier* stages of the manuscript's production and layout. After all, his single-column copying of *The Legend of Pope Gregory* (the first item in the extant manuscript, though numbered 'vi' at the tops of fols. 2–4) may, if it were an earlier production, suggest that the two-column format generally found in Auchinleck was not established by him from the outset. One might plausibly argue that this format, more generally employed for the bulk of the manuscript, may have derived, rather, from the model established by, say, Scribe 5 (that is, in booklet 5) and that it was adopted by Scribe 1 *after* he had completed his work on that booklet. If this were the case, then we would be forced to conclude that booklet 5 (begun with *Sir Beues of Hamtoun*) may have been the first in the standardized format that we now find in the majority of Auchinleck. Alternatively, if booklet 1 was a late product of Scribe 1, then one is required to ask why he abandoned at a late stage the format so generally followed elsewhere in Auchinleck. Likewise, is it purely coincidental that the first and last booklets (i.e., Scribe 2's *The Simonie*) in the present organization of the collection's booklets are the only ones in single-column format?[9]

---

[6] Robinson, 'Study', p. 129, who also holds that Scribes 2 and 4 are a single scribe: her Scribe B. The alternative numerical sequencing of scribes (as used by Kölbing and Bliss) derives from the order of their appearance in the MS as it now is compiled. Scribe 1 produced booklet 1 on his own (as he did booklets 6, 8, 9, 10, 11). Booklets 7 and 12 are the only other ones written by a single scribe, Scribes 6 and 2, respectively.

[7] In the paragraph on 'Signatures' in the page on 'Physical make-up' in Burnley-Wiggins, at http://auchinleck.nls.uk/editorial/physical.html#signatures.

[8] L. H. Loomis, 'The Auchinleck Manuscript and a Possible London Bookshop of 1330–1340', *PMLA* 57 (1942), 595–627.

[9] Of course, since we are missing the first five items of the manuscript, the present booklet 1 was preceded by at least one booklet, which *may* have been in the more usual two-column format.

While the scribal hands have been well studied (although to differing conclusions as to the number involved), and Pearsall-Cunningham, Shonk, and Wiggins have given detailed attention to a number of paratextual features (such as paraphs, catch-words, titles), little attention has been paid to the varied forms of scribal correction scattered throughout Auchinleck.[10] Beyond the apparently general attribution of the textual corrections to Scribe 1 – whether inserted intra- or super-linearly, over erasures or by altering letters, or at the end of lines – we have, in fact, left largely unexamined the variety of conventions and practices found in the correction of errors in the works of the various scribes. The received opinion holds that most, if not indeed all, corrections to the texts were the work of the compiler/editor Scribe 1.[11] But it is clear from a consideration of a few pages of the manuscript that something more varied is going on because many of them evidence differing signs and modes of deletion and insertion, for example, fols. 3v, 5v, 13v, 308r, and 324r. All these pages are the work of Scribe 1, and some of the corrections are his, but it is unlikely (given their practical variety) that they are all his. The questions therefore remain: whose corrections are they, and when in the composition and compilation of the manuscript were they made? Were they the work of others among the scribes involved in the composition of the collection, or did later readers contribute them when they sought to polish the texts that had come down to them in this collection?

A more detailed examination of these features of Auchinleck may illuminate in a small way how the collection was compiled, the relations among its scribes, and elements of its reception by early readers (and copy editors). On the basis of the differing ways of deleting errors and inserting corrections, we must at least conclude that multiple hands were involved, but, since the evidence is minimal and ambiguous, distinguishing among the correctors may prove even more difficult than identifying the number of scribes involved in the collection. And, further, identifying the various correctors with individual scribes must remain a specu-lative exercise rather than a logical (or necessary) inference: much later owners and readers of the texts may also have provided their own corrections. To complicate matters, there are, for instance, a number of places where incorrect words are marked as deleted by *two* separate means: subpunction and striking through.[12] These most obviously indicate the presence of multiple readers/correctors at work,

---

[10] Wiggins's notes on various details in her transcription and her comments on superscript insertions and misplaced lines are almost the only published discussions of these matters ('Are Auchinleck Manuscript Scribes 1 and 6 the Same Scribe?', pp. 18–19). It is worth noting that the data and numbers in my discussion (and the inventory it depends on) do not exactly correspond with hers.

[11] I have found no published statement of this view, but Oliver Pickering voiced it after I presented my earlier thoughts on 'Scribal and Paratextual Campaigns in the Auchinleck MS' at the International Medieval Congress, University of Leeds, 10 July 2000. As I show here, and as Wiggins has already pointed out ('Are Auchinleck Manuscript Scribes 1 and 6 the Same Scribe?', pp. 18–19), there are a number of instances where the corrections were demonstrably *not* supplied by Scribe 1, and others that are arguably so.

[12] Some examples: 'fley3e' (fol. 13vb, line 8); 'vp' (fol. 20va, line 22); 'wo' (fol. 61ra, line 6); 'lor' (fol. 210va, line 16); 'he' (fol. 254ra, line 5); 'her' (fol. 259ra, line 16).

one of whom did not, perhaps, understand the convention used by the other. Examining more systematically these corrections and others in Auchinleck may refine the view that someone (or ones) other than Scribe 1 played an independent – smaller yet nonetheless significant – role in the latter stages of the compilation and reception of Auchinleck.

Both deletions and insertions are accomplished in a number of distinct ways in the manuscript. Deletions are effected by scraping away, by subpunction, or by striking through the erroneous letter(s) or word(s). Table 3 below summarizes my current inventory of these various forms of deletion.[13] Of course, determining erasures is a less-than-scientific art – even if one spends considerable time examining the manuscript in person – and the numbers provided for these interventions here may be less complete than the others. A similar variety exists when we examine corrections involving the insertion of missing letter(s), word(s), or line(s). These are accomplished by writing the new text (1) in a space that has been scraped; (2) on top of existing letters/words (overwriting); (3) above the line (i.e., superscript or interlinear); (4) at the end of the line; or (5) (in the case of skipped lines) at the bottom of the column.[14] Table 1 offers my current inventory of these insertions. On the basis of letter forms, most of these can be safely ascribed to the scribes working on the main text being corrected and supplemented by the insertions. However, looking at the *ways* these insertions are supplied and marked may allow us to identify the hands involved and the timing of their contributions to the construction of Auchinleck.

Inserted lines

The most substantial corrections in Auchinleck involve the supply of missing lines, nearly all of which are self-corrections by the individual scribe writing the main text.[15] The majority of these are provided at the bottom of a column – an indication that the scribe noticed the omission while copying that column of text. This supposition is confirmed by the presence of marks in, presumably, the ink being used by the scribe. The mark is usually a brown '+', and it appears both at the point where the omitted line should be properly located and before the displaced text at the

---

[13] A more detailed list of various corrections in Auchinleck includes, so far, more than 1,000 items: see M. F. Vaughan, 'AuchinleckCorrections.xslx', at http://faculty.washington. edu/miceal/auchinleck/AuchinleckCorrections.xlsx. The inventory is still, and may remain for some time, a work in progress. There appears to be a (non-systematic) variation in the subpunction marks, and these perhaps deserve closer scrutiny. One may be able to categorize the strike-throughs to some extent: most take the form of horizontal strokes, but a few (apparently later ones) use diagonal strokes, e.g., at fol. 210va, line 16, and fol. 303vb, line 8.

[14] There are five instances, all in Scribe 1's works, where lines are inserted interlinearly (and in his hand). In three instances, no signs are used. The two in *Sir Tristrem* are *semi*-interlinear and signalled: the first (fol. 282va, line 39) has a '+' in both positions, as well as rubricated 'b' and 'a'; the second (fol. 289rb, line 31) employs only the '+' in the two positions.

[15] Cf. Wiggins, 'Are Auchinleck Manuscript Scribes 1 and 6 the Same Scribe?', pp. 18–19.

Table 1 All corrections by insertion

Scribe	Overwriting	Intralinear	Superscript letter(s)	Superscript word(s)	End-of-line	Inserted line(s)	End-of-column	Total
1 (~71%)	145 (~84%)	60 (80%)	173 (79%) / = 51 // = 1 ∧ = 1	85 (~79%) / = 31 // = 11 ∧ = 7 · = 1	17 (85%) // = 15 b+ a+ = 2	5 (100%) + = 2	13 (~81%) b+ a+ = 12 + + = 1	497 (~81%)
2 (~5%)	1 (<1%)	5 (~7%)	15 (~7%) ∧ = 4	17 (~16%) ∧ = 8	1 (5%) ~ = 1	0	0	39 (~6%)
3 (~10.7%)	11 (~6%)	3 (4%)	20 (9%) / = 4 ∧ = 1	2 ∧ = 1	1 (5%) ∧ //, // = 1	0	0	37 (~6%)
4 (~0.6%)	0	0	0	0	0	0	0	0
5 (~9.7%)	8 (~5%)	4 (~5%)	8 (<4%)	2	0	0	2 (12.5%) b+ a+ = 1 ∴ ∵ = 1	24 (~4%)
6 (~3%)	7 (4%)	3 (4%)	4 (<2%) ∧ = 3	2 ∧ = 2	1 (5%) line = 1	0	1 (~6%) .b. .a. = 1	18 (~3%)
Totals	172	75	220 ∅ = 155 (~70%) / = 55 (~25.6%) // = 1 ∧ = 9 (~4%)	108 ∅ = 47 (~44.7%) / = 31 (~27.6%) // = 11 (~10.4%) ∧ = 18 (~16%) · = 1 (~1%)	20 ∅ = 2 //, // = 15 b+ a+ = 2 ∧ //, // = 1 ~ = 1 line = 1	5 + = 2	16 b+ a+ = 13 .b. .a. = 1 + + = 1 ∴ ∵ = 1	**616**

end of the column. Fourteen of the sixteen instances employ this convention, and thirteen of these occur in texts by Scribe 1. Thirteen of the fourteen are then later marked with a rubricated 'b' and 'a', at the point of omission and at the bottom of the column, respectively; the fourteenth will be discussed below. The single instance following this convention ('a +', 'b +') in Scribe 5's work offers a slight, though perhaps instructive variation: on fol. 186vb, the original crosses are placed to the *left* of the main writing area. In Scribe 1's texts these marks regularly appear *between* the lines in the main column of text. This minor difference reinforces the sense that the '+' was the original scribe's signal in both instances. The rubricated guide letters, however, appear to be in the same hand as in the other twelve instances: whoever supplied them in Scribe 1's work also did so in Scribe 5's, and they are all most probably the work of Scribe 1.[16] In one instance, the crosses were *not* accompanied by the guide letters ('a', 'b'): at the bottom of fol. 209rb, Scribe 1 supplies *four* lines omitted above. These are preceded by a brown '+' (later rubricated), which also appears above (between lines 16–17), where the lines properly belong; these were not, however, accompanied by the rubricated 'a' and 'b', perhaps as a result of an oversight by Scribe 1.[17]

The two remaining instances of the end-of-column supply of missing lines offer more divergent variants from the above. The first anomalous instance is in Scribe 5's *Sir Beues* (fol. 197ra), where the signal in both cases is four dots arrayed in a crosslike fashion ('∴') to the left of the line-initials.[18] This is a unique mark in the manuscript, but although the form is different, the *placement* is the same as that of the '+' found earlier in *Sir Beues* (fol. 186vb) – that is, to the left of the main body of the text. It would appear that Scribe 5 employed two distinct marks to call attention to omitted lines. Finally, in Scribe 6's work, we have a final variant on these signals: on fol. 271vb, we find the rubricated 'a' and 'b', flanked by brown ink dots but unaccompanied by '+'. The red 'b' (in the left margin, between lines 19–20) has been superimposed on a brown/black 'a'. Below it is a lightly inscribed caret (with an attached horizontal line pointing to the place for inserting the missing line). These variations (in form and placement) suggest that different hands were involved in signalling the corrections for Scribes 5 and 6. But there is nothing to suggest that it was Scribe 1 or anyone other than the two scribes themselves who noticed and marked the misplacement of these lines.

While these corrections must have occurred more or less immediately as the scribes were copying, in other cases we can identify the supply of missing lines as

---

[16] In addition to the instances mentioned above (see note 14), we also find two instances where these same signals ('a +', 'b +') are used to mark the correct position for two irregularly placed bob-lines in *Sir Tristrem* (fols. 283v, 285v)], which have been inserted in the right margin by Scribe 1. These are discussed below.

[17] The '+' between lines 16–17 also has red dots added in the four quadrants. Since brown crosses were the common original mark by Scribe 1, it would appear that these rubrications are applied by a later reader.

[18] It is worth noting that this placement corresponds to the single instance of a '+' in Scribe 5's work, noted above. The four dots here before line 29 are partly obscured by the coloured 3-line initial 'I'.

occurring 'later' – but how much later cannot be determined. In most instances, however, we can assign the supplied line to the hand of the scribe of the main text being copied: the scribe noticed he had omitted a line after completing his current stint of copying. These missing lines are supplied in a few different ways. An inserted line in Scribe 6's *Otuel a Kniȝt* is placed distinctively: on fol. 269vb, the omitted line is written in the right margin, divided in two, with a line (in brown ink) drawn to the left of the upper half-line, pointing to the correct location for the supplied text. (It may be worth noting the similar line on fol. 271vb, used by Scribe 6 to mark the proper location for the end-of-column correction noted in the paragraph above.)

Scribe 1 adds five missing lines interlinearly. Although their placement makes clear where they properly belong, and three of them are accompanied by no marks, two (in *Sir Tristrem*) are signalled by the kinds of marks we have already seen him use with end-of-column insertions: one (fol. 282va) signals the insertion with rubricated 'b' and 'a', accompanied by crosses in brown ink; the second (fol. 289rb) is signalled by brown crosses alone.[19] To repeat, in all six of these cases, the evidence suggests that no one other than the original scribe was involved in the supply and mark-up of the missing lines. The scribe of the main text may not have noted the omission before the column or page was finished, but he presumably discovered the error and inserted the line not too long afterwards.

Inserted phrases, words, and letters

When we turn to less substantial insertions – omitted phrases, words, and letters – we find them handled in a number of differing ways: some are placed in the margins (more frequently in the right than the left); some are superscribed (interlinear); some are inserted within the line, often over scraped deletions of letters/words; finally, some in-line corrections are made by overwriting existing letters. On the basis of letter forms, we again are usually dealing with self-correction by individual scribes. In some instances, however, other, later hands (and not merely Scribe 1) have been involved in making the insertions.

In the case of marginally supplied omitted words, we find in two instances (in *Sir Tristrem*) that Scribe 1 provides rubricated 'b' and 'a' (accompanied by brown crosses), which, as we have already seen, he used regularly to signal end-of-column additions. He used them here in a pair of distinct instances to mark the insertion of two missing bob-lines: 'at wille' (fol. 283va) and 'on rade' (fol. 285va). Elsewhere, in the seventeen remaining instances, where single words are supplied at the end of a line for insertion earlier in that line, fifteen (all by Scribe 1) are marked (in both places) with a double virgule ('//'). The single instance in Scribe 2's stints – in *The Simonie* (fol. 329r) – supplies 'an' after a wavelike red mark in the right margin, but there is no mark in the line, between 'on' and 'oþer', where it belongs. In the final instance, Scribe 3 – in *On þe Seuen Dedly Sinnes* (fol. 70rb) – provides a marginal 'habben', which is

---

[19] Both these instances might be called *semi*-interlinear, since they are inserted above and following short bob-lines.

preceded by a double virgule, with a caret and double virgule to mark the point of insertion in the line. Significantly, however, the double virgules here are superscript in both positions, while Scribe 1's double virgules for such insertions are regularly subscript. On this evidence, the conclusion must be that scribal self-correction is the norm in all these cases. There are, in addition, a number of instances where marginal additions are made (in both left and right margins) to complete a line. Some of these are by the original scribe; others are by later editors/readers.[20]

By far the largest number of omitted words and letters are supplied in superscript (or interlinear) position.[21] Again, while most of these (on the basis of letter forms) appear to be scribal self-corrections, the variety of signals may point to the presence of copyediting intervention by others. Since the placement of these insertions is usually self-evident, we find the location for an inserted letter (or letters) unmarked nearly 70% of the time. In the case of whole words, however, the six scribes marked the location a majority (i.e., about 55%) of the time. When we turn to examine the individual practices of the various scribes, however, we discover again a number of distinct marks. In order of frequency, the marks used to identify the location for inserted letters and words are: a single virgule (~26%), a caret (~8%), or a double virgule (<5%). As Table 2 shows, the distribution of these marks among the texts of the six scribes is quite varied.

Table 2   Corrections by superscript insertions

Scribe	Superscript letter(s)	Superscript word(s)
1	unmarked: 120 (~69%) /: 51 (~29%) //: 1 (<0.6%) ʌ: 1 (<0.6%)	unmarked: 35 (~41%) /: 31 (~36%) //: 11 (~13%) ʌ: 7 (~8%) *punctus* (.): 1 (~1%)
2	unmarked: 11 (~73.3%) ʌ: 4 (~26.6%)	unmarked: 9 (~53%) ʌ: 8 (~47%)
3	unmarked: 15 (75%) /: 4 (20%) ʌ: 1 (5%)	unmarked: 1 ʌ: 1
4	None	None
5	unmarked: 8	unmarked: 2
6	unmarked: 1 (25%) ʌ: 3 (75%)	ʌ: 2
Total	220	108

---

[20] My current inventory has some twenty instances of such line-completions at the end of lines, about a half-dozen of which appear to be by later hands. There are fewer instances where insertions are made at the beginning of lines: Scribe 1 inserts 'bi' (fol. 136r), an ampersand (fol. 205v), and 'S' (fol. 286v); Scribe 2 inserts 'ʒit' (fol. 7r).

[21] Cf. Wiggins, 'Are Auchinleck Manuscript Scribes 1 and 6 the Same Scribe?', p. 18. The inventory of types and numbers given below differs from hers.

A few features deserve comment. More than one kind of mark is used in the texts of Scribes 1 and 3, where we find both carets and virgules. The caret, however, appears as the *only* mark employed to indicate the placement for superscript insertions (both letters and words) in the texts produced by Scribes 2 and 6.[22] The eight carets in Scribe 1's texts (*pace* Wiggins) deserve closer attention: seven mark the positions of supplied words and the eighth, a single letter. All of these are found in booklets that also contain work by others – that is, Scribes 2 and 5. The presence of multiple forms of signalling insertions in these composite booklets raises the question whether one of Scribe 1's collaborators (Scribe 2, say, for whom the caret is the only mark used) was also at work in correcting his contributions to these booklets. A number of these carets are associated with insertions Wiggins properly attributes to 'a later hand': both superscript words on fols. 67ra, 'ioie' (line 7) and 'held' (line 37), and likewise the inserted 'y' (in 'misseyde') on fol. 259ra, line 19. She also queries (I believe rightly) whether the 'him' inserted on fol. 258ra, line 20, is 'in another hand', and one might even extend this query to the four remaining instances of superscript insertions above a caret in Scribe 1's texts.[23] It may be fair, then, to conclude that the presence of carets in Scribe 1's texts points to these corrections as the work of someone *other* than himself. His preferred signals elsewhere, for various purposes, are virgules and double virgules.[24] Since it is usual to take Scribe 1 as the final compiler of the Auchinleck collection, these corrections deserve serious attention. A sharper eye than mine, however, would be required to determine when these corrections were introduced, and by whom: Scribe 2, Scribe 6, or someone else entirely?

The other marked superscript insertions may raise fewer, and less substantial, questions. Double virgules, for example, which Scribe 1 quite regularly employs in his texts (and Scribe 3 once) to signal end-of-line insertions (of a word or words), also are employed to mark places for *superscript* insertions. In eleven cases in Scribe 1's work, they signal a superscript *word*; in 31 (of 85) occasions in his texts, however, such superscript words are signalled instead by a single virgule. Elsewhere in Scribe 1's texts, a subscript single virgule signals approximately 30% of his superscript insertions of *letter(s)*.[25] In only a single instance in his work does a double virgule

---

[22] In the texts of Scribe 6, the single instance of an insertion with no mark – an 's' added to 'god' (fol. 275va, line 27) – may require scrutiny: the letter is similar to the form used by Scribe 1 (cf. fol. 37ra, line 19; fol. 68ra, line 10).

[23] They are: 'seyd' (fol. 158va, line 1), 'gij' (fol. 165va, line 23), 'her' (fol. 201vb, line 29), and 'it' (fol. 259ra, line 10). This last instance is not noted by Wiggins in Burnley-Wiggins, and I would argue that it is a later insertion, perhaps by the same later hand that inserted the 'y' in 'misseyde' nine lines below, which is an anomalous instance of a caret being used in Scribe 1's texts to mark an inserted letter.

[24] One further anomalous superscript insertion of a word appears above a *punctus*: 'hi~', fol. 145vb, line 33 (probably in Scribe 1's hand).

[25] In a few cases, multiple-letter insertions are marked by Scribe 1 with single virgules, e.g., 'ch' on fol. 28va, line 23, and 'de' on fol. 321vb, line 20. Also, as Shonk noted ('A Study', p. 79), Scribe 1 uses the single virgule beside a line to indicate the place for a paraph mark. Other scribes use different signs, with Scribe 6's being the double virgule.

signal inserted letters: the superscript 'þi' after 'For' (fol. 8va, line 12). This irregular sign may be the result of his momentarily taking the omitted 'þi' as the second-person pronoun; or, alternatively, this double virgule was initially intended to signal an end-of-line correction, and, after marking the spot, the corrector decided instead to add the word as a superscript. Aside from the insertions accompanied by the carets (and perhaps a few others), most of the superscript insertions in Scribe 1's texts are probably his own.

Yet another form of in-line correction involves overwriting: either to alter an existing letter into another one, or to write a new letter/word in the scraped space used to delete an error. The largest number of these appears in the stints of Scribe 1, and indeed (as far as we can determine) the hand involved in making these corrections looks to be Scribe 1's. Since this scribe contributes more than 70% of the extant manuscript, it is not surprising that his sections of the manuscript contain the greatest number of corrected errors. There may be a few instances where what appears to be a later hand is involved in such overwriting in Scribe 1's texts, but they cast little light on the process of correction.[26] In the case of letters altered by additional strokes in the texts by other scribes, the evidence also suggests that they made these alterations themselves. Likewise, most of the letters/words inserted in spaces that have been scraped are by the scribe involved in writing the main text, showing how many scribes deleted errors by scraping/rubbing, probably more or less immediately.

Of course, not all omissions and transcriptional errors have been caught by the scribes or correctors: there are a number of instances in Burnley-Wiggins's lightly edited versions of the texts on the NLS site that call attention to errors and omissions not noticed in the manuscript itself. (Adding those to the database is a job for the future.) But supplying missing letters and words, and overwriting mistaken or scraped-away graphs are not the only forms of in-line correction in Auchinleck: there are also multiple occasions where letters and words have been deleted, and not all of these instances are accompanied by corrective insertions.

Deletions

As is the case with marking corrective insertions, deletions of erroneous letters and words are also effected in two distinct ways in Auchinleck – (1) by erasure or scraping (as already mentioned), or (2) by subpunction and strike-through – and each of these two varieties present at least two distinct types. Table 3 provides a current count of these signs of deletion and their distribution among the scribes. About 96% of the cases of graphs cancelled by subpunction and strike-though, and just over 81% of deletions by erasure, are in Scribe 1's work. If we are correct in detecting his hand in making some corrections in sections of the manuscript inscribed by others, then he either paid proportionately closer attention to his own contributions, or he was not as careful in his initial inscription as were his collaborators. We have already seen, however, that some corrections in the work

---

[26] For example, the altered letters on fol. 206ra, lines 2, 10, and fol. 321ra, line 39.

of the other scribes were not his, and, furthermore, there is reason to look for another hand (or hands) in at least some of the corrections even in his sections of the manuscript.

Table 3   Corrections by deletions

Scribe	# of folios (%)	Subpunction	Strike-through	Erasure/scraping		Totals
				unfilled	filled	
1	243.5 (~71%)	73 (~99%)	47 (~92%)	116 (~82%)	80 (80%)	316 (~86%)
2	17 (~5%)	0	1 (~2%)	3 (~2%)	3 (3%)	7 (~2%)
3	37 (10.7%)	0	0	5 (~4%)	3 (3%)	8 (~2%)
4	2 (<0.6%)	0	0	0	0	0
5	33.5 (<9.7%)	0	3 (~6%)	16 (~11%)	13 (13%)	32 (~9%)
6	10 (~3%)	1 (~1%)	0	1 (<1%)	1 (1%)	3 (<1%)
Totals	343	74	51	141	100	366

Some of these deletions were made, no doubt, by the scribes at the time; others were more probably made later. It is seldom possible, however, to determine exactly when deletions of incorrect forms occurred: dating the erasures, subpunctions, or strike-throughs is virtually impossible except in cases where inserted corrections are provided. In cases of simple deletion, however, such as when doublets occur within a line, we *may* be able to conclude that the scribe himself noted the mistake and corrected on the run. But certainty, even in such cases, is difficult to come by. In many cases, for example, there exist intralinear doublets that appear to have been written continuously, and it would be difficult, perhaps impossible, to decide whether the subpunction or strike-through (usually of the first in the pair) was contemporary with the original inscription or the result of later review – and perhaps not even made by any of the scribes involved in the original transcription of the texts.

In some few cases, we *may* be able to identify a plausible sequence of steps, such as when the doublet occurs at the end of a line. For example, on fol. 157ra, line 12, we find: 'He flemeþ him his lond out of lond' ('his lond' is subpuncted with six wavelike dots). To the naked eye, the ink of 'out' looks continuous with the first 'lond', and the subpunctions do not look remarkably different. This instance might suggest that Scribe 1 noted and marked the incorrect words and proceeded to inscribe his corrected text. On the other hand, we may wonder whether the end-of-line correction on fol. 312rb, line 9, was strictly contemporary. It now reads: 'Þe ferþ hiȝt aþelred achelred' (with 'aþelred' underdotted with eight light marks, different in form from those mentioned above), while the 'a' of 'achelred' is apparently begun on top of the line-end punctus. The dots and 'achelred' look to be in a lighter ink, which suggests they might well be contemporary, but perhaps not immediately continuous with the somewhat darker ink of the original 'aþelred'. Though the timing may be in question, the hand for both the subpunction and 'achelred' is Scribe 1's, and this suggests (as is supported by other evidence below) that subpunction was this scribe's preferred mark for deletions.

But these bits of evidence do not answer a more pressing question. If indeed Scribe 1 was the supervisor and final compiler of Auchinleck, why does he employ *three* distinct means of effecting deletion of errors in his own texts? While it is, admittedly, impossible to identify different hands – if indeed there was more than one – in the case of deletions effected by rubbing or scraping, the other two cases would suggest that more than one hand was marking such deletions, since it is rather less probable that a single corrector would have employed two such distinctly different conventions, and, as we saw above, there appear to be at least two distinct styles of such marks. It remains (and perhaps must remain) an open question *when* the various instances of subpunction or strike-through were introduced into the manuscript, and the hands involved may have done so in the course of centuries rather than just days or weeks. They are not all demonstrably contemporary with the original scribes' work, except in a few cases where they are accompanied by insertions of corrected texts. When these occur in the same line, we can confidently 'date' the deletion marks. When the corrections are supplied in superscript or at the end of a line, we may need to consider a slightly wider window of time. In most of those instances, and in virtually all cases of erasures over which corrections are entered, we can indeed recognize the hand of Scribe 1. So, at least some of these marks of deletion appear to correspond with his own usage.

But which are they? The most frequent means of deleting errors in Auchinleck involves physical erasure – that is, rubbing or scraping. This method accounts for nearly two-thirds of the deletions, and might have been carried out on texts that had previously been marked by either subpunction or strike-through. Of the more than 120 items marked for deletion but not physically erased, 73 in Scribe 1's texts are subpuncted, while 47 are marked by strike-through. I have identified only a single instance of subpunction used outside the texts written by Scribe 1, and this is an erroneous correction: on Scribe 6's fol. 271rb, line 21, the 'i' in 'þei' is subpuncted. A misplaced superscript dot suggests that the corrector was intending to read 'ye', but this reading is hardly acceptable in the passage: 'To Ihesu Crist þei deden here bone' is perfectly appropriate here, and substituting 'ye' for 'þei' is not. All of this further supports the conclusion, already suggested above, that Scribe 1 probably favoured subpunction as his deletion mark. And, if he is responsible for this erroneous 'correction' of the line in *Otuel a Kniȝt*, he is not always to be trusted.

But, if Scribe 1's normal practice is subpunction, why are there so many errors deleted by strike-through in his texts? We are not helped by the deletions in the texts by other scribes since they are few: three in Scribe 5's work and one (a repeated line) in Scribe 2's *Speculum Gy de Warewyke* (fol. 41va, line 5). The meagre available evidence suggests that Scribe 5 favoured strike-through as his mark of deletion: in *Sir Beues* (fol. 200ra, line 43), we find 'So þat in a lite ~~while~~ þrawe'. The substitution of the rhyming 'þrawe' for the synonymous 'while' is in Scribe 5's hand and was likely an immediate correction. The other two deletions in Scribe 5's *Reinbrun* correct errors in his lines: cancelling 'me' and supplying the correct 'þe' immediately after (fol. 175ra, line 13); deleting the second 'seide' (fol. 173ra, line 40). However, since these comprise only three instances, and there are nearly ten times as many deletions-by-scraping in his text, we may hesitate to give them much weight. We would be on even less secure ground to claim, on the basis of the single instance in *Speculum Gy*, that this was Scribe 2's practice also: noticing and cancelling a repeated line certainly does not require insight available only to the original scribe.

Since we have already concluded that Scribe 1 favoured subpunction as his deletion mark, then it follows that cases of strike-through in his texts may well prove to be the work of another: Scribe 5, perhaps. On the basis of his two separate (and differently ordered) booklets in which he collaborated with Scribe 1, Scribe 5 is at least more intimately involved with the construction of Auchinleck than the others, and his contributions may well have extended beyond the texts that are currently ascribed to him. But, since the practice of deleting by strike-through is used by other scribes and readers in other manuscripts, we are not limited to the five scribes of Auchinleck as possible employers of this convention: these cancellations may be the work of other, even considerably later, hands.

As if these varied ways of marking deletion and making other corrections by insertion and their irregular distribution were not confusing enough, what are we to make of the half-dozen cases where an erroneous text is deleted by *both* subpunction and strike-through? All of these appear in texts by Scribe 1, and three of them provide no inserted correction to help us determine who may have been the first of these correctors. The first of these, at fol. 13vb, line 8, has 'fley3e' subpuncted (i.e., probably by Scribe 1); a later hand (perhaps not recognizing this mark of deletion) sought to solve the difficulty by striking through, with a slightly diagonal stroke, the 'l' and 'y', producing 'fe3e', which may make some better sense of the line's syntax, but does little to address the basic metrical problem. At fol. 20va, line 22, 'vp' is doubly deleted before 'breyd'. In this case, the strike-through may be original, and the subpunction later, but that is little more than speculation at this point. In any case, the double marking here, as in the previous instance, suggests that a later reader did not recognize the intention of the earlier mark. The third occurs at fol. 210va, line 16, where 'bor' was deleted by subpunction (arguably by Scribe 1), who recognized the dittography (repeating the beginning of 'borwe' earlier in the line), and whose deletion was reinforced by a later, somewhat casual '//' (with joined top). With the possible exception of the second of these, the evidence suggests that the subpunction was original, and the slanting strokes were supplied later by other readers who apparently did not understand the significance of the dots beneath the letters.

The remaining three cases do, however, provide corrections, and they reinforce the conclusion that the subpunction (by Scribe 1) was the first mark of deletion. In the case of the line-end 'wo' (fol. 61ra, line 6), both subpuncted and struck-through, with the properly rhyming 'care' added in what looks to be a later, less confident (or rushed) hand, it is difficult to determine which of the two deletion marks is the earlier. But, since the other instances suggest that later readers may have not understood the significance of subpunction, it would follow that this may also be the case here, and that the inserted 'care' (which more or less corresponds to Scribe 1's letter forms) may also be his.

One of the other two cases would appear to support the conclusion that the doubly marked deletions were the product of later misunderstanding of the significance of the earlier convention. At fol. 254ra, line 5, the first 'he' is doubly marked, with the firm subpunction resembling many others by Scribe 1. At fol. 259ra, line 16, on the other hand, 'her' is doubly deleted, between 'hir' and 'hert', and the subpunction is less firmly like Scribe 1's. We probably should hesitate to draw confident conclusions on the basis of such minute differences in the appearance of the dots beneath, or the strokes through, deleted letters. None of these doubly marked deletions, however, firmly challenges the view that Scribe 1 favoured subpunction as his preferred mark, or that the strike-throughs were later, perhaps much later, attempts to mark deletions more firmly.

Conclusions

The study of these various ways of correcting errors in Auchinleck does not in the end lead to many firm conclusions other than that there is more work to be done here. It may, however, lead us to reopen the question of whether the role of Scribe 1 as the supervisor, compiler, and corrector of this collection can continue to stand entirely unchallenged. He clearly played a major role in shaping the collection, but it is evident that many of the other scribes also made such corrections, and (most significantly) *perhaps even in Scribe 1's own texts*. The diverse signals for insertions and deletions may sustain a case for another (or others) being involved in the latter stages of this manuscript's preparation. Timothy Shonk's essay in this collection ('Paraphs, Piecework, and Presentation: The Production Methods of Auchinleck Revisited') shows how much we can learn about the construction of this compilation by examining, among other things, the distribution of its varied paraph marks. Perhaps a similar, more detailed study of the corrections inventoried here will add still more. Paratextual features of manuscripts are deservedly gaining more attention as we refine our understanding of the many contributors and many stages of composition and compilation that shaped these unique products of medieval culture.

The texts of Auchinleck define an important moment in the history of Middle English poetry around the time of Chaucer's birth. While we are gathering a rich appreciation of the scribal culture of the late fourteenth and early fifteenth centuries, we have less evidence by which to construct a satisfying picture of its antecedent a half-century earlier. The complexities attending the construction of Auchinleck continue to puzzle those of us who pursue the mystery of how it came to be. Further careful study of material, textual, and paratextual details like the patterns of correction discussed here may eventually lead us to a fuller, more detailed description of the ways in which this important collaborative enterprise arrived at its current condition in the National Library of Scotland.

CHAPTER THIRTEEN

Auchinleck 'Scribe 6' and Some Corollary Issues

Ralph Hanna

For Malcolm Parkes.

I owe my engagement here entirely to the generosity of Kenneth Dunn, head of the Manuscripts Department at the National Library of Scotland, and to the persistence of Ruth Kennedy. Having twice written directly, as best I could, about Auchinleck, I felt, at the time of the LOMERS conference, that I had nothing very useful to say to anyone about the whole book.[1] But Ruth would not let me off the hook, and we finally negotiated what she designated a 'bonne bouche', a ten-minute, late-afternoon presentation that would send conference participants to the bar, probably avid for rest and relief.

What I had to say on that occasion was an impolite presentation of the limitations of knowing this manuscript (and I would suspect, any other) mainly through its facsimile reproductions. The exhibit I offered LOMERS was entirely due to Kenneth, who has now twice (most recently in May 2014) let me spend full days handling the object itself. At this point, I take up my LOMERS script (rather miraculously found preserved on the back of sheets on which I had taken notes about the book), late in my discussion of the Burnley-Wiggins facsimile/transcription mounted on the NLS website:[2]

I

A digitized version has one real downside: reload time. The machine requirement of reloading pages estranges one from visual contact with the book, now a discontinuous sequence of images. Handling a 'live book' interposes no such discontinuity and thus allows considerably more immediate perceptual refreshment. This is the way book scholars customarily get attuned to any individual manuscript

---

[1] R. Hanna, 'Reconsidering the Auchinleck Manuscript', in *New Directions in Late Medieval Manuscript Studies: Essays from the 1998 Harvard Conference*, ed. D. Pearsall (York, 2000), 91–102, and *London Literature, 1300–1380*, Cambridge Studies in Medieval Literature 57 (Cambridge, 2005), 74–147.

[2] One should applaud Alison Wiggins's energy and industry in producing this presentation of the book, an offshoot of her extensive work on *Guy of Warwick*, originally with her late supervisor David Burnley.

– the persistent and repeated presence of similar features imposes itself on visual memory and becomes a rhythm of engagement.

I want to contrast the last time I saw Auchinleck, in the sheep flesh, as it were. I went at the book new, as if I had never seen it before – scrutiny of every page, dip in and read a little, pause over illustration, and so on. It was all quite wonderful, until … at a certain point, I realized something was wrong – that is, my visual memory was somehow disrupted. This led me to a fair amount of scuffling about to try to figure out what was responsible, comparing pages where I had been disconcerted by something, I did not yet know what, with others where I had been sailing blithely along. I discovered that what had set me off was a relatively small detail on Auchinleck fols. 268–277 – that, unlike anything else I had seen, these folios did not have a double leading-edge rule, but a single one. (I should add that, had I been an assiduous or retentive reader of the printed facsimile, which I was not, I would already have known this, as well as all the inferences that are going to follow from it.)[3]

This variation in ruling is an anomaly, and one (as I now went carefully checking through the book) not repeated elsewhere. Moreover, I fairly immediately identified this unique feature as the property of a single quire, and, when I checked which quire it was, noted that the difference in ruling interfaces with a number of other well-recognized anomalies. For this is the quire containing the unique and atelous Charlemagne romance *Otuel a Kniȝt*. The Pearsall-Cunningham facsimile identifies this as a unique effort by an Auchinleck 'Scribe 6', and this quire is further unique in being an isolated grouping of ten leaves among many consistent examples of eight leaves. Moreover, the text is not in the usual London language of the majority of the book but in that of the Worcestershire/Gloucestershire border (*LALME*, LP 7820).[4]

Certain of these anomalies are not such at all. The hand here is in fact the well-attested Auchinleck Scribe 1, merely writing in a different duct, although with some variation in the number of lines to the page (the usual 44 *and* 43). Moreover, it is unclear whether the linguistic variation offers any particular purchase in this context.[5]

---

[3] Pearsall-Cunningham, p. xiv.

[4] At least one factor contributing to the perception of multiple scribes here is the immediate juxtaposition, across an opening, of fol. 267v (Scribe 1) with the head of *Otuel a Kniȝt* at fol. 268r. The former is considerably lighter in appearance (due to fading on an exposed outer leaf of a fascicle?) and much less calligraphic. But equally, first pages, because customarily sites of display, are considerably nicer than anything else any scribe writes.

[5] These disparities are most extensively presented and discussed in A. Wiggins, 'Are Auchinleck Scribes 1 and 6 the Same Scribe?: The Advantages of Whole-Data Analysis and Electronic Texts', *Medium Ævum* 73 (2004), 10–26. In addition to the general discussion below, I would comment on but one of Wiggins's arguments: her insistence (pp. 19-20) on the unusual absence of a catchword at the end of the quire containing *Otuel a Kniȝt*. I do not find this particularly surprising. Given the absence of any subsequent quires in this segment, there is nothing in the book for a catchword to link to. Scribe 1 imposed catchwords throughout only at the end of the production (along with item numbering, presumably to accompany a contents table now lost). At this point,

Scribe 1 elsewhere writes what is taken to be a fairly consistent London language, and – following G. V. Smithers's comments, ultimately dependent on arguments mounted by Eugen Kölbing – this may have been a property of a substantial number of the archetypes from which he worked.[6] In other circumstances, the scribe may have translated into London language a number of texts he received in some other form (Northern).[7] But this does not mean he will routinely have done so, and he may have decided, as apparently also did Auchinleck Scribe 2 (who writes a quite proximate Worcs./Gloucs. language, *LALME*, LP 6940), that a literatim copy of Western materials was quite all right in this case. (There is certainly ample evidence for such behaviours with materials from this area in London at century's end, assembled by Simon Horobin.)[8]

One might contextualize these perceptions a bit by a further more general point. Every scribe writing English contemporary with Auchinleck Scribe 1 and appearing in another book (e.g., Dan Michel of Northgate, one hand in Cambridge, University Library, MS Gg. 4. 32, and the Harley 2253 scribe) clearly was engaged in writing for multiple purposes. For each of them, copying an individual book containing English was not a total pursuit, and all of them were engaged in differently 'literary' copying, usually across all three languages, and undertaken for more than one audience. I suspect that, while Scribe 1 certainly copied *Otuel a Kniȝt*, he may not have done it under the same aegis as led to the monumental Auchinleck production. Given the inclusive nature of this book, the way it sucks in a wide variety of products (and seems to respond to a multiform and changing series of textual interests), quire 38 may simply be a bit that, originally produced with other purposes in mind, ended up as a part of the rich 'whirlpool'.[9]

the scribe was certainly aware that more text should have followed here, assumed that the subsequent quire(s) might be retrievable, and kept his options open. In the event, he clearly did not succeed in finding a continuation, and he simply never returned to join the fragmentary *Otuel* to the following quire (and new textual unit).

[6] See *Kyng Alisaunder*, ed. G. V. Smithers, 2 vols, EETS OS 227, 237 (London, 1952, 1957), II, 41; Smithers relies upon E. Kölbing's extensive demonstration; see *Arthour and Merlin: nach der Auchinleck-hs. nebst zwei Beilagen*, ed. E. Kölbing, Altenglische Bibliothek 4 (Leipzig, 1890), esp. pp. lx–ciiii.

[7] See Mills in *Horn Childe and Maiden Rimnild*, ed. M. Mills, Middle English Texts 20 (Heidelberg, 1988), pp. 36, 39–43, 62–81; and the extensive discussion in R. Purdie, *Anglicising Romance: Tail-Rhyme and Genre in Medieval English Literature*, Studies in Medieval Romance 9 (Cambridge, 2008).

[8] S. Horobin, '"In London and Opelond": The Dialect and the Circulation of the C Version of *Piers Plowman*', *Medium Ævum* 74 (2005), 248–69. Cf. also my 'Studies in the Manuscripts of *Piers Plowman*', *Yearbook of Langland Studies* 7 (1993), 1–25 passim (esp. comments on dialect forms of San Marino, Huntington Library, MS HM 143).

[9] Relevant to this sense of potential variation is a fine contribution by a scholar who heard both Tim Shonk's impressive LOMERS presentation (see his chapter in this volume) and my fragile 'bonne bouche', and took up our suggestions: H. Marshall, 'What's in a Paraph? A New Methodology and Its Implications for the Auchinleck Manuscript', *Journal of the Early Book Society* 13 (2010), 39–62. Further studies like Marshall's on incidental decoration (lombards, their size, their relation to the text column, their form of flourishing – and that a small number have been missed out and filled later) would be helpful.

II

I begin extending what I said many years ago – my view that much of the Auchinleck manuscript may be composed of piecemeal leftovers from other projects – by taking up one bit of violent fallout that my 'bonne bouche' elicited. I was promptly besieged by a number of people asking how I could be so daft as to doubt a Scribe 6, particularly after Alison Wiggins's showing.[10] Of course, I knew her article. For me, however, the article ceaselessly 'begs the question', *stricto/antiquo sensu* – that is, 'engages in the logical error of *petitio principii*'. No one has ever stated that the two stints are the same in any respect, other than hand. Wiggins's argument is fundamentally, 'Yes, they are different'. But that is what we already knew, and the evidence Wiggins meticulously provides does not advance such a view beyond that. Further, it is predicated on what is manifestly not the case, an assumption of utter consistency in scribal behaviour. In contrast, close examination of scribal oeuvres routinely throws up manifold evidence of wide variation in practice, in terms both of script detail and of linguistic reproduction.[11]

I am afraid my response, which is very far from original, may be insulting, because it is going to involve a little basic palaeographical instruction. My response is not original, first, because I am returning to a *status quo ante* description of Auchinleck (five scribes, the main scribe responsible for the *Otuel* quire, as well as the overwhelming majority of the copying). Scribe 6 was largely invented in the mid-1950s by Alan Bliss, in the course of his fine doctoral study of *Sir Orfeo*.[12]

---

[10] See note 5 above.

[11] Particularly relevant here is C. Revard, 'Scribe and Provenance', *Studies in the Harley Manuscript: The Scribes, Contexts, and Social Contexts of British Library MS Harley 2253*, ed. S. Fein (Kalamazoo MI, 2000), 21–109, which discovers a certain measure of variation in the scribe's hand, here time-driven and datable on the basis of the scribe's legal copying. M. B. Parkes illustrates an outstanding example at *English Cursive Book Hands 1250–1500* (Oxford, 1969), plate 21; and cf. John Cok of St Bartholomew's, Smithfield – three distinct hands in the same volume – A. G. Watson, *Catalogue of Dated and Datable Manuscripts, c. 700–1600, in the Department of Manuscripts, The British Library*, 2 vols. (London, 1979), II, plate 414 (dated 1432). I offer a similar analysis of one of Dan Michel's stints (predicated on a different kind of stimulus), 'Dan Michel of Northgate and His Books', in *Medieval Manuscripts, Their Makers and Users: A Special Issue of Viator in Honor of Richard and Mary Rouse*, ed. C. Baswell (Turnhout, 2011), pp. 213–24 (pp. 220–2). See also M. Fisher, *Scribal Authorship and the Writing of History in Medieval England* (Columbus OH, 2012), esp. the plates at pp. 161, 166, and surrounding discussion. On linguistic variation, see such well-known examples as M. L. Samuels, 'The Scribe of the Hengwrt and Ellesmere Manuscripts of the Canterbury Tales', *Studies in the Age of Chaucer* 5 (1983), 49–65; or J. J. Smith's several studies of Doyle-Parkes's 'Scribe D', e.g., J. J. Smith, 'The Trinity Gower D-Scribe and His Work on Two Early *Canterbury Tales* Manuscripts', in J. J. Smith, *The English of Chaucer and His Contemporaries* (Aberdeen, 1988), pp. 51–69 (in reference to A. I. Doyle and M. B. Parkes, 'The Production of Copies of the *Canterbury Tales* and the *Confessio Amantis* in the Early Fifteenth Century', in *Medieval Scribes, Manuscripts and Libraries: Essays Presented to N. R. Ker*, ed. M. B. Parkes and A. G. Watson [London, 1978], pp. 163–210).

[12] A. J. Bliss, 'Notes on the Auchinleck Manuscript', *Speculum* 26 (1951), 652–8, work undertaken as part of his dissertation, leading eventually to the fine edition, *Sir Orfeo*,

Without wishing to engage in character assassination, I would offer a general comment on Bliss's perception. Anyone who has taught serious palaeography knows that neophytes (Bliss made his 'discovery' as a graduate) never, on examining a manuscript, see fewer scribes than the number actually involved. Indeed, they almost invariably respond to changes of scribal ductus by assuming that apparent variations signal the intrusion of another hand. Thus, beginners tend to assume what is not the case, that scribes are metronomes, always the same. To the contrary. Scribes frequently tire and often vary script features within a relatively set format. Moreover (and this is another reason why my presentation is far from original), two very fine professional palaeographers certainly recognized this potential difficulty; Pamela Robinson and her graduate supervisor Malcolm Parkes altogether rejected the creation of a Scribe 6 here.[13]

Both Robinson and Parkes offered this perception rather as an *ipse dixit*, without much further argumentation. But I think I understand why they did so, and here attempt to lay out the evidence, predicated on a single small script feature. I undertake this analysis with a number of caveats, well understood by palaeographers. However, the problem at issue concerns the deserved cultural centrality of Auchinleck. This has meant that the book has attracted the attention of persons who are not palaeographers. A career in literary studies teaches one textual skills and ways of translating them into statements about social utility. But to deal with manuscripts adequately requires different skills, mainly the visual ones I already mentioned. I apologize for what follows, engaging in an extensive palaeography lesson for beginners.

Both Auchinleck Scribe 1 and the putative Scribe 6 are a bit unusual within their contemporary context. They write the highly formalized script generically known as textura (or gothic bookhand). Its use, in the context of a vernacular book of the 1330s, speaks to a certain level of extremely formalized interest and presentation (shared with Scribes 2 and 5). None of the scribes I mentioned in my 'bonne bouche' as Scribe 1's clearly professional contemporaries writes the script. Rather, they use a derivative of an informal document hand, 'anglicana' (as does Auchinleck Scribe 3, for example).

As a script, textura developed from earlier formal bookhands, particularly in their less formal manifestations as the reduced script of glosses. The antecedents of the script are large, monumental, and highly formalized (twelfth-century proto-gothic). Textura, particularly outside liturgical and paraliturgical contexts (its most normal use-function until the end of the Middle Ages – and beyond, in 'black letter' typefaces), is not such, but instead reduced and packed. Comparatively, the main feature, inherited from use in glosses, is a quite substantial script compaction, in

---

2nd edn (Oxford, 1966). In fairness, Kölbing, whom Bliss here corrects, had seen this as a separate hand also (but, equally, had divided various Scribe 1 stints among different hands).

[13] See P. R. Robinson, 'A Study of Some Aspects of the Transmission of English Verse Texts in Late Mediaeval Manuscripts', unpublished B Litt thesis, University of Oxford (Oxford, 1972), pp. 128–31, extending views she ascribes to Parkes, her supervisor.

both dimensions – vertically (shortened ascenders, more closely spaced lines) and horizontally. The latter feature provides the customary definition for 'the coming/ onset of textura', datable in England to the 1180s, that script technique inelegantly known as 'biting'.

This fuzzy term describes a single feature contributing to the general duct of textura – angularity and spikiness (why it merits the nomenclature 'gothic' through analogy with architecture). One prominent way of achieving this aspect or duct is by removing from the script vocabulary the graceful curves that so mark the ancestral twelfth-century script. 'Biting' refers to a widespread tendency in textura to remove adjacent curved strokes by superimposition, the curve ')' of one letter being written over the curve '(' of the following, thereby leaving what appears simply '|' or '/'. Hence, the feature can occur after those letters with curved strokes to the right: ')', at least potentially 'b', 'd' (in textura a rounded lower loop, the form that goes back to the ancient script called 'uncial'), 'p', sometimes 'a' and 'h', and, early on, perhaps 'þ' and 'wynn'. Most usually, although not absolutely always, the conjoined following 'left curve' stroke '(' is provided by the vowels 'o' and 'e', in some hands 'a'.[14]

Achieving this effect requires a considerable care and fastidiousness on the part of the scribe, and 'biting' is not a particularly routine feature of scribes writing English – although it is for Auchinleck Scribe 1. For comparative purposes, here I want to use an extravagantly elegant and careful (as we will see, with regard to this feature, the word might be placed in inverted commas) hand, indeed the most lovely piece of vernacular textura I know before the fifteenth century. This scribe, writing about 1275, produced the text called *Ancrene Wisse* in Cambridge, Corpus Christi College, MS 402; I here use the sample (fol. 69) reproduced as the frontispiece to EETS OS 249.[15] The loveliness of this hand (particularly apparent in the ribbons of minims in his Latin) offers an unusual model of high formalization.

My examination of the plate shows the following:

After 'd' and its sibling 'eth' (simply 'crossed d'), biting with 'e' is absolutely universal: -**de** in line 2; **de**ofles 3; en**de** 4 and 5; ibun**de**n, togede**re**s 5, etc.; and oð**e**r 2, 4; nu**ð**e, oð**e**r 14. With these examples, one might join such nonce-oddments as go**des** 12 and go**dd** 26 (contrast godd 14, god 15).

---

[14] Textura 'a' and 'h' are always anomalous in this system, given that they historically represent blends of differing forms originally limited to either indigenous insular or imported scripts. Hence, depending on the scribe's sense of the graphs' underlying model, he may perceive the form as either 'curved', i.e., presenting '(' or ')' (and thus to be bitten), or the opposite. For the graph 'a', imported scripts have only notional and low left rounding (as opposed to late Anglo-Saxon square minuscule with left '('). In contrast, Anglo-Saxon 'h' has no right loop at all, but a vertical, in contrast to rounded Continental forms (by the fourteenth century, potentially influenced by fully looped strokes to the right typical of anglicana document script). 'Thorn' and 'wynn', at any point in their history, may be conceived as having wedged, rather than round, right-hand strokes.

[15] *The English Text of the Ancrene Riwle; Ancrene Wisse Edited from MS. Corpus Christi College Cambridge 402*, ed. J. R. R. Tolkien, intro. N. R. Ker, EETS OS 249 (London, 1962). On the date of the hand, see Millett's report of Parkes's views, in *Ancrene Wisse: A Corrected Edition of the Text in Cambridge, Corpus College, MS 402, with Variants from Other Manuscripts*, ed. B. Millett, 2 vols., EETS OS 325, 326 (Oxford, 2005, 2006), I, xi.

Similarly, after 'b', biting with following 'e' fails only once (beo 13), against numerous other examples: hab**be**ð, ne**b**bes 1; **be**oð, **be**oreð 3; **be**on 5, 8, and 8, ne**b**bes 8, etc.

So far as the rarity of the graph in early thirteenth-century English allows, biting is universal after 'p': s**pe**deð 18, -schi**pe**, war**pe**ð 23.

The technique also occurs, although only sporadically, in the ambivalent sequence 'he':[16] **he**he 25, **he**o 27 (but not heateð 1, helle 7, chere, heorte 9). For this scribe, none of 'a' (note the scribe's form, which is non-'('), 'wynn', or 'thorn' bites. However, there are a few oddments. Notice (the decorative?) ne**b**bes 1 (contrast hab**be**ð 1, nebbes 8); and o**þe**r 2 and **þe**t 26 at least 'kiss', if they do not 'bite' (contrast þeo, þenne, þe 1; þe (2x), þes 3; þe 6, etc.). No scribe is a metronome – script is not letter shapes alone, but also an ongoing rhythm of movement ('ductus'). One must be aware that some variation will be context-determined – for example, o**þe**r 2 may well simply echo o**ð**er earlier in the line. A certain, often considerable, amount of variation is virtually inevitable, and close examination of hands (like this one) will regularly throw up what appear anomalies, within a demonstrable continuum.[17]

Now that we have 'biting' down, we might proceed to analyse the behaviour of Scribe 1 and the figure who I am going to insist should be designated 'the artist formerly known as Bliss Scribe 6'. The surprise here is that biting is a routine feature of the hands of both. This is a surprise for two reasons. First of all, neither stint is particularly attentive to other basic features central to the 'spikiness' of textura, putting finish on minims or on ascenders; both stints are written in very competent, easily legible, yet not decorative versions of the basic script. Second, as I can say with some authority, having examined in detail nearly seventy other manuscripts written in fourteenth-century vernacular textura (many with more than one scribe, although most of the examples much later), biting is not a feature widespread in this particular script when rendering English. Far from all scribes I have surveyed

---

[16] See note 14 above.

[17] I would offer a further comment on discussion of scribal hands generally. Largely as a result of L. R. Mooney's various identifications of 'Guildhall scribes' – see L. R. Mooney and E. Stubbs, *Scribes in the City: London Guildhall Clerks and the Dissemination of Middle English Literature, 1375-1425* (York, 2013) – current conversation would seem to imply that script detail, i.e., local letter formation, identifies hands. Such is not the case, at least in part because all scribes can manage more than one script and because they are capable of anomaly, including importation of features 'foreign' to the script in which they are currently writing. Rather than script detail (part of Bliss's logic for distinguishing his Scribe 6), the same scribe is identifiable by overall aspect, i.e., recognizing the similarity of two sample hands on the basis of an examination from a distance of about 20 to 30 inches. Traditionally, the description of the local script features that underpin this identification of a similar ductus formed only a rhetorical gesture; it was intended to explain to those who had not made the identification those salient features that had contributed to the initial impression of identity. (For example, the initial identification of Doyle-Parkes's Scribe B still stands, in spite of the fact that his script in 'the Trinity Gower' universally uses a single-compartment 'secretary' 'a' generally foreign to the remainder of his work.) The detail can never be the end-all, and, although, in what follows, I am going to point to detail, I do so because I am examining a basic feature, yet one extremely unusual in the overall cultural/scribal context.

even bother with biting after 'd', and most of them ignore the remainder of the most commonplace examples. I would suspect the technique is usually taken as too labour-intensive (it requires a carefully retrograde pen movement) or as not conducive to clearly legible letter or word reproduction.

I would say first of all that my 20-to-30-inch visual scan of the two hands (see note 17) suggests strongly to me that they are the same, and significantly unlike any other fourteenth-century vernacular textura I know. Besides that general aspect, I am struck by the extent to which my scan shows the scribes indulging in 'biting' (part of what renders the hands to me significantly similar, even among the run of fourteenth-century vernacular textura). I simply report what I see on the two sides that form the opening fols. 267v–268r – that is, the end of *Roland and Vernagu* (Scribe 1) and the head of *Otuel a Kniʒt* (Bliss Scribe 6). I have supplemented this examination by surveying one mid-stint side for each: fol. 263r for Scribe 1 and fol. 271r for Bliss Scribe 6.

Both hands routinely and universally show biting, and with a broad range of agreement. They agree pretty universally in biting in the combinations BE, BO, DE, DO, HE, HO, PE, and PO; I would particularly draw attention to examples with H in combination, since, as I have indicated above, this is a graphic form that the overwhelming population of scribes I know considers entirely optional. There are equally a few designatable areas where the hands show differing features. Quite counterintuitively, because the two render the letter 'a' differently,[18] their behaviour here contrasts; Scribe 1 (with a rounded, anglicana-influenced form that one might have thought would encourage biting) virtually never bites here, while Bliss Scribe 6 (with a more 'gothic' top-knot form) does so, if sometimes inconsistently (numerous examples of BA, DA, HA, PA). Similarly, Scribe 1, although he has momentary lapses, regularly bites ÞE and ÞO, while Bliss Scribe 6 never does so. In addition, both show some odd and unusual examples: Scribe 1 has sporadic instances of DD, VE, and YE; Bliss Scribe 6 of BB, PP, OO, and OE.[19]

In actuality, I find these variations confirmatory rather than disqualifying. As my discussion above indicates, the stints provide differing behaviours in situations that have, in the history of this script feature, always been considered options. (Recall that these differences in practice all fall in an area where the highly calligraphic scribe of Corpus Christi 402 eschews biting altogether.) Simultaneously, both stints show – as, I would again insist, extremely few contemporaries do – an interest in

---

[18] This, like all the features Bliss used to distinguish the hands, is a case of choosing to generalize within separate stints a different form that is nonetheless part of the common basic script vocabulary (analogous to a linguistic variant, e.g., choosing to write 'nat' rather than 'not').

[19] These last features should be taken with a grain of salt. Because I have only sampled, rather than examined the full copying stints, the apparent uniqueness of various forms may reflect only the vicissitudes of usage available on the pages I have surveyed. For example, Scribe 1's VE shows prominently only because of the number of times he must write the name 'Vernagu'. (In my experience, biting with VE, perhaps limited to word-initial uses, occurs sporadically in isolated hands well into the fifteenth century, e.g., in the common word 'verray'.)

generalizing biting through their stints. They have simply made different choices about those places, usually considered optional, that are appropriate to extend the feature. On this basis, as well as other points that have emerged in my discussion, I see no reason not to believe in the identity of these two hands. Once again, as I argued at LOMERS, I would see the distinctions between them as representing prioritization of different features of the same script vocabulary and very likely motivated by time – that is, the two stints are temporally distinct productions of the same individual, and *Otuel* is not necessarily associated in origin with the same project as Auchinleck.[20]

III

This conclusion, broadly a consideration of 'allowable degree of variation', leads me to some more general considerations about the Auchinleck manuscript. As we are all convinced, this is a wonderful volume, an elegant and expensive book. But it is easy to overstate exactly how consistently so it actually is and exactly what norms and expectations were in place at any point in its production. The latitude of acceptable script variation I find in the hand of its major contributor, Scribe 1, leads me to offer two further examples of inconsistent production features accommodated to the whole. These are far from as minor as the scribe's decision of 'whether to bite A or not'.

Here I want to look briefly at Scribe 3, responsible for fols. 70r–104v, originally six quires, one now lost and blank leaves at the end of the last filled by other hands. Given that Scribe 4 writes only a single, booklet-ending text here (*The Battle Abbey Roll*), Scribe 3 is the only hand represented in the book but not demonstrably in touch with Scribe 1. Not only is Scribe 3's hand isolated in the book as representing documentary rather than formal training; he appears uniquely estranged from the universal format of the book – to a degree far more extreme than the one-line variations that set apart Bliss's putative Scribe 6 – and he offers a further reason for seeing the latter's variation as anodyne or meaningless.

Scribe 3 seems to have begun his work with only a vague sense of what might be considered the standing format of the volume as eventually constructed. He had a sense of the size of the sheet to be employed and of a writing area to be filled on each page, as well as some chunk of copy to reproduce. But his initial efforts in this regard could accurately be described as 'fumbling'. His first quire (fols. 70r–76v,

---

[20] In this regard, I would simply note that Scribe 1 scarcely lacks shifts of ductus, even within consecutive portions. Perhaps the grossest example occurs at the head of the stanzaic *Guy of Warwick* on fol. 146vb; see the previous discussion, and A. Wiggins, 'Imagining the Compiler: *Guy of Warwick* and the Compilation of the Auchinleck Manuscript', in *Imagining the Book*, ed. S. Kelly and J. J. Thompson (Turnhout, 2005), pp. 61–76. But nearly all of these appear to me analogous to the one at fol. 146v, the product of resuming copying after a break (and a very great number of them indicative of copying in half- or full-quire stints where the scribe has written a column, side, or folio at the opening of a subsequent quire before breaking off). For a minor glitch in formatting (45 lines, not 44) – an erroneous lapse apparently corrected – see fol. 152v.

one leaf lost) appears as if he had decided to reproduce whatever copy he had to hand as a single quire, without any recognition that this material was far from suffi- cient to fill eight leaves, in the format one recognizes as normal in the developed manuscript. The seven surviving leaves of this unit supply textual content nearly three columns short (123 text lines) of what one would expect in the book's normal format.

Moreover, there are further fairly visible glitches. The scribe does not seem to have been informed of the decorative scheme required in the book. This was a potentially serious problem, since all the scribes had to adjust their copying to accommodate decorative features. The most serious anomaly is produced by the scribe's failure to leave space for an illumination at the head of one text, *The Pater Noster Vndo on Englissch* on fol. 72r. In this case, someone (presumably Scribe 1) took the decision that illumination was more important than a neat page, and a painted Gnadenstuhl Trinity was awkwardly inserted, at reduced size, in the intercolumnar space and upper margin.

Yet this is not the single cock-up here. The main reason for believing that the scribe attempted to fill a single-quire textual space with copy inadequate for such a unit in the ongoing *mise-en-page* of the book is his persistent adjustment of page format. Through the quire, he continually reduces the number of lines per page, markedly so in the second half of the unit (from fol. 73v on). There he passes from 36–38 lines to a page, itself aberrant from normal Auchinleck format, to 33–34 lines. This adjustment allows the scribe to fill all the leaves – and to write a concluding outside leaf (fol. 76v) that matches the first leaf of the quire, with 38 lines. The scribe may have thought that this would provide a visual join with whatever was to precede or follow his stint. (Which, of course, it did not.)

These adjustments involved, it must be said, some particularly finicky work. To achieve this presentation, the scribe had to rule every page separately (rather than what one imagines to have been the normal case: ruling bifolia and/or larger units in a single go). Merely to cite the most flagrant examples: fol.71r has 38 lines, but fol. 71v has 36; fol. 73r has 37 lines, but fol. 73v has only 34. Moreover, the scribe was unusually fastidious about disguising this variousness. He ruled so as to insure that there was no visual shock for a reader of any opening during this work. Every set of facing pages has been comparably ruled and written, yet Scribe 3 varies the page content between 33 and 38 lines.

However, this effort seems to have been considered 'good enough'. It passed muster, and Scribe 3 was provided further materials for copying. He also was informed of at least some of the decorative requirements for the developing book, and took special pains with them. On fol. 78rb, he knew to leave adequate space for an illumination at the opening of *Sir Degare*. Moreover, he deliberately insured – as was not done elsewhere in the book (cf. fol. 167rb) – that the image would appear in prominent position, at the head of a column; fol. 78ra has two extra text lines so that the preceding text will end neatly at a column foot. Yet simultaneously, although he was apparently instructed that the materials he had already produced had inadequate page content, he was apparently not provided with information as to the exact format he should be following. Thus, his second quire uniformly has 40 lines to the page (except, of course, for fol. 78ra), not the usual 44 of the remainder of Auchinleck, and, in spite of the scribe's fastidiousness across openings in his first quire, the format does not visually match at either quire-bound opening: fols.76v–77r, with 38 and 40 lines; fols. 84v–85r, with 40 and 44.

As that last detail would indicate, in his third quire the scribe adapted a format in accord with the remainder of the book. From the head of this unit, with minor exceptions, he writes in Scribe 1's customary 44-line format.[21] At least one conclusion one might draw from this escapade is something about the developing nature of the book. Scribe 3 may have been involved early, before certain firm production decisions had been taken, and his various mishaps may show signs of the production team groping towards a comprehensive format for an extensive (and protracted) piece of work.

But there is another scenario that one might consider here. It is at least arguable that Scribe 3's separation from the remainder of the Auchinleck team is absolute – that is, that he was a sort of stalking horse, engaged in producing the oldest segments of the volume. Given his document-based hand, one could imagine him as a household clerk, in this case also called upon to offer recreative materials for his employer. Under such a guise, he might have 'felt' his way through to some kind of model his employer found satisfactory. And, after such a format-fixing stint, involving copying a mixture of texts but with an emphasis on 'tales', including some briefish romances, his employer might have felt that the large-scale romances he desired demanded a more professional team for their execution.

A second area of inconsistency concerns the Auchinleck illuminative programme. This is the most unusual feature of the entire production, the team apparently stimulated to imitate splash French romance manuscripts (some more than a century old) in their very English book.[22] Throughout, so far as we can tell, given the extensive pillaging, each major independent text was headed by a rectilinear image with an illustration of an important narrative episode. (And many examples lacking such openings are brief and appear to have been quire-filling late additions.)

Or so it seems. For this programme shows one area of inconsistency throughout the volume. That is, rectilinear images at text openings only seem to have appeared with utter consistency with what one may call 'internal texts', those that begin within the twelve large units in which Auchinleck was constructed. Here the handling, even in (developed) Scribe 3 portions, is utterly uniform: the image at the head of the text, the text itself introduced by a small (almost always two-line)

---

[21] The last three sides of this unit, fols. 90v–91v, have 45 lines to the page; at the very end of his stint, on fol. 104rb, the scribe left the last line blank before continuing on the verso, perhaps distracted by coming to a column-end and a section-end of his text simultaneously.

[22] For a very early example, with extensive discussion and illustration, see A. Stones, 'Two French Manuscripts: WLC/LM/6 and WLC/LM/7', in *The Wollaton Medieval Manuscripts: Texts, Owners and Readers*, ed. R. Hanna and T. Turville-Petre (York, 2010), pp. 41–56. I simply mention here one anomaly in this procedure: fol. 256vb is a heavily damaged leaf but offers evidence that, after the gold-leaf frame was laid, the size of the image – planned as unduly emphatic – was adjusted, it would appear before copying.

flourished lombard. Elsewhere, at the openings of the manuscript's booklets, things are very far from so clear-cut.

Given the losses in the manuscript – some of them, odd leaves here and there, clearly to remove the decorative work as souvenirs – generalizing is somewhat hazardous. Three of the booklets – 1, 4, 8 (fols. 1, 107a, 278) – are acephalous and obviously offer no evidence. Several of the surviving openings show exactly what one would expect from a consistent programme: the same rectilinear illumination with text-opening small lombard. Examples include booklets 6, 9, 11 (fols. 261, 281, 326).

But, as this minority of examples shows, such openings are far from universal. Several booklet-opening pages are relatively plain, marked only by large lombards: 4+ lines at booklet 2 (fol. 39); an 'I' for Scribe 3's booklet 3 (fol. 70);[23] 5 lines at booklet 12 (fol. 328). More ornately, booklet 7 (fol. 268), the *Otuel a Kniȝt* which began my discussion, resembles the previously cited examples in having been provided with an opening illustration. But it also has one of the (if not *the*) largest and most ornate lombards in the manuscript (6 lines), as well as a red-and-blue bar border.

But, just as some examples are distinctly plain, the two remaining ones are very nice. These, with champs and partial painted vine-borders at the heads of booklets 5 and 10 (fols. 176, 304) depart from the narrative mode of the remaining painted decoration. One introduces what is always seen as one of the manuscript's centre-pieces, *Sir Beues of Hamtoun*;[24] the second appears at the head of *The Anonymous Short English Metrical Chronicle*. The first has an inhabited champ, with a fairly generic image of a knight, presumably our hero;[25] the second includes an oak-leaf pattern. I'd be reasonably certain, on the basis of shapes and pigments, that at least the vinework and painted background of the champ in both are in the same hand and suggest they emanate from the same locale.

These deviations are intriguing for any variety of reasons. In terms of the aesthetics of decorating a book, they answer variously to a common rule – that is, that opening pages, while they may mirror usual practice elsewhere, are always supposed to be more emphatic than other textual breaks. They can function as contents guides in the absence of a table, for example. Thus, openings typically have larger initials than textual subdivisions, and they often show more expensive decoration – for example, champs and borders, rather than lombards and flourishing – than other breaks. In particular, the opening page of a manuscript is supposed to be more elaborate than anything else in the book.[26]

---

[23] The size of a lombard formed by an 'I' is relatively immaterial. Usual representations of the letter are always exaggerated and frequently extend along much of a column.

[24] Regrettably, the head of what may have been the manuscript's planned centrepiece, the *Guy of Warwick* sequence, is among those bits altogether lost.

[25] This image adorns the cover of this volume.

[26] For a particularly telling example of the rule, although rather far afield (shortly after 1400, probably York), one might examine London, BL, MS Cotton Vespasian E. i, where the size and quality of decoration carefully diminish throughout the book.

Given that Auchinleck as we know it was only arranged by Scribe 1 at the end of procedures, the booklet openings point to uncertainty not just about programme but also about contents and their ordering. (And, given Scribe 1's centrality, he might be expected to have 'signed off' on these various versions of opening at intervals in the ongoing production.) At various times, the book may have been imagined in very different conformations than what we have received.

In the absence of large parts of the volume, particularly decorated portions, one is here in the area of speculation. But I point out a couple of possible, if not thoroughly plausible, scenarios. Suppose one were to consider the book in terms of the model that textual openings should be more ornate versions of the basic decorative form employed elsewhere. In this scenario, a booklet opening should use rectilinear illumination in combination with some more emphatic decorative feature. In that regard, the model opening leaf would have been achieved only once in the entire production – and in a very surprising place. Only the deviant unit, formerly ascribed to Scribe 6 and headed by *Otuel a Kniȝt*, actually achieves such a presentation. This could imply that the unit was a late development, the only example in which the Auchinleck team fully achieved their desired presentation.

On the other hand, one might consider elaborate use of paint as the most emphatic form of opening a unit. In these terms, the openings to the *Short Chronicle* and *Sir Beues*, perhaps particularly the latter, stand out as especially fine (although one should admit that one's aesthetic sense and that of the book's producers, given to narrative images, might differ a good deal). Either of these might be considered a suitable opening to the full volume – the *Short Chronicle* as a way of contextualizing its British 'legendary history', *Sir Beues* as the traditional exemplar of native romance. Neither of these hypotheses admits anything like proof, but both of them point to the highly provisional, and perhaps persistently changing, nature of the production decisions underlying the book we now view.

Variations – and somewhat imponderable considerations of their effect and meaning – are inherent in dealing with the Auchinleck manuscript. In the light of such substantial examples as I outline in this conclusion, the variation allowable in a single scribal hand is a fairly minimal consideration, maybe worth only the 'bonne bouche' in which this paper originated. But the book has scarcely been exhausted of its secrets, and is certainly worthy of much more detailed examination (and probably a great deal of contention).

Bibliography

Primary sources

Alphabetical Praise of Women, in *The Auchinleck Manuscript*, ed. D. Burnley and A. Wiggins (Edinburgh, 2003), http://auchinleck.nls.uk.

A lytell geste how the plowman lerned his pater noster (London, 1510).

An Anonymous Short English Metrical Chronicle, ed. E. Zettl, EETS OS 196 (London, 1935).

Ancrene Wisse: A Corrected Edition of the Text in Cambridge, Corpus College, MS 402, with Variants from Other Manuscripts, ed. B. Millett, 2 vols., EETS OS 325, 326 (Oxford, 2005, 2006).

Anglo-Norman Dictionary, ed. W. Rothwell *et al.*, 2nd edn (London, 2005), http://www.anglo-norman.net/

Anna Our Leuedis Moder, in *The Auchinleck Manuscript*, ed. D. Burnley and A. Wiggins (Edinburgh, 2003), http://auchinleck.nls.uk.

Anonymous Short English Metrical Chronicle, in *The Auchinleck Manuscript*, ed. D. Burnley and A. Wiggins (Edinburgh, 2003), http://auchinleck.nls.uk.

The Apocryphal Lives of Adam and Eve, Edited from the Auchinleck MS and from Trinity College, Oxford MS 57, ed. B. Murdoch and J. A. Tasioulas, Exeter Medieval Texts and Studies (Exeter, 2002).

Arthour and Merlin: nach der Auchinleck-hs. nebst zwei Beilagen, ed. E. Kölbing, Altenglische Bibliothek 4 (Leipzig, 1890).

Les Arts poétiques du XIIe et du XIIIe siècle: recherches et documents sur la technique littéraire du moyen âge, ed. E. Faral (Paris, 1958).

The Auchinleck Manuscript, ed. D. Burnley and A. Wiggins (Edinburgh, 2003), http://auchinleck.nls.uk.

The Auchinleck Manuscript: National Library of Scotland Advocates' MS. 19.2.1, intro. D. Pearsall and I. C. Cunningham (London, 1977).

The Babees Book: Early English Meals and Manners, ed. F. J. Furnivall, EETS OS 32 (London, 1868).

Bevis of Hampton, in *Four Romances of England*, ed. R. B. Herzman, G. Drake and E. Salisbury (Kalamazoo MI, 1999), pp. 187–340.

The Birth of Romance in England: 'The Romance of Horn', 'The Folie Tristan', 'The Lai of Haveloc', and 'Amis and Amilun' – Four Twelfth-Century Romances in the French of England, trans. J. Weiss, FRETS 4 (Tempe AZ, 2009).

Bodel, Jehan, *La Chanson des Saisnes*, ed. A. Brasseur, 2 vols. (Geneva, 1989).

Bodleian Library, MS Fairfax 16, intro. J. Norton-Smith (London, 1979).

Cambridge University Library Ms. Ff.2.38, intro. F. McSparran and P. R. Robinson (London, 1979).

Cân Rolant: The Medieval Welsh Version of the Song of Roland, ed. A. C. Rejhon, University of California Publications in Modern Philology 113 (Berkeley, 1984).

The Canterbury Tales: A Facsimile and Transcription of the Hengwrt Manuscript with Variants from the Ellesmere Manuscript, ed. P. G. Ruggiers, intro. D. C. Baker, A. I. Doyle, and M. B. Parkes (Norman OK, 1979).

Carmen Aestivum, in *The Oxford Book of Medieval Latin Verse*, ed. F. J. E. Raby (Oxford, 1959), pp. 174–5.

Castleford's Chronicle, or, The Boke of Brut, ed. C. D. Eckhardt, 2 vols., EETS OS 305, 306 (Oxford, 1996).

La Chanson de Roland – The Song of Roland: The French Corpus, ed. J. J. Duggan *et al.*, 3 vols. (Turnhout, 2005).

Chaucer, Geoffrey, *The Riverside Chaucer*, ed. L. D. Benson *et al.*, 3rd edn (Boston, 1987).

The Chester Mystery Cycle, ed. R. M. Lumiansky and D. Mills, 2 vols., EETS SS 3, 9 (Oxford, 1974, 1986).

The Complete Harley 2253 Manuscript, ed. and trans. S. Fein, with D. Raybin and J. Ziokowski, 3 vols. (Kalamazoo MI, 2014–15).

The Cornish Ordinalia: A Medieval Dramatic Trilogy, ed. and trans. M. Harris (Washington DC, 1969).

'The Cotton Nero A.x Project', ed. M. McGillivray *et al.* (Calgary, 2010), http:// gawain-ms.ca/.

'A Critical Edition of *Sir Tristrem*, Edited from the Auchinleck Manuscript', ed. R. W. Kelton, unpublished PhD dissertation, The Ohio State University (Columbus OH, 1974).

Dante Alighieri, *The Divine Comedy of Dante Alighieri*, ed. and trans. R. M. Durling, 3 vols. (Oxford, 1996, 2003, 2011).

David þe King, in 'Kleine publicationen aus der Auchinleck-hs. V–VII', ed. E. Kölbing, *Englische Studien* 9 (1886), 49–50.

Die Kildare-Gedichte: Die ältesten *mittelenglischen Denkmäler in anglo-irischen Überlieferung*, ed. W. Heuser, Bonner Beiträge zur Anglistik 14 (Bonn, 1904).

Die mittelenglische Gregoriuslegende, ed. C. Keller, Alt-und Mittelenglische Texte 6 (Heidelberg, 1914).

Der mittelenglische Versroman über Richard Löwenherz, ed. K. Brunner, Wiener Beiträge zur englischen Philologie 42 (Vienna, 1913).

'An Edition of the Middle English Romance: *Richard Coeur de Lion*', ed. P. Schellekens, unpublished PhD dissertation, University of Durham (Durham, 1989).

The Ellesmere Manuscript of Chaucer's Canterbury Tales, intro. H. C. Shulz (San Marino CA, 1966).

The English and Scottish Popular Ballads, ed. F. J. Child, 5 vols. (Mineola NY, 1965).

The English Charlemagne Romances I: Sir Ferumbras, ed. S. J. H. Herrtage, EETS ES 34 (London, 1879).

The English Charlemagne Romances VI: The Taill of Rauf Coilyear with the Fragments of Roland and Vertnagu and Otuel, ed. S. J. H. Herrtage, EETS ES 39 (London, 1882).

The English Text of the Ancrene Riwle; Ancrene Wisse Edited from MS. Corpus Christi College Cambridge 402, ed. J. R. R. Tolkien, intro. N. R. Ker, EETS OS 249 (London, 1962).

A Facsimile Edition of the Vernon Manuscript, Bodleian Library MS. Eng. poet. a. 1, ed. W. Scase, software N. Kennedy, Bodleian Digital Texts 3 (Oxford, 2011), DVD-Rom.

Facsimile of British Museum Ms. Harley 2253, intro. N. R. Ker, EETS OS 255 (London, 1965).

The Findern Manuscript (Cambridge University Library Ms. Ff.1.6), intro. R. Beadle and A. E. B. Owen (London, 1977).

Floris and Blauncheflur, in *The Auchinleck Manuscript*, ed. D. Burnley and A. Wiggins (Edinburgh, 2003), http://auchinleck.nls.uk.

Froissart, Jean, *Chroniques*, in *Oeuvres de Froissart*, ed. J. M. B. C. Kervyn de Lettenhove, 25 vols. (Brussels, 1867–8), II–V.

Geoffrey of Vinsauf, *Documentum de modo et arte dictandi et versificandi*, in *Les Arts poétiques du XIIe et du XIIIe siècle: recherches et documents sur la technique littéraire du moyen âge*, ed. E. Faral (Paris, 1958), pp. 263–320.

—*Documentum de modo et arte dictandi et versificandi (Instruction in the Method and Art of Speaking and Versifying)*, trans. R. P. Parr (Milwaukee, 1968).

—*Poetria nova*, ed. and trans. E. Gallo, in *The 'Poetria nova' and Its Sources in Early Rhetorical Doctrine* (The Hague, 1971), pp. 13–132.

Gerald of Wales, *Concerning the Instruction of Princes*, trans. J. Stevenson (London, 1858; rept 1991).

Gower, John, *Confessio Amantis*, ed. R. A. Peck, with Latin translations by A. Galloway, 3 vols. (Kalamazoo MI, 2004, 2006, 2013).

The Greek Alexander Romance, trans. R. Stoneman (London, 1991).

Guy of Warwick, in *The Auchinleck Manuscript*, ed. D. Burnley and A. Wiggins (Edinburgh, 2003), http://auchinleck.nls.uk.

Havelok the Dane, in *Four Romances of England: King Horn, Havelok the Dane, Bevis of Hampton, Athelston*, ed. R. B. Herzman, G. Drake, and E. Salisbury (Kalamazoo MI, 1999), pp. 72–185.

Heroic Women from the Old Testament in Middle English Verse, ed. R. A. Peck (Kalamazoo MI, 1991).

Horn Childe and Maiden Rimnild, ed. M. Mills, Middle English Texts 20 (Heidelberg, 1988).

Horn Childe and Maiden Rimnild, in *The Auchinleck Manuscript*, ed. D. Burnley and A. Wiggins (Edinburgh, 2003), http://auchinleck.nls.uk.

'How the Plowman Learned His Paternoster', in *The Oxford Book of Medieval English Verse*, ed. C. Sisam and K. Sisam (Oxford, 1970), pp. 514–21.

Iacob and Iosep: A Middle English Poem of the Thirteenth Century, ed. A. S. Napier (Oxford, 1916).

The Idea of the Vernacular: An Anthology of Middle English Literary Theory, 1280–1520, ed. J. Wogan-Browne, N. Watson, A. Taylor, and R. Evans (University Park PA, 1999).

Jacobus de Voragine, *The Golden Legend*, trans. W. G. Ryan, 2 vols. (Princeton, 1993).

John of Garland, *The 'Parisiana Poetria' of John of Garland*, ed. and trans. T. Lawler, Yale Studies in English 182 (New Haven, 1974).

John of Salisbury, *Ioannis Saresberiensis: Policraticus I-IV*, ed. K. S. B. Keats-Rohan, CCCM 118 (Turnhout, 1993).

Karlamagnús saga ok Kappa Hans, ed. C. R. Unger (Christiana, 1860).

Karlamagnús saga: The Saga of Charlemagne and His Heroes, trans. C. B. Hieatt, 3 vols. (Toronto, 1975–80).

King Horn: An Edition Based on Cambridge University Library MS Gg. 4. 27 (2), ed. R. Allen, Garland Medieval Texts 7 (New York, 1984).

The King of Tars, ed. J. H. Chandler (Kalamazoo MI, 2015).

The King of Tars, ed. J. Perryman, Middle English Texts 12 (Heidelberg, 1980).

King Richard, in *The Auchinleck Manuscript*, ed. D. Burnley and A. Wiggins (Edinburgh, 2003), http://auchinleck.nls.uk.

'Kleine publicationen aus der Auchinleck-hs. III,' ed. E. Kölbing, *Englische Studien* 8 (1885), 115–18.

'Kleine publicationen aus der Auchinleck-hs. V–VII,' ed. E. Kölbing, *Englische Studien* 9 (1886), 47–50.

Kyng Alisaunder, ed. G. V. Smithers, 2 vols., EETS OS 227, 237 (Oxford, 1952, 1957).

Kyng Alisaunder, in *The Auchinleck Manuscript*, ed. D. Burnley and A. Wiggins (Edinburgh, 2003), http://auchinleck.nls.uk.

Langland, William, *Piers Plowman: The B Version*, ed. G. Kane and E. T. Donaldson (London, 1975).

—*Piers Plowman: A New Annotated Edition of the C-Text*, ed. D. Pearsall, Exeter Medieval Texts and Studies (Exeter, 2008).

The Lay Folk's Catechism, or the English and Latin Versions of Archbishop Thoresby's Instruction for the People, ed. T. F. Simmons and H. E. Nolloth, EETS OS 118 (London, 1901).

Lay le Freine, in *The Middle English Breton Lays*, ed. A. Laskaya and E. Salisbury (Kalamazoo MI, 1995), pp. 61–87.

Lestoire de Merlin, in *The Vulgate Version of the Arthurian Romances, Ed. from Manuscripts in the British Museum*, ed. H. O. Sommer, 8 vols. in 4 (Washington DC, 1908–16), II.

'Life of Adam and Eve', trans. M. D. Johnson, in *The Old Testament Pseudepigrapha*, ed. J. H. Charlesworth, 2 vols. (London 1985), II, 249–95.

Life of St Mary Magdalene, in *The Auchinleck Manuscript*, ed. D. Burnley and A. Wiggins (Edinburgh, 2003), http://auchinleck.nls.uk.

Matthew of Vendôme, *Ars versificatoria*, in *Les Arts poétiques du XIIe et du XIIIe siècle: recherches et documents sur la technique littéraire du moyen âge*, ed. E. Faral (Paris, 1958), pp. 106–93.

—*Ars versificatoria (The Art of the Versemaker)*, trans. R. P. Parr (Milwaukee, 1981).

Middle English Debate Poetry: A Critical Anthology, ed. J. W. Conlee (East Lansing, MI, 1991).

The Middle English Genesis and Exodus, ed. O. Arngart (Lund, 1968).

Middle English Legends of Women Saints, ed. S. L. Reames (Kalamazoo MI, 2003).

The Middle English Metrical Paraphrase of the Old Testament, ed. M. Livingston (Kalamazoo MI, 2011).

Middle English Religious Prose, ed. N. F. Blake (London 1972).

Minot, Laurence, *The Poems of Laurence Minot, 1333–1352*, ed. R. H. Osberg (Kalamazoo MI, 1996).

Mirk, John, *Instructions for Parish Priests*, ed. G. Kristensson (Lund, 1974).

The Mirour of Mans Saluacioun: A Middle English Translation of Speculum Humanae Salvationis, ed. A. Henry (Aldershot, 1986).

'MS Harley 2253', British Library Digitised Manuscripts, http://www.bl.uk/manuscripts/FullDisplay.aspx?index=9&ref=Harley_MS_2253.

'Nachträge zu den Legenden', ed. C. Horstmann, *Archiv* 74 (1885), 327–65.

Of Arthour and of Merlin, ed. O. D. Macrae-Gibson, 2 vols., EETS OS 268, 279 (Oxford, 1973, 1979).

Of Arthour and of Merlin, in *The Auchinleck Manuscript*, ed. D. Burnley and A. Wiggins (Edinburgh, 2003), http://auchinleck.nls.uk.

The Old Testament Pseudepigrapha, ed. J. H. Charlesworth, 2 vols. (London 1985).

On þe Seuen Dedly Sinnes, in *The Auchinleck Manuscript*, ed. D. Burnley and A. Wiggins (Edinburgh, 2003), http://auchinleck.nls.uk.

Otuel, in *The English Charlemagne Romances VI: The Taill of Rauf Coilyear with the Fragments of Roland and Vernagu and Otuel*, ed. S. J. H. Herrtage, EETS ES 39 (London, 1882), pp. 65-116.

Otuel a Kniȝt, in *The Auchinleck Manuscript*, ed. D. Burnley and A. Wiggins (Edinburgh, 2003), http://auchinleck.nls.uk.

The Owl and the Nightingale: Text and Translation, ed. N. Cartlidge, Exeter Medieval Texts and Studies (Exeter, 2001).

The Oxford Book of Medieval Latin Verse, ed. R. J. E. Raby (Oxford, 1959).

Oxford Version, ed. I. Short, in *La Chanson de Roland – The Song of Roland: The French Corpus*, ed. J. J. Duggan *et al.*, 3 vols. (Turnhout, 2005), I, I/1–338.

The Paternoster, in 'Kleine publicationen aus der Auchinleck-hs. V–VII', ed. E. Kölbing, *Englische Studien* 9 (1886), 47–9.

The Pater Noster Vndo on Englissch, in *The Auchinleck Manuscript*, ed. D. Burnley and A. Wiggins (Edinburgh, 2003), http://auchinleck.nls.uk.

Patrologiae cursus completus … series latina, ed. J.-P. Migne (Paris, 1844–64).

Pearl, Cleanness, Patience and Sir Gawain Reproduced in Facsimile from the Unique Ms. Cotton Nero A.x in the British Museum, intro. I. Gollancz, EETS OS 162 (London, 1923).

The Poems of the Pearl Manuscript: Pearl, Cleanness, Patience, Sir Gawain the Green Knight, ed. M. Andrew and R. Waldron, 5th edn, Exeter Medieval Texts and Studies (Exeter, 2007).

Poetical Works: A Facsimile of Cambridge University Library MS Gg. 4.27, intro. M. B. Parkes and R. Beadle (Norman OK, 1979).

'*Richard Coeur de Lion*: An Edition from the London Thornton Manuscript', ed. M. C. Figueredo, unpublished PhD dissertation, University of York (York, 2010).

Robert Mannyng of Brunne, *The Chronicle*, ed. I. Sullens, Medieval and Renaissance Texts and Studies (Binghamton NY, 1996).

—*The Story of England*, ed. F. J. Furnivall, 2 vols., Rolls Series 34 (London, 1887).

Robert of Brunne's Handlyng Synne, ed. F. J. Furnivall, 2 vols., EETS OS 119, 123 (London, 1901, 1903).

Roland and Vernagu, in *The Auchinleck Manuscript*, ed. D. Burnley and A. Wiggins (Edinburgh, 2003), http://auchinleck.nls.uk.

Roland and Vernagu, in *The English Charlemagne Romances VI: The Taill of Rauf Coilyear with the Fragments of Roland and Vernagu and Otuel*, ed. S. J. H. Herrtage, EETS ES 39 (London, 1882), pp. 37–61.

The Roll of Arms, of the Princes, Barons, and Knights Who Attended King Edward I to the Seige of Caerlaverock, in 1300, trans. T. Wright (London, 1864).

Roman de Thèbes, ed. G. R. de Lage (Paris, 1966).

The Romance of Emaré, ed. E. Rickert, EETS ES 99 (Oxford, 1908).

La Saga de Charlemagne: Traduction française des dix Branches de la Karlamagnús saga norroise, trans. D. W. Lacroix (Paris, 2000).

The Sayings of St Bernard, in 'Zu mittelenglischen Gedichten. VII. Noch einmal zu den sprachen des heiligen Bernhard', ed. H. Varnhagen, *Anglia* 3 (1880), 285–92.

The Sayings of the Four Philosophers, in *The Auchinleck Manuscript*, ed. D. Burnley and A. Wiggins (Edinburgh, 2003), http://auchinleck.nls.uk.

The Sayings of the Four Philosophers, in *Historical Poems of the XIVth and XVth Centuries*, ed. R. H. Robbins (New York, 1959), pp. 140–3.

The Seven Sages of Rome (Southern Version), ed. K. Brunner, EETS OS 191 (London, 1933).

Seynt Mergrete, in *The Auchinleck Manuscript*, ed. D. Burnley and A. Wiggins (Edinburgh, 2003), http://auchinleck.nls.uk.

The Simonie, in *The Auchinleck Manuscript*, ed. D. Burnley and A. Wiggins (Edinburgh, 2003), http://auchinleck.nls.uk.

Sir Beues of Hamtoun, in *The Auchinleck Manuscript*, ed. D. Burnley and A. Wiggins (Edinburgh, 2003), http://auchinleck.nls.uk.

Sir Gawain: Eleven Romances and Tales, ed. T. Hahn (Kalamazoo MI, 1995).

Sir Orfeo, ed. A. J. Bliss, 2nd edn (Oxford, 1966).

Sir Orfeo, in *The Auchinleck Manuscript*, ed. D. Burnley and A. Wiggins (Edinburgh, 2003), http://auchinleck.nls.uk.

Sir Orfeo, in *The Middle English Breton Lays*, ed. A. Laskaya and E. Salisbury (Kalamazoo MI, 1995), pp. 15–59.

The Thornton Manuscript (Lincoln Cathedral MS. 91), intro. D. S. Brewer and A. E. B. Owen (London, 1975).

Sir Tristrem, in *The Auchinleck Manuscript*, ed. D. Burnley and A. Wiggins (Edinburgh, 2003), http://auchinleck.nls.uk.

The South English Legendary, ed. C. D'Evelyn and A. J. Mill, 3 vols., EETS OS 235, 236, 244 (London, 1956–9).

The South English Nativity of Mary and Christ, ed. O. S. Pickering, Middle English Texts 1 (Heidelberg, 1975).

Speculum Vitae: A Reading Edition, ed. R. Hanna, 2 vols., EETS OS 331 (Oxford, 2008).

St Patrick's Purgatory, ed. R. Easting, EETS OS 298 (Oxford, 1991).

Statius, *Thebaid 4*, ed. and trans. R. E. Parkes (Oxford, 2012).

Susannah: An Alliterative Poem of the Fourteenth Century, ed. A. Miskimin (New Haven, 1969).

Thebaid, Books 1–7, ed. and trans. D. R. Shackleton Bailey, Loeb Classical Library 207 (Cambridge MA, 2003).

Thomas of Kent, *The Anglo-Norman 'Alexander' (Le Roman de toute chevalerie)*, ed. B. Foster and I. Short, 2 vols., ANTS 29–31 (London, 1976–77).

The Thrush and the Nightingale, in *The Auchinleck Manuscript*, ed. D. Burnley and A. Wiggins (Edinburgh, 2003), http://auchinleck.nls.uk.

The Thrush and the Nightingale, in 'Zu mittelenglischen Gedichten. XIII. Zu dem streitgedichte zwischen drossel und nactigall', ed. H. Varnhagen, *Anglia* 4 (1881), 207–10.

A Variorum Edition of The Works of Geoffrey Chaucer: Volume II: The Canterbury Tales, Part Nine: The Nun's Priest's Tale, ed. D. Pearsall (Norman OK, 1984).

The Vernon Manuscript: A Facsimile of Bodleian Library, Oxford MS. Eng. poet a. 1, intro. A. I. Doyle (Cambridge, 1987).

Vita Edwardi Secundi, monarchi cuiusdam Malmesberiensis, ed. N. Dedholm-Young (London, 1957).

The Vulgate Version of the Arthurian Romances, Ed. from Manuscripts in the British Museum, ed. H. O. Sommer, 8 vols. in 4 (Washington DC, 1908–16).

Walter Map, *De nugis curialium – Courtiers' Trifles*, ed. and trans. M. R. James, rev. C. N. L. Brooke and R. A. B. Mynors (Oxford, 1983).

Walter of Châtillon, *The Alexandreis: A Twelfth-Century Epic*, ed. and trans. D. Townsend (Peterborough ON, 2006).

—*Galteri de Castellione Alexandreis*, ed. M. L. Colker (Padua, 1978).

The War of Saint-Sardos (1323–25): Gascon Correspondences and Diplomatic Documents, ed. P. Chaplais (London, 1954).

The Wheatley Manuscript: Middle English Verse and Prose in BM MS Add 39574, ed. M. Day, EETS OS 155 (Oxford, 1921).

Wynnere and Wastoure, ed. S. Trigg, EETS OS 297 (Oxford, 1990).

The York Plays: A Critical Edition of the York Corpus Christi Play as Recorded in British Library Additional MS 35290, ed. R. Beadle, 2 vols., EETS SS 23, 24 (Oxford, 2009, 2013).

Ywain and Gawain, ed. A. B. Friedman and N. T. Harrington, EETS OS 254 (London, 1964).

Secondary sources

Aarts, F. G. A. M., 'The Pater Noster in Medieval English Literature', *Papers on Language and Literature* 5 (1969), 3-16.

Adkin, N., 'The Date of Walter of Châtillon's *Alexandreis* Once Again', *Classica et Mediaevalia* 59 (2008), 201–11.

Aebischer, P., *Des annals carolingiennes à Doon de Mayence: nouveau recueil d'études sur l'épique française médiévale* (Geneva, 1975).

Ailes, M., and P. Hardman, 'Texts in Conversation: Charlemagne Epics and Romances in Insular Plural-Text Codices', in *Insular Books: Vernacular*

Manuscript Miscellanies in Late Medieval Britain, ed. M. Connolly and R. Radulescu, Proceedings of the British Academy 201 (Oxford, 2015), pp. 31–47.

Ashe, L., 'The Anomalous King of Conquered England', in *Every Inch a King: Comparative Studies on Kings and Kingship in the Ancient and Medieval Worlds*, ed. L. Mitchell and C. Melville (Leiden, 2012), pp. 173–93.

Bahr, A., *Fragments and Assemblages: Forming Compilations of Medieval London* (Chicago, 2013).

Barker, N., *Bibliotheca Lindesiana* (London, 1978).

Baswell, C., 'Multilingualism on the Page', in *Middle English*, ed. P. Strohm, Oxford Twenty-First Century Approaches to Literature (Oxford, 2007), pp. 38–50.

Battles, D., '*Sir Orfeo* and English Identity', *Studies in Philology* 107 (2010), 179–211.

Baugh, A. C., 'Improvisation in the Middle English Romance', *Proceedings of the American Philosophical Society* 103 (1959), 418–54.

—and T. Cable, *A History of the English Language*, 5th edn (London, 2002).

Bliss, A. J., 'The Auchinleck "St. Margaret" and "St. Katherine"', *Notes and Queries* 201 (1956), 186–8.

—'Notes on the Auchinleck Manuscript', *Speculum* 26 (1951), 652–8.

Boffey, J., 'Middle English Lives', in *The Cambridge History of Medieval English Literature*, ed. D. Wallace (Cambridge, 1999), pp. 610–34.

—'Short Texts in Manuscript Anthologies: The Minor Poems of John Lydgate in Two Fifteenth-Century Collections', in *The Whole Book: Cultural Perspectives on the Medieval Miscellany*, ed. S. G. Nichols and S. Wenzel (Ann Arbor, 1996), pp. 69–82.

—and A. S. G. Edwards, *A New Index of Middle English Verse* (London, 2005).

Bradbury, N. M., *Writing Aloud: Storytelling in Late Medieval England* (Urbana IL, 1998).

Britnell, R., 'Uses of French in Medieval English Towns', in *Language and Culture in Medieval Britain: The French of England c.1100–c.1500*, ed. J. Wogan-Browne, C. Collette, M. Kowaleski, L. Mooney, A. Putter, and D. Trotter (York, 2009), pp. 81–9.

Brunner, K., 'The Middle English Metrical Romances and Their Audience', in *Studies in Medieval Literature in Honor of Albert Croll Baugh*, ed. M. Leach (Philadelphia, 1961), pp. 219–27

Bullock-Davies, C., *Menestrellorum Multitudo: Minstrels at a Royal Feast* (Cardiff, 1978).

Burrow, J. A., Notes to *Sir Thopas*, in *The Riverside Chaucer*, ed. L. D. Benson, 3rd edn (Boston, 1987), pp. 917–23.

Burrows, J. H., 'The Auchinleck Manuscript: Contexts, Texts and Audience', unpublished PhD dissertation, Washington University (Saint Louis MO, 1984).

Butterfield, A., *The Familiar Enemy: Chaucer, Language, and Nation in the Hundred Years War* (Oxford, 2009).

Calkin, S. B., *Saracens and the Making of English Identity: The Auchinleck Manuscript* (New York, 2005).

—'Violence, Saracens, and English Identity in *Of Arthour and of Merlin*', *Arthuriana* 14:2 (2004), 17–36.

Cannon, C., 'Chaucer and the Auchinleck Manuscript Revisited', *Chaucer Review* 46 (2011), 131–46.

Childress, D. T., 'Between Romance and Legend: "Secular Hagiography" in Middle English Literature', *Philological Quarterly* 57 (1978), 311–22.

Chism, C., 'Winning Women in Two Middle English Alexander Poems', in *Women and Medieval Epic: Gender, Genre, and the Limits of Masculinity*, ed. S. Poor and J. K. Schulman (New York, 2007), pp. 15–39.

Christianson, C. P., *A Directory of London Stationers and Book Artisans 1300–1500* (New York, 1990).

Clark, C., 'The Myth of "the Anglo-Norman Scribe"', in *History of Englishes: New Methods and Interpretations in Historical Linguistics*, ed. M. Rissanen, O. Ihalainen, T. Nevalainen, and I. Taavitsainen (Berlin, 1992), pp. 117–29.

Clifton, N., '*Of Arthour and of Merlin* as Medieval Children's Literature', *Arthuriana* 13.2 (2003), 9–22.

—'*The Seven Sages of Rome*, Children's Literature, and the Auchinleck Manuscript', in *Childhood in the Middle Ages and the Renaissance*, ed. A. Classen (Berlin, 2005), pp. 185–201.

Cole, K. L., 'Chaucer's Metrical Landscape', in *Chaucer's Poetry: Words, Authority and Ethics*, ed. C. Carney and F. M. McCormack (Dublin, 2013), pp. 92–106.

Coleman, J., *Public Reading and the Reading Public in Late Medieval England and France*, Cambridge Studies in Medieval Literature 26 (Cambridge, 1996).

—'Strange Rhyme: Prose and Nationhood in Robert Mannyng's *Story of England*', *Speculum* 78 (2003), 1214–38.

Cooper, H., *The English Romance in Time: Transforming Motifs from Geoffrey of Monmouth to the Death of Shakespeare* (Oxford, 2004).

—'Lancelot, Roger Mortimer and the Date of the Auchinleck Manuscript', in *Studies in Late Medieval and Early Renaissance Texts in Honour of John Scattergood*, ed. A. M. D'Arcy and A. J. Fletcher (Dublin, 2005), pp. 91–9.

Crofts, T. H., and R. A. Rouse, 'Middle English Popular Romance and National Identity', in *A Companion to Medieval Popular Romance*, ed. R. L. Radulescu and C. J. Rushton, Studies in Medieval Romance (Cambridge, 2009), pp. 79–95.

Crosby, R., 'Oral Delivery in the Middle Ages', *Speculum* 11 (1936), 88-110.

Cunningham, I. C., 'Binding', in *The Auchinleck Manuscript: National Library of Scotland Advocates' MS. 19.2.1*, intro. D. Pearsall and I. C. Cunningham (London, 1979), pp. xvi.

—'Physical Description', in *The Auchinleck Manuscript: National Library of Scotland Advocates' MS. 19.2.1*, intro. D. Pearsall and I. C. Cunningham (London, 1979), pp. xi–xiv.

—'Script and Ornament', in *The Auchinleck Manuscript: National Library of Scotland Advocates' MS. 19.2.1*, intro. D. Pearsall and I. C. Cunningham (London, 1979), pp. xv–xvi.

Cuttino, G. P., *English Diplomatic Administration* (Oxford, 1940).

Davis, N., 'Another Fragment of "Richard Coer de Lyon"', *Notes and Queries* 16 (1969), 447–52.

Dennison, L., 'An Illuminator of the Queen Mary Psalter Group: The Ancient 6 Master', *The Antiquaries Journal* 16, pt. 2 (1986), 287–314.

—'"Liber Horn", "Liber Custumarum" and Other Manuscripts of the Queen Mary Psalter Workshops', in *Medieval Art, Architecture and Archaeology in London*, ed. L. Grant, British Archaeological Association Conference Transactions 10 (London, 1990), pp. 118–34.

Dentith, S., *Parody*, The New Critical Idiom (London, 2000).

Dobozy, M., *Re-Membering the Present: The Medieval German Poet Minstrel in Cultural Context* (Turnhout, 2005).

Donaldson, E. T., 'Idiom of Popular Poetry in the Miller's Tale', in E. T. Donaldson, *Speaking of Chaucer* (London, 1970), pp. 13–29.

—*Piers Plowman: The C-Text and Its Poet*, Yale Studies in English 13 (New Haven, 1949).

Doyle, A. I., 'English Books In and Out of Court', in *English Court Culture*, ed. V. J. Scattergood and J. W. Sherborne (London, 1983), pp. 161–81.

—'Recent Directions in Manuscript Study', in *New Directions in Later Medieval Manuscript Studies: Essays from the 1998 Harvard Conference*, ed. D. Pearsall (York, 2000), pp. 1–14.

—and M. B. Parkes, 'The Production of Copies of the *Canterbury Tales* and the *Confessio Amantis* in the Early Fifteenth Century', in *Medieval Scribes, Manuscripts and Libraries: Essays Presented to N. R. Ker*, ed. M. B. Parkes and A. G. Watson (London, 1978), pp. 163–210.

Duffy, E., *The Stripping of the Altars: Traditional Religion in England 1400–1580* (New Haven, 1992).

Duggan, J. J., 'La France des Plantagenêts dans les versions rimées de la *Chanson de Roland*', in *Les Chansons de geste: Actes du XVIe Congrès International de la Société Rencesvals, pour l'étude des épopées romanes, Granada, 21–25 juillet 2003*, ed. C. Alvar and J. Paredes (Granada, 2005), pp. 205–14.

Dunphy, G., 'The Devil's See: A Puzzling Reference in the Auchinleck *Life of Adam*', *Medium Ævum* 73 (2004), 93–8.

Dutschke, C. W., *Guide to Medieval and Renaissance Manuscripts in the Huntington Library*, 2 vols. (San Marino CA, 1989).

Dzon, M., 'Joseph and the Amazing Christ-Child', in *Childhood in the Middle Ages and the Renaissance*, ed. A. Classen (Berlin, 2005), pp. 135–57.

Eberle, P. J., 'Richard II and the Literary Arts', in *Richard III*, ed. A. Goodman and J. Gillespie (Oxford, 1999), pp. 233–53.

Eckhardt, C. D., and B. A. Meer, 'Constructing a Medieval Genealogy: Roland the Father of Tristan in *Castleford's Chronicle*', *Modern Language Notes* 15 (2000), 1085–111.

Edwards, A. S. G., 'Oxford, Bodleian Library, MS Laud. Misc. 108: Contents, Construction and Circulation', in *The Texts and Contexts of Oxford, Bodleian Library, MS Laud Misc. 108: The Shaping of English Vernacular Narrative*, ed. K. K. Bell and J. N. Couch (Leiden, 2011), pp. 21–30.

—'The *Speculum Guy de Warwick*: and Lydgate's *Guy of Warwick*: The Non-Romance Middle English Tradition', in *Guy of Warwick: Icon and Ancestor*, ed. R. Field and A. Wiggins (Cambridge, 2007), pp. 81–93.

Evans, J. M., *'Paradise Lost' and the Genesis Tradition* (Oxford, 1968).

Evans, M. J., *Rereading Middle English Manuscripts: Manuscript Layout, Decoration, and the Rhetoric of Composite Structure* (Montreal, 1995).

Fein, S., 'Compilation and Purpose in MS Harley 2253', in *Essays in Manuscript Geography: Vernacular Manuscripts of the English West Midlands from the Conquest to the Sixteenth Century*, ed. W. Scase, Medieval Texts and Cultures of Northern Europe 10 (Turnhout, 2007), pp. 67–95.

—'The Fillers of the Auchinleck Manuscript and the Literary Culture of the West Midlands', in *Makers and Users of Medieval Books: Essays in Honour of A. S. G. Edwards*, ed. C. M. Meale and D. Pearsall (Cambridge, 2014), pp. 60–77.

—'Literary Scribes: The Harley Scribe and Robert Thornton as Case Studies', in *Insular Books: Vernacular Manuscript Miscellanies in Late Medieval Britain*, ed. M. Connolly and R. Radulescu, Proceedings of the British Academy 201 (Oxford, 2015), pp. 61-79.

Fellows, J., 'The Representations of Middle English Romances on English Misericords', in *Profane Imagery in Marginal Arts of the Middle Ages*, ed. E. C. Block and M. Jones (Turnhout, 2009), pp. 123–41.

Field, R., 'Patterns of Availability and Demand in Middle English Translations *de romanz*', in *The Exploitations of Medieval Romance*, ed. L. Ashe, I. Djordjević, and J. Weiss (Cambridge, 2010), pp. 73–89.

—'Romance', in *The Oxford History of Literary Translation in English, Volume 1: To 1550*, ed. R. Ellis (Oxford, 2008), pp. 296–331.

—'Romance as History, History as Romance', in *Romance in Medieval England*, ed. M. Mills, J. Fellows, and C. M. Meale (Cambridge, 1991), pp. 163–74.

—'Romance in England, 1066–1400', in *The Cambridge History of Medieval English Literature*, ed. D. Wallace (Cambridge, 1999), pp. 152–76.

Finlayson, J., '*Richard Coer de Lyon*: Romance, History, or Something in Between?', *Studies in Philology* 87 (1990), 156–80.

Fisher, M., *Scribal Authorship and the Writing of History in Medieval England* (Columbus OH, 2012).

Flood, J., *Representations of Eve in Antiquity and the English Middle Ages* (New York, 2011).

Foote, P., *The Pseudo-Turpin Chronicle in Iceland: A Contribution to the Study of the Karlamagnús saga* (London, 1959).

Fredell, J., 'The Lowly Paraph: Transmitting Manuscript Design in the *Canterbury Tales*', *Studies in the Age of Chaucer* 22 (2000), 213–80.

Gautier, L., *Les épopées françaises: Etude sur les origines et l'histoire de la littérature nationale*, 3 vols. (Paris, 1865-68).

Geist, R. J., 'On the Genesis of the *King of Tars*', *Journal of English and Germanic Philology* 42 (1943), 260–8.

Gillingham, J., 'Foundations of a Disunited Kingdom', in *Uniting the Kingdom? The Making of British History*, ed. A. Grant and K. J. Stringer (New York, 1995), pp. 48–64.

—*Richard I* (New Haven, 2002).

Görlach, M., 'The Auchinleck *Katerine*', in *So meny people, longages and tonges:*

Philological Essays in Scots and Mediaeval English Presented to Angus McIntosh, ed. M. Benskin and M. L. Samuels (Edinburgh, 1981), pp. 211–28.

—*The Textual Tradition of the South English Legendary* (Leeds, 1974).

Grimbert, J. T., ed., *Tristan and Isolde: A Casebook* (London, 1995).

Guddat-Figge, G., *Catalogue of Manuscripts Containing Middle English Romances* (Munich, 1976).

Halvorsen, E. F., *The Norse Version of the Chanson de Roland*, Bibliotheca Arnamagnæana 19 (Copenhagen, 1959).

Hanna, R., 'Dan Michel of Northgate and His Books', in *Medieval Manuscripts, Their Makers and Users: A Special Issue of Viator in Honor of Richard and Mary Rouse*, ed. C. Baswell (Turnhout, 2011), pp. 213–24.

—*London Literature, 1300–1380*, Cambridge Studies in Medieval Literature 57 (Cambridge, 2005).

—'Middle English Verse from a Bodleian Binding', *Bodleian Library Record* 17 (2002), 488–92.

—*Pursuing History: Middle English Manuscripts and Their Texts* (Stanford, 1996).

—'Reconsidering the Auchinleck Manuscript', in *New Directions in Later Medieval Manuscript Studies: Essays from the 1998 Harvard Conference*, ed. D. Pearsall (York, 2000), pp. 91–102.

—'Studies in the Manuscripts of *Piers Plowman*', *Yearbook of Langland Studies* 7 (1993), 1–25.

Hardman, P., 'Malory and Middle English Verse Romance: The Case of *Sir Tristrem*', in *Arthurian Studies in Honour of P. J. C. Field*, ed. E. Archibald and D. F. Johnson (Cambridge, 2004), pp. 215–22.

—'Popular Romances and Young Readers', in *A Companion to Medieval Popular Romance*, ed. R. L. Radulescu and C. J. Rushton, Studies in Medieval Romance (Cambridge, 2009), pp. 150–64.

Harf–Lancner, L., 'Alexandre le Grand dans les romans français du moyen âge: un héros de la démesure', *Mélanges de l'école française de Rome: Moyen Âge* 112 (2000), 51–63.

Hammill, F., *Sophistication: A Literary and Cultural History* (Liverpool, 2010).

Hauser, A., *The Sociology of Art*, trans. K. J. Northcott (Chicago, 1982).

Haywood, L. M., 'Spring Song and Narrative Organization in the Medieval Alexander Legend', *Troianalexandrina* 4 (2004), 87–105.

Heffernan, T. J., *Sacred Biography: Saints and Their Biographers in the Middle Ages* (New York, 1988).

Heng, G., *Empire of Magic: Medieval Romance and the Politics of Cultural Fantasy* (New York, 2003).

Holland, W. E., 'Formulaic Diction and the Descent of a Middle English Romance', *Speculum* 48 (1973), 89-109.

Horobin, S., '"In London and Opelond": The Dialect and the Circulation of the C Version of *Piers Plowman*', *Medium Ævum* 74 (2005), 248–69.

—and A. Wiggins, 'Reconsidering Lincoln's Inn MS 150', *Medium Ævum* 77 (2008), 30–53.

Hudson, A., *The Premature Reformation: Wycliffite Texts and Lollard History* (Oxford, 1988).

Hudson, H., 'Middle English Popular Romances: The Manuscript Evidence', *Manuscripta* 28 (1984), 67–78.

Hume, C., '*The Storie of Asneth*: A Fifteenth-Century Commission and the Mystery of Its Epilogue', *Medium Ævum* 82 (2013), 44–65.

Hunt, T., 'The Significance of Thomas's *Tristan*', *Reading Medieval Studies* 7 (1981), 41–61.

—'The Tristan Illustrations in MS London BL Add. 11619', in *Rewards and Punishments in the Arthurian Romances and Lyric Poetry of Medieval France*, ed. P. V. Davies and A. J. Kennedy (Cambridge, 1987), pp. 45–60.

Huot, S., 'Polytextual Reading: The Meditative Reading of Real and Metaphorical Books', in *Orality and Literacy in the Middle Ages: Essays on a Conjunction and Its Consequences in Honour of D. H. Green*, ed. M. Chinca and C. Young (Turnhout, 2005), pp. 203–22.

Hussey, M., 'The Petitions of the Paternoster in Mediæval English Literature', *Medium Ævum* 27 (1958), 8–16.

Jacobs, N., *The Later Versions of Sir Degarre: A Study in Textual Degeneration*, Medium Ævum Monographs, n.s. 18 (Oxford, 1995).

Jauss, H. R., *Toward an Aesthetic of Reception*, trans. T. Bahti (Minneapolis, 1982).

Johnston, M., *Romance and the Gentry in Late Medieval England* (Oxford, 2014).

Kermode, F., *The Sense of an Ending: Studies in the Theory of Fiction* (Oxford, 1966).

Kleinhenz, C., and K. Busby, eds., *Medieval Multilingualism: The Francophone World and Its Neighbors*, Medieval Texts and Cultures of Northern Europe 20 (Turnhout, 2010).

Knight, S., 'Chaucer and the Sociology of Literature', *Studies in the Age of Chaucer* 2 (1980), 15–51.

Kölbing, E., 'Vier romanzen-handschriften', *Englische Studien* 7 (1884), 177–201.

Krahl, E., *Untersuchungen über vier Versionen der mittelenglischen Margaretenlegende*, dissertation, Königliche Friedrich-Wilhelms-Universität (Berlin, 1895).

Kurath, H., S. H. Kuhn et al., *Middle English Dictionary* (Ann Arbor MI, 1954–2001), http://www.quod.lib.mich.edu/m/med.

Laing, M., 'Confusion *wrs* Confounded: Litteral Substitution Sets in Early Middle English Writing Systems', *Neuphilologische Mitteilungen* 100 (1999), 251–70.

—'*The Owl and the Nightingale*: Five New Readings and Further Notes', *Neuphilologische Mitteilungen* 108 (2007), 445–77.

Leach, H. G., *Angevin Britain and Scandinavia* (Cambridge MA, 1921).

Lewis, K. J., 'The Life of St Margaret of Antioch in Late Medieval England: A Gendered Reading', in *Gender and Christian Religion*, ed. R. N. Swanson (Woodbridge, 1998), pp. 129–42.

Loomis, L. H., 'The Auchinleck Manuscript and a Possible London Bookshop of 1330–1340', *PMLA* 57 (1942), 595–627.

—'The Auchinleck *Roland and Vernagu* and the *Short Chronicle*', *Modern Language Notes* 60 (1945), 94–7.

—'Chaucer and the Auchinleck MS: "Thopas" and "Guy of Warwick"', in *Essays and Studies in Honor of Carleton Brown* (New York, 1940), pp. 111–28.

—'Chaucer and the Breton Lays of the Auchinleck MS', *Studies in Philology* 38 (1941), 14–33.

—*Medieval Romance in England: A Study of the Sources and Analogues of the Non-Cyclic Metrical Romances* (New York, 1960).

Lusignan, S., 'French Language in Contact with English: Social Context and Linguistic Change (Mid 13th and 14th Centuries)', in *Language and Culture in Medieval Britain: The French of England c.1100–c.1500*, ed. J. Wogan-Browne, C. Collette, M. Kowaleski, L. Mooney, A. Putter, and D. Trotter (York, 2009), pp. 19–30.

Machan, T. W., *English in the Middle Ages* (Oxford, 2003).

—'Politics and the Middle English Language', *Studies in the Age of Chaucer* 24 (2002), 17–24.

Marshall, H., 'What's in a Paraph? A New Methodology and Its Implications for the Auchinleck Manuscript', *Journal of the Early Book Society* 13 (2010), 39–62.

Manly, J. M., and E. M. Rickert, eds., *The Text of the Canterbury Tales: Edited from All Known Manuscripts*, 8 vols. (Chicago, 1940).

McGerr, R., *Chaucer's Open Books: Resistance to Closure in Medieval Discourse* (Gainesville FL, 1998).

McIntosh, A., 'Is *Sir Tristrem* an English or a Scottish Poem?', in *In Other Words: Transcultural Studies in Philology, Translation, and Lexicology Presented to Hans Heinrich Meier on the Occasion of His Sixty-Fifth Birthday*, ed. J. L. Mackenzie and R. Todd (Dordrecht, 1989), pp. 85–95.

—'The Middle English Poem *The Four Foes of Mankind*', *Neuphilologische Mitteilungen* 79 (1978), 137–44.

—M. L. Samuels and M. Benskin, with M. Laing and K. Williamson, *A Linguistic Atlas of Late Mediaeval English*, 4 vols. (Aberdeen, 1986).

Mehl, D., *The Middle English Romances of the Thirteenth and Fourteenth Centuries* (London, 1969).

Mills, M. 'The Composition and Style of the "Southern" *Octavian*, *Sir Launfal* and *Libeaus Desconus*', *Medium Ævum* 31 (1962), 88-109.

Mooney, L. R., and E. Stubbs, *Scribes in the City: London Guildhall Clerks and the Dissemination of Middle English Literature, 1375-1425* (York, 2013).

—D. W. Mosser, E. Solopova, and D. H. Radcliffe, *The Digital Index of Middle English Verse*, http://www. dimev.net.

Mordkoff, J. C., 'The Making of the Auchinleck Manuscript: The Scribes at Work', unpublished PhD dissertation, University of Connecticut (Storrs CT, 1981).

Morey, J. H., *Book and Verse: A Guide to Middle English Biblical Literature* (Urbana IL, 2000)

Morgan, N., 'Old Testament Illustration in Thirteenth-Century England', in *The Bible in the Middle Ages: Its Influence on Literature and Art*, ed. B. S. Levy (Binghamton NY, 1992), pp. 149–98.

Nichols, A. E., *Seeable Signs: The Iconography of the Seven Sacraments 1350–1544* (Woodbridge, 1994).

Norris, R. C., *Malory's Library: The Sources of the Morte Darthur* (Cambridge, 2008), pp. 95–113.

Olson, C. C., 'The Minstrels at the Court of Edward III', *PMLA* 56 (1941), 601-12.

Olson, L., 'Romancing the Book: Manuscripts for "Euerich Inglische"', in K. Kerby-Fulton, M. Hilmo, and L. Olson, *Opening Up Middle English Manuscripts: Literary and Visual Approaches* (Ithaca NY, 2012), pp. 95–151.

Owst, G. R., *Literature and Pulpit in Medieval England* (Cambridge, 1933).

Oxford English Dictionary, http:// www.oed.com.

Parkes, M. B., *English Cursive Book Hands 1250–1500* (Oxford, 1969).

—'The Influence of *Ordinatio* and *Compilatio* on the Development of the Book', in *Medieval Learning and Literature: Essays Presented to Richard William Hunt*, ed. J. J. G. Alexander and M. T. Gibson (Oxford, 1976), pp. 115–41.

Partridge, S., 'Minding the Gaps: Interpreting the Manuscript Evidence of the *Cook's Tale* and the *Squire's Tale*', in *The English Medieval Book: Studies in Memory of Jeremy Griffiths*, ed. A. S. G. Edwards, V. Gillespie, and R. Hanna (London 2000), pp. 51–85.

Paul, N., *To Follow in Their Footsteps: The Crusades and Family Memory in the High Middle Ages* (Ithaca NY, 2012).

Pearsall, D., 'Contents of the Manuscript', in *The Auchinleck Manuscript: National Library of Scotland Advocates' MS. 19.2.1*, intro. D. Pearsall and I. C. Cunningham (London, 1979), pp. xix–xxiv.

—'Literary and Historical Significance of the Manuscript', in *The Auchinleck Manuscript: National Library of Scotland Advocates' MS. 19.2.1*, intro. D. Pearsall and I. C. Cunningham (London, 1979), pp. vii–xi.

—'The Whole Book: Late Medieval English Manuscript Miscellanies and Their Modern Interpreters', in *Imagining the Book*, ed. S. Kelly and J. J. Thompson (Turnhout, 2005), pp. 17–29.

—'Towards a Poetics of Chaucerian Narrative', in *Drama, Narrative and Poetry in the Canterbury Tales*, ed. W. Harding (Toulouse, 2003), pp. 99–112.

Pearson, D., *English Bookbinding Styles 1450–1800* (London, 2005).

Pearson, R., 'William Morris Interrupted Interrupting Chaucer', in *Chaucer's Poetry: Words, Authority and Ethics*, ed. C. Carney and F. M. McCormack (Dublin, 2013), pp. 158–84.

Phiddian, R., *Swift's Parody* (Cambridge, 1995).

Philips, S., *Edward II* (New Haven, 2010).

Phillips, H., '*The Book of the Duchess*: Structure and Consolation', *Chaucer Review* 16 (1981), 107–18.

—'Merry, Merry Men and Greenwood: A History of Some Meanings', in *Images of Robin Hood: Medieval to Modern*, ed. L. Potter and J. Colhoun (Newark NJ, 2008), pp. 83–101.

Pickering, O., 'Stanzaic Verse in the Auchinleck Manuscript: *The Alphabetical Praise of Women*', in *Studies in Late Medieval and Early Renaissance Texts in Honour of John Scattergood*, ed. A. M. D'Arcy and A. J. Fletcher (Dublin, 2005), pp. 287–304.

Pollard, A. W., and G. R. Redgrave, eds., *A Short-Title Catalogue of Books Printed in England, Scotland, and Ireland and of English Books Printed Abroad 1475–1640*. 2nd edn, rev. W. A. Jackson, F. S. Ferguson, and K. F. Panzer, 4 vols. (London, 1976).

Porcheddu, F., 'Edited Text and Medieval Artifact: The Auchinleck Bookshop and "Charlemagne and Roland" Theories, Fifty Years Later', *Philological Quarterly* 80 (2001), 465–503.

Prestwich, M., *The Three Edwards: War and State in England, 1272–1377*, 2nd edn (London, 2003).

Pringle, R. V., 'An Early Humanity Class Library: The Gift of Sir John Scot and Friends to St Leonard's College (1620)', *The Bibliotheck* 7 (1974), 33–55.

Purdie, R., *Anglicising Romance: Tail-Rhyme and Genre in Medieval English Literature*, Studies in Medieval Romance 9 (Cambridge, 2008).

—'The Implications of Manuscript Layout in Chaucer's *Tale of Sir Thopas*', *Forum for Modern Language Studies* 41 (2005), 263–74.

Putter, A., 'Metres and Stanza Forms of Popular Romance', in *Companion to Medieval Popular Romance*, ed. R. L. Radulescu and C. J. Rushton, Studies in Medieval Romance (Cambridge, 2009), pp. 111–31.

—and K. Busby, 'Introduction: Medieval Francophonia', in *Medieval Multilingualism: The Francophone World and Its Neighbors*, ed. C. Kleinhenz and K. Busby, Medieval Texts and Cultures of Northern Europe 20 (Turnhout, 2010), pp. 1–13.

Réau, L., *Iconographie de l'art Chrétien*, 3 vols. (Paris, 1956).

Reichl, K., 'Orality and Performance', in *A Companion to Medieval Popular Romance*, ed. R. L. Radulescu and C. J. Rushton, Studies in Medieval Romance (Cambridge, 2009), 132–49.

Rejhon, A. C., *Cân Rolant: The Medieval Welsh Version of the Song of Roland* (Berkeley, 1984),

Revard, C., 'Oppositional Thematics and Metanarratives in MS Harley 2253, Quires 1–6', in *Essays in Manuscript Geography: Vernacular Manuscripts of the English West Midlands from the Conquest to the Sixteenth Century*, ed. W. Scase, Medieval Texts and Cultures of Northern Europe 10 (Turnhout, 2007), pp. 95–112.

—'Scribe and Provenance', in *Studies in the Harley Manuscript: The Scribes, Contexts, and Social Contexts of British Library MS Harley 2253*, ed. S. Fein (Kalamazoo MI, 2000), 21–109.

Riddy, F., 'Middle English Romance: Family, Marriage, Intimacy', in *The Cambridge Companion to Medieval Romance*, ed. R. L. Krueger (Cambridge, 2000), pp. 235–52.

Rikhardsdottir, S., *Medieval Translations and Cultural Discourse: The Movement of Texts in England, France and Scandinavia* (Cambridge, 2012).

Robinson, P. R., 'The "Booklet": A Self-Contained Unit of Composite Manuscripts', *Codicologica* 3 (1980), 49–69.

—'A Study of Some Aspects of the Transmission of English Verse Texts in Late Mediaeval Manuscripts', unpublished B Litt thesis, University of Oxford (Oxford, 1972).

Rothwell, W., *et al.*, *Anglo-Norman Dictionary*, 2nd edn (London, 2005), http://www.anglo-norman.net.

Runde, E., 'Reexamining Orthographic Practice in the Auchinleck Manuscript through Study of Complete Scribal Corpora', in *Variation and Change in English Grammar and Lexicon: Contemporary Approaches*, ed. R. Cloutier, A. M. Hamilton-Brehm, and W. Kretzschmar, Jr (Berlin, 2010), pp. 265–87.

Saintsbury, G., *A History of English Prosody from the Twelfth Century to the Present Day*, 3 vols. (New York, 1906).

Salter, D., "'Born to Thraldom and Penance": Wives and Mothers in Middle English', in *Writing Gender and Genre in Medieval Literature: Approaches to Old and Middle English Texts*, ed. E. Treharne (Cambridge, 2002), pp. 41–59.

Salter, E., *Fourteenth-Century English Poetry* (Oxford, 1983).

—'*Piers Plowman* and "The Simonie"', *Archiv* 203 (1967), 241-54.

Samuels, M. L., 'The Scribe of the Hengwrt and Ellesmere Manuscripts of the *Canterbury Tales*', *Studies in the Age of Chaucer* 5 (1983), 49–65.

Sandler, L. F., *Gothic Manuscripts 1285–1385*, 2 vols. (Oxford, 1986).

Scattergood, [V.] J., 'Authority and Resistance: The Political Verse', in *Studies in the Harley Manuscript: The Scribes, Contents and Social Contexts of British Library MS Harley 2253*, ed. S. Fein (Kalamazoo MI, 2000), pp. 163–201.

—'Literary Culture at the Court of Richard II', in *English Court Culture*, ed. V. J. Scattergood and J. W. Sherborne (London, 1983), pp. 29–43.

—'Political Context, Date and Composition of *The Sayings of the Four Philosophers*', in J. Scattergood, *Manuscripts and Ghosts: Essays on the Transmission of Medieval and Early Renaissance Literature* (Dublin, 2006), pp. 95–106.

—'Validating the High Life in *Of Arthour and of Merlin* and *Kyng Alisaunder*', *Essays in Criticism* 54 (2004), 323–50.

Schaefer, U., ed., *The Beginnings of Standardization: Language and Culture in Fourteenth-Century England*, Studies in English Medieval Language and Literature 15 (Frankfurt am Main, 2006).

Scott, K., 'A Mid-Fifteenth-Century English Illuminating Shop and Its Customers', *Journal of the Warburg and Courtauld Institutes* 31 (1968), 170–96.

Scottish Book Trade Index, http://www.nls.uk/catalogues/scottish-book-trade-index.

Shonk, T. A., 'BL MS Harley 7333: The "Publication" of Chaucer in the Rural Areas', *Essays in Medieval Studies* 15 (1998), 81–9.

—'The Scribe as Editor: The Primary Scribe of the Auchinleck Manuscript', *Manuscripta* 27 (1983), 19–20.

—'A Study of the Auchinleck Manuscript: Bookmen and Bookmaking in the Early Fourteenth Century', *Speculum* 60 (1985), 71–91.

—'A Study of the Auchinleck Manuscript: Investigations into the Processes of Book Making in the Fourteenth Century', unpublished PhD dissertation, University of Tennessee (Knoxville TN, 1981).

Skårup, P., 'Contenu, Sources, Rédactions', in *Karlamagnús saga: Branches I, III, VII, et IX*, ed. K. Togeby *et al.* (Copenhagen, 1980), pp. 333–55.

Sklar, E., '*Arthour and Merlin*: The Englishing of Arthur', *Michigan Academician* 8 (1975), 49–57.

Smith, B. H., *Poetic Closure: A Study of How Poems End* (Chicago, 1968).

Smith, J. J., *The English of Chaucer and His Contemporaries* (Aberdeen, 1988).

Smithers, G. V., 'Another Fragment of the Auchinleck MS', in *Medieval Literature and Civilization Studies in Memory of G. N. Garmonsway*, ed. D. A. Pearsall and R. A. Waldron (London, 1969), pp. 192–209.

—'Two Newly-Discovered Fragments from the Auchinleck MS', *Medium Ævum* 18 (1949), 1–11.

Smyser, H. M., '*Charlemagne and Roland* and the Auchinleck MS', *Speculum* 21 (1946), 275-88.

—'The List of Norman Names and the Auchinleck Bookshop', in *Mediaeval Studies in Honor of Jeremiah Denis Matthias Ford*, ed. U. T. Holmes and A. J. Denomy (Cambridge MA, 1948), pp. 257–87.

Spearing, A. C., *Readings in Medieval Poetry* (Cambridge, 1987).

Spencer, H. L., *English Preaching in the Late Middle Ages* (Oxford, 1993).

Steingrimsson, S., 'Árni Magnússon', in *The Manuscripts of Iceland*, ed. G. Sigurðsson and V. Ólason (Reykjvík, 2004), pp. 85–99.

Stenroos, M., 'A Middle English Mess of Fricative Spellings: Reflections on Thorn, Yogh and Their Rivals', in *To Make His Englissh Sweete upon His Tonge*, ed. M. Krygier and L. Sikorska (Frankfurt am Main, 2007), pp. 9–35.

Stones, A., 'Two French Manuscripts: WLC/LM/6 and WLC/LM/7', in *The Wollaton Medieval Manuscripts: Texts, Owners and Readers*, ed. R. Hanna and T. Turville-Petre (York, 2010), pp. 41–56.

Strohm, P., 'Passioun, Lyf, Miracle, Legende: Some Generic Terms in Middle English Hagiographical Narrative', *Chaucer Review* 10 (1975), 62–75, 154–71.

Summerfield, T., '"And she answered in hir language": Aspects of Multilingualism in the Auchinleck Manuscript', in *Multilingualism in Medieval Britain (c. 1066–1520): Sources and Analysis*, ed. J. A. Jefferson and A. Putter, with A. Hopkins (Turnhout, 2013), pp. 241–58.

Tarlinskaja, M., 'Meter and Rhythm of Pre-Chaucerian Rhymed Verse', *Linguistics: An Interdisciplinary Journal of the Language Sciences* 121 (1974), 65–87.

Taylor, A., 'Fragmentation, Corruption, and Minstrel Narration: The Question of the Middle English Romances', *Yearbook of English Studies* 22 (1992), 38-62.

—'The Myth of the Minstrel Manuscript', *Speculum* 66 (1991), 43-73.

Thompson, J. J., 'The *Cursor Mundi*, the "Inglis tong", and "Romance"', in *Readings in Medieval English Romance*, ed. C. M. Meale (Cambridge, 1994), pp. 99–120.

Traugott, J., '*A Tale of a Tub*', in *Modern Essays on Eighteenth-Century Literature*, ed. L. Damrosch, Jr (New York, 1988), pp. 3–45.

Turner, M., 'Guy of Warwick and the Active Life of Historical Romance in *Piers Plowman*', *Yearbook of Langland Studies* 23 (2014), 3–27.

Turville-Petre, T., *England the Nation: Language, Literature, and National Identity, 1290–1340* (Oxford, 1996).

Tyerman, C., *England and the Crusades, 1095–1588* (Chicago, 1988).

—*God's War: A New History of the Crusades* (Cambridge MA, 2006).

Vale, J., *Edward III and the Cult of Chivalry: Chivalric Society and Its Context, 1270–1350* (Woodbridge, 1982).

Vaughan, M. F., 'Chaucer's *Canterbury Tales* and the Auchinleck MS: Analogous Collections?', *Archiv* 242 (2005), 259–74.

—'AuchinleckCorrections.xslx', at http://faculty.washington.edu/miceal/auchinleck/AuchinleckCorrections.xlsx.

Wakelin, D., 'When Scribes Won't Write: Gaps in Middle English Books', *Studies in the Age of Chaucer* 36 (2014), 249–78.

Wallace, D., *Chaucer and the Early Writings of Boccaccio*, Chaucer Studies 12 (Cambridge, 1985).

Walpole, R. N., 'Charlemagne and Roland: A Study of the Source of Two Middle English Metrical Romances, *Roland and Vernagu* and *Otuel and Roland*', *University of California Publications in Modern Philology* 21 (1944), 385-451.

—'The Source MS of Charlemagne and Roland and the Auchinleck Bookshop', *Modern Language Notes* 60 (1945), 22–6.

Watson, A. G., *Catalogue of Dated and Datable Manuscripts, c. 700–1600, in the Department of Manuscripts, The British Library*, 2 vols. (London, 1979).

Watson, N., 'Christian Ideologies', in *A Companion to Chaucer*, ed. P. Brown, Blackwell Companions to Literature and Culture (Oxford, 2000), pp. 75–89.

Webb, D. M., 'Woman and Home: The Domestic Setting of Late Medieval Spirituality', in *Women in the Church*, ed. W. J. Sheils and D. Wood (Oxford, 1991), pp. 159–73.

Wiggins, A., 'Are Auchinleck Scribes 1 and 6 the Same Scribe?: The Advantages of Whole-Data Analysis and Electronic Texts', *Medium Ævum* 73 (2004), 10–26.

—'Imagining the Compiler: *Guy of Warwick* and the Compilation of the Auchinleck Manuscript', in *Imagining the Book*, ed. S. Kelly and J. J. Thompson (Turnhout, 2005), pp. 61–73.

Windeatt, B., 'Literary Structures in Chaucer', in *The Cambridge Companion to Chaucer*, ed. P. Boitani and J. Mann (Cambridge, 2003), pp. 214–32.

Index of Manuscripts Cited

General Index

This index contains the topics, names of people, and titles of works discussed in the text and footnotes. It does not include references to works or authors cited in the Bibliography and not discussed further.

Manuscript Culture in the British Isles